MODERN JURISPRUDENCE

The second edition of this book provides a concise and accessible guide to modern jurisprudence, offering an examination of the major theories as well as highlighting principal themes such as legality and justice. Together with new material, the second edition explores the historical developments and ideas that give modern thinking its distinctive shape. A key feature of the book is that readers are not simply presented with opposing theories, but are guided through the rival standpoints on the basis of a coherent line of reflection from which an overall sense of the subject can be gained. Chapters on Hart, Fuller, Rawls, Dworkin and Finnis take the reader systematically through the terrain of modern legal philosophy, tracing the issues back to fundamental questions of philosophy, and indicating lines of criticism that result in a fresh and original perspective on the subject.

Modern Jurisprudence

A Philosophical Guide

Second Edition

Sean Coyle

·HART·
PUBLISHING
OXFORD AND PORTLAND, OREGON
2017

Hart Publishing
An imprint of Bloomsbury Publishing Plc

Hart Publishing Ltd
Kemp House
Chawley Park
Cumnor Hill
Oxford OX2 9PH
UK

Bloomsbury Publishing Plc
50 Bedford Square
London
WC1B 3DP
UK

www.hartpub.co.uk
www.bloomsbury.com

Published in North America (US and Canada) by
Hart Publishing
c/o International Specialized Book Services
920 NE 58th Avenue, Suite 300
Portland, OR 97213-3786
USA

www.isbs.com

HART PUBLISHING, the Hart/Stag logo, BLOOMSBURY and the
Diana logo are trademarks of Bloomsbury Publishing Plc

First published 2017

© Sean Coyle 2017

Reprinted 2018, 2021

Sean Coyle has asserted his right under the Copyright, Designs and Patents Act 1988 to be
identified as Author of this work.

British Library Cataloguing-in-Publication Data
A catalogue record for this book is available from the British Library.

ISBN: PB: 978-1-50990-561-4
        ePDF: 978-1-50990-562-1
        ePub: 978-1-50990-563-8

Library of Congress Cataloging-in-Publication Data

Names: Coyle, Sean, author.

Title: Modern jurisprudence : a philosophical guide / Sean Coyle.

Description: Second edition. | Oxford, United Kingdom ; Portland, Oregon : Hart Publishing Ltd,
an imprint of Bloomsbury Publishing Plc, 2017. | Includes bibliographical references and index.

Identifiers: LCCN 2017024450 (print) | LCCN 2017025513 (ebook) | ISBN 9781509905638 (Epub) |
ISBN 9781509905614 (pbk. : alk. paper) | ISBN 9781509905621 (ePDF)

Subjects: LCSH: Law—Philosophy—History—20th century. | Jurisprudence—History—20th century.

Classification: LCC K230.C69 (ebook) | LCC K230.C69 M63 2017 (print) | DDC 340/.1—dc23

LC record available at https://lccn.loc.gov/2017024450

Typeset by Compuscript Ltd, Shannon
Printed and bound in Great Britain by TJ Books Limited

To find out more about our authors and books visit www.hartpublishing.co.uk. Here you will find extracts,
author information, details of forthcoming events and the option to sign up for our newsletters.

We shall not cease from exploration
And the end of all our exploring
Will be to arrive where we started
And know the place for the first time.

TS Eliot, 'Little Gidding' V

Preface to the Second Edition

The second edition of *Modern Jurisprudence* affords an opportunity to add a much needed chapter on the legal theory of Thomas Aquinas, and to revise or rewrite material elsewhere. The major changes are to chapters two and five, but there are many smaller changes in other chapters to aid readability, and additions to the suggested reading. I am very grateful to the team at the Hart imprint of Bloomsbury for the opportunity to make these changes, big and small.

As to the purpose and ambition of this book, the introductory words of the original preface still stand, and are preserved immediately below. I hope that the book proves useful to every person into whose hands it falls.

SC
University of Birmingham
April 2017

Preface to the First Edition

This book is primarily intended for students taking university courses in Jurisprudence or legal philosophy, but it may be useful to persons in other fields, or at other stages of legal education, who wish to deepen their engagement with topics in legal and political philosophy.

Within the structure of the modern law degree, Jurisprudence is usually taught either as a compulsory subject studied in the second year, or (more usually) an elective course in the third year. With this in mind, I have forsworn the customary introductory exhortation, beloved of jurisprudence textbooks, asking 'why study jurisprudence?': as presumably (if you are reading this book) you have already made an informed decision to do precisely that, or else you were not given the choice and found yourself thrust through the door whether you liked it or not.

For readers of both kinds, there obviously already exist very many textbooks offering guidance in what is, irreducibly, a complex and challenging subject. The point of departure of *this* book, which is based on the jurisprudence courses I taught at UCL, Durham and Birmingham, derives from the sense I have that jurisprudence students do not simply want to be presented (as it were, democratically) with a range of difficult, mutually contradictory standpoints and theories amongst which they are urged to make up their own mind, especially perhaps when feeling some intuitive attraction to all of them. Perhaps not unreasonably, many readers wish for a sense of direction when otherwise it is difficult to know where to turn. Certainly when studying the law of contract (for example), the lecturer's audience is not simply presented with numerous, diverging lines of authority and instructed to think its own way through the thicket of conflicting judgements and interpretations. Contract textbooks provide no less a deliberate interpretation of the law: one view out of many possible reconstructions that is held out, however defeasible it may be, as being the correct way to look at things. (That is, as the historian AWB Simpson reminds us, the reason why we buy them all.) Why should it be any different with jurisprudence?

In this book, therefore, I have not hesitated to state how I think the central questions of jurisprudence should be understood, and where this takes us. I have not presented a series of theories relatively independently of one another, as on an equal footing, but have tried to indicate a coherent line of reflection from which sense of them can be made. At the same time, it is important not to think of jurisprudential questions as capable of dispositive 'answers'. It is the primary characteristic of philosophical questions that they cannot be resolved, proved or disproved, once and for all. These are the widest questions one can ask: setting no limits to the depth or the breadth of enquiry, not because human minds are forever removed from ultimate truths, but because there is no end to the task of interrogating the understanding of such truths. There is no point beyond which it becomes impossible further to deepen one's reflection upon, and engagement with, ideas such as justice or of right.

It goes without saying that I have simplified arguments here and there, given the introductory intention of the book, but (I trust) without actual distortion. Though I hope that readers will feel encouraged to make their way systematically through the book, fully exploring the deeper issues raised, it is possible for the reader in a hurry to skip directly to those passages, mostly in the second part of the book, that discuss the writings of particular legal philosophers of modern times. For both sorts of readers, my hope is that this book provides some orientation in this endlessly fascinating subject, and sheds a measure of light upon some of its concerns.

SC
University of Birmingham
September 2013

Contents

Preface to the Second Edition vii
Preface to the First Edition ix

1. Justice, Law and History 1
   Morality 4
   History 7
   Law 11
   Situating Jurisprudence 16

   PART ONE: FOUNDATIONS

2. Origins of the Western Jurisprudential Tradition 21
   A Basic Division 23
   Aristotelian Political Thought 30
   The Abandonment of Aristotle 34
   Suggested Reading 37

3. Jurisprudence: The Classical Tradition 39
   Positive Law 40
   Natural Law 42
   The Relationship Between Natural Law and Positive Law 46
   Justice and Determination 49
   Human Knowledge of Natural Law 50
   Suggested Reading 52

4. The Emergence of 'Modern' Political Thought 53
   Hobbes's View of the Human Condition 54
   Law and Society 59
   The Political Context of *Leviathan* 62
   A Divided Inheritance 67
   Suggested Reading 70

5. Images of Law from Grotius to Kant 72
   Grotius as a Natural Lawyer 75
   A New Framework 79
   Suggested Reading 90

PART TWO: DEBATES

6. Positive Law, Positive Justice: Hart 93
    The Basic Dimensions of Hart's Positivism 99
    The Nature of Law 104
    Law and Morality 110
    Natural Law 112
    Justice and Equality 118
    Suggested Reading 123

7. Justice in the 'Real World': Dworkin 125
    The Philosopher-Judge 127
    Could the Law be an Expression of Something Other than
      'Integrity'? 136
    Objectivity, Truth and Scepticism 146
    Philosopher-Kings and Philosopher-Judges 148
    Suggested Reading 149

8. Justice and the Liberal State: Rawls 151
    Rational Reflection and Questions of Method 154
    The Problem of Justice 158
    The First Principle of Justice 164
    The Second Principle 168
    The Basic Structure in Context 174
    Suggested Reading 176

9. Justice and the Common Good: Finnis 177
    Introducing the Political Philosophy 177
    The Basic Goods 181
    The Status of Practical Reasonableness 186
    Order, Community and Justice 188
    Justice and Rights 201
    The Overall Direction of Finnis's Account 207
    Suggested Reading 209

10. Justice and Legality: Fuller 211
    Legality and Justice 212
    Justice and the Institutional Reality of Law 222
    Eunomics: The Theory of Good Order 227
    The Direction of Fuller's Thought 232
    Suggested Reading 235

11. Justice and Legal Order: Further Reflections.................................... 237
    Natural Right and Natural Law.. 237
    The Origin of the Law's Authority... 245
    Legal Order and Positive Law... 251
    Summing Up.. 256
    Suggested Reading 258
12. Conclusions? 259

Index.. 265

1

Justice, Law and History

THE STARTING POINT for this book is a series of questions about the nature of law and its relationship to justice. Scholars and students of law in English-speaking countries, and elsewhere in the world where the English legal tradition has been received, are familiar with the characteristic division between statute and common law. Statute law comprises those written standards and bodies of rules that have been enacted and laid down; whereas the common law, variously described as 'case law', 'judge-made law' and 'unwritten law', forms that part of the legal system in which judges apply, interpret and clarify the law. In carrying out this role, the courts in some sense develop the law, so that a body of doctrine and principle grows up around the enacted rules.

Understood in these terms, the relationship of law to justice may already seem tolerably clear: the rules enacted by legislative bodies (even those that are directly and democratically elected) may be fair or unfair; it is the part of the courts in applying the rules to ensure that justice is done by giving effect to them in a measured and balanced way, according to established principles and doctrines such as *volenti non fit iniuria*, 'equity will not aid a volunteer' and so forth. At the same time, the courts are constrained by principles of statutory interpretation to give effect to the written law. Hence, both the general rules of law and the particular decisions of the courts may at times conflict with one's own sense of what is truly just, or right, and at other times coincide with it.

Familiar as it may be, this picture is unsatisfactory in several respects. To begin with, let us consider what it means, in modern times, to be under the governance of law. Used to the peace and prosperity of liberal society, citizens in the West experience law simultaneously in a remote and in a more immediate way. 'Free' societies grant a great deal of liberty to individuals to order their lives as seems preferable to them. But those same societies also erect a system of rules, enforceable through official institutions, to govern certain kinds of behaviour: both crimes and civil wrongs. For most people, such laws will seem remote from everyday experience, since it is only when they are transgressed that their importance bears down on one. And how many of us, in our lifetime, find ourselves in the position of a litigant, or in the dock?

This sense of remoteness perhaps contributes to the image of law and justice described above.

But in another sense, the presence of law is felt in a more immediate way. Importantly, indeed increasingly, each person considers herself or himself to be a possessor of 'rights'. These rights, however imprecisely understood, pertain at once to those arrangements and resources that are necessary for a tolerable standard of living (needs that require to be fulfilled, benefits to which one feels entitled), and to freedom from interference, both by the state and one's neighbours. No doubt the nature and scope of such rights becomes much bowdlerised in popular discussion; but behind them lie two ideas of considerable importance. The first is that it is the function of the state to secure certain material conditions of prosperity for its citizens, as well as other goods such as peace, liberty, bodily integrity and so forth (the 'common good'). The second is that the state is itself subject to law, and not simply the source of all law. But what does this mean? Often, we think that a person's rights derive from the state, as determined by the enacted state law. Yet if the state is limited in the extent to which it can interfere with a person's rights, is this to say that the state is itself *limited* by law, a bearer of legal responsibilities towards its citizens which cannot be overcome simply by changing the enacted law?

Another way to put this is to ask whether the state has duties of justice towards citizens. In putting this question, it becomes necessary to ask what is meant by 'justice'. Is justice merely the cultural ideal of a political community, or does it denote some permanent, objective standard against which to measure the actions of states, and of individuals? If it is a cultural artefact, does justice have *legal* power to restrain the actions of the state, or merely the force of political rhetoric? If justice is an objective concept, how must it be understood and what are its implications?

Through the academic study of law at university, law students come to have a much more sophisticated and detailed understanding of the way in which the law impacts upon, and deeply structures, daily life. They learn to analyse everyday transactional behaviour in terms of the concepts, rules and doctrines of contract law that give them their stable form: concepts seldom explicitly called upon—and sometimes transgressed—in everyday contexts (such as the purchase of petrol), but nonetheless present as assumptions that structure such occasions. Law students also learn about property, about the complex rights and responsibilities that define ownership, and they learn significant bodies of constitutional and administrative law. Yet the constraints imposed by the requirements of professional qualification, and prolonged conditions of social peace and stability, conspire to remove the deeper questions of justice from the attention of most students and their lecturers. All too often, the study of law (perhaps especially public law) can even suggest that one must *contrast* the body of 'black-letter' rules, as such, with questions about their justice or injustice.

The structure of legal education can therefore reinforce the intuitive picture of law and justice that I described at the beginning. But in thinking about that picture, it must also be remembered that, if litigants expect a judgment according to law, they also think of the function of the judge as doing justice to the interests (indeed the rights) of the litigants. As the eminent legal historian AWB Simpson put it, 'In the common law system no very clear distinction exists between saying that a particular solution to a problem is in accordance with the law, and saying that it is the rational, or fair, or just solution.'[1] But even where this is remembered, how often, in the study of law, is the idea of justice examined in relation to the questions raised at the end of the preceding paragraph, or yet others that might be raised about its nature?

University courses in jurisprudence take these questions (and others) as their focus. Indeed, the connection between the 'black-letter' law and questions of fairness, justice and so on is indicated by the fact that the term 'jurisprudence', in the legal cultures of the West, has a dual meaning. On one hand, it refers to the body of judicial arguments and decisions which inform the application of legal rules. We speak, for example, of 'the jurisprudence of the International Court of Justice' as a means of referring to that institution's past decisions, and the reasons which inform them. Jurisprudence in this sense is connected to the idea of legal *doctrine*: that aspect of law which is concerned not with explicitly formulated rules, but with the systematic connections that may be made between them. Thus, in the law of tort we subsume various particular rules and decisions under the broader intellectual category of 'nuisance'. Others we treat under the heading of 'negligence' and so on. We think of these categories not simply as convenient labels, but as bodies of thought that are capable of systematic study. Such systematic study in turn influences and shapes our interpretation of the rules.

On the other hand, 'jurisprudence' is used as an alternative name for the philosophy of law. Here, the focus is not upon the correctness of particular doctrinal assertions, but upon wider questions of the nature of law itself. Even for lawyers, the law itself and the activity of legal reasoning rest upon a framework of ideas that are not usually themselves invoked in ordinary doctrinal argument. A lawyer involved in a case of nuisance with respect to the use of land, for instance, is not immediately concerned with questions of the basis of the law's power and authority to interfere in the lives of ordinary citizens; nor will he see it as his job to go into the moral question of what the limits (if any) of such a power should be. Such questions are nevertheless implied by the existence and operation of law, and although much legal practice can proceed perfectly well without giving any thought to them, it is these and

---

[1] AWB Simpson, 'The Common Law and Legal Theory' in AWB Simpson (ed), *Oxford Essays in Jurisprudence*, 2nd Series (Oxford, Clarendon Press, 1973) 79.

similar questions which form the primary concern of the legal philosopher. Accordingly, the principal aim of the subject is not to improve one's practical skills as a lawyer (though it is sometimes claimed that philosophical study positively affects one's general ability to reason and to judge and interpret incisively). It is instead to foster an awareness of the deeper implications and suppositions of legal practice. As a lawyer one is involved in these implications whether aware of them or not. Deeper scrutiny of the various suppositions upon which the practice of law is founded transforms one from an unthinking servant of whatever values they represent, into one whose practice is conducted with a full knowledge of the broader issues and problems involved.

If doctrinal argument is indeed linked to broader assumptions of political power and morality, then may we not come to regard legal reasoning as ultimately connected with reflection on moral or political values, or perhaps even as *itself* a species of moral or political reflection? Furthermore, does not the assumption that law is concerned with the idea of justice suggest precisely such a connection? Some of the theories we shall be looking at in this book, which form the 'central debates' in current jurisprudence, concern just this question of whether law is intrinsically associated with morality. One who denies the claim that law consists in something more than a series of rules designed to meet the needs of various occasions does not, therefore, demonstrate the irrelevance of jurisprudential assumptions. In reality, such a person grounds their position in a number of jurisprudential assumptions about the nature of law and legal reasoning.

MORALITY

In thinking about the question of the law's relationship to morality, it is not only *law* that needs to be understood more clearly, but also morality itself. Increasingly, citizens of liberal societies regard moral belief as a matter of opinion rather than of truth. Each person has their own understanding of what is morally permissible, of 'good' and 'bad' action, which may coincide and diverge with the beliefs of others at numerous points. It is said that nobody's insight into these matters is more privileged or superior to anyone else's, so that all opinions must be respected. Given this situation, it may seem as if the law should avoid giving priority to any specific moral viewpoint (or idea of justice?), but confine itself to creating liberal social conditions that allow each person to live their life in their own way, and in accord with their own beliefs.

These beliefs are increasingly commonplace, and in a certain sense are very easy to hold. But philosophical reflection has the power to transform beliefs, often by bringing to light the wider and most profound implications of thoughts that normally lie unexamined. The views stated in the preceding paragraph raise a number of questions. What does it mean, for example, to show respect for divergent opinions? If this means to refrain from pressing one's own beliefs where they meet with disagreement, does this act of refraining not actively disrespect one's own beliefs? Is it not simply the lazy avoidance of arguments that need to be made and sincerely considered: to stand up and be counted? Or perhaps more worryingly, is it a tacit acceptance of the idea that moral opinions are not rational at all, but mere emotion, sheer inarticulate stirrings of the heart that are incapable of being other than juxtaposed to one another? Do we really believe these things?

Much of the time, the idea of morality as 'mere opinion' seems to proceed from the specifically liberal ideal of live-and-let-live: a desire not to apply or force views upon those who do not accept them. But let us again reflect, and examine the nature of this belief: when we say 'live and let live', is this *objectively* good to do, a better way of conducting oneself socially than other alternatives, or is it just one possible social arrangement equally as good, bad or (thus) as insignificant as any other? Those who live by such liberal maxims imply that the liberal outlook has a certain moral priority over other alternatives (else they quickly become embroiled in contradiction).[2] Consider the reality in 'open' societies of religious freedom. Where such freedom exists, neither apostasy nor heresy is a capital offence. Is this not, all things considered, a better situation than one in which belief (or its outward expression) is coerced, and disagreement suppressed? But this leads to further questions. Can the maxim of live-and-let-live be applied to the extent that equal blessing is given to those regimes or individuals who seek to destroy the very foundations of tolerance?

The fact is that, on reflection, the ideal of live-and-let-live cannot be pursued without limits. It cannot be asserted that all forms of life are equally valid, all outlooks worthy of respect. One can perhaps hold such a view in the abstract, but it falls apart when subjected to close scrutiny. The respective priorities of murderers and their victims do not represent an irresolvable clash between opposing 'moral points of view'. We do not, in relation to these differing priorities, need to find some way of demonstrating respect to both. The murderer who kills in order to remove obstacles to his desired goals; the thief who acknowledges no moral restrictions upon pursuit of wealth or coveted objects; the rapist who commits violent assault in order to satisfy the demands of lust or cravings of power: these are attitudes of mind that are incapable of commanding respect. To be the resisting victim of such attacks is not to worry whether one's determined resistance manifests 'disrespect' of the rapist's 'values', or perpetrates an injustice towards the attacker. Such attacks

---

[2] That is to say, if liberal values have no especial significance, the ground of the desire not to force or impose values on others in virtue of their disagreement entirely disappears.

are not themselves manifestations of any value, but the extinction of life or the annihilation of one's values.[3] Thus, to be the victim of an outrage is to comprehend the utter emptiness of the idea that 'it may be wrong for me, but right for him'. By extension then, are such acts any less an outrage, any less condemnable, when directed against others rather than oneself? Is the evil of such acts magnified or diminished by their systematic pursuit by organs of government and the state? Should one feel hesitance in condemning regimes which implement or oversee ethnic purges, the systematic raping of women, the confiscation of property or suppression of liberty?

Very often, the hesitancy to condemn such practices seems to flow from an outlook of 'cultural relativism'. But cultures are no more brute givens than the opinions of individuals, and no less inarguable or incapable of criticism.[4] The failure to cry out against injustices when directed to other victims and not oneself, is nothing but an extreme form of moral cowardice: the fear of upsetting cultural sensitivities induces all too easily a moral panic which silences criticism. But is this finally anything other than a failure of one's moral duty to ensure justice in one's own life? The presence of political power, or of historic cultural norms, seems to impress the modern mind in a way that the realities of its effects do not. How often do we dismiss the precarious plight of vulnerable groups in a repressive or unjust society, deeply aware of the culturally embedded practices that create such 'values', but forgetful of the narrowness of lives lived under the rule of injustice, the precariousness of each individual's situation, or very real instances of daily suffering? The status of a practice as the product of a 'culture' does not render its values impervious to rational criticism!

> Keep the truth which thou hast found; men do not stand
> In so ill case here, that God hath with his hand
> Signed kings blank-charters to kill whom they hate, ...
> Fool and wretch, wilt thou let thy soul be tied
> To man's laws, by which she shall not be tied
> At the last day?[5]

Modern minds nevertheless struggle with the ideas of culture and of history. This is perhaps due to a feeling that one's own moral perspectives in

---

[3] Ordinary language mirrors this: we do not speak of a 'better and more perfect murderer' but of a 'worse and more terrible' one. The murderer's 'values' are not intelligible as positive goals that one may move towards and manifest more *excellently*, but only as inversions of good things from which one has fallen away.

[4] One must consider too the image of the human being implied by relativism. As Fuller once observed, if man's 'nature' is entirely shaped by his cultural environment (such that he does not possess a well-defined 'nature' at all), then any interruption of that cultural environment—any transformation, development or disturbance of it—would cause man to disintegrate, making it entirely unclear what he will become, or what his new characteristics will be: see ch 10 below.

[5] John Donne, *Satires* III.89–95.

being (inescapably) both culturally and historically situated, render all under-standings finally uncertain, and haunted by the spectre of 'bias'. It is there-fore important to understand precisely the place of history in jurisprudential thinking.

HISTORY

We cannot truly understand our 'modern' situation, and the values and assumptions that inform it, unless we know something of the historical con-ditions that contributed to its production. Indeed, a major purpose of this book is to overturn the image of jurisprudence as a set of contrasting theories that are essentially free-floating or ungrounded in immediate concerns. Such 'positions' did not materialise out of nothing, but have an origin and a history behind them. By exploring and understanding this historical development, we increase our understanding of the significance of these important intel-lectual traditions, of which the currently dominant theories are merely the latest expression. For example, the argument about whether the law can be said to embody a coherent moral position can only arise if the law is assumed to possess a systematic character. But from whence does this assumption arise? And what were the social or intellectual conditions which made that assump-tion possible (or inevitable)? As we shall see, the image of law as a systematic body of rules and principles is a relatively recent one, consequent upon certain historical conditions in sixteenth- and seventeenth-century Europe. Without knowledge of such conditions, it is impossible to appreciate the full meaning and significance of the numerous arguments surrounding the law's systematic character.

But at the same time, philosophical questions never reduce entirely to his-torical questions. It is the domain of historians to consider the beliefs, opinions and doctrines that people have held concerning matters such as justice and 'the good life': how and why they arose, what conditions sustained them or led to their decline, and what social, economic or cultural currents might explain these processes. Yet the question of what justice itself *is*, what form or forms of life are genuinely and actually 'good'; these need to be separated from the historical enquiry into the opinions, doctrines or theories which assert that there are such phenomena, and what they entail. One might try to capture this distinction by saying that there can be a history of opinions, of what certain people or cultures believed or no longer believe about these matters, but not technically speaking a history of 'justice' itself, as the object of those beliefs.[6]

---

[6] See in particular J Finnis, *Natural Law and Natural Rights*, 2nd edn (Oxford, Clarendon Press, 2011) 24.

I have much sympathy for this, but it should not lead us to be forgetful of the fact that ideas such as 'justice' and 'the good life' mean nothing in the abstract, if left unconnected with the life of what ancient philosophers referred to as 'the city'. The 'good life' is (as it were) not only a *form* of life, but also a form of *life*. It requires a context. It is not, as Saint Augustine reminded his friend Nectarius, the task of human beings merely to dream pleasing dreams of justice, but actually to achieve its manifestation in this life.[7] Justice cannot *be* justice unless it has a history, a set of concrete historical facts of human action that lead to its satisfaction and fulfilment. Likewise, the 'good life' is nothing if not a set of arrangements, of conditions that demand to be instantiated in the here-and-now. It is not a 'good' that is entirely otherworldly, postponed until the next life. In saying that justice and the good life require a city, the classical philosophers did not mean to refer directly to actual cities such as Athens or Alexandria. 'City' in this sense meant a metaphysical, or ideal city. But if the world has not witnessed or hosted a perfect example of the ideal city, our starting point for speculation is nevertheless firmly rooted in the conditions of this world. Images of justice are images of cities that could exist practically, and be manifested historically.

Historical sensitivity is especially important in the light of these considerations. Our sense of justice, and of what it is to lead a good or worthwhile life, do not really have any independent starting points for speculation, but grow out of reflection upon the imperfections of current practices and arrangements. Justice can be thought of as demanding some transmutation of current practices. How great an inversion of current priorities and attachments is demanded? Do we think of the world, and of human history, as *utterly* devoid of any justice, and of any elements of a good and worthwhile way of life? For the most part, we do not: but then how do we ensure that our deliberations on justice do not simply amplify or idealise particular cultural biases, or reflect the assumptions that inform 'how we do things around here'? This is why historical awareness is of such importance.

The intellectual conditions of any historical era (including the present) will tend to favour certain ideas, placing some questions at the centre of enquiry whilst marginalising or altogether suppressing others. As citizens of a liberal and democratic society, we have learnt to value ideals of rights and liberty. We think of rights and liberties as things that are important to us, and as things we in some measure *possess*. But it was not always so. Indeed, the notion of 'rights' as personal possessions or attributes is one that developed only against the background of considerable political crisis. Similarly, the notion that democracy is a desirable form of government is a comparatively recent one.

---

[7] Augustine, Epistle 91, 4.

What brought about this fundamental change in outlook? Can this change be viewed as 'progress'? Or is it simply the latest turn in an ongoing historical journey to somewhere else? Our present jurisprudential debates cannot be separated from these broader questions. In the first part of this book we shall be looking at some of these questions, and examining some of the history of the subject. In doing so, we will see that many of the assumptions that inform the jurisprudential theories of the present day have their origins in important historical debates concerning the nature of society, and of the human being; of the nature of law and its role in society; the idea of 'the state' and its politics; questions of religion and theology; indeed the question of the nature of the human condition itself.

The philosophy of concepts such as justice and the good life is not therefore reducible to cultural history or anthropology. All societies, in all places and times, have entertained ideas about law, justice and the ideal state. It is the task of philosophy to evaluate cultural ideas and practices, and certainly not to remain neutral between aspects of different cultures that are opposing. Philosophy is inescapably about truth (*philo sophia*), and the lover of wisdom must place truth above culture. That which is good in one's own culture is to be loved because it is good, and not because it is one's own culture. To those who argue that it is impossible to escape the subtle influences and biases of one's own culture, one must oppose the very character of argument itself. Argument is not the same as flag-waving. A vision of justice is not the blanket assertion of the superiority of one's own cultural values, but a considered, rational reflection on what is good rather than bad in one's culture. Reasonable persons possess the capacity to be moved towards the truth. To engage in argument and in critical thought at all, is to exhibit confidence in the power of reason to overcome error, and lead to truth. All cultures manifest injustices and imperfections to some extent, sometimes considerably, but few or none represent a complete absence of all that is good or worthwhile. When the philosopher criticises cultural practices, the opposition is not between two mutually contradictory sets of cultural ideals, but a set of concrete historical practices and a body of ideas that stand in criticism over all historical practices.

Law itself represents an idea that transcends the numerous historical manifestations of social order to which we give that name. We know intuitively that the law of Athens and the law of Germany are substantially different, but each is yet an instance of 'law'. Is it possible to reflect upon or identify those aspects that unite these (and other) examples, those aspects which make them examples *of law*? Can one analyse and clarify a general concept of law? HLA Hart, one of the most famous legal philosophers of the twentieth century, for example, stated that the theory of law offered in his most famous book, *The Concept of Law*, is intended to be general 'in the sense that it is not tied to any particular legal system or legal culture, but seeks to give an explanatory and clarifying account of law as a complex social and political institution'.[8] One of Hart's disciples, Joseph Raz, similarly claims that:

> It is easy to explain in what sense legal philosophy is universal. Its theses, if true, apply universally, that is, they speak of all law, of all legal systems; of those that exist or will exist, and even of those that can exist or never will. Moreover, its theses are advanced as necessarily universal.[9]

On the face of it, Raz's claim is more prescriptive than Hart's. Whereas Hart seems simply to be describing the general character of his own theory, Raz asserts that no proper jurisprudential conception of law can be other than fixed, or universal. Raz seems to be assuming an image of jurisprudential argument in which a variety of opposing concepts of law, each of which must be described in terms that do not depend upon references to the specific properties of actual legal systems, are weighed against one another. But if we adopt that image, then the standards we use in order to select the 'correct' theory must be somehow internal to the set of arguments upon which the theories are constructed, not rooted in the intellectual traditions of which actual legal arrangements are part.

The idea of fixed concepts does not sit well with other claims that legal philosophers have made about law. An American philosopher of law, Lon Fuller, once wrote of the activity of a legal philosopher as representing 'his part in the eternal process by which the common law works itself pure and adapts itself to the needs of a new day'.[10] Similarly, Ronald Dworkin in his influential book *Law's Empire* refers to the 'old trope' of the present law 'gradually transforming itself into its own purer ambition'.[11] If the law itself is believed to be capable of self-transformation in this way, why should it be thought that there are fixed or 'universal' concepts capable of capturing the idea of law? Indeed, such variances between conceptions of law at different stages of history are not simply a matter of broad understandings of 'law'. Particular branches of law themselves undergo transformation, so that what seems to be the very essence of (say) contract law at one time may seem inessential or even altogether absent from the same body of law at another time. The historian AWB Simpson in fact pointed out just this: 'any attempt to investigate the medieval law of contract in terms of modern legal theory would be perfectly futile, for it could only lead to the ridiculous conclusion that no law of contract then existed'.[12] Thinking about law must exhibit historical sensitivity, if it is to avoid such errors.

---

[8] HLA Hart, *The Concept of Law*, 3rd edn (Oxford, Clarendon Press, 2012) 239.
[9] J Raz, 'On the Nature of Law' (1996) *Archiv fur Rechts und Sozialphilosophie* 1, 1–2.
[10] L Fuller, *The Law in Quest of Itself* (Chicago, Foundation Press, 1940) 140.
[11] R Dworkin, *Law's Empire* (London, Fontana Press, 1986) 400.
[12] AWB Simpson, A History of the Common Law of Contract: The Rise of the Action of Assumpsit (Oxford, Clarendon Press, 1975) 5.

How then should philosophical analysis of law be understood? One might regard it in these terms. Philosophy is indeed a search for general or 'universal' ideas (of law, or of justice or the good life): ideas that are universally or generally true, rather than being internally valid relative to a particular culture. But the correct way to gain an understanding of such ideas is not to prescind from all particularities and all actual instances or manifestations of the concepts one wishes to comprehend. It is to seek a deep, detailed and sensitive understanding of those ideas as they appear in the social practices that are closest to one's experience. Such an understanding must above all be critical; but one can only 'ascend' to philosophical truth from the examination of one's present experience, and what led to it, not through relentless abstraction from all experience.

LAW

Modern jurisprudential debate concerning the nature of law is informed by two major distinctions. On the one hand, jurisprudence is frequently presented as an ongoing battle between the two rival traditions of natural law and legal positivism. On the other, it is not unusual to find the subject divided into categories of 'analytical' and 'normative' jurisprudence. It is sometimes asserted that the second of these distinctions derives from the first: it is the nineteenth-century positivist Jeremy Bentham who is principally associated with the explicit division of the subject in this way. Bentham famously asserted that the question of how law is to be described, as a social institution, is separate from that of whether that institution is just, unjust, corrupt etc. The positivists' separation of law and morality therefore seems to invite the distinction between descriptive and normative enquiries, whereas natural law doctrines, in which the institution of law is itself taken to embody a moral idea, would seem to exclude the possibility of separate enquiries. And yet perhaps this is overhasty. Whether or not one is a natural lawyer, it seems intelligible enough to distinguish enquiries into the nature of law that are primarily intellectual from those that are predominantly practical in seeking to recommend some specific set of laws or rights on moral grounds.[13] A natural lawyer, therefore, might pursue an account of the nature of law that shows it to be intrinsically moral and incapable of being described except through the use of moral categories and ideas. In so doing, she will have made a contribution to 'analytical' jurisprudence, without necessarily saying very much about which concrete set of rights, duties, liberties and so on are to be morally preferred.

---

[13] See, eg, Finnis (n 6) 18.

What can be said, by contrast, of the first distinction, between natural law and positivism? To those encountering jurisprudential debates for the first time, natural law, often initially (though erroneously) presented as the theory that 'an unjust law is no law', will appear to many as straightforwardly false, whereas positivism, with its separation of law from considerations of its merit or demerit, seems straightforwardly true. Certainly, these descriptions are very broad, and more subtle statements of each alternative may have the effect of introducing doubts concerning the other, whilst investing themselves with greater plausibility. Yet do such argumentative niceties do more than disguise an obvious truth, apparent from the outset, that positivists are basically correct? But if that is so, what in our thinking makes it 'obvious'? And if the intuitive answer is indeed the right one, what explains the continuing attraction that is felt towards natural law doctrines, and how did that intellectual tradition ever come to form a significant part of our Western legal inheritance?

My earlier remarks on justice and right were partly intended to introduce a set of questions that demonstrate an equally (or perhaps even more) fundamental set of instincts about the law's connection with justice. In a very complex system of laws, it is highly unlikely that every provision that applies to one's situation will prove satisfactory to one's own personal sense of justice. Thus, though I said that litigants demand, and expect, justice to be done to their rights and interests, it is clear that in some, perhaps many, cases, some litigants will deem the outcome in law to be unjust. Is this enough to confirm the positivist's contention that 'law' as such is separate in understanding from justice? Or should one say that law amounts in the end to a body of reasons for decision, and that one can scarcely understand the reasons offered for any decision at law except by supposing them to be motivated by or directed towards justice to the litigants' interests? Therefore, if certain decisions, when considered impartially and fully, represent a failure or a travesty of justice, their fault lies in their being precisely a travesty *of that ideal* that is demanded; a failure to manifest exactly that property which forms part of the set of expectations that inform one's idea of 'law'.

These questions require an appreciation of the wider social and historical context in which ideas about law are situated. If the claims of legal positivism often hold more initial appeal, or seem to demand acceptance over the other possibilities, this is not something that occurs in isolation from the rest of our thought but constitutes part of our whole vision of the world. The jurisprudential arguments that we find the most persuasive are generally those that fit most closely with our wider understandings. In other instances, jurisprudential theories can lead us to question our pre-existing view of things, and even radically alter our view of the world. But in either case, the jurisprudential insights must be accommodated within the complete picture, and do not remain wholly aloof from it.

In the history of Western civilisation, the character of law and legal practice has been strongly influenced by jurisprudential argument. We think of law as possessing systematic qualities, for example. When we study legal textbooks on contract or the law of property, we are not presented with a mere list of rules or decisions bearing no relationship to one another. Rather, the law is expounded as an ordered whole, the particular rules and cases being related to one another on the basis of more general structural ideas, categories and principles. The complexity of law is largely a function of the potentially endless ways in which rules and decisions can be collectively interpreted in the light of more general ideas (such as that of 'mistake' in contract, or an 'easement' in property). But the understanding of law as a systematic body of principles and doctrines is relatively recent in origin, and owes its existence in large part to the tradition of natural law thinking.

It had been a commonplace of political thinking in Western Europe that the moral basis of the community and its accumulated wisdom were to be found expressed above all in its politics, rather than its laws. One of the greatest Western texts on ethics, the *Nicomachean Ethics* of Aristotle, reminds us that although all people acknowledge happiness or 'wellbeing' (*eudaimonia*) to be the ultimate aim of life, they disagree about what this aim entails: a life of temperance, justice and virtue, a life in pursuit of glory, or a life of material satisfactions? Given this dissonance in the common life of the community, laws are needed in order to guide each person towards the virtuous life: but the laws are not the source of virtue, which springs from the life in common. In England itself, the presence of local and regional customs persisted in spite of kingly law-codes until the era of Henry II, the period from which most historians date the existence of a truly national law: a single body of writs and remedies that could be administered by courts throughout the realm, as a kind of national custom distinct from the statutes enacted by king's own council.[14]

There is no doubt that these developments paved the way for a system of legal justice, but it was a long time before the law came to be understood as providing an especially significant source of insight into the good life. As late as 1771, Blackstone was to write of his ambition in compiling the *Commentaries* (that of 'reducing our laws to a system') as involving 'a method in many respects totally new'.[15] Indeed, it is here for the first time that the task

---

[14] See, eg, RC Van Caenegem, *The Birth of the English Common Law*, 2nd edn (Cambridge, Cambridge University Press, 1988).

[15] Blackstone, *Analysis of the Laws of England* (Oxford, Clarendon Press, 1762) v.

of devising 'schemes … for digesting the laws of England' are explicitly and consciously equated with systematic ambitions that would allow for the contemplation of law as a complete and ordered whole.[16] A very different picture of the legal order was present in the traditional common law scholarship of the fifteenth and sixteenth centuries. The legal writings of this period were organised around the assumptions and preoccupations of legal practice, and hence emphasised procedure and remedies. The focus on matters of immediate practical significance meant that there was no pressing reason to regard the law as an ordered system; and, by and large, it did not occur to legal commentators to do so. The majority of the legal writings of the time consisted in the form of abridgements and glossaries, and where a systematic presentation of the rules did seem desirable, this was usually limited to the arrangement in alphabetical order of possible heads of action.

The form of legal scholarship practised by the traditional common lawyers did not encourage the construction of more ambitious classificatory schemes. The rules were seen as emerging, not from more general principles, but from long usage and experience. There was in consequence no reason to assume that the accumulated body of rules and customs should amount to a coherent and ordered system. The law simply reflected a set of evolved responses to a variety of social problems: a circumstance which led to the law being described as 'a wilderness of single instances'.[17]

From the beginning of the seventeenth century, in the writings of Grotius, Locke, Rousseau, Kant and others, the emphasis shifted from the idea of law as a collection of remedies to the idea of law as a system of interlocking rights. This intellectual shift required the development of a systematic jurisprudence. Law came to be seen as a system of horizontal and vertical patterns of entitlement. The idea that every individual was possessed of rights and duties, towards both other individuals and the state, gave rise to the notion of formal equality: that each person was essentially equal in the eyes of the law. Law thus came to be depicted as a systematic body of rights, established according to general principles of equity of which the positive rules are mere instances. It is this vision of the legal order that is at work in Blackstone's *Commentaries*, a work often regarded as a typical example of early eighteenth-century natural law scholarship.

It is from such a vision that the present tensions within jurisprudence, between natural law and legal positivism, came to prominence. Once law is seen as being governed by rational principles, the 'rules' come to be regarded as related to those principles deductively, rather than as evolving only gradually

---

[16] ibid vii and iv.
[17] Alfred Lord Tennyson, 'Aylmer's Field' in *The Collected Poems of Alfred Lord Tennyson* (Ware, Wordsworth Editions, 1994) 581.

and in response to single instances. But since the general principles can be interpreted in different ways according to the moral values and purposes they are held to serve, the idea of posited rules becomes important. Legal rules, we are tempted to think, are set apart from open-ended moral debate precisely in that they are ascertainable and final. It then becomes plausible to conceive of law in terms of a body of authoritative standards, laid down by human beings, which might serve morally good ends or morally bad ones.

The tension between these inherited traditions (the positivist perspective which emphasises articulated rules, and the notion, derived from natural law, of law as a body of rational principles) has shaped our received views and attitudes towards legal writing. Blackstone's *Commentaries* are part of a tradition that views the legal commentator as systematically expounding the law: his propositions are understood as describing the legal order, conceived as a body of general principles, definitions and doctrines. But once this has been recognised, the question of the basis of the treatise writer's propositions becomes pressing. Such propositions cannot be said to derive their authority from their conformity to standards of reason or justice; rather, they can claim to possess authority only insofar as they are an accurate statement of judicial decisions or legislative provisions. But if this is so, why not jettison altogether the idea of transcendent principles, and realise instead that legal rules have their origin in court rulings and Acts of Parliament? The source of legal rules becomes important. The focus of legal thinking shifts from the content to the form of legal rules.

The role of textbooks, on this view, is reduced to the reporting, clarifying and ordering of the mass of rules that emanate from these sources. The textbook writer's propositions are no longer regarded as possessing any intrinsic authority. Bentham in particular viewed textbooks with distaste. He saw their peculiar mix of exposition and justification as apt to mislead the unwary reader into believing that the law consists of principle rather than command. Latter-day positivists have abandoned Bentham's hostility to principle, but have in the main retained this account of authority. Rational or systematic reconstruction of the legal order according to systematic conceptions (such as rights) is seen as a matter of interpreting and applying *rules*. At the same time, however, we continue to regard the common law as a distinctive body of principles and ideas, essentially different in character from statute law.

Much of modern legal theory is concerned with reconciling these conflicting ideas. The systematic and coherent quality of law comes to be seen as more a matter of squaring overlapping policies, than of expounding an underlying moral vision. The law is regarded as pursuing various, often interrelated, projects (such as compensation, deterrence and protection of the environment); the job of the commentator is, then, to present the law so as to give expression to the policy served by the rules in such a way that the law's other projects are not undermined. Hard cases may arise where policies conflict, or where it is impossible to articulate, on the basis of a general policy, a sufficiently specific principle governing particular circumstances. In such cases, it is consistency of approach and purpose, rather than the articulation of an underlying moral vision, that is seen as supplying the grounds for decision. These ideas have not gone unchallenged, but it is from such ideas that the distinctive concerns of modern legal philosophy flow. Where legal reasoning is viewed as expounding an underpinning moral theory, problems associated with judicial discretion do not arise. But where the courts are seen as giving effect to underlying policies, we must begin to face difficult questions about the appropriateness of judges deciding upon the meaning, scope and relative merits of related policies.

I raise these issues in order to show that although the fundamental questions of justice and the life of the community are permanent and unchanging, the forms in which they receive expression are subject to all kinds of shifts and changes. It is the task of philosophy to question these forms of thought, and to reflect upon their significance. Even at the present day, there are important theories which pursue the idea of justice largely outside the context of law. Rawls's monumental and hugely influential book, *A Theory of Justice*, has set the agenda for much thinking on the subject of justice in recent times. But it contains nothing that could be said to amount to a theory of *law*. Even John Finnis, an important modern figure in the natural law tradition, pursues the idea of justice through a 'grammar of rights' which derives not primarily from juridical concerns but instead 'provides a way of expressing virtually all the requirements of practical reasonableness'.[18] These requirements in turn are 'only analogically law',[19] so that the very idea of 'natural law' is a 'rather unhappy term' and can even be 'inconvenient'.[20] Against these positions, modern writers such as Ronald Dworkin and Lon Fuller have urged upon legal scholars the view that law and legal institutions are firmly at the centre of our attempts to unravel the problem of justice. We must ask ourselves: is there something about law (as an institution) that forms part of the very requirements of justice; or must we in the end direct our thoughts to politics, perceiving law only as the instrument of values derived from elsewhere?

SITUATING JURISPRUDENCE

Western jurisprudence forms part of a rich and important cultural inheritance. We need to understand that inheritance if we are to make sense of

---

[18]   Finnis (n 6) 198.
[19]   ibid 280.
[20]   ibid 374, 437.

modern-day jurisprudential debates. But at what point can one be said to be studying 'modern' jurisprudence rather than exploring its history? When, in other words, does modern jurisprudence begin? If we understand this to mean, 'which are the major texts that we study, now?', we are likely to conclude that modern jurisprudence began in the 1960s, in the writings of HLA Hart. Hart's work (and the subsequent responses to it) certainly did bring about a significant shift in perceptions of what jurisprudence is about. But Hart's classic book *The Concept of Law* and other later writings contain important discussions of earlier legal philosophers such as Jeremy Bentham, John Austin and Hans Kelsen. As it is against this earlier framework of ideas that Hart is reacting, one might say that a complete understanding of Hart's theories is impossible without knowledge of these earlier writers. We would then be forced to say that the distinctive concerns of modern jurisprudence grew out of late nineteenth-century debates on law. But if we instead mean to identify the point at which the concepts and categories of modern thinking began to emerge and take shape, then our starting point is much earlier: in the social, political and intellectual debates of the late seventeenth century.

The seventeenth century marks an important watershed in legal and political thought. It is here that we begin to encounter concepts, ideas and questions that set the terms of the political and jurisprudential debates that we pursue today. It was here that the structure and character of the modern state came to be defined, and here also that the importance of private individuals, pursuing agendas of their own was clearly perceived. Out of these developments grew our present notions of justice, liberty and individual rights. And from this a new and distinctively modern understanding of the role, nature and position of law in society came to prominence. One of the most seemingly intractable arguments in modern jurisprudence concerns the relationship between law and morality. Is it necessary (Hart asks) that law reproduce or embody certain moral demands? If so, what is the extent, and the basis, of this correspondence? And if not, how must the relationship between laws and morals be characterised? These questions are widely debated within the subject. But what is less clearly understood is the extent to which our answers depend, not only upon our perceptions of what law is, but also upon our conception of morality and its place in human affairs.

We tend to think of morality as being similar to law, at least in form. Many people would say that morality consists of moral *rules*. We also frequently speak of moral 'duties' and sometimes even of moral 'rights'. These are first and foremost legal ideas, and indeed it perhaps only makes sense to ask whether law can *embody* moral obligations if we think of morality as having this essentially law-like form: either our legal duties are the same as our moral duties, or they are not. If they are not, then we are effectively living under two sets of obligations which may at times conflict. Yet *must* we think of morality in such terms? Historically, such a conception of morality is in fact quite recent, and gained much of its present form in the context of the religious controversies of the European Reformation. Even from this example we can begin to see that an exploration of the history of jurisprudential ideas is not cleanly separable from a philosophical study of the ideas themselves. For in setting such ideas within the broader context of their evolution, we gain deeper insights into the assumptions they involve, the extent of their bearing on human affairs, and (perhaps) their truth. Jurisprudential debates are conducted within a particular framework of ideas. Unless we are prepared to examine the nature of the framework itself, the reasons and conditions of its existence, we become mere mouthpieces for older, inherited ideas.

In the first part of this book, therefore, we will be exploring the origins and development of some of the central concepts and ideas of modern jurisprudential argument. We will examine, for example, the emergence of 'legal positivism' and its rivals, and trace the development of thinking on justice, morality and right, as well as the foundations of the liberal democratic state itself. Such investigations will reveal the true depth and scope of the current jurisprudential debates that are described in Part Two, as well as (hopefully) making them more accessible and intelligible.

The exposition in Part Two is arranged in terms of chapters devoted to prominent thinkers in the modern literature. There are sound reasons for arranging matters this way, rather than by dividing the discussion into discrete issues, such as 'rights', 'justice', and so on. In the first place, university courses on jurisprudence are typically organised on this basis, examining each writer in turn. Students using this book for guidance will accordingly find it easier to locate the information they are looking for. At a deeper level, it is difficult (especially for those coming fresh to the subject) to achieve a solid understanding of substantive ideas such as justice apart from the intellectual systems and contexts in which they figure. The meaning of 'justice' for a writer such as Hart, for example, cannot be made clear without also knowing that he is a positivist, and hence must be understood in relation to what he says about law, adjudication and other matters.

Part One

Foundations

2

Origins of the Western Jurisprudential Tradition

JURISPRUDENCE IS A practical subject. It sits alongside ethics and political theory, the parts of philosophy that are concerned with right action or, equivalently, how to live. Ethics is arguably the most fundamental of the three, and there is no clear line between it and political theory or jurisprudence. Political theory is concerned with the way in which ethical values are to be enshrined and pursued by a community, and with the question of what form of life is the 'good life' for human beings. Jurisprudence is concerned, amongst other things, with identifying the point or purpose of law, its moral basis, and the ethical values it embodies and promotes. Other types of enquiry into law, such as those of 'descriptive jurisprudence', are in fact conceptually dependent upon the kind of practical enquiries discussed here.[1]

The great questions of Western jurisprudence can indeed be understood as questions about the objectivity (rational necessity) of certain moral demands, including the demands of justice. This is not to say that all moral judgements are rationally necessary: in matters such as sentencing, for example, there is scope for competing reasonable points of view. But the rational necessity of numerous moral demands clearly has an important bearing on one's understanding of law, the basis of the law's authority, legal justice and so on. Hart's legal positivism is almost certainly the product of his moral scepticism, for example.[2] It is therefore important to consider the question of moral necessity directly, in an attempt to overcome the pervasive moral scepticism of our times.

To those who are tempted by moral scepticism (the view that all moral 'values' are social—or indeed personal—constructs), modern ethical philosophy has evolved a number of ways of overcoming doubt. I will mention only two here. The first (to be examined in more detail in Part Two) is directed

---

[1] See, eg, J Finnis, *Natural Law and Natural Rights*, 2nd edn (Oxford, Clarendon Press, 2011) 3–18. On descriptive jurisprudence, see ch 6 below.

[2] HLA Hart, *The Concept of Law*, 3rd edn (Oxford, Clarendon Press, 2012) ch IX.

to those who worry that our moral thoughts and beliefs are influenced, in inextricable ways, by our cultural or personal experience. If every person's morals are a product of their culture or upbringing, what entitles us to impose our moral beliefs on other communities, or even other persons in our own communities? In short, who are we to judge? Against this concern, the political philosopher John Rawls proposes the following solution. Imagine a group of people are put into a situation in which they are deprived of all personal knowledge about themselves and their beliefs: a so-called 'original position', in which no one knows details such as their race or gender, whether they will be wealthy or poor, sick or healthy, old or young (etc) and even what their 'values' will be: in other words, what their conception of the good life is. In such a situation, each person must settle questions of justice, and devise a set of reasonable laws, without the influence of any conscious or unconscious bias: deprived of all such knowledge, they must reason from behind a 'veil of ignorance'.

The outcome of such deliberations will be examined properly in Part Two. Here, I merely wish to point out this method's suitability for overcoming the moral sceptic's worry that unconscious bias affects all our moral thinking, rendering it unreliable or unreasonable. For, although it is obviously impossible to deprive ourselves of knowledge of who we are, and what we believe, it is possible—and potentially fruitful—to consider what persons in the original position would think about questions of justice and lawfulness. Even if some very difficult moral questions remain, such a method might at least be practical in answering some basic, but important, conclusions about the demands of justice and personal freedom.

But some moral sceptics are motivated by a different, and more fundamental concern: that there are simply no moral values at all, but merely projections of our feelings or desires. This is a more radical claim, and one, in fact, that stands as much in need of proof and justification as any philosophical thesis. Is it really the case that the murderer's interest in killing is every bit as valuable as his victim's desire to live? Against this view, the philosopher Robert Nozick raises the example of a machine that generates experiences for one plugged into it, that satisfy every desire that the person might have.[3] As long as the person remains comatose and attached to the machine, they will experience the gratification of all their desires, whatever they happen to be. Yet at least the majority of people would regard a life of unconsciousness, plugged into the machine, as a terrible life, and a waste of life. For the 'experiences' are of course not real but only simulated. Even if (having been plugged in) it is impossible for a person to *know* they are in the machine (they believe that

---

[3] R Nozick, *Anarchy, State and Utopia* (New York, Basic Books, 1974) 42–45.

what they are experiencing is real) it remains the case that such a life is not to be admired or called a good life. Why is this? It is surely because nothing truly *valuable* occurs in the life of the person attached to the machine. They perform no deeds or actions, experience no *true* friendship with others, indeed do not truly *live*, in the normal sense of the word. Having one's brain stimulated to simulate such experiences is no substitute for the real thing. But if this is true, then there are real values (such as life and friendship) as distinct from apparent values, that is to say, evils that can appear as values to the unreasonable. And the murderer's delight in killing is precisely such an evil, desired by a disordered mind as a good.

Here we have a simple demonstration that life contains certain good or valuable ends, to be pursued, as well as certain evils or disvalues to be avoided. The defender of moral scepticism, it would seem, has the much harder (indeed impossible) task of establishing—despite appearances—that delight in killing is every bit as valuable as other desires, such as the desire to preserve life.

These two abilities—the ability to transcend in one's thinking the particular values of one's own community, and the ability to distinguish real from false values—are central to the activity of ethics. Only one who understands them is aware that law can be something other, and more valuable, than a mere expression of state power. Yet these thoughts do not answer, but merely raise, the classical questions of ethics: what is the good life? How should I act? Accordingly, the ancient philosophers, Plato and Aristotle, devote their ethical works to the question of the good life. This focus helps us to see that law (along with all human purposes) is directed to furthering and maintaining the common good of the community. The phenomenon of law is intelligible only given this central purpose: though law can be used as an instrument of evil, or of repression, these two possibilities are not equal; the law's instrumentality for evil is comprehensible only as a failure or distortion of its true purpose to uphold the common good. For it replaces that common good with a lesser good: the good of the ruler, or of a ruling faction. And these narrower ideas of the good are qualified versions of, and thus parasitic upon, the true idea of good.

A BASIC DIVISION

There have come down to us from the ancient philosophies two alternative ways, or methods of reflection, that allow us to transcend our own community's values, and to distinguish the truly right from the truly wrong. Many of the central debates in jurisprudence can in fact be seen as a continuation of the argument between these two alternative modes of reflection. The first, originating with Aristotle, takes its orientation from the idea that, if we are to understand law, politics, or the bearing of these systems of thought on society, we must look at the world. To understand the meaning of justice (for example), one can only examine the justice or injustice of people's actions, reflecting on what makes actions just or unjust, and on their repercussions. Contemplation of justice apart from its worldly associations tells us nothing: just as the mere idea of an ingenious well-functioning machine reveals nothing of the problems and malfunctions one is likely to encounter in its construction and actual operation. Ethics, law and politics are of the world.

But an opposing tradition of thought, deriving from Plato, is orientated by reference to a different idea. Discussing justice in the *Republic*, Plato observes that most human thinking and action involves a corruption or distortion of justice. Worldly influences (such as greed or fear) constantly disrupt the vision of justice, causing us to identify it with those things that tend to support our personal interests and wellbeing. Thus, time after time, Socrates (Plato's narrator) is forced to stand against the popular but erroneous view that justice is merely a weapon of the weak against the strong, and that it is better to commit injustice than to suffer it. Faced with a thousand false teachings, with everything that can mislead the mind or pull it into error, the philosopher must turn away from the world, away from popular beliefs. Understanding lies not in observation but in the mind's contemplation of unchanging ideas. Although one can scarcely avoid the worldly implementation of these ideas, always in application the true values become distorted, confused, qualified. The world cannot be a source of true ideas. Ethics, law and politics belong to philosophy.

Which of these two traditional ways of thinking about values such as justice is the right one? This is a question every jurisprudential scholar and student must face, and decide. A history of jurisprudential ideas from classical Greece to the present day could well be framed in terms of this fundamental opposition. This is not such a work; but here I will explore the bearing of this opposition on subsequent thinking.

First in the *Gorgias* and then, later, in the *Republic*, Plato defends ethics and justice from the callow men of Athens who think that these ideas merely bewitch the strong, who would otherwise take all that they want, and advance the position of the weak, who are naturally to be exploited. In the former work, Socrates successfully argues that ethics is not mere rhetoric, the art of persuading people of ideas even when they are false, but in fact identifies moral truth. In the latter, he is asked to define justice, against the proposal that justice is simply what is good for the strong. Socrates patiently explains that justice is that which makes a person wise and good, and that the just person lives a happier life than the unjust person.[4] But when he is asked to define what justice is, Socrates says that he can do so only by building a conception of an

---

[4] Plato, *Republic* 338c–352d.

ideal society: for justice is intrinsically a social phenomenon, but all present, actual societies are more or less ruined by corrupt practices and unjust ways of living. Thus, in order that human behaviour should be guided towards what is good and to shun that which is evil, it is necessary that its guiding values be drawn from outside human practice itself. Human action cannot be its own guide: to deny this proposition is to eliminate the idea of goodness as anything more than 'what we happen to do around here' (and to regard evil as merely that which is disliked or detested).

If we are to guide human behaviour by some other standard than 'what is done around here', what is that standard to be? Both Plato and Aristotle make the same reply: reason. But they differ over the character of reason. For Plato, our reason must transcend the practices that we are required to judge, orientating our judgement by reference to ideals or archetypes of which actual practices are imperfect instances. This is Plato's famous theory of Ideas [*eidos*], as described in the *Republic* by the following analogy.

For Plato, the visible world, the world of ordinary experience, is analogous to a cave in which we are imprisoned. Forced to gaze only at a blank wall, the denizens of the cave watch shadows projected on the wall by things moving before a fire which lies behind them towards the mouth of the cave, and they begin to ascribe forms to these shadows. This, Plato says, is as close as the cave-dwellers ever come to perception of reality. The philosopher, by contrast, is one who realises that the shadowy forms are not in fact elements of reality, but comes to knowledge of the real forms which cast the shadows, thereby escaping the cave. In Plato's image, the world of ordinary perception and experience is but a pale echo of reality in its highest form, a set of conventional ideas conceived about Forms (or archetypes) that are known only through the imperfect examples that we encounter in the material world. It is these archetypes which are the object of genuine knowledge, just as our knowledge of the properties of geometric figures pertains to the *ideal* sphere or cube, not the various approximations we draw and study upon the page.

The theory of Ideas rendered Plato's philosophy congenial to the Christian jurists of later centuries, who saw in it a resemblance to their own understandings, concerning the relationship between the transitory and changeable world of mere sensation and the eternal, unchanging order of God's Kingdom. This was nowhere more the case than in Saint Augustine's vision in *De Civitate Dei* (*Of the City of God*).

In the *City of God*, Augustine differentiates between two 'cities' (ie, communities characterised by an agreement or relationship between many minds). On the one hand, there is the earthly city, in which human beings remain focused upon earthly needs and rewards; and on the other, the city of God, which represents both the heavenly kingdom of the afterlife *and* a dimension of present life insofar as it is present in the good works and charitable acts of the faithful.

The city of God is thus understood in two aspects, first in its perfection as the eternal heavenly community, and secondly as it exists within the earthly city where it is 'on pilgrimage'. Again, the idea of a 'city' in this image is not meant to refer to actual cities (such as Rome) but to the idea of community as an ordered arrangement of minds. It is in this sense that Augustine can speak of the city of God as being present and at work within the world. 'In truth', Augustine says, 'those two cities'—ie, ways of thinking an acting together— 'are interwoven and intermixed in this era, and await separation at the last judgment'. Augustine distinguishes the earthly and heavenly cities according to their objects of love: 'In one city, love of God has been given first place, in the other, love of self'. Speaking of the love that binds humankind to the earthly city, he writes: 'This then is the original evil: man regards himself as his own light, and turns away from that light which would make man a light if he set his heart on it.'[5]

Augustine's vision of the two cities is underpinned by the same division between transitory and eternal objects that informs Plato's metaphor of the cave. The legal order of a state is a human creation, with its own ends and purposes; but if it also aims to be just, it must reach beyond itself and set its sights on the eternal prize. Politics, the practical arrangement of human societies, can of course be a sordid business. The earthly city knows corruption, violence and conflicts of many kinds. This is, of course, the result of those whose eyes are fixed upon earthly goods, temporal and fleeting, the trappings of worldly advancement and success that many crave but only few can achieve. No society can avoid the need for laws which govern access to earthly goods, and for the regulation of mundane arrangements. But Augustine's concern is to make heavenly salvation also an end of politics, even amidst these sinful realities. We must, in this way, strive to perceive the purer form of law (the divine law that is normative for the Christian) within the imperfect law of the earthly kingdom. This idea is one which recurs in various forms throughout the history of Western jurisprudence. It is present, for example, in the positivist distinction between law as it is, and law as it ought to be. It is still more explicit in Dworkin's injunction to seek for the 'law beyond law',[6] and in Fuller's famous statement in his evocatively titled book, *The Law in Quest of Itself*, that the judge must 'play ... his part in the eternal process by which the common law works itself pure and adapts itself to the needs of a new day'.[7]

Here it is possible to see an interpretation of various modern jurisprudential theorists as pursuing a Platonistic agenda. Platonism is characterised by a type of dualism. We have values that are derived from intellectual sources

---

[5] Augustine, *De Civitate Dei* (*Of the City of God*) XIV.13.
[6] R Dworkin, *Law's Empire* (London, Fontana Press, 1986) ch 10.
[7] L Fuller, *The Law in Quest of Itself* (Chicago, Foundation Press, 1940) 140.

that are worldly, subjective, local; and values that are eternal, celestial, immutable. Those that are immutable are not completely separate from the worldly domain, for they have a presence within it. But they also transcend that domain, and their presence within it is but a partial, imperfect echo. Is it necessary to believe in a supernatural realm of values and meanings in order to preserve the idea of genuine value? It might seem so: if there is no more than the material world of our experience, then our judgements about what is good and evil, right and wrong, just and unjust (and so forth) are at bottom mere shared conventional understandings. All very well, perhaps. But if values are no more than conventional, then we are forced to admit that, say, slavery is evil only because we generally agree that it is so; once upon a time we did not. For as long as it was considered acceptable, slavery was in every conceivable sense good. There are some who might be able to live with this conclusion. And yet it is necessary to go further. If slavery is morally right or wrong only by the lights of human convention, then we have no reason at all (except perhaps sentiment) for preferring one judgement to the other. It follows that we can advance no opinion about the value of things that is not equally as valid as it is contradictory. In denying a supernatural realm of value, it seems that we bring about the destruction of all values. There is, however, an alternative possibility.

I referred to the Platonic world-view which underpins the Augustinian philosophy as a type of dualism, of Heaven above and Earth below. But it is also informed by a temporality that is central to its character. There is in fact an inherent temporality in Christian thought, which describes an initial Fall (into sinfulness), the eventual coming of Christ as redeemer, and finally salvation for sinful human beings. Strongly present within this temporal framework is the idea of a journey back to God, via the pilgrimage through this world, just as the philosopher in escaping the cave must undertake his own journey. But although it is implicit in the Christian account, a temporal framework is not an inevitable feature of an explanation of the human condition. The Aristotelian account, in particular, is based rather upon a teleology that is not essentially temporal. It is this which explains the hostility of early Christian natural lawyers to the Aristotelian philosophy.

Some explanation is necessary. Aristotle's philosophy addresses the world of natural being. It seeks to understand the botanical properties of plants and the actions of animals as well as subjects such as ethics and 'human sciences'. Indeed, the natural philosophy includes the study of the human being, who is himself considered as a natural being. This stands in some tension to the Judeo-Christian picture of the world, in which the human being is not a natural being but a being made in the image of God. Nature itself is not *mere* nature, but a created order which must be understood by reference to the supernatural processes which govern it and brought it into existence.

The focus of enquiry within the Christian-Platonistic tradition is therefore upon the abstract world of the Forms (Eternity), with little of importance to be said about the material world of ordinary experience. Aristotle, on the other hand, presents a natural philosophy in which the material world is thought to contain its own principles of operation. We must therefore look to it, and not elsewhere, for understanding. The beings of this world are held by Aristotle to contain their own potentialities, and therefore as seeking ends that are defined by their own nature rather than by external laws. Thus, it is the purpose of the acorn to grow into an oak tree, and of everything to flourish according to its own kind. Human beings are thereby presented in the Aristotelian philosophy as possessing the capacity to achieve their highest good *in this life*, without intercession from the beyond.

Christian theologians were alive to the dangers inherent in the Aristotelian position. For it seemed that no room existed in this teleological picture of the world and its processes for God as an influence (benign or otherwise) upon the destinies of the beings within it. This opposition did not last forever. Partly under the influence of Arabic scholarship, through which the first translations of Aristotle's texts were made available for study in Europe, the Church gradually moved from a situation in which the works of Aristotle must *not* be studied, to one in which the study of Aristotle is *required*. This depended, of course, upon the reconciliation of Aristotelian doctrines with the Christian framework of thought; and the resulting synthesis is of the first importance in Western jurisprudence. The most important figure in effecting this reconciliation was Thomas Aquinas.

Philosophical knowledge for Aristotle derives from the contemplation, not of some other-worldly domain of Forms, but of the material world itself. The question Aquinas asks is: *how* do we understand the world? Imagine watching a garden grow. You notice the different rates of growth of the various kinds of plants, trees and flowers. Some are brightly coloured, others less so. Some attract insects whilst others do not, and so on. But Aquinas says you understand yet very little until you know *why* it grows, and *where* it is growing to. One must understand, as it were, the directionality of nature: both its teleology, and its cause. It will be remembered that in the Platonic philosophy, the focus is on that which is eternal and unchanging, with the transitory and ephemeral objects of the material world being considered as but pale and fleeting echoes of eternal forms. Aquinas (following Aristotle) reverses this priority: the animation of the natural order is not regarded as incidental and unimportant, but vital to understanding. All things move. What, then, moves them? It is through acquaintance with the natural order that one approaches a knowledge of God (the first mover).

Fuller's image of the law 'working itself pure', as well as Dworkin's allusion to the 'law beyond law' can also be understood in this way. They can stand as images of the ideal form of law that exists, only incompletely and in corrupted form, in the law that we have. As the acorn may become an oak tree, so it is the purpose of law to develop into a deeper, more satisfying expression of its own inner values (such as justice). But in the case of law, it is we, as human beings, who must achieve it.

I will not for the moment consider which of these interpretations (the Aristotelian or the Platonic) best reveals the meaning of these modern theories. One must not assume, however, that they are merely alternative expressions of the same idea, leading to the same end. The Platonic interpretation lends itself quite readily to a view according to which we are required to align our actual, imperfect laws with a definite set of principles that constitute an independent and free-standing moral perspective on the world. Such principles are themselves essentially law-like, comprising general standards which must be applied to the variable particulars of human practice. (We might think of them either as constituting the law of God, as a kind of divine legislator, or else—perhaps if we are atheists—as laws that are in some sense *rationally* necessary.) From this standpoint, we can ask the natural lawyer's traditional questions: to what extent morality is realised within the law, and whether an unjust 'law' is genuinely binding upon those subject to it. But we can think of law and morality in another way. With Aristotle, we might conceive of moral understandings as being grounded in historical practice, and therefore as being reflected in those institutions, such as the law, that are directed towards good ends. Law, though imperfect, achieves a modicum of justice and good order; and it is by reflecting upon the character of these achievements that we form an idea of what is good, or just. According to such an image, law is guided not by some well-defined set of principles, understood in abstraction from actual arrangements, but by an archetype,[8] just as, in drawing geometric figures we are guided by the archetype of the perfect sphere or triangle. But our ability to conceive of the archetype is nevertheless possible only by contemplating the approximate and imperfect figures that we are actually able to produce. Knowledge of the archetype, in other words, comes not from acquaintance with what is perfect, but from the knowledge that all existing examples are imperfect.

When most people think about morality, they probably have in mind something approximating to the first of these views, in which morals are regarded as moral *laws*, standing in judgement over human actions, which may be kept or broken. It is therefore worth spending some time considering the views on law, morality and the state contained in Aristotle's *Politics*. Ultimately, Aristotelian ethical doctrines were to fall comprehensively out of favour: so much so that it is possible to think of the jurisprudential and

---

[8] See NE Simmonds, *Law as a Moral Idea* (Oxford, Oxford University Press, 2007).

political theories of modernity as a specific rejection of Aristotle. The interesting question is of course *why* this happened, and whether, in departing from Aristotelian ideas, modern theories marched firmly down the wrong path into error and confusion. For the moment, it is necessary to begin by examining the vision of human life and human society at the heart of Aristotle's *Politics*.

ARISTOTELIAN POLITICAL THOUGHT

Aristotle's thought contains a philosophy of nature. His political philosophy also begins with nature. At the beginning of Book I of the *Politics*, Aristotle says that the state is a creation of nature, because 'man is by nature a political animal'.[9] What drives Aristotle to this judgement? In the first place, the survival of the human race obviously depends upon human beings forming unions and becoming what he calls 'companions of the manger' and later 'companions of the cupboard'. Families are natural units in the sense that they are necessary for the bare requirements of life. But the nature of a thing is defined not by what is merely necessary to its existence, but by 'what each thing is when fully developed'.[10] And because a state is formed where many families coexist together for mutual advantage, one may say that it 'originat[es] in the bare needs of life, and continu[es] in existence for the sake of the good life'. Why the 'good life'? Because what is natural for the human being (the need for society with others) can also be said to be what is good for him, that is, required for his flourishing. Aristotle therefore contemplates the nature of a good that is essentially social in nature, being of a kind that can be realised only in common. Requiring a nexus of social and political institutions to foster and maintain it, the nature of 'the good' is then thought to be reflected in the character of those institutions (such as the family, the market, the law and so on) that constitute forms of human association. It is for this reason that Aristotle takes the view that established arrangements and institutions, such as law, form an archetype which serves as a focal point for knowledge of morality and the good.

It is tempting, and quite usual in modern times, to begin an account of politics with the individual and then to consider how diverse individuals can come together to form a body. Aristotle stands at the head of a tradition of thinking which begins at the opposite end: he asks, rather, how we can come to view ourselves as individuals. '[T]he individual', Aristotle says, 'when isolated, is not self-sufficing; and therefore he is like a part in relation to the whole'.[11]

---

[9] Aristotle, *Politics* I.2.
[10] ibid.
[11] ibid.

One who, by nature, is without society must either be above or else below humanity ('either a beast or a god'). Having established this priority, Aristotle proceeds to ascribe ethical significance to the state. For according to his teleology, it is not the mere being of a thing but its full development that determines its nature. Consequently, he is able to state that civilised society represents the *perfection* of the human being. 'For man, when perfected, is the best of animals, but, when separated from law and justice, he is the worst of all.'[12] This leads Aristotle to the following conclusion: '[J]ustice is the bond of men in states, for the administration of justice (which is the determination of what is just) is the principle of order in political society.'[13]

The two sentences at the end of the preceding paragraph reveal a dual aspect of law. On the one hand, individuals must learn how to be virtuous and good by being encouraged to act rightly. Becoming habituated to good ways of acting, they will come (through experience) to love what is good. (If this sounds unlikely, then reflect upon the way in which one's moral character is formed through a combination of parental direction and instruction from early teachers.) In this way, our evaluative judgement, which might otherwise focus on the mere pleasure and pain that certain actions hold for us, is initially guided towards the right objects. Continual reinforcement then fosters the inculcation of excellence-forming habits of behaviour. This aspect of law relates to what Fuller calls a 'morality of minimum duty'; or (as with Aristotle) law as it is contemplated as a principle of social order. On the other hand, law also possesses an aspirational aspect, or as Fuller terms it, a 'morality of aspiration'.[14] In speaking of the administration of justice in connection with the perfection of the human being, Aristotle links the realm of law and justice with the wider range of questions concerning virtue and prudence. Hence, just as Augustine makes Heaven an end of politics, Aristotle places questions of excellence at the centre of the enquiry. Human nature is intrinsically sociable; and it therefore finds expression in the range of social institutions around which society coheres. If, moreover, human nature is perfected through society, then scrutiny and careful interpretation of institutions will yield a conception of excellence which may form a basis for moral judgement and criticism.

It is often said that, whereas Aristotle's theory is of a kind that is directed towards a single, unified conception of 'the good', by contrast modern theories of law and politics have tended towards a view in which each individual pursues his or her own idea of the good, so that each such idea may vie and conflict with others. In this way, the idea of a highest good, or *summum bonum*,

---

[12] ibid.
[13] ibid.
[14] L Fuller, *The Morality of Law*, rev edn (New Haven CT, Yale University Press, 1969) ch 1.

was eventually to disappear from politics. In fact, this is something of a simpli-fication, and may be a source of significant misunderstanding.

Both Aristotle and (later) Aquinas retained an understanding of the com-plexity and variety of human arrangements. One could in no wise equate in this way a 'highest good' with a *single* form of life that is understood to be uniquely correct, or optimal, or as the mode to which all others gravitate or aspire. How ought this notion of 'highest good' be understood? Consider first the position of individual human beings. It is clear that individuals can pursue all sorts of things that they deem to be 'good' for themselves, in provoking feel-ings of satisfaction. Some of these (eg, immoderate indulgence in rich foods and fine wines) are incompatible with others (such as health). Aristotle wants to say that our *highest* good must be understood by reference to the practice of virtue: in this example, moderation (temperance). This exercise of restraint is not pointless self-denial, but promotes the good of healthy life, which is a deeper and more permanent source of wellbeing than the short-term pleas-ures of the table. The latter are all too quickly forgotten, and if allowed to gain a hold over us they will ruin both our character (in making us a slave to our passions) and our broader wellbeing. The good or worthwhile life, under this conception, is the life of the flourishing agent. Put into more modern terms, each agent is thought to realise his wellbeing by aligning his actions with what Finnis calls 'forms of human flourishing'.[15] Each person may differ in the way that they participate in these forms of flourishing (one person preferring to indulge her talents as a scholar, whilst another develops her excellence in sport, or in the creation of works of art, for example). But what constitutes the flourishing life is nevertheless determined by the general characteristics of the human being. (We can imagine this somewhat analogously to the dynamic bal-ance controls on a piece of music equipment: just as we can alter the balance between bass, treble tones and those in between by increasing or decreasing their level via a series of sliders, so we can vary the level of our involvement in various forms of flourishing activity, as our talents and time allow.) If we examine this situation, we will discover that the essential forms of human flourishing are of a kind that can only be pursued and realised in common: in society. It is because of this basic alignment of prudence and wellbeing with the flourishing life of the agent that Aristotle is able to claim, at the beginning of the *Politics*, that the state 'aims at the highest good'.[16]

This reference to the highest good should not be misunderstood. The good of each individual and the good of the community must not be elided. As Aquinas points out, happiness equates to the *perfection* of a rational animal,

---

[15] Finnis (n 1) ch 2. Though see my later discussion in ch 11, which casts doubt on the close-ness of Finnis's position to that of Aristotle.

[16] Aristotle, *Politics* I.1.

which for human beings is one's personal relationship with God: something that cannot be true of the community as distinct from the individuals within it. Yet it is only in community that human beings can explore their potentialities fully. Hence, if human beings are to be placed in a flourishing condition, the community must take as its object the common good of its members, who will require peace, stability and opportunities to pursue the objects of the good life mentioned above. The suggestion that the modern world is characterised by recognition of a plurality of goods, none of which can claim to be the 'highest' good that is proper to man, is therefore not to be distinguished from the older tradition of thinking on the ground that it refuses to identify a specific form of life as the one uniquely appropriate or somehow to be singled out from the rest as 'the right way to live'. Nevertheless, the emergence of deep divisions in the political and religious life of Europe from the sixteenth century onwards produced important shifts in thinking away from the intellectual tradition epitomised by Aristotle.

The fracturing of old certainties gradually led to a concern with politics as a domain of *disagreement*, and the thought that each person's pursuit of their own conception of the good life was by no means guaranteed to result in a *common* good, except perhaps in a very thin sense. Might not these ideas of the good be genuinely opposing, implying radically different and incompatible visions of the kind of society required for their fulfilment? Increasingly doubtful was the Aristotelian/Thomist position that the common good of a society is characterised by the shared, rational pursuit of modes of human flourishing. Instead, rationality came to be seen as the logical fitting of means to desired ends in pursuit of one's own, private conception of the good in a world where plural notions of the good compete for dominance. An altered picture of law therefore emerged, which has more in common with the 'minimum duty' aspect of the Aristotelian picture than with its aspirational character. The potential for conflict between opposing forms of the good, and the likelihood therefore of collisions between those bent on their pursuit, gives rise to the need for an organised framework of rules and entitlements. Rather than seeking to give priority to one (or some) of these goods over the others, such rules instead limit the level of impedance that one person's attempts to secure what is good for them can have upon another person's attempts to further theirs. Politics, in other words, is the search for a reasonable balance between interests that are constantly shifting and opposing, not the realisation of a shared way of life. The 'common good' of the community comes to be equated only with those minimal base lines that are necessary so as to enable individuals living in close proximity to pursue anything: social stability and peace, law and order, and forms of mutual forbearance.

Subsequent thinking on law and politics has devoted much attention to the specific characteristics of these minimal base lines of social cooperation.

One of the most significant questions concerns the extent to which even such minimal commitments can come into being only where created and imposed by *law* (ie, through the exercise of political authority), or whether they constitute that minimum form of justice to which human beings must commit themselves if any ordered existence is to be imaginable (and thus in some way exist prior to enacted forms of law). The following chapters of this book explore these questions as they appear in the thoughts of Aquinas, Hobbes, Grotius and later thinkers on law and politics in the West.

THE ABANDONMENT OF ARISTOTLE

These shifts in European culture played a large part in the waning significance of Aristotelian ideas. But some of the key thinkers of the Reformation, including Luther and Calvin, had begun already to institute a line of thought that was overtly hostile to Aristotle. '[T]his defunct pagan' (wrote Luther), 'has attained supremacy [in the universities]; impeded, and almost suppressed, the Scriptures of the living God. When I think of this lamentable state of affairs, I cannot avoid believing that the Evil One introduced the study of Aristotle'.[17] Why the reversal?

Consider what Aristotle says about the life of the flourishing individual. By pursuing excellence, we enhance our wellbeing. We come to a knowledge of what constitutes an excellent and worthwhile life by examining and considering the fabric of institutions which reflect our shared human nature. But who is to say that what we will discover there is actually *good*? What if these institutions reveal a nature that is *not* good and just, but evil and corrupt? How are we to know the difference? Given these contingencies of the human situation, must we not rather follow Plato and Augustine in contemplating the moral life in the starry heaven of eternity? Aristotle is justified in deriving a knowledge of the good from experience of this world only if he correctly assumes human nature to be itself essentially good or benevolent. Here, we must remember that Aristotle's philosophy is indeed underpinned by a metaphysical conception of the human condition (one that regards the human situation from its position within the wider rationally ordered cosmos). His political philosophy emphatically belongs to his broader philosophy of nature, in which all aspects of earthly activity are teleologically ordered (ie, ordered towards their end or perfection).

It is this aspect of Aristotle's philosophy of nature that proved so objectionable to the writers of the Reformation, who broadly preferred Plato as an

---

[17] Martin Luther, 'Twenty-Seven Proposals for Improving the State of Christendom' in J Dillenberger (ed), *Martin Luther: Selections From His Writings* (New York, Doubleday, 1961) 470.

intellectual model. Aristotle's philosophy belongs to a tradition which regards things, actions and so on as possessing in themselves good or bad characteristics. We can understand and evaluate the worth of objects by reference to their place in a universe, or cosmos, that is rationally intelligible and capable of interpretation. The early Christian writers and those of the medieval period who absorbed Aristotle's teachings into their writings, developed a conception of natural law that was at first associated with the intellect and understanding. It addressed a created order in which goodness is imagined to be the product of God's nature rather than His arbitrary will. Is honesty good because God commands honesty, or does God command honesty *because* it is good? In the former case, it seems that we can understand nothing about *why* honesty is good. We can merely *know* it to be so because it is God's will. If on the other hand, we think of goodness as belonging to God's nature as a perfect being, and that God commands us to be honest because it is His nature to command what is good, then the goodness of virtues such as honesty can be understood as something distinguishable from their status as willed commands. Were the source of natural law to reside in God's will alone, there could be no moral understanding, but simply obedience. But if the morality of things is distinguishable from their status as divine laws, then moral wisdom becomes possible. And Aristotle's account is, in the first place, one of how we acquire and develop moral *wisdom*.

Contrast this notion with the standpoint of Luther: 'What God wills is not right because He ought, or was bound, so to will; on the contrary, what takes place must be right, because He so wills it.'[18] To hold otherwise, Luther supposes, is to commit the heresy of believing there to be a higher source of authority than God. Calvin makes the point explicitly:

> For if [God's will] has any cause, something must precede it, to which it is, as it were, bound; this is unlawful to imagine. For God's will is so much the highest rule of righteousness that whatever He wills, by the very act that He wills it, must be considered righteous.[19]

Ethical understanding, from this perspective, consists not in the interpretation and scrutiny of established institutions and practices, but in an attitude of pious acceptance of God's will. Nature, similarly, presents a context for moral reflection 'in its givenness, but not in its intrinsic orderliness or purposefulness'.[20] Here, we can perceive a decisive shift away from Aristotelianism, and towards a Platonistic standpoint. The visible world is to

---

[18] Martin Luther, 'The Bondage of the Will' in J Dillenberger (ed), *Martin Luther: Selections From His Writings* (New York, Doubleday, 1961) 196.

[19] John Calvin, Institutes of the Christian Religion, Book III, xxiii.2.

[20] J Porter, *Nature as Reason: A Thomistic Theory of the Natural Law* (Grand Rapids MI, Eerdmans Publishing, 2005) 44.

be viewed as more or less corrupted and imperfect; righteousness a matter of withdrawing one's thoughts from material things and elevating one's gaze to the heavens. But having become thus unspotted from the world, the object of one's gaze is not understanding, but faith. God's ways are 'wholly incomprehensible and inaccessible to man's understanding'.[21] (Isaiah 55:8 proclaims: 'For my thoughts are not your thoughts, saith the Lord'.) Luther is thus led to the Protestant doctrine of justification by faith alone: it is each person's responsibility to come to knowledge of righteousness by private study of the Bible.

It should be apparent that the Lutheran view of the world brings about a certain impoverishment of moral thinking. Luther's theology transforms the Aristotelian world of natural processes and ends in a morally inert realm of brute facts, the significance of which depends upon values that are drawn from elsewhere. Moral ideas, as the natural lawyer Samuel Pufendorf later wrote, 'do not arise out of the intrinsic nature of the physical properties of things, but they are superadded, at the will of intelligent entities, to things already existent and physically complete'.[22] In this way, morality came to be seen as a separate and autonomous outlook upon the world, Pufendorf adding 'That reason should be able to discover any morality in the actions of a man without reference to a law, is as impossible as for a man born blind to choose between colours.'[23] This depiction of morality as a self-standing body of moral *laws* that exist essentially separately and apart from the practices over which they stand in judgement, has continued to dominate political thinking long after the specifically theological premises which led to it have been forgotten. It is, in particular, this conception of morality that gives shape and definition to the theories of writers such as Rawls and Dworkin, which will be examined in Part Two of this book. Insofar as they are heirs to the developments charted in this chapter, modern political theories operate within an essentially Protestant view of the world, and indeed deserve to be termed Protestant political theories. Dworkin, in particular, observes that the notion of political obligation that is central to his legal theory '[is] a ... Protestant idea: fidelity to a scheme of principle each citizen has a responsibility to identify, ultimately for himself, as his community's scheme.'[24]

When modern-day theories of law address the question of the relationship between law and morality, it is in the main to this Platonistic-type image of morality that they refer. But it is worth noting that Plato himself suggested that

---

[21] Luther, 'The Bondage of the Will' (n 18) 200.
[22] S Pufendorf, *De Iure Naturae et Gentium* (*Of the Law of Nature and Nations*) (London, 1749) I.1.5–6.
[23] ibid I.2.6.
[24] Dworkin (n 6) 190.

the philosopher who has 'escaped the cave' will have a difficult time in trying to apply his insights to the mundane world of human practice. Part VII of the *Republic* contains some depressing images about the likely degradation of the philosopher's character as he grapples with earthly realities and vested interests. Forced into compromises and continually subject to dark and depraved influences, the philosopher will lose sight of truth long before he manages to accomplish anything. The world will remain resistant to his messages, and incalculably greater than he. Sometimes, Plato suggests that the wisest man will seek a kind of monastic life, free from the snares and entrapments of a wicked world. But in taking this course, the philosopher evades his responsibilities and does not achieve true greatness.

The modern theories I have spoken of retain little of this pessimism. They treat justice, 'integrity' and other political values as genuine possibilities on the earthly plane, to some considerable extent already instantiated in Western societies. One's 'community's scheme' is not to be despised but celebrated, even as one aspires to its further refinement. Society's institutions and practices are not dark and depraved, but enlightened. What assumptions underpin this optimism?

In this chapter I hope to have demonstrated that a Platonistic image of morality is not inevitable. Although it is both familiar and largely unquestioned, it deserves to be thought about, engaged with and critically reflected upon. Its assumptions deserve to be examined, not least when combined with an underlying optimism about Western moral and political values. Careless of their commitments, can modern jurisprudential theories long ignore such questions without projecting themselves into abstraction, or collapsing under the weight of internal contradictions?

SUGGESTED READING

POLITICS IS OF THE WORLD

Aristotle, *Politics*, Book I, 1–2; Book II, 1–7.
—— *Nicomachean Ethics*, Books I and II.

Background Reading

MF Burnyeat, 'Aristotle on Learning to be Good' in AO Rorty (ed), *Essays on Aristotle's Ethics* (Berkeley CA, University of California Press) 69–92.
S Darwall, *British Moralists and the Internal 'Ought' 1640–1740* (Cambridge, Cambridge University Press) 1–9.
L Fuller, *The Morality of Law* (New Haven CT, Yale University Press, 1964) ch 1.

A Kenny, *Aristotle on the Perfect Life* (Oxford, Oxford University Press) chs 1–2.
NE Simmonds, *Central Issues in Jurisprudence*, 4th edn (London, Sweet & Maxwell) 1–8.

POLITICS BELONGS TO PHILOSOPHY

Plato, *Republic*, Books VI–VII.
—— *Gorgias* 461b–505d.

Background Reading

JL Ackrill, *Essays on Plato and Aristotle* (Oxford, Oxford University Press) ch 15.
R Kraut, 'The Defence of Justice in Plato's *Republic*' in R Kraut (ed), *The Cambridge Companion to Plato* (Cambridge, Cambridge University Press) 311–37.
DD Raphael, *Concepts of Justice* (Oxford, Oxford University Press) ch 4.
G Santas, *Plato, Aristotle and the Moderns* (London, Blackwell) chs 3–5.

3

Jurisprudence: The Classical Tradition

IN ORDER TO understand a debate, it is often necessary to return to a point before the controversy emerged. This is no less the case with the controversy between 'natural law' and 'legal positivism'. It was in fact natural lawyers who first developed the idea of positive law, as something distinct from the law of nature.[1] Despite ongoing twists and turns of debate, the modern outlook concerning these ideas continues to be shaped by the epoch-making works of two writers: John Finnis (on the side of natural law), and HLA Hart (on the side of legal positivism). Their works will be considered in Part Two of this book. Over the course of the next four chapters, we will examine not only the origins of these ideas, but also understandings of positive and natural law that differ in some important (and oft-ignored) ways from their modern incarnations.

It ought to be emphasised, however, that our reasons for examining the earlier treatments are not merely historical or comparative. As Finnis himself points out, the subject matter of investigation is not the history of beliefs about natural law (or positive law), but natural law (or positive law) itself. Consider that over the centuries, people have believed many strange and contradictory things about the earth's relationship to the sun. A historian might spend happy hours studying these beliefs and how they changed over time; but this would tell her nothing about the reality of that relationship. Similarly, it may be useful to gain knowledge of the beliefs people have held concerning natural law, or positive law; but the ultimate subject of enquiry is natural law, or positive law, itself.

Both Hart and Finnis hold views about the errors of the thought of their forebears in the natural law and positivist traditions. Their own positions are—at least to some degree—a reaction to these perceived errors. In the case of Hart, the errors to be corrected are those to be found in Aquinas and Hobbes, and in earlier positivists such as John Austin. In Finnis's case, the

---

[1] Certainly, as we shall see, Aquinas possessed such a notion. Finnis persuasively argues that the idea of positive law was first given clear expression as early as 1130: *Collected Essays of John Finnis*, IV.7, 174–75.

errors are those not only of Hart(!) but also of later writers in the tradition inaugurated (to some degree) by Thomas Aquinas (1225–74): in particular, the Spanish Jesuit writer Francisco Suarez (1548–1617) and the Dutch Protestant, Hugo Grotius (1583–1645). In order to discover what was at stake, we will look in some detail at the positions of Aquinas, Grotius and Hobbes. The present chapter will focus on Aquinas.

POSITIVE LAW

Aquinas offers a definition of law in Q.90.4 of the *Summa Theologiae*'s Prima-secundae Pars (I–II).[2] He says that a law is 'nothing except a rational [precept] directed to the common good of the community, created and issued by one responsible for the care of the community'.

Let us notice several things about this definition: (1) it is not actually a stipulated definition, but a conclusion from arguments Aquinas has made in the preceding three Articles; (2) a law is '*nothing except*' this, in other words anything that lies outside these terms falls outside at least the central definition of law; (3) it is a definition of a law *as such*: it covers all possible types of law, including natural law and positive law; (4) the reference to 'common good' *seems* to signify a point of controversy between natural law and positivist theorists, as positivists wish to acknowledge the possibility and existence of kinds of law that contravene the common good of the community. In fact, the appearance of disagreement is false: natural lawyers also wish to point to the existence of unjust or tyrannical laws (as we will see below). The point, for the natural lawyer, is that this definition explains the basis for our recognition of something as a law: it is a law *insofar as* it fulfils the terms of this definition. A law that departs from one of the elements of this definition (eg, by legislating against the common good) is, precisely by this measure, a *deficient* law, an *unjust law*. Yet Aquinas would agree, in most cases, that an unjust law is, for this very reason, *a kind of law*.

Aquinas has two terms for describing positive state law: human law (*lex humana*) and positive law (*lex positiva*). But if there is a law of nature, why is there a positive law in the first place? There are several reasons. First, positive law is responsible for articulating the immediate conclusions of natural and divine precepts: for instance, from the commandment against killing, to the

---

[2] Aquinas's *Summa* is cited by Part [I, I–II, II–II, III], Quaestio [here 90], and Article [here 4]. Each article is further subdivided into objections—ie, the arguments Aquinas will discuss [arg 1, arg 2 etc]; the Sed contra [sc]—reply to the objections from authority, with which Aquinas is not always in full agreement; the main body of Aquinas's reply [c], and specific replies to objections [ad 1, ad 2 etc].

indictment of murder and other kinds of homicide, rules of self-defence and so forth. Second and relatedly, there are many matters in relation to which the natural and divine law are ambivalent or where various different arrangements are compatible with justice. In these situations, the relevant provisions derive their binding force mainly or completely from having been set down by a ruling authority. An example would be a system of property rights: these systems differ from place to place, and from time to time, but all have a common function of upholding justice and securing prosperity in a community.

Third, a community's common good is composed partly of matters that are objectively good for all societies (such as internal peace, justice and prosperity), but also some matters that are the outcome of the community's own cultural identity and choices. Matters of the second kind, such as perhaps state patronage of the arts, are matters not for natural law but for positive law.

In the fourth place, positive law is required in order to differentiate between the duties one owes to one's community as a *citizen*, and the virtuous practices that make one a good *person*. For example, generosity and care and concern for others are virtues that make a person good. But the positive state law does not require that we pay our taxes willingly out of love for others, but only that we do pay them, however unwillingly.[3] Aquinas is clear that human law does not compel all virtue, nor repress all vices: it pertains only to those virtues (like justice) and acts (such as robbery or murder) that have a serious effect on others within the community.

The purpose of positive law, as we have seen, is the common good of the whole community, and the moral goodness of its members only to the extent that this concerns other citizens. The point of law, in other words, is *justice*. But, to return to the matter of unjust law, what would Aquinas say if, for example, certain laws of a community were unjust, or if an entire legal system were perverted against the common good for the benefit of a tyrant?

The image of natural law found in Hart suggests that a central belief of natural lawyers is that an unjust law is not a law at all (*lex iniusta non est lex*). Tellingly, Hart is quite unable to find a source for this doctrine![4] The reality is that Aquinas and other natural lawyers held that certain types of seriously unjust law remain a part of the enacted state law, but are not binding *in conscience*. Their argument was therefore not that such laws 'are not laws', but that such laws are only binding at the level of the state's coercive control over its citizens' actions. There might be moral imperatives of conscience for disobeying laws of this kind (eg, a command to kill the innocent), and submitting

---

[3] *Summa Theologiae* (hereafter *ST*) I–II.95.1c; I–II.95.2c and ad 3.

[4] The closest is Augustine, *De Libero Arbitrio* I.11: 'for me, a law that is not just does not conform to the appearance of law' (*nam mihi lex esse non videtur quae iusta non fuerit*). See also *ST* I–II.96.4c.

oneself to the consequences (imprisonment, death). But in many other cases, Aquinas counsels that one should obey even an unjust law in order to avoid civic disturbance or scandals (eg, foregoing one's rights in the name of social peace). None of this involves the claim that unjust laws are 'not laws at all'. The closest Aquinas comes to that proposition is his statement that the proclamations of a tyrant, issued altogether against the common good of the community, 'have more in common with' acts of violence than with (proper) laws.

From this it can be seen that Aquinas took great care to distinguish between various kinds of unjust law, far from denying its existence or possibility. He does this because the aim of his treatise is to offer advice to all persons (especially Christians) on their obligations, including in difficult situations where their obligations to the state and those of morality conflict. This is why Aquinas's response to the problem of unjust law is to distinguish between different states of conscience. He is not interested in denying the reality of the state's power of enforcing unjust law against persons who transgress it for the sake of good.

NATURAL LAW

Aquinas's theological ethics builds upon the eudaemonist tradition begun by Aristotle, being concerned with the interrelated concepts of 'end' and 'good'. As a first step, Aquinas responds to a series of questions intended to reveal our supreme end (return to God in the afterlife). Following an analysis of human acts, he then considers the virtuous ends that lead us towards God, and the vices that lead away from God. Before considering each of the virtues in detail, he interposes a treatise on laws (*ST* I–II.90–108), which includes the treatment of natural law. The purpose of this treatment is to describe how even pagans and pre-Christian peoples who never possessed the truth of revelation, can nevertheless attain a knowledge of moral truth and the possibility to live a virtuous life.

Aquinas distinguishes four kinds of law: (i) the *lex aeterna*, God's eternal law for the heavens and earth, which remains unfathomable to human beings; (ii) the *lex divina*, the part of eternal law that has been divinely revealed to humans, for example through God giving the Ten Commandments to Moses, or through Christ's teachings in the Gospels; (iii) the *ius naturale*, the natural law that is 'the participation of eternal law in a rational creature'; (iv) *lex humana*, or human law. The natural law is the part of eternal law that is knowable through human reason alone, independently of revelation.

Recall the definition of law that Aquinas gives, above: 'a rational precept directed to the common good of the community, created and issued by one responsible for the care of the community'. How does natural law fit in with this definition? Let us first examine the issue of promulgation: in what sense is natural law issued to human beings? Aquinas notes that any precept or measure—if it is to direct the actions of those subject to it—must exist not only outside the subject (eg, as a legislated provision) but also *in* the subject as an active principle. In much the same way, Hart speaks of rule-following as having an 'internal aspect' in addition to the externally observable behaviour (as we will discuss later).[5] So when one obeys the law against theft, one so to speak 'gives the rule to oneself' in order to guide one's behaviour: a form of self-regulation essential for all law. In the case of natural law, Aquinas says it is promulgated to us by the fact that God has placed it into human minds, so that it can be naturally apprehended.[6] This means that promulgation does not resemble one person's command to others; it consists instead in: (i) God's infusion into us of inclinations towards types of goodness and away from evils (such as pain); and (ii) the fact that humans have the reflective capacity to apprehend their own nature.

Aside from promulgation, what does it mean to say that natural law is a 'rational precept'? In order to understand this, it will be necessary to consider the difference between speculative reasoning and practical reasoning. Speculative reasoning is concerned with the truth of matters of fact, and with coming to know how things are. Practical reasoning is concerned with action, and with coming to know means and ends in order to change how things are. The difference is important, because those who incline to moral relativism often base their belief that there are no objectively determined moral values on the fact that the truth of moral propositions cannot be demonstrated in the same way as propositions of fact. Here we would do well to remember Aristotle's advice, that it is not wise to look for a demonstration in one category that is only appropriate to another category. For the scholastics, the way we apprehend or grasp practical matters differs from the way in which we grasp speculative matters of fact. In particular, our grasp of practical matters does not derive from matters apprehended by the speculative intellect.

Aquinas clarifies the point like this: the first and most basic idea that is grasped by the speculative intellect, is *being*. The idea of being is included in all other things that are apprehended by the mind. Therefore, the first precept of the speculative intellect is one based on the idea of being and non-being, namely 'nothing can be simultaneously affirmed and denied'. This precept is an indemonstrable precept: it is incapable of demonstration because it is impossible to *show* that it holds of all things, in virtue of their infinity. (Think of the atoms on the farthest star.) Yet its truth is self-evident, for anyone who

---

[5] *ST* I–II.90.1 ad 1; and see ch 6 below.
[6] *ST* I–II.90.4 ad 1.

grasps the idea of *being* also grasps this truth. This is an example of a self-evident truth that is universally understood (even if only implicitly by many people). But Aquinas warns that some truths that are self-evident, are yet evident only to the learned, who understand the terms contained in it. As an example, the truth that 'angels are not bounded within some space' is self-evident, but its self-evidence is only apparent to those who understand that angels are not physically embodied.

If the idea of 'being' and the precept that 'nothing can be simultaneously affirmed and denied', are the absolutely first things grasped by the mind, what then are the first things grasped by the mind when reasoning *practically*? Aquinas says that the first thing to fall within the understanding of the practical intellect is *good*, because all agency is directed to an end, which has the intelligible significance of good. That is to say: in any deliberation about action, if an agent elects to pursue an end, it *must* be because they consider the attainment of the end *on some level and in some way* good. Hence, the primary precept of practical reason is one based on the intellection of good, namely that good is that to which all things incline. (Plants do this unconsciously, animals on the basis of instinct, humans through appetite and reason.) Aquinas therefore announces the primary precept of law: *The good is to be done and pursued, and the bad is to be avoided.* All other precepts of natural law are based on this one.

One important facet of Aquinas's position deserves to be singled out at this point. The mode of reasoning about natural law is not driven by any ideological or political aim: it is pre-political and non-ideological. We can think of ideologies or political standpoints as narrowing the field of moral discourse by asserting assumptions (eg, 'a human being is *homo economicus*') or affirming conclusions ('workers ought to own the means of production'). The associations of the word 'ideology' suggest a certain resistance to entirely unrestricted thought, just as those of the word 'politics' suggest a moderation (if not modification) of moral thought by pragmatic considerations of circumstance or constituency. In contrast, the identification of natural law precepts involves no reference to ideals or political ideas. The primary precept simply follows from the incontestable proposition that everyone who acts, acts for the sake of an end which they consider (in some sense) to be good.

Does this mean that the references to 'good' and 'bad' in the primary precept are references to ordinary, non-moral goods and bads? It may certainly seem so: one's continuing existence is a good, to be secured through one's efforts to survive (eg, by looking both ways before crossing the road), just as ill health is a bad, to be avoided (if one can). Furthermore, Aquinas offers a hierarchy of natural law precepts that he says accords to the order to be found amongst our natural inclinations: first, the inclination to continue in existence, from which we understand that the means to preserve life, and of warding off threats to life, belong to natural law. Then follow matters that 'nature teaches all animals', such as union of male and female, and the raising of children; and finally, specifically human inclinations such as the desire to live peacefully in society, and to perceive the truth, and avoid error. As will be seen later, John Finnis relies upon this passage in order to suggest that natural law is concerned with the pursuit of human goods such as life, sociability, marriage and practical reasonableness: pre-moral goods.

Ultimately however, this is not the purpose of Aquinas's remarks. Borrowing a useful distinction from Finnis, it can be said that the reference to 'good' and 'bad' in the primary precept includes non-moral goodness and badness is a secondary sense, but refers to moral goodness and badness in the primary, or focal sense. Like Aristotle and the Stoics before him, Aquinas differentiates between different notions of good: (i) that which is good because it is pleasurable, such as the taste of good wine; (ii) that which is good because it is useful in attaining some further good, such as an aeroplane ticket in visiting a friend; (iii) that which is good in itself, and is enjoyed for its own sake. This third class, the so-called 'noble good' (*bonum honestum*) is the intended reference of the primary precept. In a loose sense, it incorporates 'natural' goods such as life and marriage, but noble goodness in the strict (focal) sense pertains to moral good specifically. Thus the 'good' that ought to be done and pursued, is first and foremost moral good.

The great majority of Aquinas's ethical philosophy is to be found in his treatment of the virtues, especially his extensive discussion of particular virtues such as justice and fortitude in the Secunda-secundae of the *Summa Theologiae*. The purpose of moral philosophy is to recount the virtuous acts that lead us towards our supreme end, and the vicious acts that lead us away from it. Why then does Aquinas add a natural law doctrine into the middle of this moral philosophy? The answer is threefold:

1. First, as mentioned above, it explains how individuals or peoples who never possessed the revealed truths of Scripture, nevertheless possess a knowledge of virtue. This explains in particular how pagan philosophers like Aristotle and Plato could have developed an ethical philosophy that anticipates Christian morality, without the aid of Christ's teachings.

2. It is concerned specifically with virtuous actions ordered to the common good of the community, such as sociability, that are essential for every community. As such, natural law is compatible with (and indeed a basis for) the various different ways of living seen across the world. The common good of a community consists *partly* in politically chosen aims that are culturally specific, but partly in goods that every community requires to pursue: goods including peace, benevolence to fellow citizens (*concordia*), repression of criminality, justice, prosperity, enforcement of bargains and so on. The doctrine of natural law explains how the pursuit of these goods

is naturally an end of every society, even otherwise wicked societies, or those governed by a tyrant.

3. It explains the basis upon which the positive state law must be obeyed. Insofar as the positive law is in accord with the common good of the community, it is also in accord with natural law. Hence, to prioritise one's own interests to one's legal duties of justice, is to act against the natural law. One's political disagreement with the goals of the state is not a sufficient reason for disobeying the state law. Only in the very gravest circumstances is it permissible to disobey the law; for, as we have seen, even unjust law upholds the goods of internal peace, safety and tranquility, which are to be preferred even to one's own just rights in order to avoid disturbance and outcry.[7] It is only where the law commands an immoral act, or is orientated away from the common good of the community and instead towards the tyrant, that it ceases to bind in conscience.

In short, natural law is concerned primarily with the virtuous goods and ends that make a person truly good—good without restriction—and gives consideration to natural (non-moral) goods insofar as they assist the virtues. Finnis's modern natural law theory, on the other hand, gives the impression that natural law centres upon natural goods, and considers virtue only in regard to how such goods are to be pursued and obtained.[8] Furthermore, natural law does not touch upon every question of ethics and human good, but concerns the good (and proper end) that is common to all human beings, in all places and at all times.[9]

THE RELATIONSHIP BETWEEN NATURAL LAW AND POSITIVE LAW

As we have already seen, Aquinas holds that posited human laws that contravene natural law (eg, by legislating against the common good) are not binding in conscience; though they obviously 'bind' citizens in the usual sense that transgression incurs a state punishment such as imprisonment. But Aquinas also explores the possibility of positive state laws that are enacted in line with, or even *in addition to* the demands of natural law.

Accordingly, Aquinas mentions two ways in which positive state law derives from precepts of natural law.[10] In the first way, positive laws derive from natural law precepts as a conclusion from premises: for example, from the

---

[7] See *ST* I–II.96.4c and ad 3; I–II.97.1 ad 2; II–II.117.6c.

[8] See ch 9 below.

[9] On the difference between natural law's permanence and human law's mutability, see *ST* I–II.97.1c and ad 1.

[10] *ST* I–II.95.2c.

Commandment against killing, to laws framing the indictment against murder and other forms of homicide, along with rules specifying certain defences. In the second way, positive laws derive from natural law precepts by virtue of determining generalities: a process Aquinas likens to an architect's creative freedom within the bounds specified by the general form of a house. Thus, natural law requires (as a matter of justice) that criminals are punished; but the natural law does not specify what the punishments ought to be: this is left open to determination by the positive law. The force of such determinations does not come from reason alone, but from the fact of their having been laid down as human laws.

With the exception of Hart, legal positivists have generally been slow to recognise the natural law content of positive law. Yet a great many laws have the purpose of supporting the moral common good of the state, consisting in the human goods of peace, justice and prosperity. For instance, positive laws prohibiting theft and murder, and other criminal vices, offer clear examples of laws that contribute directly to the upkeep of peace within a state. They do so by removing causes of unrest between persons, and by temporarily removing from society persons who commit forbidden acts. But no less, the laws of property, contract and tort make an important contribution to a society's peace and justice.

A modern reader of late-scholastic treatises such as Grotius's *De Iure Belli ac Pacis*, or Luis de Molina's treatise *De Iustitia et Iure*, will be surprised to encounter long and intricate discussions of contract law, as well as tort and property, in works allegedly of natural law. For example, Grotius devotes two entire chapters of his work to the nature of promises and contracts.[11] His discussion touches upon the nature of a binding promise (eg, whether it is possible to make a binding promise through the agency of another);[12] of issues concerning acceptance and communication of acceptance;[13] and whether an extorted promise binds the promisor.[14] Why does Grotius's text read like a contract law textbook at this point? To understand why, it is necessary to remember that for natural lawyers like Aquinas and Grotius, peace and justice form part of the objective common good of the state. Grotius's discussion of contract attempts to explain one element of social peace and justice: the keeping of agreements.

The natural lawyers were aware of the importance of contract and tort to facilitate internal social peace by requiring a citizen who breaches a contract to restore the other party to their original situation, or to compensate

---

[11] Grotius, *De Iure Belli ac Pacis* II.11–12 (hereafter *DIBP*).
[12] *DIBP* II.11.12.
[13] *DIBP* II.11.14–15.
[14] *DIBP* II.12.7.

another for harm that he or she has caused through their fault. By restoring justice between the parties, causes of contention are extinguished, and peace between the parties is restored.[15] Indeed, restoration to equality is the purpose of contract law: 'The natural law demands that there be equality in all contracts, such that one who receives less, acquires a right of action arising from the inequality'.[16] Grotius reports these aspects in a work on natural law, because he aims to expound what is contained in the objective common goods of peace and justice. For the most part, these will be matters upon which human beings already agree, at least tacitly. Thus, the state government will—in most cases—have legislated the rules that are necessary to retain peace and justice for the community. Grotius expounds the natural precepts that are already realised in human behaviour to some degree.

This aspect of equality in contract law is one not often considered. Peace (and of course, justice) requires that each person avoid giving offence to those amongst whom they must live in harmony.[17] Such causes of offence are not necessarily crimes (ie, offences against the whole community, such as murder or theft, or other actions that make the community more unsafe), but may constitute harms to one's neighbour. The distinction between criminal law and the law of obligations reflects the fact that certain types of behaviour disturb the peace of the entire community (even if they do not cause actual harm to persons: as with attempted crimes), whereas other types of behaviour disturb one's peaceful relations only with one other person, whilst leaving social peace intact. For example, causing loss to one's neighbour through breaking an agreement is an injustice that does not amount to a crime. Yet it still requires correction, in the form of an act of *restitutio*, for equality to be restored. This restitution also restores peaceful relations between the litigants.[18]

In fact, the act of performing one's contracts serves justice and peace also in other ways. Not only does it keep one on a peaceful footing with one's neighbours, it also serves the general common good of the community in two ways: (i) it serves the end of prosperity for the community, by extending trade and business between people; and (ii) it allows for people to come together to participate in realising aspects of the common good that are culturally specific, as opposed to naturally given. For example, the provision of public buildings such as schools and universities, or churches or synagogues, all require a basis of contract law in order to be brought into existence.

---

[15] In an extreme case, see *Addison v Chief Constable of West Midlands Police* [2004] 1 WLR 29.

[16] Grotius, *DIBP* II.12.8; on equality in other aspects of contract see II.12.9–13.

[17] See Aquinas, *ST* I–II.94.2c; II–II.79.1c. (The link between these passages has been largely unexplored.)

[18] Grotius argues restitution is also necessary in relation to criminal acts, beyond receiving punishment: *DIBP* II.1.1.

As a specific example of positive law that contributes to social peace and justice, consider the 1925 property legislation, particularly the (now) 2002 Land Registration Act. At a first glance, this is merely a particularly technical statute concerned with the transfer of title to property. Yet, there are numerous ways in which it facilitates peace and justice. By establishing which kinds of right can exist in land, and the particular rights that are consistent with each type (eg, alienability in a freehold or quiet possession in a lease), the positive state law informs citizens of their corresponding duties against interfering in the rights of others. It does this in particular by specifying the formal requirements that must be met in order for a right to be created, transferred or otherwise invested in its owner.[19] This creates a basis for justice, understood in the classical sense of abstaining from that which pertains to another, or alternatively, giving to each person their right,[20] by determining the extent of each person's right.

The positive state law also legislates to protect owners and purchasers of land from fraud,[21] and through the recognition of equitable interests, from having one's right extinguished without one's fault (as in the principle of 'overreaching').[22] It is worth stating this point: abstention from acts of fraud and protection from bad-faith actions of others is an important component not only of justice, but also of peace between persons in a community. They are naturally given ends. Yet, a system of registered title is not a naturally given end! It is a possible means by which a society can positively legislate to achieve the ends of peace and justice. Thus, it represents an important *determination* of the natural law's precepts concerning peace, justice and prosperity. For this reason, pre-modern natural lawyers rightly regarded property law as an indispensable basis for a state. The situation without clear rules of ownership and division of rights is one of anarchy.

JUSTICE AND DETERMINATION

As we have already seen, Aquinas readily agrees that unjust positive laws exist, and even that entire legal orders may be unjust if under the rule of a tyrant. A sense of the complexity of injustice is given, however, at the beginning of his treatment of justice itself. For there, he states that the Latin word *ius* first of all denotes the just thing itself (*ipsam rem iustam*), but in a secondary sense applies to the art by which it becomes known what is just (ie, legal or

---

[19] See, eg, Law of Property Act (LPA) 1925 s 1. See also Grotius, *DIBP* II.6.1–2 and 14.
[20] Grotius, *DIBP* Proleg § XLIV; Aquinas, *ST* II–II.58.1c.
[21] eg Land Registration Act (LRA) 2002 Sch 3(2) and Sch 8.
[22] LPA 1925 s 2(1).

moral science), as well as the administration of justice by a judge 'even if his sentence is unjust'.[23] For example, I may lawfully—even in a sense morally—claim rights of ownership created and recognised by (positive) law, even if the community's scheme of property law is substantively unfair.

This gives us some idea of how difficult and complex questions of injustice can be. Many consumers know, on some level, that many of the things we buy (including food and clothing) are produced and manufactured under conditions of injustice (long hours, low wages, adverse conditions) in other parts of the world. Because we can scarcely do without these things, many people are, in a sense, complicit in injustice: especially when we favour the lower prices consequent upon such practices. Furthermore, a properly adequate analysis of human vulnerability may reveal the injustices in our own communities.

None of these matters affects the validity of a community's determined rules (ie, positive laws). If one person A steals another person B's property, that is still an act of injustice of A against B. Upholding such a rule restores justice in one sense, whilst continuing to reinforce injustice in a wider sense (within or/and beyond the community). Perhaps many rules, in this way, contain some taint of injustice, whilst *at the same time* upholding a reasonably just system of laws through their ordinary operation. Such rules tend to take effect as part of a highly integrated body of law, so that the task of rooting out injustice becomes particularly complicated and problematic. Again, the history of land law provides examples of legal rules that operate reasonably justly in some cases, but are unjust with respect to certain groups (eg, certain kinds of purchaser) in others. The story of the courts' difficult efforts to overcome such injustices can be read in any property law textbook.

HUMAN KNOWLEDGE OF NATURAL LAW

Finally, it is necessary to address the issue of human knowledge of natural law precepts. Aquinas first of all draws a distinction between the most general precepts of natural law, which are completely unchanging and valid for all times, and certain secondary precepts that are more specific quasi-conclusions from the general precepts, which are true for the most part, but admit of exceptions.[24] As an example, it is a principle of justice that loans and deposits are returned to their true owner. But certain circumstances may intervene whereby a deposit is not to be returned: such as a weapon to a drunken person, or an enemy of the people. Aquinas says that the more one descends to levels of detail and particularity, the more one encounters errors, both because

---

[23] *ST* II–II.57.1 ad 1.
[24] *ST* I–II.94.4 and 5.

errors of reasoning produce incorrect conclusions, but also because more spe-cific precepts are valid only for the most part (*ut in pluribus*), but not universally.

Aquinas then employs this distinction in his answer to the question whether human knowledge of natural law can fail, ie, whether our knowledge of natu-ral law can ever be expunged totally from the heart. His reply is that, in the case of the most general precepts, considered in the abstract, they can in no way be deleted from the human heart; but they can be obscured or rubbed out in the context of a particular action, where due to sinful passions our reason is prevented from applying the precept to a particular question of practice. However, in regard to the secondary precepts, these can be entirely deleted, whether because of evil predilections or because of depraved customs and corrupt dispositions.

Aquinas's insistence that a basic knowledge of natural precepts is always present within the human heart (even if not always obeyed), follows Aristotle in explaining moral culpability as a matter of a faulty will, as opposed to the Socratic/Platonic idea that moral fault is a problem of the intellect's igno-rance of true virtue, ie, a matter of not having grasped the *Form* of virtue. Aquinas is saying that every person has the most general and primary precepts of the law; if they lack the detailed moral knowledge applicable to the specific case, this is generally due to a fault of one's will, in deflecting one's reason or obscuring one's knowledge of rightful action. Unlike Plato, Aristotle and Aquinas accept that one may have a good knowledge and understanding of virtue, and yet act contrary to justice. For them, the most difficult problems of moral philosophy do not surround the issue of what morality demands, but rather of actually doing what one knows to be right, and avoiding what one knows to be wrong.

Are people very different today? It does not seem so. The vast majority of people know and understand that certain types of behaviour are seriously wrong: they obey the law (against assault, for example) not through fear of punishment, but because they believe it is the right thing to do. The law articu-lates a moral purpose with which most people already agree. On the other hand, when people do break the law, perhaps by committing small acts of dis-honesty, they perform such acts in the full knowledge that they are wrong, not in ignorance. They perceive that some particular advantage can be gained, or more easily gained, through a dishonest act, and reason that the size of the advantage offsets the reasons for not committing a relatively trivial immoral act. But such reasons are mere rationalisations; the perpetrator of the immoral act is under no illusions that one should forego the advantage if it cannot be achieved by honest means. Over time, however—as Aquinas warns—the per-son who gives in to the immoral act will shortly become an expert at quieting their conscience, and will lose the will to be good: again, even though they have not completely lost sight of the fact that the dishonest act is wrong.

SUGGESTED READING

Aquinas, *Summa Theologiae* I–II.90–108; II–II.57–63.

Background Reading

S Coyle, 'Natural Law in Aquinas and Grotius: An Ethics for Our Times' 97 (2016) *New Blackfriars* 591.

J Finnis, *Aquinas: Moral, Political and Legal Theory* (Oxford, Oxford University Press, 1998).

T Irwin, *The Development of Ethics*, vol 1 (Oxford, Oxford University Press 2007) chs 16–24.

A Lisska, *Aquinas's Theory of Natural Law: An Analytic Reconstruction* (Oxford, Clarendon Press, 1997).

R McInerny, *Ethica Thomistica* (Washington DC, CUA, 1997).

SJ Pope (ed), *The Ethics of Aquinas* (Washington DC, Georgetown University Press, 2002).

J Porter, *Nature as Reason: A Thomistic Theory of the Natural Law* (Grand Rapids MI, Eerdmans Publishing, 2005) esp chs 1–2.

J-P Torrell, *Aquinas's Summa: Background, Structure and Reception* (Washington DC, CUA, 2005).

4

The Emergence of 'Modern' Political Thought

THE POLITICS OF the classical world had centred upon the idea of the 'good life'. At the heart of juridical enquiries was the question of how law could facilitate, or produce, that form of life. 'Modern' jurisprudence takes its distinctive form from an entirely different conception of the political realm. How can law produce or maintain order in a world of doubt over moral values? What form shall law take when each person strives to pursue their own conception of the 'good life' in competition with others? How shall the capitalist live with the crusader for social equality? Can or even should all ideas of 'the good' be accommodated?

Perhaps the first thinker to elaborate such ideas was Thomas Hobbes (1588–1679), who in the course of a long life produced one of the most important works of Western political thought, the *Leviathan* of 1651. Political thinkers of Hobbes's day were the heirs to a subtle and complex interpretation of human life which lay at the heart of medieval Christian civilisation. This was the vision of the human race, and the material world it inhabits, as products of the creative act of God. But through original sin, men in seeking to become gods themselves became separated from God, and were diminished. Thereafter, the human race being corrupted knew hardship and strife, leading lives which were separated from the source of their original happiness.[1] But a limit was also set upon human misery and self-destruction, for to human beings was offered the possibility of redemption: divine grace, given to those who acknowledged their imperfection and sought to limit the worst excesses of their desires, would bring a final salvation.

The ideas of Fallen humankind and of the need for redemption and of salvation are the central symbols of Europe's intellectual heritage, the background against which the history of political and legal thought developed. They are representative of the human condition as a predicament, and both law and politics relate to the context of this predicament. Philosophies of law and of politics concerned the extent to which the legal and political

---

[1] See Genesis 3:15–24.

order contributes to the alleviation of the human situation. Two traditions of thought in particular gave shape to the intellectual background out of which Hobbes's great work emerged. The first of these was the Christian philosophy of Saint Paul and Saint Augustine. Paul regarded human nature as morally ambiguous: the logic of humankind falling away from God suggests the initial greatness of the human being, and so the potentiality of its recovery; whereas the cause of the Fall, being a sin of pride, recalls the human being to his imperfection. This dilemma is expressed clearly by Paul: 'For I do not do the good I want, but the evil that I do not want is what I do' (Romans 7:19). In this way, Paul articulates a question that is central to Western jurisprudential thought, namely the extent to which human effort, especially in law and politics, can bring about an improvement in the human situation. How far, in other words, is law a redemptive force in human affairs, as opposed to a useful tool for the management of a predicament from which there is no escape?

Augustine presents a still more radical split between the higher and base aspects of the human character. *City of God* speaks of the human being as the simultaneous inhabitant of two 'cities', one earthly and the other heavenly.[2] Relations in the earthly city are determined by the provisional peace established by the law, an uneasy armistice between contending interests.[3] Those of the heavenly city are the result of perfect love, projected (at least in part) into a Platonic 'other realm', and stressing the permanent inadequacy of the achievements of justice in the legal and political arrangements of earthly societies.

The other great tradition was that which sprang from Aristotle's *Ethics*. Aristotle and the ancient writers on ethics belonged to the older world-view which focused upon the question of how we can lead an excellent and valuable life. Consequently, their ethical thought gave a central place to the idea of the 'good life', and explored the ways in which politics and law might foster and sustain that life. Requiring political institutions for its realisation, the nature of the good life was thought to be intrinsically social, capable of full expression only within the bounds of a common existence rather than something capable of pursuit by individuals in isolation. Within this picture, law formed part of a nexus of institutions which foster and pursue the common good. Hobbes's work challenges nearly every aspect of this political vision.

HOBBES'S VIEW OF THE HUMAN CONDITION

Political philosophy, as Hobbes understood, is the illumination of the universal predicament through the contemplation of the particular and transitory

---

[2] See the discussion in ch 2 above.
[3] See R Niebuhr, *Man's Nature and His Communities* (London, Geoffrey Bles, 1966) 31.

concerns of the age.[4] The vision of law and society at the heart of *Leviathan* draws upon the Pauline conception of the person in its most negative mood. It is an account of man's smallness, imperfection and mortality, and considers what law must be in the light of these characteristics. The human being is presented as a solitary creature, but one who inhabits a world in which he is not alone, and finds himself under constant threat from others of his kind. The source of this insecurity is human desire: each person, Hobbes tells us, is driven by his 'appetites', some of which are permanent and common to all (such as hunger and thirst), but others are more fleeting and changeable. It is impossible given the constitution of the human body that all our appetites can be satisfied. Still less is it possible that the same objects should always stimulate in us the same appetites and aversions.[5] For what we desire is not a final end-state in which all our desires are extinguished (that, says Hobbes, is death), but a never-ending series of material comforts. We thus live in a state of perpetual desire, and (because the world contains the resources and objects of our desires) a constant state of hope of fulfilling our desires.

By nature, we are created roughly equal in terms of strength, wit and native cunning. Though it is true that some individuals are stronger, faster or more intelligent than others, none is so superior in mind or body that they could not be overcome by the organised efforts of a few others. Even the most powerful man must sleep sometimes, or become sick, and therefore must fear even the weakest. From this rough equality in abilities, Hobbes argues that there arises a similar equality in hopes of attaining what we desire. And so if two men desire the same object (which they cannot jointly enjoy), they must find themselves in competition with one another. This image of solitary human beings in perpetual competition with one another represents, in Hobbes's view, the natural state of mankind: were one to imagine a situation in which there were no laws, and no man-made social conventions of any kind, the result would be this 'war of all against all'.

Hobbes's vision of what is 'natural' to the human situation, once all artificial (man-made) conventions are stripped away, is startlingly bleak. In one of the most famous passages of the book, he paints a vivid picture of what such a situation would be like. Though we might be initially attracted by the idea of a state of complete freedom, the reality is that this 'right of anyone to anything' eliminates altogether any security from harm or maltreatment that laws and conventions establish: such a right extends 'even to one another's bodies'. The only bodily security a person possesses in the natural condition is 'what their

---

[4] Hobbes, *Leviathan*, ch 32.
[5] ibid ch 6.

own strength and their own invention shall furnish them withall'. In such a condition, Hobbes says

> there is no place for industry, because the fruit thereof is uncertain: and conse-
> quently no culture of the earth; no navigation, nor use of commodities that may be
> imported by sea; no commodious building; no instruments of moving, and remov-
> ing such things as require much force; no knowledge of the face of the earth; no
> account of time; no arts; no letters; no society; and which is worst of all, continual
> fear and danger of violent death; and the life of man solitary, poor, nasty, brutish
> and short.[6]

Some of these consequences may appear more significant than others, but altogether, they create an image of humankind as having collapsed into primitivism. Without arts of building, tool-making, farming and so on, life is reduced to a nomadic, hand-to-mouth existence. Without common bonds of language and mutual understanding, people become unreadable to one another, so that 'man becomes wolf to his fellowman'. Just as when encountering a wild animal, one lacks any sense of what another's intentions might be: having stripped away all common speech, and all conventional understandings, interpreting the facial expressions of another human being becomes as difficult as trying to read the face of the wolf. Consequently, the only rational response to an encounter between two men in this natural state is to employ violent, pre-emptive attack as a form of defence. Against this background, there can be no industry, and no collective or organised endeavour of any kind, such as might alleviate the grim and solitary conditions of the state of nature.

Should Hobbes's argument be accepted? Though it outraged the reading public upon its release in 1651, there are not lacking in our own time those who endorse a very similar sense that, when stripped back to its basics, human life is 'every man for himself'. One sometimes encounters individuals who liken the human condition to the law of the jungle, and who regard the laws, conventions and manners which restrain the worst excesses of human selfishness as an artificial veneer, hiding 'true' human nature. It is not unheard of for some to suggest that laws and conventions should be abolished, so that we can be 'more true to our real character'. Would such an existence be 'more honest'? (Those who say this typically lack Hobbes's understanding of how grim things would really be if everyone were to become 'true' to themselves in this way; or else they really mean to suggest that they should be free to do as they please, whilst the rest of us, like ignorant sheep, follow the law.) At the heart of this understanding of the human condition is a particular vision of the role of law in human affairs: law is a set of artificially created (man-made) rules, imposed upon otherwise 'free' individuals so that a common life in conditions

---

[6] ibid ch 13.

of peace and order is made possible. It is in this vision of law and human nature that one finds the first seeds of 'legal positivism'.

I asked whether Hobbes's vision of human nature should be accepted. It is sufficiently dark and pessimistic to be attractive to those who like to regard themselves as 'realists'. But is it true? Hobbes's view depends upon separating what is 'natural' from what is 'artificial'. Human nature is the residue left behind after all else has been taken away, consisting in little more than (roughly equal) bodily strength, wit and characteristic desires. Yet in stripping away all that unites us and makes us mutually intelligible, are we not left with something unnatural? Is it not precisely our manners, languages and culture that define us as human? From the earliest times, human beings have been presented not as solitary creatures, but as social animals. Rather than eliminating law, custom and culture from an account of human nature, should we not instead reflect upon the form and substance of our social institutions and cultural inheritance, as a mirror in which we find our own essential character reflected? This very different understanding of the human being as a social being lay at the root of Aristotle's philosophy; and it is the same conception that we find in Hobbes's near-contemporary, the natural lawyer Hugo Grotius.[7]

For the moment, let us explore Hobbes's view of law further. The idea of a 'natural condition of humanity' was fairly common in seventeenth-century philosophy, though different writers held distinctive views about its character. In Hobbes's own characterisation of it, the natural state was one of absolute freedom, in which each person had a natural right to everything, the goal being self-preservation. This natural right Hobbes called 'the Right of Nature', and because each person's right simultaneously extended over everything, the result is lawless chaos and a perpetual and total war of each against all. It follows that the only way to escape from the natural condition is for everyone to lay aside their right to everything, by voluntarily alienating or restricting large areas of liberty. From being initially completely autonomous, individuals must surrender control of their lives to 'an arbitrator or judge, whom men disagreeing shall by consent set up, and make his sentence the rule thereof'.[8] This is, of course, easier said than done. Imagine a situation such as Hobbes describes. Each person uses pre-emptive attack as their only form of defence. Though you (and perhaps the others) would like to live in peace, it would clearly be foolish for you to disarm voluntarily unless the others did so too. And it would be dangerous also to honour any agreement to disarm simultaneously, for the prudent man would suspect treachery (and having foreseen its possibility, again seek to pre-empt it).

---

[7] See ch 5 below.
[8] *Leviathan*, ch 6.

Hobbes was aware of the difficulty, and argued as follows. The hostile conditions of the state of nature render pre-emptive attack the only prudent form of self-defence. But we should be careful to distinguish what is rational, or prudent, in the short term from what is rational in the long term. We might accept, therefore, that pre-emptive attack is necessitated by the immediate conditions in which we are forced to act, whilst also recognising that such actions serve only to perpetuate those same conditions. Because, as rational creatures, we are capable of taking this longer view, we can come to understand that although nature may have placed us in these desperate conditions, there is nevertheless a possibility of escape from them. This possibility, Hobbes says, consists 'partly in the passions' and 'partly in [the] reason'. The passions that incline men to peace consist in the fear of premature death, and the desire for commodious living. Reason, on the other hand, 'suggests articles of peace' through which men may reach agreement. These, says Hobbes, are called Laws of Nature. But perhaps the problem is greater than Hobbes thought. If we are truly, by nature, unreadable to one another, how are any such intentions to be communicated? Indeed, since it is language that communicates our own thoughts to ourselves, how can we even formulate such ideas in our own heads? Hobbes is right to say that language is a social, and not a private, phenomenon. But if the solitary existence we lead in the natural condition precludes language, can we be said (in those conditions) to be rational animals at all? Would we not be mere creatures of instinct?

This is a genuine and troubling difficulty for Hobbes. But putting it to one side for the moment, let us concentrate upon his main argument, for it contains many themes and ideas that still find resonance today. The right of nature, Hobbes says,

> is the liberty each man hath to use his own power, as he will himself, for the preservation of his own nature; that is to say, of his own life; and consequently, of doing anything which in his own judgment and reason, he shall conceive to be the aptest means thereunto.[9]

A law of nature, on the other hand, is a general rule or precept by which one is restrained from doing that which is destructive of one's life. Hobbes states that many tend to confuse law and right,

> yet they ought to be distinguished, because Right consisteth in the liberty to do, or to forbear; whereas Law determineth and bindeth to one of them: so that Law and Right differ as much as obligation and liberty, which in one and the same matter are inconsistent.

We tend to think of rights as being determined by law (and hence speak of 'legal rights'), and so are likely to find Hobbes's usage somewhat strange.

---

[9] ibid ch 14.

But it is this contrast between right and law that allows Hobbes to assert the following of the state of nature:

> To this war of every man against every man, this also is consequent; that nothing can be Unjust. The notions of Right and Wrong, Justice and Injustice, have there no place. Where there is no common power, there is no law: where no law, no injustice ... Justice and Injustice are none of the faculties neither of the body nor mind ... They are qualities that relate to men in society, not in solitude.[10]

In other words, justice and injustice (and other moral values) are to be understood as artificial products of social convention. They are established by law, not something intrinsic to the human mind or body. Here we touch upon one of the central questions pondered by philosophers and jurisprudential thinkers: to what extent are moral values intellectual creations (like languages or poems), or naturally existing phenomena that are apprehended rather than invented by the human mind: *nomos* rather than *physis* in Plato's language? Hobbes broadly implies the former, holding that morality makes sense only within the context of shared social relationships. And it is with the establishment of these relationships that Hobbes is concerned.

These are the central ideas out of which Hobbes's views on law and society emerge. Human nature is essentially solitary, driven by desire and fearing death above all else. But human beings are not alone, and are forced to conduct their strivings in near proximity to others of their kind: this is the human predicament. It is a predicament that makes men natural enemies to one another, and increases the fear and continual danger of violent death. This predicament is not the result of an original sin or of human depravity, but comes from nature itself. Yet human nature, which is the source of the predicament, also offers a means of escape: and its first awakening is the recognition of the predicament itself (just as, for the Christian, repentance is the first step towards forgiveness).[11] In deepening our understanding of the predicament, we are led to more general precepts which suggest that, by mutually limiting the extent of our pursuit of felicity, we increase its certainty. These general precepts thus guide us to what might properly be called our salvation: society, and peace.

LAW AND SOCIETY

In contrast to the view, inherited from Aristotle, that man is a social being, Hobbes presents society as wholly artificial and not the natural condition

[10] ibid ch 13.
[11] See the excellent discussion by Michael Oakeshott in his introduction to the Touchstone edition of *Leviathan*.

of mankind. Law, too, is the product of artifice. It consists in rules that are explicitly created, or laid down, by a recognised authority. Given the natural equality and autonomy of human beings in their natural state, it becomes apparent that authority can only be created through agreement, namely a collective decision by each to subject their individual will to that of an 'arbitrator or judge whom men disagreeing shall by consent set up'. In effect, each person renounces their right of self-governance, and transfers it to a sovereign ruler, insofar as matters of peace and collective security are concerned. Clearly, this ruler cannot be a natural person (who like all others desires only to satisfy his own desires) but an 'artificial man': the Leviathan, or state. The sovereign ruler is thus not a man, but an office. And it may be an office consisting of one person or of many; a monarch or a parliament. And the constitution of the office may also take on many forms: of aristocracy, dictatorship, theocracy, democracy etc. But in none of these cases is it the function of the sovereign ruler to interpret the various desires of his subjects and act accordingly. He does not 'represent' them, but is responsible for maintaining peace and good order, and pursues those actions and policies which lead to that end.

There are several obvious differences between the vision of the state offered by Hobbes, and that which is familiar within a modern liberal democracy. Hobbes's vision is, to begin with, a minimalist view of statehood (sometimes called a 'nightwatchman state'), for the function of the state is concerned exclusively with the maintenance of peace and order. The provision of material comforts, economies of scale, minimum standards of living, of health, hygiene and so on; none of these is the responsibility of the state, except insofar as they impinge upon the issue of peace and order. Similarly, the function of law is limited to the creation and maintenance of social order, and is not concerned with the realisation of social policy goals or the promotion of specific moral values. Law is simply a system of clear and deliberately chosen rules, which together create a stable framework within which each person is able to formulate and pursue projects of their own, whilst observing certain boundaries established by the rules. It is in the nature of such projects to compete and destructively interfere with one another: my pursuit of my goals will inevitably impact upon and impede your pursuit of yours. The rules are necessary in order to limit the level of interference so that my efforts do not completely *exclude* yours (and vice versa). A legal system can function effectively only when the vast majority of its subjects recognise its authority, and they will continue to do so only so long as it is seen to offer some level of protection to their interests.

Nevertheless, the civil authority (or sovereign) envisaged by Hobbes is unconditional. Though its remit is limited, its right to rule is absolute. Having once authorised the sovereign's right to rule, that authorisation cannot be taken back by the individuals who gave it. (In the same way, one who complains that he did not himself take part in the original agreement which founded the sovereign office, does not thereby make himself independent of the sovereign's authority, but merely becomes an outlaw, putting himself beyond the protection of law and society.) These sentiments have contributed to Hobbes's reputation as an absolutist. He is effectively saying that there is no 'contract' between the ruler and the ruled, such that the agreement might be breached and sovereignty remitted back to the populace. Though the sovereign's function is to rule for the benefit of the peace and security of subjects, there is no suggestion that subjects have the right to challenge or resist a sovereign whose actions are not conducive to that end, or which exceed it. On the whole, one would expect the civil law to conform to the 'laws of nature' which are conducive to peaceful relations between persons. But the validity and authority of the law do not in any way depend upon their correspondence with these natural laws. It is not wisdom, Hobbes says, but authority that makes a law. Legal validity depends neither upon the wisdom of the laws, nor directly upon their propensity to secure peace, but purely on its being the command of the sovereign. And, since justice and injustice have no meaning outside of law, there can be no question of a law being 'unjust'. Law establishes what is just.

No doubt Hobbes's views on law will seem rather unattractive. We might accept Hobbes's suggestion that the 'freedom' of the natural condition is an illusory freedom: that unconstrained pursuit of all goals means failure in attaining any of them, and that it is only through the imposition of certain limits to freedom that a genuine freedom is established. (This is a suggestion that runs throughout modern legal and political philosophy.) But we might nonetheless consider that such freedom is bought at an extremely high price. Even if it is not automatically the case, it would seem as if Hobbes's ideas at least encourage flirtation with totalitarian governance. For example, on the subject of free speech Hobbes acknowledges that individual subjects might hold opinions that are critical of the law or the state, or which envisage some major upset of the status quo. The state can and should do nothing about people's inward beliefs. But, says Hobbes, quite the opposite is true where such opinions are expressed aloud, especially if before large numbers of people. Here, outward beliefs should conform to the official position of the state. And if, for instance, unity of religious belief is considered by the state as a precondition of peace and order, then religious divisions are not to be tolerated, and should be punishable by law.

Sounds distasteful? There are, of course, examples of totalitarian and authoritarian regimes across the world. Of these, some (such as communist regimes) demand allegiance to a particular political programme or ideology. Others are more overtly religious in orientation. But it would be a mistake to think of Hobbes as pursuing either kind of ideal. He is ostensibly offering an answer to the question of what law *must* be in human societies. Ought we to dismiss him utterly? Might it not be that our own laws and our own society resemble Hobbes's vision much more closely than we care to admit? That the rhetoric of choice, and of liberal values and the 'open society', is but a comforting illusion? What Hobbes offers is a brilliantly acute analysis of power, and the suggestion that it is ultimately power that validates all social and legal arrangements. In order to appreciate fully Hobbes's argument in *Leviathan*, it is necessary to examine the conditions in which it was written.

THE POLITICAL CONTEXT OF *LEVIATHAN*

Hobbes characterised his own political philosophy as the illumination of the universal human predicament through contemplation of the particular historical situation. The historical situation into which *Leviathan* was launched was that of the English Civil War. It is against this background that its claims must be understood. The immediate causes of the Civil War were numerous, partly concerning the autocratic tendencies of Charles I, and partly also the rumoured Catholicism of his heirs. These concerns had led in 1649, two years before the appearance of *Leviathan*, to the king's execution, and by 1651 to the establishment of a republican regime in England. To contemporaries, the outcome and final end of the war were still in doubt at that time, and there was little reason to suppose that the bitter divisions between Royalists and Parliamentarians (which had set communities, and even families, against themselves) were at an end. Hobbes's England was a community in turmoil, gradually disintegrating from within: a time in which, it appeared, man was indeed as a wolf to his fellowman. Judged against this background, Hobbes's claims about a 'state of nature', devoid of law, order, peace and trust, possess a new resonance. We might see the 'natural condition', not as a primitive situation that exists prior to the foundation of the political state, but as a condition that we (as civilised beings) might fall into, if our political and religious divisions are not held in check. The authoritarian character of Hobbes's philosophy of law is explained by reference to the need, felt much more clearly and closely in times of political turmoil than in times of extended peace, to stamp out disagreement and encourage uniformity.

It is not hard to follow Hobbes's concerns. The divisions of belief that had led (by a long road) to the terrible violence of the Civil War, had already begun a process of social fragmentation, setting family against family, and even families against themselves. In such conditions, government of the realm becomes impossible. Economic growth ceases. The fruits of labour and industry become uncertain. No single direction in politics or sense of community unites the people. The cultural life of the nation stagnates. Its achievements are reversed, and life is lived in a climate of fear and suspicion. The cause of all this, in a sense, is not that people possess varying points of view, but that they are allowed to give free expression to them and to pursue their realisation. Suppose those rifts are not suppressed, but are instead allowed to grow unchecked. Each faction might then find itself hopeful of imposing its point of view upon the rest of society by force. And where the state has lost its monopoly on the use of force to order relations in society, these factions will prove difficult to hold together, resulting in further fragmentation and division. If this process is allowed to continue indefinitely, its logical conclusion is the state of nature: a free-for-all conflict of each against all, in which cultural achievements have been completely reversed, to the extent that language itself is lost. This ultimate loss of 'common humanity' is begun precisely where the seeds of division are sowed: the point at which one's fellow citizen becomes an 'other', an opponent, not a neighbour.

It may seem an exaggeration to regard the state of nature as the ultimate consequence of a permissive society, and perhaps it is. But it must be remembered that our own perceptions, as the inheritors of extended periods of social peace, differ quite significantly from those who find themselves in the midst of civil war. This is especially true of our perceptions concerning authority, freedom and toleration of diversity. What to us might appear an abstract possibility may in other circumstances be felt as a real and present danger. The required leap of imagination is considerable. But for Hobbes's philosophies of law and government to be relevant to our times, it is not necessary that they paint a recognisable or even desirable picture of modern societies. It is enough that they reveal something about us, some permanent aspect of the human character and condition, manifested partially in, but never completing, our political thought. In the case of Hobbes, this is the necessary centrality of an authoritative framework of law for the governance of a society characterised by the reality of pluralism.

Hobbes was amongst the first European thinkers to consider the juristic implications of a Protestant society. Prior to the Reformation, legal thought was shaped in large part by assumptions about human nature deriving from Plato, Aristotle and the Scholastics. The influence of Aristotle in particular loomed large over European thought up until the early modern era. As we saw in chapter three, the Aristotelian philosophy depicted the human being as a social animal: one who is understood completely only within the context of society, and whose rationality and perfection are unimaginable outside such a context. The Good of the human being was, irreducibly, a common good. To this picture of human beings and human society, the early Christian writers added a further dimension. Drawing upon similar elements in the Hebrew tradition, the ultimate felicity of humankind was deemed to consist in knowledge of God, and the path towards His mercy and redemptive grace was to be found in the pursuit of the most basic of Christian duties, love of one's neighbour. In Saint Augustine, for example, we find the thought that love of neighbour and love of self contain each other, for in each case we learn to love what is good despite the indelible presence of imperfections (in both one-self and others). From this perspective, Hobbes's departure from this classical tradition of thought is not so great. He too insists upon the need to explore a 'common humanity', and to resist the tendency to explore our differences, making issues of them. And yet there are also pronounced differences between Hobbes and his Western predecessors.

The classical and medieval legal writers addressed a European civilisation as yet unmarked by major religious divisions. (Religious threats as such were external, and prompted Crusades against the cultures of the East.) But in the post-medieval world, internal doctrinal schisms within the European church could no longer be contained by the ecclesiastical authority of the institutional Church itself, resulting in intense political and ideological battles between the Catholic Church and the various reformed congregations. The theology at the heart of the Protestant churches emphasised a doctrine of personal grace. Ultimate salvation was no longer a matter of obedience to imposed collective tradition, but of personal engagement with the Bible and the effort to live according to its message. Each individual was thought to possess the means to their own salvation, and to lead the 'good life' was to pursue one's own conception of the good in one's own way. But if this is the case, how can one avoid making issues of the different conceptions of the good which divide us? Are these not disagreements which precisely concern what each person thinks as being 'good'? To suggest that each person must determine the good for himself or herself is not to suggest that all such conceptions are equally valid, and to be tolerated or celebrated as instances of diversity. Even 'love of neigh-bour', from this perspective, can become closely connected with sentiments of aggressive conversion of those in error to the true way.

It is this changed context that Hobbes is addressing in *Leviathan*. The brutal-ity of Civil War politics was for him a microcosm of the human condition. In this condition, it is law rather than neighbourly love that acts as the cement by which society is held together. Law is not in this sense the embodiment of a collective attempt to secure and give expression to an agreed common good. It is a framework of imposed rules for the maintenance of peace and order in a world in which each person strives to pursue their own good in their own way. It is law for a world in which a person may gaze into the face of a fellow human being and no longer find there reflected an image of himself. Rather, Hobbes's world is a world of relative strangers and cool, arm's-length relation-ships. One frequently encounters the suggestion that law, on Hobbes's account of it, forms a framework of rules that is neutral as between competing concep-tions of the good. Indeed, for law to fulfil the function that Hobbes sets for it (to maintain order in a world of competing goods) something of that character might seem to be implied. The powerful form of legal authority in Hobbes's philosophy will, after all, be acceptable only to prudentially reasonable individuals who realise that their attempts to impose subjective interpretations of virtue are likely to be unsuccessful and destructive. For example, I may have a violent objection to pushbikes being ridden in parks, or I might have a strong desire to ride my bicycle where I like. But if I believe that asserting this right may lead to uncontrolled outbursts of violence or anarchy then I may instead accede to what I believe is an unjust law. Even if I felt that I might prevail through violence on this issue, I might consider that the application of this might-makes-right attitude more generally would lead to my defeat on issues I cared more about (property ownership or electoral reform, say). But I will only make this calculation if I feel that the values promoted by the legal system as a whole are values worth maintaining in the face of doubts or disputes about the merit of particular rules.

And yet the matter is not so clear-cut. For what if, instead, we concentrate on precisely those more deeply held issues? From almost the moment of the creation of the Anglican Church in the century before Hobbes's *Leviathan*, and with few periods of respite, English Catholic theology was held to constitute a form of treason in its acknowledgment of papal authority in divine matters over that of the king. Such an acknowledgment is in direct opposition to the foundation of the state's political authority in Hobbes's account of it. It carries the suggestion that one is to be directed by two masters, each of whose 'sentence' is to be the 'rule' of the subject. There is, in such terms, no possibility of the law's remaining neutral between two opposing ideas of the good: law, being the instrument of the state, excludes English Catholicism absolutely.

Hobbes's own attitude towards the political authority of the Church is reflective of this conclusion. From the beginning of the Civil War, the king's own advisers were divided over how to secure victory. One faction believed the preservation of the Anglican Church to be of one piece with the preservation of the monarchy, and thus to be made central to all royalist policy. The other (following the example of Henry IV in France) believed that the Church should be sacrificed if necessary for the survival of the monarchy.[12] Hobbes's theology, as set out in the third and fourth parts of *Leviathan*, left no independent role for the Church either in the administration of the Sacraments, or in scriptural interpretation. His views amounted to an emaciated Anglicanism: the consequence of the state's power to determine all ecclesiastical appointments was that ordination itself held no special status (no more than is involved, say, in the appointment of a judge or other state official).

---

[12] See R Tuck, *Philosophy and Government 1572–1651* (Cambridge, Cambridge University Press, 1993) 320. There were Catholics amongst the royalist party, and they too had an interest in the refutation of extreme papalism.

Indeed, the sovereign office, as the source of all ordinations, is competent itself to fulfil any religious office and to perform any sacrament.[13] The key tenet of the Christian Church, that of the apostolic succession, was therefore broken.

These arguments serve to highlight a profound precondition of political stability in the modern world, which nevertheless is now seldom felt or noticed: the need for a religious settlement enshrined by law. (Only in Northern Ireland, of all the polities of Europe, does this issue reach the surface of ordinary politics.) This is a dimension of legality that, by its nature, cannot be 'neutral' as between opposing conceptions of justice or the good. Hobbes's own arguments do, however, prefigure the religious situation of present-day Western society in important ways. We must not forget that the Hobbesian state is the 'nightwatchman state', so that whilst the sovereign is the final arbiter of the meaning of scriptural, as well as other contested texts, the authority of that interpretative office extends only to what is deemed necessary for the continued survival of ordinary citizens. The result is a surprising amount of scope for toleration amongst various Christian points of view, based upon a minimalist view of Christianity. In Hobbes's ecclesiology, the prime danger to the individual soul is the entanglement of the Christian message with 'vain philosophy' espoused by clerics. Hence, 'there ought to be no Power over the consciences of men, but of the Word itself'.[14] The premise is, of course, Lutheran; but its effect is nevertheless to grant much latitude to private conscience.

In the course of the century and a half after the publication of *Leviathan*, religious toleration came to be an established condition of political life in England. This came about not because of ideological pressure from the direction of liberalist thought, but due to a number of interwoven factors leading to the gradual diminishment of the Church's political authority and relevance. It came to be recognised that the state's power might coerce populations in certain forms or methods of worship, but it could never compel belief. In England, the long and conscious search for a peaceful political settlement necessitated the eventual recognition of mutual concessions to rights of worship, congregation and so on. There had been, moreover, a tradition of anti-clerical thought in Britain which, though social in orientation rather than political, led eventually to the erosion of close relations between Church and State. Politics and law eventually became largely secular institutions. It was indeed the inner logic of Protestant thought, summed up in Hobbes's phrase that there should be no external power over the consciences of men, that led to the declining importance of religion in the political societies of the West. But it was this also

---

[13] *Leviathan*, ch 42.
[14] ibid ch 47.

which made possible the stable religious settlement that had seemed so remote at the time of *Leviathan*'s composition.

We who inhabit modern, multicultural societies, might be supposed to have left such problems behind to the extent that they are no longer relevant to us. But this is not the case. Such developments effectively combine to create the central problems of the jurisprudence of the present day. Its context and assumptions, like those of Hobbes, are essentially Protestant.

So long as Protestant thought retained its theological aspect, each person's understandings could be conceived as private determinations about the correct means of participating in and achieving a basic good (entry into the Kingdom of Heaven) presupposed as an ultimate end. Private 'conceptions of the good' functioned in reality as mere constituents of a unified, but complex ethical ideal. As morality became increasingly separated from moral theology, under the pressure of Protestant ideas, a secular concern with the individual began to emerge for which the capacity for autonomous reflection signalled genuinely opposing forms of the good. For we can think of each person's understanding of the means of achieving salvation as the adoption of a 'form of life'. It then becomes possible to view such understandings not simply as causal mechanisms for the realisation of some postponed good, but as constituents of a good life in their own right. Protestantism allows scope for fundamental conflict amongst these differing forms of the good. The central problem for the jurisprudential and political thought of the present day is thus how to reconcile the recognition and pursuit of these diverse forms of the good with the need for political stability and social order.

A DIVIDED INHERITANCE

It is often remarked that Hobbes, and his near-contemporary Hugo Grotius, are the first distinctively 'modern' philosophers of law and politics. There is some justice in this. What marks them out as 'modern' is above all the revolutionary character of the question that drives their thought, rather than the answers they offer (which in many ways remain anti-modern). Grotius and Hobbes stand at the head of two opposing traditions of thought directed at answering the question of how to reconcile pursuit of diverse forms of the good with the need for stability and order. Such a question does not arise within the ethical philosophy that derives from Aristotle. The possibility that the good of each individual was genuinely divergent from others, and incapable of subsumption under a 'common good' of the community, was unimaginable in that context. One might exhibit certain virtues or excellences to the exclusion of others, of course, so that we might ask whether (for example) the life of the statesman is better than that of the scholar.[15] But there was no possibility that my pursuit of excellence in statecraft denies or excludes the value of your scholarship. It was only with the development of a Protestant conceptual framework that genuine oppositions became possible. Both Grotius and Hobbes can be seen as offering varying responses to Aristotle from within Protestant Christianity.

Protestantism was in the main hostile to Aristotle. Hobbes's vision of law and state represents a comprehensive assault on Aristotelian doctrines of all kinds. Grotius was more moderate, seeking to retain as much of the Aristotelian framework as was compatible with his Protestant beliefs. The effect of the new framework ushered in by Hobbes and Grotius, however, was to emphasise the distinctiveness of the questions raised by the circumstances of 'modernity', and this led to a decline of interest in Aristotle, and the perception of the classical tradition of reflection upon ethics as irrelevant to the new understandings. It would be a mistake, however, to think of 'modern' jurisprudence as having instituted a decisive break with Aristotelian concerns and ideas.

It is indeed true that the Hobbesian image of government is drastically different from that offered by Aristotle. Aristotle's ethical philosophy is premised upon a rich and detailed account of human nature, of the human being as a rational and social animal for whom government is in some sense a natural state. Hobbes reduces human nature to a few propositions about equal vulnerability, insatiable wants and self-value. Hobbesian men conceive wants, strategise about their fulfilment and take decisions about the appropriate courses of action purely on their own terms. When first we encounter them in the 'natural condition', their personalities and individual priorities are shaped by their position as lone agents, without common structures of meaning and mutual intelligibility to influence their determination. The collective governance of such persons can be founded only upon each of them forming a comprehension of the potential benefits of peaceful and organised coexistence, and then including its creation amongst their several priorities, subordinating their other wants to it. Although the initial enthusiasm for peaceful governance may derive from intellectual considerations (belonging to the agent's reason), the actual creation, and thus the basis, of a regime of governance resides in the will. We might therefore be led to assume that the questions that may be asked of such forms of governance, in respect of its foundations, authority, legitimacy and so on, are somewhat removed from the Aristotelian reflections upon human nature and the human condition encountered in chapter three. Being the product of an act of free will, does not governance have essentially nothing to do with nature? Must we not instead confine our

---

[15] See, eg, Plato's discussion in Part VII of the *Republic*.

attention to the content of human choices, and the various implications that arise from them?

However that question is answered, it is unhelpful and artificially limiting to regard the questions at the heart of 'modern' understandings of law and government as excluding those posed by Aristotle. To regard a certain body of philosophical speculation as dead rather than living is often merely to have absorbed a particular set of claims or assumptions to such an extent that one can no longer bear to doubt their veracity. For one in this position, theses that are in fact opposing seem to demand not the arguability but the exclusion and suppression of the rival standpoint. Traditions of thought that are continuous therefore come to be represented as discontinuous. The continuity between the classical and modern traditions can be seen fairly clearly. We might regard Hobbes and Aristotle as being interested in where the line must be drawn between what is 'natural' in the human situation or consequent on the supposed rational nature of human beings, and what is adventitious or produced through freely willed actions which have as their starting point the determinations of 'individuals'. Hobbes and Aristotle both devote themselves to explaining upon which side of this line collective government belongs.

For a long time, scholars of political theory criticised 'contractarian' theories such as Hobbes's on the ground of the unreality of the original compact that was said to bring about government and social peace.[16] Societies are not founded by a contractual agreement, and it is of limited value as a means of explanation of the basis and legitimacy of government. But it is possible to develop this into a broader point. Suppose it is said that no act of will is required for the 'acceptance' of legal or governmental authority. Suppose in other words that we set out to oppose not only social contractarian theories but more broadly all theories that locate the legitimacy of law and government on the voluntary and individualist side of the line. Hart's claim that the efficacy of a legal system is ultimately dependent upon popular acceptance of its existence; Dworkin's statement that it is up to each person to determine 'for himself' the range of standards that form the basis of governance in his community; Rawls's arguments concerning the way in which the legitimacy of the standards (such as justice and equality) by which a community is governed are to be conceived: all come down, despite many differences, on the same side of the dividing line we have been contemplating.

---

[16] See my discussion above, for the need to treat the 'contract' metaphor with some care: it pertains to the original donation of power as a voluntary act, and not the character of the subsequent relationship of governor to governed. Indeed, care should further be taken in assuming that all those thinkers conventionally banded together under the banner of 'social contractarians' regard the form and function of the 'contract' in the same way.

Understood this way, it is clear that none of these theories can avoid the need to answer Aristotle's question simply by dismissing its relevance. It is perfectly possible to entertain the suggestion that the ordinary citizen's 'acceptance' of political authority (in the sense of his habitual preparedness to submit to various laws and ordinances, some of which he may find oppressive or inconvenient to his aims), depends upon no act of will at all, but upon some other habit of mind in relation to which the consideration of opposing choices is wholly absent. Perhaps there is nothing more to legitimacy than that, finding ourselves, as it were in the middle of a situation into which we are born, we may seek to intellectualise the reasons for that compliance which is (without having chosen it) already part of our personal and shared experience. Perhaps government is, after all, 'natural' to human beings.

This returns us firmly to the question posed at the beginning of this chapter, namely the relationship of law to the human condition. For Hobbes, reflection upon the human condition reveals nothing at all about the substance of the law. Law is to be understood as artifice, an imposed (or 'posited') solution to the problems afflicting the human predicament. Being an imposed instrument, nothing of any significance about human nature is to be read there. In both its negativity and its separation of law from sources of moral illumination, Hobbes's positivism represents a significant break with Aristotelianism. Grotius, as will become clear in chapter five, retains much more of the Aristotelian framework. If the human condition resembles for him a predicament then so too is it a journey: one the goal of which is the greater realisation of the good in human affairs, and for which the good (for all its variety and conflicting expressions) can be secured only in the context of collective endeavour. And it is through law that both the predicament and the journey are to be understood.

SUGGESTED READING

The Classical Picture

Augustine, *City of God*, Books I, IV–V and XIX.

Background Reading

A Fidora, 'Augustine to Aquinas (Latin-Christian Authors)' in B Davies and E Stump (eds), *The Oxford Handbook of Aquinas* (Oxford, Oxford University Press, 2012).

E Fortin, 'The Political Thought of St Augustine' in L Strauss and J Cropsey (eds), *History of Political Philosophy*, 3rd edn (Chicago IL, University of Chicago Press, 1987).

—— 'Augustine, Thomas Aquinas and the Problem of Natural Law' (1978) 4 *Mediaevalia* 179.

E Perreau-Saussine, 'Heaven as a Political Theme in Augustine's *City of God*' in M Bockmuehl and G Stroumsa (eds), *Paradise in Antiquity: Jewish and Christian Views* (Cambridge, Cambridge University Press, 2010).

T Smith, 'The Glory and Tragedy of Politics' in J Doody, K Hughes and K Paffenroth (eds), *Augustine and Politics* (Lanham MD, Lexington Books, 2004).

THE EMERGENCE OF MODERN POLITICS AND LAW

Hobbes, *Leviathan*, chs XVIII–XIX, XXXII and XLVI.

—— *Dialogue Between a Philosopher and a Student, of the Common Laws of England.*

Background Reading

MH Kramer, *Hobbes and the Paradoxes of Political Origins* (London, Macmillan, 1997) ch 2.

Martin Luther, 'The Bondage of the Will' in J Dillenberger (ed), *Martin Luther: Selections From His Writings* (New York, Doubleday, 1961).

M Oakeshott, 'Introduction' to the Simon & Schuster edition of *Leviathan*.

NE Simmonds, 'Between Positivism and Idealism' (1991) 50 *Cambridge Law Journal* 308.

5

Images of Law from Grotius to Kant

IN CHAPTER FOUR, it was observed that Hobbes was a kind of 'legal positivist': his legal philosophy depends upon a view of law as a set of rules that have been posited or laid down. Such laws can have any content, as long as they promote the value of social peace. But Hobbes was a kind of natural lawyer, too: he believed in a primordial equality of all persons, and in a set of 'theorems of prudence' (natural laws) according to which human beings could escape the harsh and violent primordial condition. This vision of natural laws is a long way from Aquinas's. It will be remembered that natural law, for Aquinas, is the human being's participation in eternal law, a mode of participation based upon reason working practically to identify and pursue human goods. For Hobbes on the other hand, practical reason exists in service to the faculty of desire: we identify something as good *because* we desire it; we do not desire it *because* it is good. The laws of nature, then, for Hobbes, are mere insights into better and more advantageous ways by which we (you, I and others) can secure the things we desire: such as peace and a comfortable life.

It is rightly said that, insofar as Hobbes possesses a natural law theory, it is a Protestant natural law theory. To say this is to make a point about the end or purpose of law. In Aquinas, the ultimate object of natural law (indeed all law) is the common good: a good that is none other than the good of all individuals that make up the community. Hobbes does not believe in a common good in this sense. Natural laws merely point to a method of achieving social peace: a peace that will allow each individual to formulate and pursue their own understanding of the highest good in their own way. Peace is, no doubt, a common good of all persons, but as we have seen, Hobbes does not consider peace as dependent upon justice: instead, justice is the name given to whatever rights and duties are enacted by the positive state law.

If we are not careful, however, the distinction between 'Catholic' and 'Protestant' natural law can be highly misleading. For it may seem that we are thereby designating two different kinds of law, applicable to two different kinds of people. But in reality, in making this distinction, we are talking about two different theories *about* natural law, for there is only one natural law. If Hobbes is right in his thinking, it must follow that Aquinas is wrong, and vice versa. It is preferable therefore to speak of Catholic and Protestant *perspectives* on natural law.

The difficulty of using these terms is amply demonstrated in relation to the subject of this chapter, the Dutch jurist Hugo Grotius (1583–1645). Grotius was a Remonstrant (a form of Arminian Protestantism), but his works on natural law remain strongly within the tradition of Aquinas and Aristotle. The principal difference from Aquinas is simply the level of focus and detail in relation to questions of law and natural law. Whereas the *Summa Theologiae* is—as its title suggests—a work of theology, Grotius's most famous work, *De Iure Belli ac Pacis* (*Of the Law of War and Peace*) is a work on law. Its scope is therefore similar to QQ 90–108 of the *Summa Theologiae*'s Prima Secundae Pars. It consequently leaves out much of the topic of final or ultimate end, and matters such as grace and the theological virtues. Instead, it gives a much more extensive discussion of positive and natural law in relation to the law of and between communities (positive state law and the *ius inter gentes*).

Though a near-contemporary of Hobbes, Grotius wrote his major works when much younger. (Hobbes came to write on philosophy only in middle age.) Intellectually, as well as historically, Grotius's works are closer to the scholastic writers of the generation before Hobbes. Again, this chronological precedence does not imply anything about the texts themselves, which continue to meet one another at the timeless level of ideas, not of history. But it demonstrates that Grotius was writing in a tradition of thought extending beyond the scholastic philosophers back to Aquinas and Aristotle.

The difference between the Hobbesian and Grotian traditions is perhaps most visible in relation to their views on the general character of law. Hobbes, as we have seen, thinks that the law—that is, the posited law of the state—can have any content, at least as long as it preserves social peace and order. The rights and obligations of citizens, as well as the nature of justice itself, entirely derive from the content of these posited laws. Grotius, for his part, follows Aquinas in recognising the positive state law. There are very many matters on which the state legislator and courts have competence to create laws to answer the ordinary problems of social life. Indeed, they possess a duty to legislate, for the sake of the common good. However, as we shall see, Grotius thinks that there are intrinsic limits to the state's authority to enact laws. This results in a conception of the general character of law as a system of rights that are logically prior to such enactments.

As both Hobbes's and Grotius's positions should remind us, it is in one sense wrong to *contrast* positivist doctrines concerning enacted rules with the proposition that law embodies intrinsic ideas. In laying down the rules, a sovereign government may itself be guided by a particular vision of justice which it deems to be independent of its own authority, and which it seeks to implement through its enactments. But the logic of Hobbes's position is to invert this image, placing authority above justice and regarding the latter as the contingent expression of the former. Equally, the law might be seen as an instrument for the establishment, not of some particular moral ideology or theory of justice, but merely of a reasonable accommodation of conflicting interests, seeking to strike an acceptable balance between them. Here, what is 'acceptable' cannot be determined in advance, but depends entirely upon the character and strength of the opposing interests that are in need of reconciliation. As we have seen, Grotius for his part does not deny the need for authoritative enactment as a feature of the legal protection of a system of rights, but he deems the authority of such a system to precede the enactment.

The subsequent history of legal positivist thought, particularly from the time of Bentham onwards, has focused almost exclusively upon the supposed contingency of the relationship between law and morality. But it is in fact the idea of law as a body of posited rules (versus the image of a system of logically prior rights) that is of most interest and significance. The significance of this is best appreciated if we consider the relationship between law and the activity of legal scholarship. Legal writing in the modern era presupposes that the law possesses a systematic quality. Basic textbooks as well as the most sophisticated treatises proceed on the assumption that the law is not simply a mere assemblage of rules, principles and decisions, no matter how well organised, but something more than that: an integrated and coherent whole. Much of the effort of the textbook writer is directed towards explaining individual rules and decisions as elements of a broader system of goals and principles, not as the application of self-standing and quite separate considerations. Such explanations go beyond the reported content of decided cases and of statutory provisions. Their meaning lies precisely in their deep systematic properties. Just as the physicist's experimental data mean nothing until accompanied by an interpretation which makes sense of the whole, so the legal scholar attempts to reveal something of the substance of the law which goes beyond a mere recital of particular rules and decisions. The legal historian AWB Simpson once noted that it is not uncommon for different textbooks on the law of contract, or of tort, to diverge in their interpretation of the law (eg, the nature of the law on the matter of a common mistake by both parties). But this divergence, he reminds us, is why we buy them all: not because one author is uniquely aware of a rule or decision of which the others are ignorant, but because of the differences of emphasis and interpretation each writer places upon the various elements, and for the alternative characterisation of the whole that results.[1]

The point about such writings (familiar as they are) is that they are most at home with a view of law that differs quite sharply from that of Hobbes.

---

[1] AWB Simpson, 'The Common Law and Legal Theory' in AWB Simpson (ed), *Oxford Essays in Jurisprudence*, 2nd Series (Oxford, Clarendon Press 1973).

They fit neatly into a theory for which authoritative rules and decisions give determinate but incomplete expression to a body of rights and general ideas of justice which are logically prior to the rules. The legal scholar's arguments, on this view, aim at expounding the more general ideas in the light of the more specific authoritative expressions. As we have seen, the determination of law for Hobbes is by contrast a matter for the sovereign alone. Its authority entirely depends upon its being enacted or decided by those officially charged with its determination. But the writer of the textbook or scholarly treatise does not typically think of his arguments as concerning what any particular group of officials believes to be the law. Rather, the arguments are to be taken as demonstrating what is the law, either by drawing out the law's implicit content or by reflecting upon what the law must be in the light of a given reading of the rules, decisions and so forth. These activities are superficially reconcilable with the Hobbesian view if one remembers that, for Hobbes, all legal propositions represent an opinion about the law, the truth of which depends entirely upon whether they accurately capture the sovereign will. But this does not disturb the sense that there is a deeper incompatibility between Hobbes's view of law and the activity of the legal writer. For, once again, the legal scholar's explanations are not at all directed at clarifying authoritative statements of the rules (still less at mere reportage). They concern instead the attempt to comprehend the meaning and significance of particular rules and decisions in the light of their contribution to the wider body of principles and standards against which they must in turn be understood.

Underlying these divisions are important assumptions about the nature of the law's authority and purpose. On the one hand, we have in Hobbes's vision an image of law as imposing a specific resolution of the problem of conflicting forms of the good (however this is achieved). Legal scholarship might suggest many things about the quality of justice implied by the rules, but general reflections on the character of justice establish nothing about the content of the rules: the fact that justice might demand such-and-such demonstrates not one thing about the law's actual arrangements. On the other hand, Grotius offers a vision of law for which the resolution of conflict between competing forms of the good is to some extent a matter of the nature of the beings pursuing them. This nature, for Grotius, hinges upon a basic premise of juridical equality, and it is against the background of this basic equality that the law's content is to be worked out.

GROTIUS AS A NATURAL LAWYER

Hobbes, it will be recalled, regarded the natural condition of human beings as one of continual warfare resulting from mutual diffidence and distrust.

Grotius, by contrast, retains the Aristotelian assumption that human beings are essentially sociable, driven by impulses that tend to draw us together rather than divide us. He adds to Aristotle's account of the human *telos* a theological dimension, claiming that the naturalness of forms of association is to be found in the proposition that God wishes human beings to thrive, and multiply. Just as Aristotle regarded the state as arising from the 'bare needs' of life, Grotius depicts a process whereby states form and flourish in pursuance of human survival. We can imagine an initial situation in which small groups of extended families band together for safety. If we conceive their knowledge and collective skills to be slight and primitive, it is likely that such groupings would lead a sparse and nomadic existence, consuming the natural resources of one area and moving on to another. But as a proto-community grows bigger, it also becomes slower and less easily moved around. Thus at some point, a community of a certain size will become static, and will need to discover a means of sustaining itself by organising and renewing the resources available to it. Agrarianism must develop; but both it and the stasis that prompts it require conceptions of *ownership*, over and above mere *use*. Property, Grotius therefore suggests, is at the root of the political system, and forms the foundation of the state.

Comparison of the Grotian position with that of Hobbes is instructive. A condition in which there is no property (ie, no distinction of 'mine and thine' in Hobbes's terms) is one of basic equality. God gave the world to human beings, Grotius says, so that they may use its bounty for their nourishment. Each person, therefore, is by nature equally free to use and consume these resources. No one person is *more* (or less) entitled to worldly goods than any other. Equality had of course been at the root of Hobbes's philosophy; but the consequences Hobbes draws from the premise of initial equality are essentially negative. For him also, each person is equal in that none has more right than another to the things of this world. But Hobbes interprets this to mean that everyone in a state of lawlessness has an absolute right to everything. It is this image of a chaotic situation of mutually opposing, overlapping rights to the same earthly things that leads Hobbes famously to *distinguish* the realms of law and right. Law does not fulfil the conditions of an already-present system of rights, but must be thought of as modifying and restricting those rights so as to bring order to a chaotic world.

Grotius, by contrast, sees law as giving definite expression to a systematic body of rights, found already in nature, that do not conflict. Unlike Hobbes, Grotius thinks of equality as implying a coherent system of limited rights. If each person is by nature equal, this must mean that no person can, by nature alone, be thought of as the property or subject of any other. But if none is naturally the slave of another, this must mean that each person's right is not unlimited, but is rather confined within certain naturally determined bounds.

If I am not a slave, it is because there is domain (as it were, of self-ownership) within which I am at liberty to order my own affairs and actions. This domain (of one's own, *suum ius*) establishes certain protective rights, essentially to life and the liberties of seeking and using that which sustains it, that constitute a line beyond which others may not trespass. Each may pursue his own course so long as he does not impinge upon the *suum* (right to one's own) of another. If a person acts within the scope of her rights, she does not violate those of others. Howsoever an institution of property ownership develops in society, Grotius suggests, it must do so in a way that continues to respect the domain of one's own.

One who is impressed by the Hobbesian vision will immediately ask what, if such limited rights exist, the chances are of anybody actually conforming their behaviour to them. Would each person not instead completely disregard such limits? And even if there are some who would otherwise be guided by them, would not the actions of others who are bent upon infringing such rights necessitate a general disregard of all rights, as a condition of survival?

It is here that the importance of the political state is made clear. For there are certain things that are impossible for individuals acting alone or together to achieve, without the coercive authority of the state: such as enforcing rights, for example. This properly falls to the state to ensure, along with other matters that pertain to the common good of all citizens: for example, preserving and enforcing peace; defending against external enemies of the community; ensuring that harms are compensated in some way, and that crimes are suppressed and punished; and regulating matters that pertain to the welfare of all members of the community. Only the state is capable of safeguarding these goods. In so doing, the state acts to protect each person's fundamental right (*suum ius*); but the limit of the state's authority is proscribed also by that very same right: the right of each person to the things that are necessary in order to live. Such fundamental rights constitute important baselines beyond which the state cannot step. A law that sacrificed one individual's fundamental right in order to give advantage to others, would be without legitimate force, in being ultra vires. Similarly, an individual who is starving could take the food of another without committing theft: for in extremis, property reverts back to the common condition that held in the beginning of human existence.

These restrictions on the power of the state, largely absent from Hobbes's philosophy, are significant and important in regarding the state as possessing both negative and positive duties (ie, duties of non-interference and duties of assistance). The matters which pertain to the state to enforce are matters of commutative justice: matters that are not decided according to distribution, but on the basis of the characteristic qualities of the person(s) to whom they are owed. They are matters that lie at the basis of every community's common good, and are present—at least to some extent—in any form of association stable enough to be called a community. Yet, this still leaves open a wide range of possible ways in which the common life of the community may develop. 'Just as there are several ways of living', Grotius says,

> and everyone may choose which he pleases of all those sorts; so a people may choose what form of government they please: neither is the right which the sovereign has over his subjects to be measured by this or that form, of which divers men have divers opinions, but by the extent of the will of those who conferred it upon him.[2]

All may be regarded as giving differing expressions to these innate ideas, and therefore as being 'patterned after nature's plan'.

Like Aquinas, Grotius regards the natural law as something open to reason, something capable of being rationally apprehended by human minds reflecting on action. Natural laws are not sheer determinations of God's will, but discoverable aspects of the divine intellect. Murder is not wrong because God decreed it so; rather God decreed it because it is—demonstrably—wrong, ie, wholly unreasonable. If this were not so, there would be no possibility of saying *why* crimes such as murder are wrong. Thus, Grotius says that:

> What we have been saying [about the natural law] would have somewhat the same status even if we should concede that which cannot be conceded without the uttermost wickedness, that there is no God, or that the affairs of men are of no concern to Him.[3]

Grotius was not the first natural lawyer to say this, but his statement of the thesis is probably the most famous. It is so because of the effect it had on future generations of political philosophers, who saw Grotius as establishing a division between the rational *content* of the natural law, and that which gives it obligatory *force*.

Grotius's aim was the elucidation of a body of laws that are universal, and must therefore be supposed to apply to those amongst whom the Word of God had not yet been received. But the separation it establishes, between rational content and obligatory force, was later to become an important intellectual basis for philosophies of politics that *excluded* ideas of natural law. The later writers, who included Hume and Bentham, were to observe that these 'natural laws' were in fact no more than 'laws' of human happiness. One did not need a theology to understand that each person should seek to maximise their own happiness. Thus, the basis of morality came to be seen by these philosophers as no more than the pursuit of happiness, whatever that might be. Because the causes of each person's pleasure and pain differ (one's meat being the other's poison), notions of 'the good' were transformed into measurable and equally valuable units of 'utility'.

---

[2] Grotius, *De Iure Belli ac Pacis*, I.3.8.
[3] ibid Prolegomena, II.

In this way, Grotius's account lent itself to an interpretation that provided an intellectual ground of *positivist* philosophy. But equally, one might work out the implications of Grotius's position in another way, as pointing to the ground of morality lying wholly within the realm of human reason. This was to be the inspiration for the line of thinking that culminated in Kant's philosophy of law, for which the ultimate source of moral insight was not nature or the created world, but human reason alone. In this new system of philosophy, questions of human good did not inform an understanding of the rights which each person possesses; instead, questions of right were prioritised to those of the good.

A NEW FRAMEWORK

Grotius, as we have just seen, pursues the essentially Aristotelian thought that moral and political reflection are guided by concentration upon historical experience, whilst making specific departures from Aristotle in relation to the idea of justice. Humans are not to be viewed as having *invented* society, the state, or its central institutions. They are to be supposed as engaging in various practices and relationships that are quite natural to their situation which *then*, in retrospect, have certain meanings attached to them. Ideas of law, of property and so on, are the expression given to phenomena that have already taken shape, unnoticed, on the human landscape, just as one who is hungry does not suddenly become hungry but rather becomes suddenly aware of a hunger that has been growing, unnoticed, for some time. And it is via this process of reflection upon our collective situation that we come to understand what justice is: 'abstaining from that which is another's'.

The character of the philosophy to be found in Kant's writings on law and justice is altogether removed from this framework of thought. Aristotelians will typically view collective institutions such as the law, the economic marketplace, the Church and so on, as potent sources of moral reflection in their own right, to be prized for the light that they are capable of throwing upon a form of human association. Kant, by contrast, is engaged in a process of intellectual clarification that seeks to recover the concepts that *underlie* this historical experience. This amounts to a form of 'human anthropology' which attempts to identify general *laws* of human reason, and of human existence. Historical forms of association, being *objects* of governance by these laws, can offer only limited insight into their substance. (For might not the historical efforts of human beings fall short of what is required in terms of these laws?)[4]

---

[4] Kant does not himself go so far as his intellectual descendants of the present day, in downplaying a context of 'ordinary understandings' as a source of moral insight. See I Kant,

The object of this human anthropology would be an understanding of the human condition in its normative aspect: the identification of the conditions by which human beings *ought* to live. There is a strong resemblance in this respect between Kantian thought and Augustine's vision of the Two Cities. Both are essentially Platonic, and hence dualist, understandings of history and politics. But there is nevertheless an important difference between Augustine's world-view and that of Kant and his modern successors. Whereas the 'normative' meaning of the world is in Augustine's view a divine matter, and hence fundamentally *outside* history, Kant locates this meaning in reason itself. For Augustine, we must acknowledge our sinfulness and smallness, and humble ourselves before God's infinite goodness and mercy. Only through Grace can we come to perfection. For Kant on the other hand, it is we who must, and indeed can potentially, by our own efforts, achieve maturity and autonomy over our base desires, becoming master of them. The question of how we ought to live is to be settled by laws that we give to ourselves: laws that would reign supreme in their universality even over God Himself: 'Even the Holy One of the Gospel must first be compared with our ideal of moral perfection', Kant writes, 'before he is cognized as such'.[5]

For Kant and for his successors in the Western tradition down to the present day, the meaning of the human condition is to be found not in theology, but in reason itself. If Kant's positioning of laws of reason above 'the Holy One' seems remarkable, it is no more so than the philosophical doctrines that he set out to challenge by means of it. On the one hand, Hobbes, and the German natural lawyers Pufendorf and Thomasius, adopted an 'Epicurian' image of the human being as a creature driven by passions which make him dangerous and self-destructive, and hence in need of 'external' governance by law and state. On the other hand were Aristotle, the scholastics and Grotius, for whom the human being is a rational animal, whose rational and moral characteristics are *reflected* in collective social arrangements such as law, family, the market etc. For these writers, the law of nature was a law of *human* nature, congenial towards and tending to realise human flourishing. 'The good' of human beings, thus understood, comes to the same thing as the moral law, or that which ought to be done. Sin, no matter how great the fleeting fulfilment it gives to base desires, was accordingly conceived as a wound to one's inner nature and wellbeing.

Kant's thinking on law and politics belongs to neither of these frameworks. The human being is to be considered as an intellectual being who resides

---

'Groundwork of the Metaphysics of Morals' in M Gregor (trans), *Practical Philosophy: The Cambridge Edition of the Collected Works of Immanuel Kant* (Cambridge, Cambridge University Press, 1996) 4:404, 59.

[5] ibid 4:408, 63.

nonetheless in the sensible world. An image of man as a passionate and dangerous animal is not altogether outside the truth, but represents a state of immaturity that must be transcended through a process of self-transformation. Being a creature of intellect and of reason, the human being is capable of representing to itself considerations of an abstract and general nature, apart from the particular circumstances of the world. But the human being is *also* a creature of sense, and inhabits a world which demands certain responses that must be made to its varying circumstances. This dualistic nature of human beings is essential to Kant's moral theory. Lacking the rational aspect that holds us apart from the world, a person would be capable of representation 'only as subject to the natural law of his needs'.[6] Subjection of this kind amounts to slavery to one's animalistic, worldly nature. Consequently, Kant is led to say that the 'good will' is one that is 'free': that is, free of subjection to its worldly associations.

We might think of the will as being shaped by experience. But 'experience' is not something that is 'given' to us, and towards which we are as passive receptors. We confront the world from a standpoint that is inescapably human. Its 'objectivity', the independence of many of its operations from human control or influence, belongs to a conceptual framework of understanding that is inseparable from our being acted or impinged upon by it. To have knowledge of the world is to have intellectualised it, so that it holds meaning for us. 'Experience' is precisely this intellectualised product of our relationship to what is external to us. This world demands to be responded to in numerous ways. We can therefore think of the world as an endless source of influences upon the mind's determinations, in the sense that responses are constantly demanded to stimuli from outside ourselves. By the 'unfree' will, Kant has in mind a will that takes its *principles* of action from these outside sources (eg, the desire for rich foods, or attraction towards potential sexual partners: imagine the ruin which would come to one's character from making sexual attraction the *basis* of all one's goals and actions). Such influences, 'as sources of needs, are so far from having an absolute worth … that it must be the universal wish of every rational being to be altogether free of them'.[7] The free or autonomous will is one that gives to itself its own laws. But the will that suffers its volitions to be determined by its reactions to the world belongs to the man who is 'subject to the natural law of his needs'.

> The will in that case does not give *itself* the law; instead the object, by means of its relation to the will, gives the law to it. This relation, whether it rests upon inclination or upon representations of reason, lets only hypothetical imperatives become possible: I ought to do something *because I will something else*.[8]

---

[6] ibid 4:439.
[7] ibid 4:428.
[8] ibid 4:441 (some emphasis added).

Freeing itself from these snares, the will becomes autonomous. It will be truly self-determining. Its only guide in moral matters will be pure reason: I ask only, can my maxim stand as a universal law, one that is not conditional upon inclinations, needs, or any context of reaction to the circumstances of the world?

The philosophies of Machiavelli and Hobbes had shown the true and bitter consequences of viewing men as passionate creatures in need of 'external' governance: philosophies in which the realm of public interaction resembles the school playground, to be governed and organised by ultimately despotical masters on behalf of those who, lacking maturity, cannot be relied upon to safeguard their own best interests. For Kant, the role of moral philosophy is the achievement of maturity and hence autonomy, a state in which man ceases to require the 'external' governance of others and lives rather by the 'internal' governance of reason. In this way, Kant claimed, the individual becomes free in being subject only to laws that he himself imposes. Such laws are to be guided by the 'categorical imperative': 'Inexperienced in the course of the world, incapable of being prepared for whatever may come to pass in it, I ask myself only: can you also will that your maxim become a universal law?'[9]

As we saw earlier, Grotius's philosophy differed from Hobbes in supposing there to be a natural domain of non-overlapping rights that exists prior to any laws laid down by the sovereign. Grotius derives the content of these rights from reflection on the characteristic needs and desires of human persons as created beings: we are created equal by God, and meant by His law to survive and flourish in this world. Hence, each person enjoys a foundation of 'fundamental right' *suum ius*. Kant also conceives of law as taking the form of a body of non-overlapping domains of entitlement, but he does *not* derive the content of these rights from any reflection upon human nature. The content of such rights is to be determined by the categorical imperative alone, that is, by a reason that considers only what is universal. The outcome of such deliberations must in consequence hold true not just of humans, in virtue of whatever is particular to their nature, but of *any* rational creature (be he monster or god). The consequences of this shift in thinking are enormous. Let us examine them one at a time.

1. Kant's suggestion that one who is 'inexperienced in the course of the world' may nevertheless achieve moral wisdom puts his thought on a radically different path from that of Aristotle (and Grotius). No longer is the world of human action and society to be regarded as a potent source of moral insights. It represents instead a morally inert realm that is subject to governance by standards that derive from elsewhere. Pufendorf had laid the foundations for

---

[9] ibid 4:403.

such a view: distinguishing between 'physical' and 'moral' entities, he states that moral entities stand apart from the causal nexus, and 'do not arise out of the ... physical properties of things, but they are superadded, at the will of intelligent entities, to things already existent and physically complete'.[10] We are not, consequently, to think of objects or actions in this world as possessing intrinsic moral properties. Rather such properties arise from the *interpretation* of those objects and actions. The further implication of this view is that moral ideas cannot act upon behaviour as a cause, for instead all behaviour is conditional upon the exercise of will.

Moral philosophy in Kant's hands becomes a fundamentally different type of enquiry. Jurisprudential writers of the present day who follow Kant tend to regard it as a mistake to suggest that law may itself provide a starting point for reflection into morality or the nature of the good life. Law is to be viewed instead as a domain of practices to which ethical insights are to be *applied*. Even those writers who reject any firm distinction between law and morality exemplify this tendency. Thus, we find Dworkin arguing that 'mere conventions' can tell us nothing about the moral nature of our practices: the fact that a culture has been historically committed to a certain way of thinking or acting contributes not one bit to a demonstration that such practices are desirable or morally right.[11] Obviously, the fact that 'this is what we do around here' does not demonstrate that a practice is morally right, but it is something different to suggest that scrutiny of a context of historical practices offers no *guidance* to our moral deliberations. Ordinarily we think of experience as capable of teaching us various things ('the burnt hand teaches best'). This refers, inevitably, to our *interpretation* of experience rather than a mute reception of external stimuli. We are not as plants, acted upon by the elements and lacking any awareness of what affects us. Our intellect allows us scope to enquire into the meaning of the situations in which we find ourselves. Aristotle's philosophy belongs to a tradition that regards the world as intelligible and meaningful, and it is for us to uncover that meaning. So long as this is the case, it is easy to see why our actions have a moral significance. But if all meaning in the world is 'superadded' by the will of intelligent beings (the world *itself* lacking intrinsic intelligibility or meaning), then it becomes much less obvious what moral values, as products of the will, have to do with facts or actions that are, in themselves, morally inert.

2. Kant suggests that one's moral duty is defined by reference to the categorical imperative. Each putative moral maxim must be subjected to the test of

---

[10] S Pufendorf, *De Iure Naturae et Gentium* (*Of the Law of Nature and Nations*) Book I.1.5–6.
[11] See R Dworkin, *Law's Empire* (London, Fontana Press, 1986) ch 2.

whether it is capable of re-description as a universal law. Only if we are able and willing to subject each person equally to a given standard (including ourselves), no matter what the particularities of their situation, can the fruit of our will be described as a moral law. In giving laws to itself, the will becomes free, for it then needs no external governance but only that of reason itself. Suppose each person must reflect on the nature of the good: the 'freedom' of the will depends upon each person determining for himself or herself what is good, rather than relying upon 'external' sources of authority. What, one might then ask, guarantees that each person will converge in their judgement on the nature of the good? If meaning is not present but superadded, in other words, why should we ever be supposed to agree upon the meaning to be assigned to things and actions?

Kant of course requires of any moral law that it be universal. But since reasonable people can be expected to differ just as vociferously over what is universal as over what is good, it would seem as if the requirement of universality advances us no further. The autonomous will is one that is rational, but we must not think of reason as something *external* to the will. Were we to concede rationality as being something that determines the will 'from outside', then we have effectively returned to an Aristotelian conception of the world as a domain in which intelligibility is present rather than 'superadded'. We are thus in the position of having to explain how wills that are genuinely autonomous and self-determining can nevertheless share a sense of what is 'rational'. And it is by no means clear that the convergence in judgement of such wills upon standards agreed to be 'rational' or 'universal' could be more than a fortuitous contingency. This question will arise again later in the book, as it is important to understand how modern writers on law and politics, such as Dworkin and Rawls, have wrestled with this Kantian inheritance.

3. One question that Kant's philosophy of law imposes upon us, concerns the proper place of jurisprudence in intellectual life. Must we think of jurisprudence as a branch of moral philosophy, or as a social science that is largely distinct from questions of morality? On the one hand, it is possible to think of law as a source of order and security for the civic community. The function of the state (on this view) might be conceived as extending only to ensuring the peace and defence of its citizens, both from external enemies (foreign states) and internal strife (from one's neighbours). Both Hobbes's and Pufendorf's theories of law (and also to an extent Grotius's) are of this kind: the bitter experience of religious civil wars in Europe had convinced the 'civic' jurists that human beings require governance not by reason, but by *law*. So long as politics is thought of as directed towards the salvation of the community, law is likely to function as an instrument of confessional conflict. Separating law from the moral and intellectual judgements about the nature of the good is

then a condition of social peace. After reading Pufendorf at university, the German jurist Thomasius formed the conviction that the series of religious civil wars in Europe had been brought to an end, not by the triumph of 'universal reason', but by the settlement imposed by *law* and *state*.[12]

Initially, Kant's philosophy of law might seem to resemble this image, insofar as he relegates the importance of law to the defence of the security of the civic community. Those who have achieved enlightenment, or moral maturity, can be thought to have transcended the need for the external governance of law, and live instead according to the internal governance of reason. The only civic role for law can therefore be the collective defence of such individuals from external enemies. But the implications of Kant's position are in fact quite different from the picture of civic jurisprudence just explored. For on the other hand, we might conceive of law as the guardian of the purity of the *moral* community. The existence of a domain of non-overlapping rights is for Kant a consequence of exactly that private pursuit of moral regeneration that is consequent upon reflection on the good. In regarding the achievement of social peace as contingent upon this exercise, Kant effectively transforms all political debates into rational ones about the nature of the good. He therefore resurrects an approach to politics that might otherwise have been thought to have perished with the Reformation, by associating the idea of moral progress with that of moral maturity.

4. How ought we to regard the idea of human progress? The classical and early Christian philosophers had focused upon the improvement of the individual soul, and the idea of eternal salvation in the next life. Life in *this* world was thus regarded variously as a predicament and a journey (or pilgrimage) to the hereafter. The image of the two-fold man related to this dualistic picture: man is represented as both a spiritual being, created by God, and a sensual creature, whose worldly passions are capable of leading him to act in ways that offer a wound to his spiritual wellbeing. One who is true to his nature as a created being should therefore remain unspotted from the world, and love rather what is transcendent and eternal.[13]

Within the Kantian philosophy, the two-fold nature of man is interpreted instead according to the division between passions and the demands of *reason*. Because this reason is normative for all rational beings (god or man), there is nothing about it that especially concerns the relationship of human beings to God. Even the Holy One of the Gospel is subject to its demands. This worldly focus (that is, the ethical focus on worldly actions) is compounded by Kant's attitude towards moral development and enlightenment. In his

---

[12] See I Hunter, *Rival Enlightenments* (Cambridge, Cambridge University Press, 2001) ch 1.
[13] See ch 2 above.

essay, 'An Answer to the Question: What is Enlightenment?'[14] Kant defines enlightenment as 'the human being's emergence from his self-incurred minority'; minority in turn being 'inability to make use of one's own understanding without direction from another'.[15] A public, Kant thought, should aim to become self-governing, in that it should be capable of giving to itself its own laws. Only by doing so could it be 'free': free, that is, of external moral direction by guardians, and by traditions and old prejudices. The thought is that these 'guardians' have themselves developed the ability to 'think for themselves' on the moral questions facing society. Kant wants the 'unthinking masses' to do the same, though he admits that 'a public can achieve enlightenment only slowly'.[16] To impede such enlightenment is 'a crime against human nature, whose original vocation lies precisely in such progress'.[17] Thus, shall 'People gradually work their way out of barbarism of their own accord if only one does not intentionally contrive to keep them in it'.[18]

In passages such as these, Kant seems to be proposing a picture of human history as a journey, from barbaric and uncivilised beginnings to the highest states of enlightenment and civility. It is an image, therefore, of human perfectability within the world: the refinement of human existence, and thus society, in historical time. We might contrast this picture with that of the classical and medieval writers on ethics, for whom (in different ways) the perfectability of the human being lay in a degree of *detachment* from the world. For them enlightenment meant, not the ability to give oneself laws, but humble submission to God's laws. It may be that Kant's own ambitions in ethics were not radically divorced from this older image of ethical improvement. But the focus of his enquiry, upon the historical human journey, has inspired modern writers to such a degree that 'the just society' has become *itself* the object of worship as the ultimate source of good. The words of Francis Fukuyama are an especially plain expression of this shift in priorities: he regards the modern, liberal democratic state with commitment to human rights and free market practices as representing the *final* form of human society, standing 'at the end of history'.[19]

The branch of theology that is concerned with end-points and ultimate conditions is called eschatology. Within traditional Christian eschatology, the final perfection of the human being (ie, its ultimate salvation) is something that occurs only beyond the circles of this world. It concerns not the perfection

---

[14] See Kant (n 4) 17–22.
[15] ibid, 8:35.
[16] ibid, 8:36.
[17] ibid, 8:39.
[18] ibid, 8:41.
[19] F Fukuyama, *The End of History and the Last Man* (Harmondsworth, Penguin, 1993).

of, or attachment to, institutions in the earthly city, but the soul's love of the heavenly city. And this final salvation is not brought about by purely human efforts (even the best of which are not free of sin), but by the gift of God's grace. The gradual disappearance of religious perspectives from politics and political theory might give the impression that eschatology is irrelevant to present understandings, but in fact there is real value in regarding the process as one of the replacement of one eschatological vision by another. A political theory like that of Fukuyama's, the ultimate object of which is the ideally just society, represents a vision of human perfectibility within the world, and by human efforts alone. 'Salvation' becomes the progressive escape from present injustices, in the race towards the brighter future. As I have said, the extent to which Kant himself can be identified with this ambition is less clear than in the case of modern-day writers such as, say, Rawls. But it is nevertheless Kantian categories and concerns that bring about this monumental, yet largely unnoticed, shift in Western thinking.

5. How is the relationship between morality and 'the good' to be understood? Earlier, I mentioned in passing that there is within Aristotelian ethical thought a perception that moral goodness is aligned with what is good for human beings. By acting well, we promote our own happiness or wellbeing. Acting badly, we give injury to ourselves. Taken within the context of Christian theology and natural law, we can make sense of this alignment by observing again the two-fold nature of human beings. On the one hand, we are physical beings inhabiting the realm of sensation and matter. Our interactions with this world can bring both physical pain and physical pleasure (both of which may be harmful). On the other hand, we are spiritual beings capable of living the life of the intellect. Spiritual goods (closeness to God, nobility of character etc) are both the goal and the reward of virtue, and represent the proper direction for human thought and action. One who fails to remain 'unspotted from the world' may achieve a kind of pleasure (one that stimulates the senses), but fails to nourish the spirit. And since it is the spirit, or character, which maketh the man, such emptiness can be sustained only by repeatedly renewing the sensory experience, chasing fleeting ghosts of happiness which never last or truly satisfy.[20]

But suppose we leave on one side the religious dimension to this image. Grotius forces us to contemplate this possibility, for (it will be remembered) he claims that his general account of human nature and the moral life would hold true even if there were no God. We may then be tempted to raise the question of why the sensory pleasures should not weigh more heavily than

---

[20] This is of course quite close to the image of human nature found in Hobbes's *Leviathan*: see ch 4 above.

the spiritual ones. Imagine a person who often acts in ways that we consider immoral. He lies, cheats, bullies and sometimes steals to get what he wants, and is incredibly self-centred. Assuming he also generally gets away with it, is it correct to think of such a person as being less 'happy' than one who devotes herself to good causes, lives a life centred upon her relationship with others, and who values good manners, honesty and justice? We might think so, if we consider some famous lines of Sir Walter Scott:

> High though his titles, proud his name,
> Boundless his wealth as wish can claim;
> Despite those titles, power, and pelf,
> The wretch, centred all in self,
> Living, shall forfeit fair renown,
> And, doubly dying, shall go down
> To the vile dust, from whence he sprung,
> Unwept, unhonor'd, and unsung.

But are we doing anything more here than equating happiness with good character? Performance of good actions might well invest the doer with an inner sense of satisfaction, born of the knowledge than one has acted well. What right have we to think of this form of spiritual contentment as of greater quality to that enjoyed by the shallow, selfish man? Is sociability (for example) any *more* a wellspring of happiness or wellbeing than misanthropy? It is clear that in some cases, to do the right thing is to invite hardships or suffering to oneself that might be avoided by pursuing a more selfish course. Do worldly comforts count for less than the knowledge that one has acted rightly?

I leave this question as one to ponder and argue over. For present purposes, we need only be aware that an important line of philosophical thinking has held the moral life to be one that is deeply agreeable to the human character. The wise man will therefore find happiness in his virtue; and, if he is wise, he will find conformity to the moral law no struggle. By contrast, the man who pursues shallow worldly pleasures is a fool.

Kant's standpoint on morality is vastly different. For him, obedience to the moral law *must* be a struggle. If one is to act morally, Kant insists, one must do so only for the sake of the moral law, and not for the benefit of any other objects that may be consequent upon such obedience. Thus, if we obey the moral law in order to ensure our spiritual salvation before God; or if we act because we value goodness and the quality of being good; or if the aim in acting is the production of a satisfactory outcome; in all such cases, Kant says, we do not *genuinely* act morally, but for a mixture of motives that are bound up with our own wellbeing.[21] Consequently, Kant is led to the striking

---

[21] See Kant (n 4) 4:390.

conclusion that there has never, in human history, been a true example of moral action.

This, as we have already seen, places Kant onto a radically different path from that of Aristotle, for whom moral understanding proceeds from contemplation of characteristic wants and needs. If no human action has ever been truly moral, then history provides no starting point for ethical reflection. But what is remarkable about Kant's position is the implication it has for our understanding of moral character. Almost paradoxically, Kant is suggesting that a young man who (for example) visits his sick elderly relative in hospital out of compassion or love, or in order to bring relief or pleasure to the relative, is *less* moral than one who does so resentfully, being motivated out of nothing but a sense of duty. The faint sense of paradox arises precisely because we normally think of the 'good man' as one who *enjoys* being good. Surely (we ordinarily think) one who resents having to be good, and who finds no substantive value in moral obligations, is a good example of someone who is morally unenlightened. Kant's error, one may suppose, lies in the extreme voluntarism involved in deepening the division made by Grotius, between the juridical realm of right and justice, and the broader ethical domain of love, virtue and charity. HLA Hart captures something of this hint of paradox when he writes that

> it is plain that most likely to abandon their moral beliefs when these are shown to have a subjective source are those whose moral sentiments have been formulated apart from concrete situations and kinds of conduct, and have become focused on general principles and theories or on the divine will or on whatever is taken to be a general authoritative source of all moral right and wrong. The moral monster who thinks there is nothing morally wrong in torturing a child except that God has forbidden it, has a parallel in the moralist who will not treat the fact that the child will suffer agony as in itself a moral reason enough.[22]

It might be that the sense of oddness attaching to Kant's assertion (that one must act morally only because it is the moral law, and not because it is good), is sufficient to incline you to reject his doctrine. But we ought not to be too hasty in this judgement. For it is perhaps the case that the survival of morality depends upon there being some kind of distinction between 'what is good for human beings' and what they ought to do. Can morality survive if it is intelligible only in terms of the success or fulfilment of human nature? How are we then to discriminate between human nature as understood by the Nazis, and human nature as envisaged by (say) the Pope or the Dalai Lama? The point is

---

[22] HLA Hart, 'Who Can Tell Right from Wrong?' *New York Review of Books* 33:12 (17 July 1986); quoted in A Perreau-Saussine, 'An Outsider on the Inside: Hart's Limits on Jurisprudence' (2006) 56 *University of Toronto Law Journal* 371, 387.

not a sceptical one. We are not asking, what would become of morality if there were nothing other than human choices. We are asking, rather, what would become of morality if the guiding ideal to which our actions are directed were conceived as the perfection or final flourishing of human nature. Such ideals may stand outside or beyond human nature as such; but if they represent teleological end-points, then our understandings of morality are shaped by the extension or deepening of the natures we already possess. Can our world indeed survive without a conception of morality that is, in some contexts, *opposed* to the deepest natural human inclinations? That is the supposition that is pursued by Kant, and it is one that should not be lightly dismissed.

SUGGESTED READING

H Grotius, *De Iure Belli ac Pacis* (*The Rights of War and Peace*), Prolegomena (preliminary discourse) and Book 1.

I Kant, 'Groundwork of the Metaphysics of Morals' in M Gregor (trans), *Practical Philosophy: The Cambridge Edition of the Collected Works of Immanuel Kant* (Cambridge, Cambridge University Press, 1996).

J Locke, *Two Treatises of Government*, Second Treatise, esp chs I–IX.

—— *Essay Concerning Human Understanding*, Book II, 2 and 33; Book III, 9 (para 7).

Background Reading

S Buckle, *Natural Law and the Theory of Property: Grotius to Hume* (Oxford, Clarendon Press, 1993) 16–35 and ch 3.

P Haggenmacher, *Grotius et la Doctrine de la Guerre Juste* (Geneva, Graduate Institute Publications, 1983).

C Korsgaard, *Creating the Kingdom of Ends* (Cambridge, Cambridge University Press, 1996).

O O'Neill, *Constructions of Reason* (Cambridge, Cambridge University Press, 1990).

S Pufendorf, *De Iure Naturae et Gentium* (*Of the Law of Nature and Nations*) Book I, chs 1–4.

JB Schneewind, *Moral Philosophy From Montaigne to Kant* (Cambridge, Cambridge University Press, 2002) 1–32.

R Tuck, *Philosophy and Government, 1572–1651* (Cambridge, Cambridge University Press, 1993) chs 5–7.

Part Two

Debates

6

Positive Law, Positive Justice: Hart

IN THE FIFTH of his lectures on jurisprudence, John Austin (1790–1859) famously claimed that 'the existence of law is one thing; its merit or demerit is another'.[1] Austin's statement may strike us as obviously true. One can point to many examples of laws that reasonable people deem to be unjust, or of dubious merit. But the truth of Austin's claim may seem less straightforward when we reflect upon some of its implications. If the existence of law is a question distinct from its merits, then one must be able to find the law without any reliance upon moral judgements. Is this the case? Examining cases on the law of torts, for example, one might be struck by the extent to which determinations of the courts as to the law to be applied hinge upon considerations of the extent of duties owed to the victim, the onerousness of obligations of care, or of what was reasonable in the circumstances. Indeed, is not litigation concerned in one sense with the justice of the demands being made by the claimant and defendant?

Aware of these dimensions to legal thought, the version of legal positivism offered by HLA Hart (1907–92) emphasises a different idea: that of the contingency of the relationship between law and morality. In chapter IX of *The Concept of Law*, Hart contends that 'it is in no sense a necessary truth that laws reproduce or satisfy certain demands of morality, though in fact they have often done so'.[2] This statement appears to leave room for the possibility that certain legal arguments or decisions of the court might be concerned with the elucidation or justification of moral ideas. But it is nevertheless the case that Hart shares with Austin a belief that legal positivism is concerned above all with the nature of the connections between the domains of law and moral thought. Earlier theories of the nature of law were occupied with a different question: to what extent law consists exclusively of rules and arrangements that are posited, or laid down, establishing a merely conventional justice.

The earliest juridical philosophies sought an understanding of those standards of reason or justice that are in some sense natural to human societies, in

---

[1] J Austin, *The Province of Jurisprudence Determined* (London, Weidenfeld & Nicholson, 1832) 185.
[2] HLA Hart, *The Concept of Law*, 3rd edn (Oxford, Clarendon Press, 2012) 185–86.

being directed towards the wellbeing of the community and the soundness and legal virtue of its internal arrangements. The establishment of certain communal conditions was essential for the pursuit of human flourishing or happiness. The private good of each individual could be subsumed under the common good of the community, its shared rational and ideological commitments to developing a common way of life, as the only real path to their fulfilment. If the human being was by nature a social animal, then his most basic need was that of *order*. But classical jurists in the Aristotelian and Platonic traditions believed that stable order was nevertheless possible only if it embodied a measure of justice. Order implies rationality. Thus, the conditions required for human flourishing are not infinite as to the form that they can take. The end of a community's rational and ideological commitments must be orientated to the pursuit of good order (*eunomia*), unless society ultimately unravel itself. It was therefore quite clear to the ancient jurists that if the flourishing life is proper to man, it is yet necessary that he labour in order to achieve it by crafting laws and policies for the direction of social life. But all too often, the positive arrangements and standards that men lay down for themselves can go against justice, standing in opposition to the life that is properly appointed.

In the hands of the Christian jurists of the medieval period, this distinction grew in sophistication and altered in its significance. The life that is ordained for human beings is present in God's eternal law (*lex aeterna*). But humans, removed from the mind of God, do not perceive His eternal will, and it remains unfathomable to them. Yet God's law is not only the product of His will, arbitrary and unrestrained by any consideration, but is shaped by His perfect nature. Consequently, it is possible for human beings to participate in the eternal law in virtue of their rational nature. They can gain knowledge and understanding of a 'natural law' (*ius naturale*). The importance of this is worth exploring.

For the Christian writers, the primary source of human understanding of God's law is revelation. Through the Decalogue and through biblical texts, a part of the eternal law is revealed directly to human beings. But the part of the law that is thus revealed (*lex divina*) is in many ways less than the law that is needed for the guidance of human action. Its commandments are general; its beatitudes are aphoristic. Much that pertains to the way human beings must act in concrete situations remains hidden. We are called upon to be just, but it is unclear precisely what justice involves. As explained in chapter five above, if the divine law arose purely out of God's own 'free' will, the only possible response to it would be obedience (or disobedience). We could not question the justice or wisdom of the law, but only accept it: God's announcement of the law would determine what is just and unjust, and would alone constitute the reason for the justice or injustice of certain actions.[3] There would be no other 'reasons'. But the very 'freedom' of God's will is exercised in the light of His goodness, justice and mercifulness. These are properties of His nature, reflected by, and not mere products of, His will. It is therefore open to human beings to reflect upon God's nature and goodness as a source of further moral insight. God's creative act (the natural order of the world) can itself be comprehended as a good. Human beings in belonging to this creation can come to understand their proper place within it. Their needs for food, clothing, shelter and community are not accidental but can be interpreted as an extension and fulfilment of natural order. Reflecting on these needs, it is possible to understand the actions and forms of life that tend to secure or increase them, and those which limit or deny them. Thus, human beings through reflection upon their own worldly situation can form a deeper understanding of how to live, so that the 'natural law' could almost be spoken of as a law of human flourishing.

At the hands of writers such as Aquinas, therefore, the classical assumption that the correct way to live was to pursue the life of virtue, and that this would bring happiness, was given a specifically theological underpinning. God did not create humankind only for them to suffer and die. His law is not set against the happiness and welfare of human beings, but ensures their very flourishing. Measures of happiness are no doubt possible for those who turn away from goodness; but true fulfilment can only be found by living virtuously, by practising the Christian virtues. Above all, human societies must strive to uphold the common good. The purpose of the state is to ensure the flourishing of its members. The earthly law, the law that human beings create for themselves and for the governance of their social arrangements (*ius positivum*) is therefore intended to articulate human understanding of natural law as it applies at the concrete level: a detailed 'working out' of natural law. Positive law can in this sense add to natural law, but would lose its validity to the extent that it contravenes natural law.

The idea of 'positive law' therefore predates the development of 'legal positivism' by a considerable interval of time. It was above all the disintegration of the Aristotelian framework of political thought that gave rise to the development of positivist thought. In the wake of the Reformation, the political realities of Europe created conditions in which political societies could no longer be seen as underpinned by shared rational understandings of a 'common good' that must be pursued collectively, through shared commitments and ideals. The internal socio-political arrangements of European states were structured around the simultaneous pursuit of a plurality of individual 'goods'

---

[3] Recall that Hobbes attributes a similar power to the earthly ruler, the 'mortal god' of the state.

that tended to limit or impede one another. The need for a framework of authoritative, clearly delineated rules was paramount. Posited law alone was relevant. Lacking agreement on the life that is 'good' or 'proper', individuals had to create their own arrangements. Nothing could be inferred from the character of these arrangements: they did not pursue an 'order' that is natural to man, but represented an imposed framework of governance designed to secure the internal peace and stability of society. From amongst the numerous forms of social ordering that spring from the human will, none reflect arrangements or conditions that serve the 'natural' or 'proper' ends of human beings, but only ends that are selected by human wills.

In the centuries after Hobbes, philosophers in the British intellectual tradition made more direct and deliberate attacks on further aspects of natural law thought. Natural lawyers in the era after Aquinas held largely to the view that the *ius naturale* could be considered as a law congenial to human flourishing. One might almost say, as noted above, that the natural law constituted the law of human happiness. Writers such as Hume (1711–76) and Bentham (1748–1832) were sceptical of the need for such 'natural law' explanations. They noted that whilst the deontic or imperative force of law continued to derive from its divine origin (that it stems from God's will is the reason we *must* obey it), the actual substance of the law was drawn instead from human reason: namely, rational reflection upon our own situation, and what is required in order to make it bearable, comfortable and conducive to human wellbeing. But then why (one might wonder) do human beings need any further motive, aside from its tendency to promote their wellbeing or happiness, to obey that law? Accordingly, the entire theological framework could, it seemed, be removed from the picture without disturbing the substance of established moral and political ideas. All one needed to say was that the purpose of law is to maximise human wellbeing.

At the same time, the new doctrines did not leave existing ideas of law entirely undisturbed. Placing political understandings on a more 'scientific', less obscurely metaphysical, basis allowed philosophers to see more clearly how law can be made to advance the common good. On the one hand, the notion of 'the common good' could itself be treated in a more scientific way. Once it is understood that there is no natural hierarchy amongst various contentious conceptions of the good, it becomes possible to understand the common good as little more than an accumulation of 'units' of 'utility'. You and I may disagree about the nature of the good life. I think the good life consists in amassing knowledge by reading books. You think it is about all-night parties and live-for-now consumerism. If it proves impossible simultaneously to fulfil both desires (there are too few trees to provide *both* paper for my books *and* wood to fire the power stations necessary to sustain your consumption), then society must choose the alternative that maximises utility overall.

If more people agree with you than agree with me, then utility is maximised by using the wood for power stations. There is no 'deeper' ethical question about which idea of 'the good' is 'better': human beings just happen to find utility in different things. Utility for you might result in disutility for me (and vice versa). The clear-sighted thinker understands that, in such circumstances, the correct approach for law is to try to maximise the amount of utility in society overall.

Utilitarianism has many more elaborate and complex forms: preference utilitarianism (maximisation of preference-fulfilment); motive utilitarianism (inculcating utility-maximising decision-making traits, such as honesty); negative utilitarianism (ensuring the least suffering for the greatest number); and others. All forms of utilitarianism are united by their consequentialist assumptions: the moral worth of an action is determined only by reference to its resulting outcome. The morality of an action, its relative weight vis-a-vis other possible actions, can therefore be determined only after knowing all its consequences. This gives utilitarianism immense intuitive appeal. It also suggests that actions and arrangements do not have moral properties 'absolutely', but only in relation to other possibilities. They are not 'good' in any ultimate sense, but only better or worse than something else. The project of deciding which alternative is the best, or optimal choice for society to pursue was called by Bentham 'censorial jurisprudence'. Amounting to a vision of the way law ought to be, it must be sharply distinguished from 'expository jurisprudence', the examination of the law as it actually is. The natural lawyer's use of the terminology of '*ius*' had operated to obscure this distinction, by making it unclear whether one was referring to the law or right as it is written down and applied, or intending to denote 'the just situation' itself—or indeed whether it was possible to distinguish these senses at all.

Bentham was bitter in his attacks upon earlier jurists, especially Blackstone, who had striven to represent the common law as an articulation of the natural law. Henceforward, the law was not to be understood as a systematic body of rights, which had to be debated and delineated according to underpinning justifications and notions of justice and entitlement. Such arguments represented glosses on the law, the unauthoritative pronouncements of treatise writers (such as Blackstone) pursuing 'censorial jurisprudence' under the guise of exposition. Labouring under this image of law, writers ever treated hard-edged rules and decisions as mere fragments of larger rights, giving partial expression to the system of rights as a whole. Instead Bentham insisted that the law must be understood to extend only to the enacted provisions and decisions of authoritative institutions. The hard-edged rules were not partial expressions of anything, but a complete expression of the law as it is. The doctrinal writer's 'rights' were nothing other than the writer's subjective ideas concerning the moral implications of the body of rules. Natural law was nonsense, obscuring clear-sighted moral visions of what ought to be done. But the vision of law as the expression of rights shaped by natural law represented the highest and most refined form of this nonsense: 'nonsense on stilts' as Bentham put it.[4]

Seeking to explain the idea of law on the basis of more down-to-earth phenomena, Bentham offered the definition of law as 'an assemblage of signs declarative of a volition conceived or adopted by the sovereign in a state'.[5] Nothing could be more 'positive' than this! Law is 'an assemblage of signs': it has an official and unmistakable written form. Truly it can only be found in the written texts of statutes and official records of court decisions. Any 'interpretations', glosses or explanations of these written propositions are not law, because they change the written form, substituting an unauthoritative and variant form. A different 'assemblage of signs'.

Austin's conception of law too gives a central role to the 'sovereign', but one might say that his famous definition is less concerned than Bentham with questions of form, and places the focus more exclusively on questions of origin: law is defined as the 'command' of the sovereign. (The two sentences, 'Hand over all the money!' and 'Empty the till!' could plausibly be said to embody the same command, but they obviously involve rather different 'assemblages of signs'.) In another sense, Bentham and Austin share a common concern, to present law as a kind of 'social fact'. From the end of the seventeenth century, across Europe but perhaps especially in England, the idea that the legitimacy of sovereign rule derived from a hypothetical 'social contract' was regarded as a false and dangerous idea. If government rested on the consent of the governed, then the people could—hypothetically—rise up and resist the rule of an unpopular or tyrannical sovereign, withdrawing their consent. Bentham's and Austin's philosophies represent instances of a line of thinking that was not hypothetically vulnerable to acts of dissolution. Sovereignty itself stood outside the scope of law and even of questions of legitimacy. It derived not from contract or consent, but from social fact: the fact that the people exhibit the regular tendency to obey the sovereign's commands. Furthermore, the legitimacy of the sovereign was no longer tied to a respect for each person's 'natural rights'. Increasingly, government came to be regarded as unconditioned.

---

[4] Austin also advocated a utilitarian ethics, but interestingly it is one that restored God's will to a central role in moral thought. Human beings are required to follow God's law, but possess only that part of the law that has been revealed to them. Where this law is silent, 'we must construe [His command] by the principle of utility'. Austin (n 1) Lecture IV.

[5] J Bentham, *Of Laws in General* (ed HLA Hart, London, Athlone Press, 1970) 1.

THE BASIC DIMENSIONS OF HART'S POSITIVISM

It was Bentham rather than Austin who had the greater influence on Hart. Not only did Hart publish a famous series of essays on aspects of Bentham's philosophy, he also became an editor of Bentham's work later in his career. But it is Austin's work, rather than Bentham's, that forms the starting point for Hart's reflections on the nature of law in his most famous book, *The Concept of Law*, originally published in 1961.

Hart's immediate influences were nevertheless closer to home, bound up with the Oxford 'ordinary language' philosophy of the 1940s and 1950s, and the enthusiasm for 'conceptual analysis'. Amongst the principal ideas of the new philosophy was the belief that traditional enquiries into the nature or essence of things were deeply mistaken. Human knowledge of the world derives from our ability to conceptualise it: in other words, from language. Instead of seeking to understand the 'nature' of a 'right', one should examine and analyse the *concept* of a 'right' as it appears in our thought. Conceiving of rights as ideal or metaphysical entities, one does nothing except chase empty phantoms (as Bentham would have said). Hart instead intends to use 'a sharpened awareness of words to sharpen our perception of the phenomena'.[6] Sympathetic to Austin's aims in placing law on the level of social fact, he nevertheless demonstrates that Austin's concepts fail to account properly for the obligatory character of law.

If law is underpinned by nothing except habit and fear, then one is obliged to say (as Austin does) that the 'binding' force of the law is simply the fact that one who disobeys is likely to suffer the application of a sanction. But this cannot be all there is to the notion of legal obligation. For one thing, my lawbreaking might go undetected. For another, I may have a legal obligation to perform my side of a contract, but you might choose to waive your right to performance. More depressingly, I might die before you have the chance to sue me. But in each of these cases, it seems wrong to suggest that (by avoiding the 'sanction'), I never had an obligation in the first place. It is true that Austin speaks only of the 'likelihood' of having a sanction applied; but the point is that the *reason* for applying the sanction is the breach of the legal obligation, it is not the *ground* of that obligation. These reflections may well prompt us to fall back on ideas of the law's moral character, seeking an explanation of the legitimacy of the law's obligations and sanctions. Hart wishes to avoid this. He wants to demonstrate that legal obligation can after all be understood as a 'social fact' (not a species of moral obligation requiring a moral vision

---

[6] Hart (n 2) v. (Hart is quoting the Oxford philosopher JL Austin here).

of the nature of law), but that legal obligations are genuinely prescriptive of behaviour and not simply predictive of likely outcomes.

In the first place, Hart sets out to demonstrate that the notion of a 'command' does not throw much light on the actual experience of law and legal practice. True to his intentions in 'sharpening our awareness' of words, he draws a distinction between the condition of being under an obligation, and the condition of being obliged to act in some way. By threatening to shoot you, I can certainly place you in a position where you have no alternative but to hand over the money. In that sense one could say without too much argument that I have 'obliged' you to hand over the money. But it would be incorrect to say that you possessed an 'obligation' to hand it over. Such 'orders' lack a standing quality that attaches to genuine 'commands', a distinction that Austin seems to be unaware of. In speaking of 'commands', Austin has something much more like the gunman's orders in mind. These ideas are capable of shading into one another (the gunman may correctly be said to 'give an order' to a henchman, and in that sense issue a command), because in some cases the order attaches not simply to a threat in the face of non-compliance, but to a stable structure of hierarchical authority. Hart concedes that the proper, quasi-military notion of 'command' is much closer to the idea of law than the gunman's order. But he instantly dismisses it as therefore unlikely to shed much useful light on law. The element of authority involved in law is the precise aspect of law that obscures explanations of the law's nature. It does not elucidate the nature of law to compare it to the military commander's exercise of a function that depends upon a similar respect for authority.

How shall one account for the respect for authority that appears to be central to laws and military commands? The answer cannot be found in the presence of threats, if only because a military general may have the power to give out orders without having the power to punish disobedience (that may fall to a court martial or tribunal). At the same time, one cannot say that the general's authority derives from any moral obligation on the part of his men to respect military orders. What is it that enables us to speak of law as imposing obligations, rather than simply 'obliging' people to act in certain ways under threat of sanction? Hart suggests that the answer lies with the idea of accepting a rule.

Austin's jurisprudence had rested upon the presence of generalised habits amongst the population to fall in with commanded orders of the sovereign. The regularity that is presupposed by the idea of a 'habit' is present in many aspects of social life not immediately connected with law. Many people regularly go out drinking on a Friday night. But one could not accurately describe this situation by saying that 'it is a rule' that people must go out on a Friday night. On the other hand, people regularly pay their taxes, and speak of this as obeying a rule. What is the difference? In both cases, one could observe a regular pattern of conduct. Many people engage in both activities. But unlike the habit of going out on Fridays, the presence of a rule is characterised by more than a 'mere regularity' of behaviour. The regularity constitutes what Hart calls the 'external aspect' of a rule, its observable aspect. But for a rule to exist there must also be an 'internal aspect': the fact that people accept the rule as a standard that ought to be complied with, and as a standard for criticism when it is disobeyed. It is above all the presence of this 'normative' terminology (words such as 'ought', 'should', 'must' and so on) and its appropriateness to certain situations that marks out the presence of rules. People do happen to go out on Fridays, but it is false to conclude that they *must* do so. It is the same normative terminology that allows us to speak of legal rules 'imposing obligations' or 'conferring rights'.

The idea of acceptance of a rule (the presence of a critical and reflective attitude) separates law from habits and orders, on the one hand, but Hart says that it also absolves us of the need to seek out moral explanations of the basis of law on the other. The law's authority does not derive from morality, but from acceptance. It remains on the level of social fact.

At the same time, it will be remembered that legal positivism was itself a response to the fact that modern societies tend to be characterised by widespread *disagreement* about the appropriate standards for governing conduct. A clear and stable framework of authoritative rules was required precisely because people cannot agree on what is permissible, what ought to be done and so on. In the same way, the army commander's men do not accept the commander's orders because they necessarily 'accept' the wisdom or necessity of those orders (they may regard the orders as unreasonable or excessive, or anyway unwelcome). What they 'accept' is the authority of the commander. Hart's argument is that this notion of accepting or recognising authority is to be explained as the acceptance of a *rule* instituting or confirming the authority of the relevant office. It is this which makes the commander's orders 'valid' orders, irrespective of their content.

Hart has a similar argument concerning legal validity. The validity of legal rules does not stem from popular acceptance of the standards they embody. (Perhaps most people pay their taxes very reluctantly.) In Hart's terminology, the validity of legal rules derives from acceptance of an underpinning 'rule of recognition' that 'specif[ies] some feature or features possession of which by a suggested rule is taken as a conclusive affirmative indication that it is a rule of the group to be supported by the social pressure it exerts'.[7] Hart is not prescriptive of the kind of 'features' that are to be taken as conclusive. In an early society, he suggests that the presence of a rule carved on a public monument might suffice. But this does not allow for much flexibility or systematic

---

[7] ibid 94.

complexity. Therefore, in more sophisticated societies, the identifying characteristics of rules are likely to make reference to their originating from certain
recognised *sources* of law, such as statutes or decisions of courts. Indeed, the
criteria of recognition might well (as in most Western societies) involve a recognised hierarchy obtaining amongst the sources.

It might occur to us that, on reflection, most law students do not begin
their course of study with an already-present knowledge of the hierarchy of
sources in (say) English law. It is one of the things they are required to learn.
For most people then, knowledge of the sources of English law (including
custom as a subordinate source) is not common knowledge and therefore not
something about which there is very widespread 'acceptance'. For Hart therefore, the presence of the rule of recognition is explained by its acceptance
amongst officials as an appropriate standard of criticism. Hart does not state
exactly what he means by an 'official', but we might take him to mean those
official officers involved in the administration and creation of law at all levels.
Since it is these officers who apply the law in accordance with recognised
procedures and formalities (eg, treating statute as the superior source of law,
deciding cases according to established law rather than subjective whim and
so forth), it is their acceptance which grounds the rule of recognition. The
rule is present, as before, both in the regularity of official conduct, but also
in their 'internal attitude' in accepting the rule as a standard that ought to be
complied with.

The rule of recognition seems to satisfy the need, so passionately defended
by Hobbes, for publicly ascertainable rules demanded by modern pluralistic
societies. Legal validity does not depend upon or reduce to private moral
judgements. At the same time, one could say that the rule of recognition also
amounts to a significant departure from Hobbes's ideas about law. The need
for acceptance and conformity to certain standards on the part of 'officials'
distinguishes law from open-ended power. Law is not power alone but also
legality, the limitation of the operation of that power. And yet law does not
demand that power be exercised for specific purposes (such as ensuring the
common good), only that it take a specific form. Is it disturbing that the very
limits to power that are demanded by the idea of law lie in the hands of the
same state that wields it? That law can be considered an instrument that can
be used for good or evil ends? A full discussion of this question is deferred until
chapter ten. In the meantime, it is worth noting that Hart additionally claims
that the efficacy of a functioning legal system depends upon widespread compliance. That is to say: the existence of law depends upon arrangements instituted and observed by the mighty machinery of the state; but its successful
functioning requires popular obedience. This distinction is necessary in order
to ensure that explanations of authority do not rest with notions of habit, and
thus bring Hart full-circle back to Austin's starting point.

The rule of recognition itself is of a kind to which Austin's model of 'commands' pays little attention: rules that are power-conferring rather than duty-imposing. Hart refers to duty-imposing rules (such as prohibitions of the criminal law) as 'primary rules', whereas he calls power-conferring rules 'secondary rules'. The rule of recognition is power-conferring in this sense, because it specifies the conditions under which laws may be enacted, recognised, interpreted and so on. But the law contains other rules of this type. Rules of property law that make provision for the creation of wills and transfers of title provide one example, as do the laws of contract. Hart speaks of these as 'rules of change', because they allow one either to vary one's own legal position, or to vary that of another. Austin was of course himself aware of the existence of the laws of property and contract, but he endeavoured to analyse them by reference to the same notion of sanction-based orders that he applied to all rules. In this case, the 'sanction' would be the failure of the instrument to take its intended legal effect: the nullity of the will, the voiding of the contract and so on. Austin's mistake can be explained by the lack of subtlety in his analysis—precisely that lack of 'sharp awareness' of distinctions and shifts of usage that Hart demanded. Clearly, it is intrinsic to the nature of all rules that they are behaviour-enjoining. The rule of recognition, for example, enjoins officials to act in a certain way. But the enjoining of behaviour is not the same thing as the imposition of a duty. No one is under a duty to create a will or contract after a certain form, simply because no one is under a duty to create a will or contract at all. The nullity that results from failure to obey formal requirements for the creation of wills or contracts is not intended as a punishment, but arises from the very nature of formal instruments. For there to *be* contracts and wills, subject to legal regulation and with certain established effects, these must take a certain form. One must be able to distinguish them from other kinds of agreement which do not enjoy any legal effect. (Something cannot be a contract simply because one party says it is.) It follows from the need for formalities in the creation of legal instruments, that transactions which do not obey the formal requirements simply do not create the instruments.

This brings us to a third kind of secondary rule: rules of adjudication. The law's established rules, doctrines and principles (including its various formalities) demand to be applied in specific cases. The rule of recognition empowers officials to find and interpret the law, but what happens where the established doctrines do not appear to lead to an unambiguous conclusion? It is not open to the court to declare a *non liquet*. In such cases, Hart says that the judge is empowered and indeed obliged to decide the case under the authority granted by rules of adjudication. If this sounds reasonable, it is nevertheless the aspect of Hart's position that has given rise to the most critical discussion. Think about it: in the absence of clear law, the court's judgment in the instant case would have to depend on precisely those contentious matters of morality and social policy that the law itself (in the eyes of positivists) was meant to supplant. More than anything, parties to a legal dispute go to court seeking a vindication of their rights. If the solution is (as it were) an invented one, in what sense is it a decision 'in law'? In what sense does it uphold, or adjudicate, the extent of a person's rights?

Aspects of this situation fall to be discussed in later chapters dealing with critics of Hart's position. It is, however, clearly in line with the assumptions from which the positivist tradition started: that the law is correctly represented as a body of deliberately created rules. It is not a system of underlying rights of which the rules are to be treated as 'fragments' or partial expressions. Instead one can speak of 'rights' only analogically as clear implications arising from the rules.

THE NATURE OF LAW

The philosophies of law encountered in the work of Hobbes and Bentham were inimical to the idea of common law. If law were the will of a sovereign, then 'interpretations' of that will should not be allowed to blossom into an alternative source of law: legal 'doctrine'. Consequently, the common law tended to be understood by positivists as the arena in which courts *apply* statutory provisions to specific cases, rather than an autonomous source of legal reflection with its own distinctive priorities and principles. Hart's position is on the whole more receptive to common law understood in more systematic terms.

In a passage headed 'The open texture of law', Hart points out that large societies depend upon 'general rules, standards and principles' addressed to classes of person or of act or thing, rather than 'particular directions' given to individuals.[8] The very existence of law therefore 'depends on a widely diffused capacity to recognize particular acts, things, and circumstances as instances of the general classifications which the law makes'. If it were not possible to communicate general standards of conduct in this way, without the need for further direction, 'nothing that we now recognize as law could exist'.

This innocuous-sounding passage is in fact rich in implications. For example, we are accustomed in the West to regard personal freedom as a natural and altogether unremarkable condition. Hart can be understood as pointing out that this condition in fact depends upon the fact that we are governed, and capable of being governed, at a general level. Our freedom to choose between various contingencies that lie open to us is the product of what philosophers

---

[8] ibid 124.

in the Kantian tradition called our 'autonomy': the fact that we are capable of deciding things for ourselves, applying rules to ourselves, and do not require the direction of others. Our actions do not await the explicit permission of outside authorities, in virtue of the fact that we are capable of understanding the general rules that are laid down for us. Human beings are above all *rational*, and it is this capacity that enables governance in the form so familiar to us. For example, we know that homicide is forbidden by law. There are, of course, thousands of imaginative ways of killing a person: shooting, stabbing, beating, dismembering, freezing, crushing, burning, suffocating, strangling and so on. I am sufficiently rational to understand that my beating you to death with the hardback second edition of *The Concept of Law* falls under the class of act denoted by the legal definition of homicide. I do not require 'further direction' from outside in order to know this. Consequently, I do not need to clear all my potential actions with some outside authority before putting my plans into action. If this sounds entirely mundane as an observation, then recall that the rationale behind a political philosophy such as that of Hobbes was focused on the need for obedience as the citizen's first duty, and the avoidance of 'interpretation'. Hart is pointing out that obedience is itself an intellectual act. It is in one sense itself an act of 'interpretation'.

Does this threaten the very idea of positivism? Obliged to reason from generalities which one must apply to one's situation, is one not ultimately reliant on the systematic framework of moral assumptions that Hobbes suggested were insufficient as a basis of social order? In the passage on 'open texture', Hart reconciles the need for such judgements with an underlying positivism in a way that attempts to reveal *both* the law's humanly-created nature *and* its systematic form. Moving away from a concern only with enacted law, he observes that:

> Two principal devices, at first sight very different from each other, have been used for the communication of such general standards of conduct in advance of the successive occasions on which they are to be applied. One of them makes a maximal and the other a minimal use of general classifying words. The first is typified by what we call legislation and the second by precedent.[9]

Both precedent and legislation are to be considered as intrinsic to the nature of the law's guidance and functioning. The differences between the operation of these 'devices' is illustrated by an analogy that Hart proposes, of a father instructing his son to remove his hat on entering a church. Hart suggests that the operation of legislation resembles the father laying down a verbal rule to his son ('Every man and boy must remove his hat on entering a church') in advance of the occasion on which it is to be applied. The operation of

---

[9] ibid.

precedent is revealed by supposing the father gives no verbal rule at all, but performs the action himself (removing his hat), expecting the son to comply by emulating the action. This expectation is based upon the fact that the son can be supposed to respect the father as an authority on the proper form of behaviour in social situations (and not a crank experimenting with outrageous new ideas), and watches the father's actions in order to learn what to do. Precedent, in other words, is to be understood as a form of authoritative example.

Hart observes that communication of general standards by example seems to leave open a range of possibilities 'and hence of doubt' about the standards being set out. Exactly what aspects of the situation demand to be emulated? Does it matter whether the hat is removed slowly or hastily? That the father used his right hand and not his left? That the hat is stowed under the seat rather than on a hatstand or on the empty pew next door? The father leaves the hat off during all the time he is in the church; is this significant or can the hat be placed back on the head once inside the door? Is the purpose of the action indeed explained by the fact that it is not raining inside the church, negating the need for the hat, and nothing more? Or, if removal of the hat is mandatory, is the implication that a hatless person must *purchase* a hat before being allowed to enter the church? One could go on indefinitely. Perhaps these examples might incline us to wonder why the father (here representing the previous line of decisions) should leave the son (the judge in the instant case) foundering amid so many perplexities. Why not just tell the son outright what is demanded: every male is expected to remove his hat on entering a church? Why not just lay down an explicit rule?

In fact, the son is not really all that lost in perplexity. It has been many years since men have habitually worn hats, and perhaps not many of us go to church. Nevertheless, I suspect most or indeed all readers of Hart's book would have understood immediately, without need of further explanation, the precise action required. One knows that the removal of the hat, as a sign of respect, is the point of the father's action. Everybody understands that the use of the left or right hand is immaterial, just as are the many possibilities for storage of the hat inside the church. We all know this, because we share a common set of understandings and values that are so entrenched as not to require any explicit announcement. These background understandings inform our actions and deliberations at all points, allowing people to understand one another without any significant effort. If I enter a shop to buy chocolate, the owner does not immediately pounce or call the police when I remove the chocolate from the shelf. He understands that (in normal circumstances) I intend to take it to the till to pay for it. When I hand over a ten-pound note, I do not need to explain that I require change along with the chocolate, and that I am not offering to buy the bar for that amount. Social situations such as this proceed smoothly and even without the need for any spoken words at all (try it), because of the presence of a rich stock of values and understandings on which we all draw in giving meaning to the situations that confront or involve us.

On this basis, the son's deliberations can focus pretty accurately on what is required. The context of ordinary unverbalised understandings effectively reduces the *possible* interpretations of the situation to *plausible* ones. At the same time, variant interpretations are not altogether eliminated. It remains open to question whether the father is removing his hat out of respect for his God (as we might first suppose), or whether he is an atheist attending a wedding or funeral, and performing the action out of respect for the beliefs of those in the congregation. Again, perhaps the father has no respect for the beliefs, thinking them foolish, but complies out of a desire to avoid censure or criticism. Hart suggests that reasoning from authority (the contemplation of a range of specific examples) guides the court's deliberations without disposing of the question in advance. Legal reasoning is not 'mechanical'. It does not consist simply in the automatic 'application' of rules to particulars. Inescapably, legal reasoning is a process of *judgement*.

On the face of it ('at first sight' as Hart puts it), reasoning from authoritative *rules* seems to guide reasoning in a more rigid way. The son in the example is not left in doubt as to what is required, but is given the criteria for action in explicit verbal form. He has only to recognise particular instances of the verbal terms in order to apply the rule. And yet on reflection, it turns out that these two 'principal devices', though superficially different, are in fact underpinned by a deeper and profound similarity. Application of verbally formulated rules is no more mechanical, no less a process of judgement, than reasoning from precedent. This is not simply because verbal rules might refer to such ideas as 'reasonableness' or 'foreseeability', but because language generally possesses an 'open texture'. Even the most mundane words exhibit this property. Hart invites the reader to imagine a rule prohibiting vehicles from a public park. Clearly this will apply to cars, lorries and buses, for example. But what about a mountain bike, or a skateboard, or a rowing boat? At some stage, reference must be made to the point or purpose of the rule in determining its application. The language of the rule itself does not 'claim its own instances'.[10]

Suppose a case arises in which a person is convicted of driving a car through the park, presumably as a shortcut to escape traffic congestion on a homebound commute. A court would have little difficulty in applying the rule. One can readily imagine a judge making obiter remarks about the extreme danger to users of the park (many of which will be children), and the selfish actions of the driver in breaching rules instituted for their protection. Now imagine that at some later time, somebody suffers a cardiac arrest in the middle of the

---

[10] ibid 126.

park, and an ambulance crew rush to respond, driving the ambulance into the very heart of the park. Would a court be likely to treat this in the same way as the first case? Undoubtedly not: a judge would be likely to observe that the rule was put in place as a safety measure to protect both the users of the park and the park's grounds from harm. It could not have been the intention to exclude emergency services from answering calls and dealing with on-the-spot situations. On the other hand, what would be the situation if a radio station's traffic helicopter persistently hovered in the air above the trees? On the one hand, there are no real safety issues involved. One could say that commercial air traffic in general passes over parkland all the time, albeit at greater altitude. Nevertheless, it is conceivable, if the helicopter frequently flew low over the park, that a court might seek to broaden their interpretation of the rule. The rule exists to ensure the reasonable enjoyment of the park's amenities. Noise and downdraft from the helicopter all but prevents reasonable use of the park: scaring small children, ruining the park's tranquility and so on. Enjoyment of the park requires not only safety, but also freedom from extreme noise and disturbance.

Could this broader reading of the rule lead to further extensions of the scope of the rule? For example, could an 'environmental' understanding of the rule be used to prevent the use of rowing boats on the lake, which might threaten fragile grasses along the banks, or interfere with the nesting sites of water birds? Might skateboards or mountain bikes constitute a nuisance to those who like to stroll along the park's paths? Here the court might end up restoring a narrower reading of the rule, refocusing deliberation on issues of safety and amenity. Or perhaps it will be said that the rule exists for a variety of different reasons, demanding a balance between different considerations which might come into conflict. Or again, perhaps the different purposes do not have equal or merely circumstantial priority, but demand to be ranked into some hierarchy or order. (One could go on.)

Hart's example demonstrates that the application of hard-edged statutory rules is no more 'mechanical', involves no less a process of judgement, than does the use of precedent. Indeed, as even the highly simplified considerations above show, application of explicitly formulated rules quite quickly become encrusted with various exceptions, considerations and extensions which occur in the very course of their application. Invariably, a body of jurisprudence (legal doctrine) grows up around posited rules, so that the deliberately created aspect of law can scarcely be separated in practice from the law's systematic aspect as an expression of reason (or reasoning). At the same time, Hart urges his readers to an awareness of the essential indeterminacy of aim that is characteristic of deliberately posited rules. The introduction of the rule is not a random, arbitrary phenomenon, but has an end in view. It is intended to settle some question or other. But by introducing the rule, there are also many things that we have not settled, because it is impossible to anticipate or account for all ends to which the rule might be related. Insofar as the rule settles certain matters (the car driven through the park), it is possible to speak of their being an agreement in judgements on the matter. The rule guides our reasoning, by specifying the criteria to be applied. Other dimensions of the morality of the situation are to be excluded. In this way, the presence of written laws does indeed replace an inchoate moral consensus with authoritative standards on which all can rely.

It is possible to be misled by the idea of an 'agreement' in judgements, or the notion of 'settled' law. Neither situation is dispositive of contentious questions that might arise. The nature of the agreement is a kind of *convergence*, which might fragment at various points. This might not be very troubling. You and I might disagree about the relative priorities involved in the rule banning vehicles from the park. I say it is primarily about safety, whereas you think it is primarily about conservation of the park's delicate environment. Faced with a case of a car being driven through the park, there is no need to pursue these divergent views: we both agree this involves a breach of the rule. Despite the lack of deeper agreement, our judgements converge. The presence of the rule serves an important purpose in allowing us to proceed without having to entertain any of the deeper, contentious reasons. But at some point, competing outlooks will reassert themselves where the application of the rule proves indeterminate.[11] Hart insists that the operation of statute and precedent (indeed, all sources of law) produce a certain openness in the law, resulting in the 'need for the further exercise of choice in the application of general rules to particular cases'.[12] No system of law is so complete or comprehensive that it does not leave to judges a certain responsibility for the further development of the law in ways that are bound to be contentious.[13]

One might be tempted to believe that the fundamental claim of positivists is nonetheless correct. Perhaps one can maintain that the presence of formalised rules considerably narrows the scope of this judicial discretion, in restricting the criteria to be applied. Legal decisions are not mechanical but involve judgement; but this is nevertheless a process of legal judgement rather than open-ended moral judgement. The rule's announcement of the criteria to be applied ensures that the judgement that is required always operates within certain limits, must always pay attention to established legal doctrines and

[11] ibid 128.
[12] ibid 129.
[13] See ibid 130: '[A]ll systems, in different ways, compromise between two social needs: the need for certain rules which can, over great areas of conduct, safely be applied by private individuals to themselves without fresh official guidance or weighing up of social issues, and the need to leave open, for later settlement by an informed, official choice, issues which can only be properly appreciated and settled when they arise in a concrete case'.

ideas (such as reasonableness, foreseeability and so on). Don't be so sure: the issue of whether mountain bikes (which after all may cause significant injury to others in a collision) are legally excluded from the park may even touch on such fundamental questions as individual liberty. Can one not say that even reasonable safety concerns should not be allowed to make significant encroachments on my liberty to ride my bicycle where I like? Where might such arguments end?

LAW AND MORALITY

I have alluded to the extent to which legal judgements do, or do not, involve considerations of a decidedly moral nature. But can this question be answered before morality itself is properly understood? All societies seem to contain limitations upon certain forms of behaviour, such as the use of violence, observance of notions and practices of property ownership and so forth. Limits of this kind, when taken together, appear to be essential to the very existence and endurability of social order, allowing human beings 'to live continuously together in close proximity'.[14] Students of moral philosophy encounter numerous theoretical standpoints that attempt to account for this phenomenon. That of Aristotle, as we have seen in Part One, insists upon a close connection between morality on the one hand, and human needs and interests on the other. Utilitarians may argue for a narrower connection, suggesting that nothing can count as a moral rule or principle unless it can be demonstrated to redound to human happiness or wellbeing. Hart wishes to prescind from all such standpoints, adopting a 'broader view' of morality in the light of its defining characteristics: the relative importance given to moral rules versus other forms of social pressure or expectation; the immunity of moral principles from deliberate change; the voluntary nature of moral offences; and the 'special' form of moral pressure which involves appeals to respect for the principle itself, aside from threats or considerations of fear or interest. Hart admits that standards classified as 'moral' in this way might sometimes come into conflict with the 'narrower' understandings proposed by moral philosophies such as utilitarianism (which might condemn certain rules as barbarous or unenlightened). But Hart suggests that his proposal has the virtue of bringing a certain form of social rule under one banner, avoiding the need 'to divide in a very unrealistic manner elements in a social structure which function in an identical manner'.[15]

At the same time, moral considerations of various kinds may give rise to different sorts of expectation. Those standards which define obligations and

---

[14] ibid 181.
[15] ibid 182.

duties constitute the bedrock of morality, but societies also contain more broadly defined moral ideals. We do not *demand* that people exhibit saintly virtues of patience or benevolence, whereas we demand that people perform their duties. But we recognise the performance of virtuous actions as a kind of moral excellence. Hart's characterisation of virtues as 'supererogatory' and 'ancillary' is by no means uncontroversial: classical philosophies in particular treated the cardinal virtues as exactly those dispositions of the rational character upon which the individual's moral life hinged. Equally, Hart suggests that a society's morality 'may extend its protections from harm to its own members only, or even only to certain classes, leaving a slave or helot class at the mercy of their masters' whims'.[16] In this sense, a society's morality itself may become the object of moral criticism if it seems to depart from standards of rationality or generality. Given these complexities and differences, Hart begins the ninth chapter of his book ('Laws and Morals') with a warning, that '[t]here are many different types of relation between law and morals, and there is nothing which can be profitably singled out for study as *the* relationship between them'.[17]

Hart is happy to concede that the development of law ('at all times and places') has in fact been profoundly influenced both by conventional moral standards and social ideals, and by 'critical morality' (those standards by which a society's conventional moral practices are themselves subjected to criticism). However, Hart emphatically wishes to resist the claim, which he thinks is all too often confused with the foregoing admission, that a legal system *must* exhibit 'some specific conformity' with morality or justice, or must depend upon a widely held conviction that there is a moral obligation to obey it. The purpose of the discussion of chapter IX is intended to refute this latter claim, and to defend legal positivism against the doctrines of the natural law tradition.

The definition that Hart offers of 'legal positivism' at the beginning of this chapter has led to considerable debate and controversy. I propose to ignore these later debates as much as possible, both because readers are unlikely to derive much benefit from a discussion of their complexities, and because a lengthy digression would obscure rather than clarify Hart's argument and concerns. The definition Hart offers is as follows: 'Here we shall take Legal Positivism to mean the simple contention that it is in no sense a necessary truth that laws reproduce or satisfy certain demands of morality, though in fact they have often done so'.[18] His aim is to defend positivism against two rival understandings:

i. classical theories of natural law, according to which 'there are certain principles of human conduct, awaiting discovery by human reason, with which man-made law must conform if it is to be valid'; and

---

[16] ibid 183.
[17] ibid 185.
[18] ibid 185–86.

ii.   a 'less rationalist' view of morality according to which legal validity is connected with standards of equality and justice.

Hart's way of defining these oppositions is not entirely helpful. Both employ a concept of 'legal validity' that is not immediately known in ordinary legal practice. In practice, 'validity' is an idea most often associated with questions of procedural correctness, or the proper exercise of functions or powers. It does not appear for example in the language of natural law, which does not ask about the conditions of 'valid law' or legal validity, but about the conformity of positive law to the *ius naturale*, or the extent of one's obligations in conscience to abide by positive law. These are not equivalent questions: Hart's notion of 'valid law' is defined in terms of 'acceptance' and the rule of recognition. The question of whether *law* is connected to standards of equality and justice, or to the common good, is not the same as the question of whether a rule must so conform in order to be 'recognised' as 'valid'.

Some of the deeper objections to Hart's claims will be considered in later chapters. For the moment, let us examine Hart's argument itself.

NATURAL LAW

Hart rightly observes that the notion of morality as consisting of standards of rightness that are discoverable by human reason is not self-standing, but derives from a general conception of nature as possessing intelligibility, purpose or direction. On the other hand, modern secular thought possesses an altogether different idea of nature, devoid of purpose and possessing no order and no forces that cannot be scientifically explained and experimentally confirmed. There is no 'order' beyond the 'order' that can be scientifically observed or implied. In consequence, these arguments about the character of morality are not likely to be open to final resolution. Can one do no more than oppose these alternative images of worldly and universal order to one another?

In a way that is reminiscent of the earlier standpoints of Hume and Bentham, Hart suggests that the fundamental core of natural law thinking is not logically dependent upon a metaphysical framework 'which few could now accept'.[19] Consequently, he sees it as possible to extract certain 'elementary truths' of natural law thinking that are 'of importance' for understanding of law and morality, 'disentangling' them from their metaphysical framework in order to restate them in 'simpler' terms.

---

[19] ibid 188.

At the heart of the earlier metaphysical view of the world was the idea of teleology: nature, but also things in nature, exhibit purposefulness and are conceived as possessing a proper goal or end (*telos*). This is as much true of acorns, which achieve their proper end by becoming oak trees, as of human beings whose *telos* (according to Aristotle) is to lead the good, or flourishing, life, which is coeval with the life of virtue. There might be a thousand reasons why an acorn may fail of its purpose. Too much rain, and the acorn will rot in the ground. Too little, and it will wither. It may be consumed, or crushed, or land on barren soil, or become diseased. In all these cases, one could say that the acorn failed in its purpose, did not reach its optimum state. But we continue to think of its optimum state as the oak tree. We do not (without much thoughtful reflection) consider that the acorn possesses many (or perhaps no) optimal states of which the oak tree is merely one, decay and disintegration representing other equally viable 'optimum' states. Similarly, Aristotle conceives of the life of virtue as the proper, or appointed end of human beings. Human beings may create for themselves many actual 'ends', as well as being subject to disease and premature death like the acorn. A person may become a liar, a drunkard, a coward, a recluse and many other things. But in such cases the person has failed in their purpose, turning away from their true or proper end.

Hart is sceptical of this mode of reasoning, dismissing it even as 'somewhat comic' when applied to elements of a supposed natural order that are inanimate. But Hart also draws attention to the fact that modern thinking considers human beings as having purposes of their own devising, which they consciously adopt and pursue, and do not have a specific optimum state or end that is somehow set for them in advance. This is a fundamental shift in thinking: no longer is it supposed that human beings desire certain things (a commodious life, virtue and other things) because it is their good or end; but it is thought now that certain things constitute goals or ends because we desire them.

At the same time, Hart concedes (or perhaps warns) that the earlier teleological assumptions continue to influence the way in which people ordinarily think and speak about themselves and the world. It is, Hart says, latent in the identification of certain things as constituting human 'needs' that it is 'good' to satisfy; and we similarly classify certain things as 'harms' or 'injuries'. We do not accidentally happen to desire food and rest, but these are necessary for us: they constitute human *needs*. When we call such needs 'natural', it is to distinguish them from needs that are merely conventional (such as the need for luxury possessions or fame: so-called 'false needs'). Underlying these 'natural' needs is nothing pertaining to the human being's status as a rational animal or a moral being. All are drawn from biological priorities that human beings share with all animals. Above all they rest upon 'the tacit assumption that the proper end of human activity is survival, and this rests on the simple contingent fact that most men most of the time wish to continue in existence'.[20]

If we were to leave the argument at that point, Hart suggests that what we would have is a very attenuated natural law theory. This would still fall considerably short of what most natural lawyers would want to claim, because survival (*perseverare in esse suo*) was only the most basic element in a much richer ('and far more debatable') conception of the proper end for the human being. But Hart wants to go further than this in rejecting natural law. In a clear indication that he did not intend his thesis as a 'very attenuated version of natural law', Hart goes on to say that we can, when speaking of survival,

> discard, as too metaphysical for modern minds, the notion that this is something antecedently fixed which men necessarily desire because it is their proper goal or end. Instead we may hold it to be a mere contingent fact which could be otherwise.[21]

Once again: it is an end for us only because, and insofar as, we do happen to desire it. This provides an underpinning (however contingent) for our analytical assumptions about law and governance. For we can assume that what we are dealing with are social arrangements designed collectively to secure our 'continued existence'.

Hart's argument is effectively designed to resolve the tension between two ideas that are both seemingly attractive, perhaps even unarguable, but also in tension with one another. On the one hand, the humanly created nature of our laws tends to imply that there is no permanent, necessary content to law. All is the product of human convention, and therefore contingent and revisable. But on the other hand, it appears that all legal systems everywhere (those recognisable to us as systems of 'law') do seem to share certain characteristics that might even seem to constitute part of our conception of law: laws prohibiting homicides, regulating access to resources, recognising ownership of property etc. Are these not indeed permanent or necessary features of law? Are they not absolutely fundamental to the order that law secures, such that the absence of that order would betoken also the absence of an effective legal order?

Hart's reply is as follows. Any questions concerning the arrangements by which human beings live together *must* begin by assuming survival as an aim. Once this assumption has been granted, one can proceed to some 'very obvious' generalisations about human beings. As long as these continue to hold true, there will be certain rules and arrangements which must be reflected in our created modes of social organisation if that organisation is to be viable.

---

[20] ibid 191.
[21] ibid 192.

Indeed, these arrangements 'do in fact constitute a common element in the law and conventional morality of all societies'.[22] From the fact that human beings are vulnerable, subject to deliberate and natural harms, it follows that limitations must be placed upon violence and the infliction of bodily harm. This is absolutely necessary given the way human beings are, but falls short of belonging to the very idea of law because it remains contingent upon our continued, collective interest in survival, and also upon continued susceptibility to physical harm (we might evolve into beings invulnerable to attack). Hobbes had pointed to the fact that all human beings are approximately equal to one another, despite minor variations in physical strength and intellectual ability. In a clear reference to Hobbes, Hart argues that this fact entails the necessity of a system of mutual forbearances. Being limited each in their own fashion, human beings absolutely require order above all else, one founded on a domain of compromise between their various interests. No individual is strong enough to accomplish all that they desire alone. At the same time as she is reliant on the cooperation of others, the human being is also characterised by limited altruism (the limited but not entirely absent interest in the wellbeing and interests of others). Hence, human beings cannot be relied upon to create a spontaneous domain of compromise of their own. Law demands to be of the nature of a coercive system for the organisation of social life: again, so long as survival continues to be an overarching goal. The limited understanding and strength of will possessed by most people entails that such coercion requires to be backed by an equally orderly system of sanctions. Finally, the fact that human beings live in a world of limited resources entails the need for order in the matter of the fulfilment of basic human needs such as clothing, shelter, food and so on. It is as a consequence of this that legal order must involve conceptions of property, and invoke the systematic regulation of ownership after some design or pattern. As Grotius observed, the particular arrangements of different societies may exhibit great variety concerning the manner of distribution, and in determining in whose hands ownership lies. But all societies demand absolutely some legal organisation and recognition of property.

Is Hart's argument convincing? On the one hand, Hart maintains that the substance of legal rules and doctrines is indeed contingent, despite the remarkable degree of convergence exhibited by legal systems across the world in prohibiting murder, administering property ownership and so on. This is so because none of those substantive provisions belong to the very idea of 'law' itself. They are not necessary truths about law, but derive from elsewhere: from the overarching human desire for survival. On the other hand, Hart can call

---

[22] ibid 193.

upon the deep human instinct for survival to explain why such a remarkable degree of convergence in fact obtains. So deeply ingrained are these traits that we can hardly avoid thinking and speaking of them as being 'natural' or 'necessary'. Yet it remains: were the human desire for survival to diminish, or were certain features of human beings or of the world to change, the substance of legal arrangements might look very different.

Having claimed that the desire for survival is, in fact, contingent (despite appearances to the contrary), Hart goes on to explain that survival nevertheless has 'a special status' in relation to human thought:

> For it is not merely that an overwhelming majority of men do wish to live, even at the cost of hideous misery, but that this is reflected in whole structures of our thought and language, in terms of which we describe the world and each other. We could not subtract the general wish to live and leave intact concepts like danger and safety, harm and benefit, need and function, disease and cure; for these are ways of simultaneously describing and appraising things by reference to the contribution they make to survival which is accepted as an aim.[23]

But if this is the case, in what sense is the 'end' of survival not 'discoverable by human reason'? Hart's use of the phrase 'awaiting discovery by reason' might suggest a kind of passive reception of the human intellect to outside phenomena that somehow impinge upon it, much as the eye receives light. In that sense, we might well wonder how the intellect can discover moral truths. Writers within the 'classical' natural law tradition (the object of Hart's criticism) instead conceived of reason as an active faculty, a processing or intellection of the world. Aristotle and Aquinas both remark upon the human being's status as a linguistic animal: it is the possession of language that gives to the human being a knowledge of good and evil.[24] It is language that fits the human animal as specifically a *political* animal. There is not, as it were, an experience of the world *and then* an intellection or speaking of it. Rather, the experience consists in our speaking of it. Thus, if we discover that the aim of survival is presupposed in entire structures of thought and language—presupposed in our very knowledge of and understanding of the world, and of human beings—then how can one resist the claim that survival is for us an 'end' discoverable by reason, an objective good-for-man? Our notions of harm and injury (to take Hart's example) speak to the way in which we conceive of our relationships to others. Everything from our actions towards those we love (and wish to save from harm) to our actions towards enemies (to whom we wish to do harm) suggest that survival is understood as intrinsically valuable to human beings.

Hart's suggestion that structures of thought and language might change, if the human condition were to change in some fundamental way (making us

---

[23] ibid 192.
[24] Aristotle, *Politics* I.

invulnerable), is quite misleading. Hart suggests that such changes would be reflected in the structures and priorities of social arrangements, which might no longer require systematic controls upon the use of violence. That might be so; but is not jurisprudence meant above all to focus on the nature of law within the human condition? Indeed, is it not part of an attempt to reflect upon and understand that condition? One might recall Aristotle's observation in the *Politics* that a person who does not stand in need of society is either a beast or a god, either sub-human or super-human. It would quite miss the point to suggest that everything Aristotle has to say on the subject of politics is 'entirely contingent' upon human beings continuing to require society for their existence and flourishing: Aristotle's claim is precisely that a social nature is a necessary feature of what it means to *be* human.

Similarly, Hart's insistence that survival is an 'aim' that is contingent and 'might be otherwise' deserves to be questioned. If its contingency depends (as Hart says) upon entire structures of thought and language with which it is fundamentally and thoroughly intertwined—if in short it represents a basic building-block of our relationship with and knowledge of the world (and each other)—then it is far from clear that any contrary outlook is actually imaginable to us. One cannot steadily and soberly imagine an alternative viewpoint, for the very reason that the value of survival is presupposed by all practical reason and understanding.[25] Human beings may embrace death for all sorts of intelligible reasons, including self-sacrifice in the service of others, heroism, fear of pain or of a long and difficult illness, despair and so on. But none of these reasons invoke the worthlessness of life as such as the reason for seeking its extinction. Rather the underlying belief is that insurmountable obstacles stand in the way of one's own ability to participate fully and meaningfully in that good (in the case of illness or despair), or that certain other values (including the value of others' lives) may take priority over one's own life. In the latter case, self-sacrifice and heroism are remarkable and significant acts precisely because the thing being laid down in service of other values (ie, one's life) is itself so precious.

This train of thought might take us in several directions. Is survival (*perseverare in esse suo*) the only value that is presupposed by human reason and action in this way? Or is it, as the natural lawyers indeed argued, only the first stratum in a richer conception of the human condition and of human ends? Might it not lead to a concern with broader conceptions of the 'flourishing' life? Alternatively, is survival itself intelligible as a distinct value apart from conceptions of the 'good' or 'worthwhile' life? If this should prove to be the case, is the life without (say) knowledge less valuable than the life of one who

---

[25] See J Finnis, *Natural Law and Natural Rights*, 2nd edn (Oxford, Clarendon Press, 2011), and the discussion in ch 9 below.

is learned in some, or a number of, fields? Are all lives equally valuable? In all cases, what else might be deduced about the character of law and legal arrangements, against the background of these richer conceptions of human goods or ends? Might this not lead us to reject Hart's dissociation of law and morality, to embrace the possibility that it is indeed necessary that laws reproduce or satisfy certain demands of morality? There is no reason (in advance of much thought on the matter) why the inevitably contentious character of these richer legal visions should be taken for their contingency. Not everything that is true or necessary is obvious, incontestable, unarguable.

JUSTICE AND EQUALITY

Having conceded a 'minimum content' of natural law as the foundation of legal systems, Hart devotes the rest of chapter IX to a consideration of further senses in which law might be said to be 'necessarily' connected to morality. A basic feature of law is its concern with justice. Lawyers are familiar with the idea that like cases demand to be treated alike, but also devote much thought, judgement and writing to the determination of the presence or absence of similarities between shifting sets of particulars. Is it the fulfilment of justice to give each person an equal share in some finite resource, such as a birthday cake? Or must we distinguish between fully grown adults, who require a comparatively larger intake, and children who consume relatively less, so that each receives a portion in relation to his or her size? There again, should those who bought the most thoughtful or expensive presents be rewarded in proportion to their generosity, or is this an irrelevant consideration? The question of how to treat people as equals is enormously complex. Earlier in the book, Hart points out that:

> The connection between this aspect of justice and the very notion of proceeding by rule is obviously very close. Indeed, it might be said that to apply a law justly to different cases is simply to take seriously the assertion that what is to be applied in different cases is the same general rule, without prejudice, interest, or caprice.[26]

Yet the connection between justice and the very notion of following rules should not, Hart suggests, lead us to conclude that questions of morality are intrinsic to law. It remains that courts may apply certain rules unjustly, or indeed Parliament may enact unjust rules, conferring benefits unevenly or on a favoured group to the detriment of others. It is plain, Hart says, 'that neither the law nor the accepted morality of societies need extend their minimal protections and benefits to all within their scope, and often they have not done so'.[27]

---

[26] Hart (n 2), 161. See ch VIII in general for Hart's treatment of justice.
[27] ibid 200.

In order for a regime to maintain itself in power, it is necessary that it confer benefits on some of its citizens. (Recall that Hart said popular acceptance was necessary for a functioning, effective legal system.) But it is possible that a very organised 'master group', in possession of significant resources and characterised by high levels of solidarity, can dominate and maintain in a position of permanent inferiority a 'subject group', denying it basic protections or advantages, and limiting its ability to organise.

Does this not go against what Hart admits about the 'very close' connection between justice and the idea that the law consists in stable, certain 'general' rules? We have already seen that the process of applying rules to specific cases is neither mechanical nor arbitrary: it is, inescapably, a matter of *judgement*. This process is one which often displays 'characteristic judicial virtues' of 'impartiality and neutrality in surveying the alternatives; consideration for the interests of all those who will be affected; and a concern to deploy some acceptable general principle as a reasoned basis for decision'.[28] Yet for all their importance and centrality to received 'canons of interpretation', Hart reminds us that these principles 'have been honoured nearly as much in the breach as in the observance'. But consider: insofar as one breaches these considerations, departs from these virtues, does one's decision not represent precisely an arbitrary (or perhaps a mechanical) one? The idea of 'judgement' and offering a 'reasoned basis for decision' are one and the same. The unreasoned decision is an automatic or arbitrary one. Indeed, as Hart goes on to admit:

> [T]he contention that a legal system must treat all human beings within its scope as entitled to certain basic protections and freedoms, is now generally accepted as a statement of an ideal of obvious relevance in the criticism of law. Even where practice departs from it, lip service to this ideal is usually forthcoming. It may even be the case that a morality which does not take this view of the right of all men to equal consideration, can be shown by philosophy to be involved in some inner contradiction, dogmatism or irrationality.[29]

But if Hart is right about judgement being an inescapable feature of following and applying rules, then the commitment to a reasoned (non-arbitrary) decision is more than mere 'lip service'. Might these considerations, which Hart says 'might well be called moral' not be considered an intrinsic property of the administration of law? Hart is of course right to say that legal orders have flouted these principles of justice. But what does this tell us? Does it reveal any more than that legal systems have failed, either through the limitation of human insight and impartiality, or else deliberate effort, to offer a perfect

---

[28] ibid 205.
[29] ibid 206. I explore this further in ch 9 below.

instantiation of that rationality that is intrinsic to legal judgement? Hart insists that this demonstrates the lack of a 'necessary connection' between law and morality because his focus is on the question of the 'validity' of legal rules. Iniquitous or unjust rules may be applied and recognised as 'valid' law. Yet if we prescind from the question of the validity of unjust rules, might we not come to see that the 'rational' nature of legal judgement, invoking as it does notions of justice and equality, remains intrinsic to the very idea of law, so that an entire *system* of governance, if it were utterly bereft of rational and conscious concern for defensible, intelligible grounds of decision, would scarcely resemble 'what we now recognize as law'?

Hart seems to accept something of the sort a little earlier in his discussion. Statutes may be understood as a kind of shell, and 'demand by their express terms to be filled out with the aid of moral principles' in much the same way as 'the range of enforceable contracts may be limited by reference to conceptions of morality and fairness' and liability for civil and criminal wrongs may be judged according to 'prevailing views of moral responsibility'. If viable legal systems are, as Hart suggests, dependent 'in part upon such types of correspondence with morals', then '[i]f this is what is meant by the necessary connection of law and morals, its existence should be conceded'.[30] Furthermore, the principles of natural justice (impartiality in respect of the application of general rules, undeflected by prejudice, interest or caprice), which are synonymous with the idea of 'legality', represent what Lon Fuller calls an 'inner morality of law': Hart says that 'we may accept' this as a necessary connection between law and morality, though observes that '[i]t is unfortunately compatible with very great iniquity'.[31]

In spite of these concessions, Hart wants to maintain that governance through law is not an intrinsically moral idea. Authority itself, though not resting entirely on the 'mere power of man over man', is not yet created or cemented by a moral obligation, but depends upon acceptance. But the 'internal attitude' need not be a moral one. People's allegiance to the law 'may be based on many different considerations', including 'calculations of long-term interest; disinterested interest in others; an unreflecting inherited or traditional attitude; or the mere wish to do as others do'.[32] As a result, Hart 'think[s] it quite vain to seek any more specific purpose which law as such serves beyond providing guides to human conduct and standards of criticism of such conduct'.[33]

---

[30] ibid 204.
[31] ibid 207. Hart's acceptance of this idea is in fact less straightforward than it might appear from this passage. Hart in fact argued in print with Fuller on this issue: see ch 10 below.
[32] ibid 203.
[33] ibid 249.

This argument could be turned another way. The 'power of man over man' alone is not the same as governance through law. The characteristic form of the latter requires (in Hart's view) the cooperation and voluntary 'acceptance' of persons in society, even if the law's protections do not extend to all. Those who voluntarily accept the authority of law may indeed have numerous reasons for doing so, or perhaps in some cases may indeed have no conscious reasons, being unreflective. But these attitudes are sustainable only given a basic assumption: that the law in some way furthers or protects their fundamental interests. I will remain 'disinterested' in my interest in others, for example, only insofar as their lifestyles are not bought at the expense of all that I hold dear or necessary to my own. Similarly, an unthinking attitude of obedience is likely to be the luxury of someone whose interests are untroubled by undue restrictions and arbitrary impedances. If my deepest interests become threatened, will I not begin to ponder? Such attitudes can only exist, one might say, only where the law serves the general good.

History does indeed contain terrible examples of societies in which minorities, and even sometimes downtrodden peoples as a whole, are subjected to depredations and terrors, being deprived of liberty, property and the protection of law. It is abundantly clear that institutional and regulatory form can be given to the measures by which people are alienated from their ordinary existences. But here we might ask a question. Does the existence of law—understood to conform to principles of legality or 'natural justice'—aid and accelerate such processes, or does it stand in their way? As Kristen Rundle recalls, some narratives of the Holocaust run along these lines:

> By 1938, the Jewish subject of Nazi law had been living under an oppressive, grossly discriminatory and incrementally pathological legal order for over five years. But even in the early months of 1938, there were still authorities to report to and rules to follow, forms to fill out and sign—including, crucially, those associated with the April 1938 decree that required all Jews to declare and register their property holdings—and officials to receive and process them. In these structures, so the testimonies and memoirs tell us, one found at least some threads of stability; or, one might suggest, of the possibility of a continuing 'daily life'. But over the course of that year, the modes of Nazi oppression expanded in their variety and escalated in their effects. And then, on the night of 9–10 November, there was wanton destruction and defilement, brutal violence and murder, arbitrary arrest and transportation to concentration camps for no apparent crime. This, we are told, is when 'daily life' ended.[34]

Contestable and complex though such interpretations are, they give to us a sense of the contentiousness of Hart's own position. We might call attention

---

[34] KA Rundle, 'Law and Daily Life: Questions for Legal Theory from November 1938' (2012) 3 *Jurisprudence* 429.

to the specific regulatory measures by which Jews and others were deprived of property, status and basic liberties, recognising that these were enacted against the background of a legal order that continued to regulate other aspects of life for ordinary Germans in the usual way. But we can also direct attention to the combined and systematic effect of the range of such measures, which (as Hart puts it) operate to deprive a certain group within society of the benefits and protections of law. If we remain on this plane of engagement, then we might consider that the effect overall is an interruption to the principles of legality and natural justice characteristic of ordinary legal judgement. And if we concede this, we may consider that the regime that has deliberately so departed from or interrupted those principles has, precisely in so doing, decreed that a part of its rule has thenceforward been withdrawn from the constraints of legality, and applied as sheer force or power. Is the regime that does this, which regards itself as no longer bound to rule according to and within the limits of law, any different from the regime which enacts, with procedural propriety, a statute declaring that intent directly, namely to rule without legal limitation and in defiance of legally established rights? And, if any government did enact such a statute, can one say that its terms could be held without contradiction to constitute 'law' as we understand it?

There is perhaps no easy answer to such questions. Certainly, one cannot resolve the issue by offering a stipulative definition, as Hart himself recognises: 'Plainly we cannot grapple adequately with this issue if we see it as one concerning the complexities of linguistic usage'.[35] Hart's solution is to ask, of any given way of conceptualising the matter, whether it will aid our understandings:

> If we are to make a reasoned choice between these concepts, it must be because one is superior to the other in the way in which it will assist our theoretical inquiries, or advance and clarify our moral deliberations, or both.[36]

Hart's approach exhibits an underlying functionalism: the concept to be adopted is the one that allows us to group and consider together as 'law' all those rules that are valid according to the formal tests of a system of primary and secondary rules, over one that would exclude certain rules on moral grounds even if they exhibited all the other characteristics of laws as part of 'a system of rules generally effective in social life'.[37] Is this so straightforward and

---

[35] Hart (n 2) 209. The issue Hart has in mind here is slightly different from the one I have raised, but relates to the issue of whether the rule of law can become so iniquitous that it can no longer be obeyed, and whether it follows this that its propositions are not 'valid' rules of law.

[36] ibid.

[37] ibid.

value-neutral? On what grounds do we determine whether our theoretical deliberations have been 'clarified' rather than obscured, by a particular scheme of conceptualisation? How rich or austere, simple or complex, should our conception of social function be? It seems, in the end, that our impression of such things cannot avoid appealing to conceptions of the human condition, and the aspects of that condition (such as survival, but possibly others as well: justice or the good life), that it is the function of the rules to advance and protect.

SUGGESTED READING

The Background to Hart's Positivism

J Austin, *The Province of Jurisprudence Determined* (1832, various edns) Lectures I and V.
HLA Hart, *The Concept of Law*, 3rd edn (Oxford, Clarendon Press, 2012) esp chs 1–3, 6 and 7.
—— *Essays in Jurisprudence and Philosophy* (Oxford, Clarendon Press, 1983) chs 2 and 3.

Background Reading

J Finnis, 'HLA Hart: A Twentieth-Century Oxford Political Philosopher' (2009) 54 *American Journal of Jurisprudence* 161, §§ I and II.
N Lacey, *A Life of HLA Hart* (Oxford, Oxford University Press, 2004).
N MacCormick, *HLA Hart* (London, Edward Arnold, 1981) I.
SFC Milsom, 'The Nature of Blackstone's Achievement' (1981) 1 *Oxford Journal of Legal Studies* 1.
C Orrego, 'Gains and Losses in Jurisprudence since HLA Hart' (2014) 59 *American Journal of Jurisprudence* 111.
G Postema, *Bentham and the Common Law Tradition* (Oxford, Clarendon Press, 1986) 256–62.
P Schofield, 'Jeremy Bentham and Nineteenth Century Jurisprudence' (1991) 12 *Journal of Legal History* 58.
NE Simmonds, 'Between Positivism and Idealism' (1991) 50 *Cambridge Law Journal* 308.
AWB Simpson, 'The Common Law and Legal Theory' in AWB Simpson (ed), *Oxford Essays in Jurisprudence*, 2nd Series (Oxford, Clarendon Press, 1973).

Law as an Instrument of the Good Life?

HLA Hart, *The Concept of Law*, 3rd edn (Oxford, Clarendon Press, 2012) ch 9.

Background Reading

C Orrego, 'HLA Hart's Understanding of Classical Natural Law Theory' (2004) 24 *Oxford Journal of Legal Studies* 287.

A Perreau-Saussine, 'An Outsider on the Inside: Hart's Limits on Jurisprudence' (2006) 56 *University of Toronto Law Journal* 371.

——'Bentham and the Boot-Strappers of Jurisprudence' (2004) 63 *Cambridge Law Journal* 346.

S Perry, 'Hart's Methodological Positivism' in J Coleman (ed), *Hart's Postscript: Essays on the Postscript to the Concept of Law* (Oxford, Oxford University Press, 2001).

NE Simmonds, 'Legal Validity and Decided Cases' (1981) 1 *Legal Studies* 24.

E Skidelsky, 'The Strange Death of British Idealism' (2007) 31 *Philosophy and Literature* 41.

7

Justice in the 'Real World': Dworkin

IN THE SEVENTH Part of the *Republic*, Plato sets out his argument for the advisability of placing society in the hands of philosopher-kings. It is possible to regard the legal philosophy of Ronald Dworkin (1931–2013) as pursuing in some ways a similar idea, that it were best for the administration of the law to lie in the hands of philosopher-judges.

This immediately suggests a vision of the nature of law that is fundamentally at variance with that of legal positivists. It will be recalled that positivists insist upon the necessity of a framework of certain, stable rules that are both ascertainable and distinct from open-ended moral-political judgements. Indeed, the traditional separation of legal- and open-ended, moral-political judgement precedes by some distance of time the development of distinctive positivist concerns. Common lawyers of the medieval and early-modern periods referred to the law as 'the artificial perfection of reason'. By this they meant to suggest that although 'the common law is nothing else but reason', it is something distinct from 'every man's natural reason'.[1] It is artificial not only because it has been fashioned at the hands of many men, but specifically in virtue of its greater perfection:

> [I]f all the reason that is dispersed into so many several heads, were united into one, yet could he not make such a law as the law in England is: because by many successions of ages it hath been fined and refined by an infinite number of grave and learned men, and by long experience grown into such a perfection, for the government of this realm.[2]

The artificiality of legal reason was intended as a comment upon the law's wisdom, but it also functions as a limit upon the exercise of men's 'natural' reason. James I is reported to have cried: 'Reason is too large. Find me a precedent and I will accept it'.[3] The accumulated reasonings of so many 'grave and learned men' had the effect of establishing concepts, doctrines and principles

---

[1] See Coke, The First Part of the Institutes of the Laws of England I.2.6.138.
[2] ibid.
[3] Quoted by G Postema, *Bentham and the Common Law Tradition* (Oxford, Clarendon Press, 1986) 15.

for the direction of subsequent thought. The reception of these understandings into the legal tradition gave to lawyers a certain structure to their deliberations. It was not necessary (indeed not in accordance with 'the law') to
address the respective claims of the litigants from a blank canvas, considering
every matter that might conceivably come into mind. The lawyer's notions of
justice, of reasonableness and fairness, are orientated by a thousand doctrinal
ideas and conceptions which give them shape and direction. Ideas of justice
and fairness are endlessly debatable in philosophy. The lawyer's doctrines do
not settle these ideas, but give to them a certain form and consistency. Indeed,
the very limitation of legal argument according to its established criteria
serves an indispensable condition of formal justice, that like cases demand to
be treated alike.

From the perspective of traditional common law thinking, judges, howsoever grave and learned, do not need to be philosophers. One can admit this
without invoking any suggestion that legal reasoning is discontinuous with
moral or political reasoning. Take the law of contract by way of example.
When deciding whether a valid, enforceable contract exists between A and
B, lawyers refer to a range of concepts and principles such as the presence
or absence of valuable consideration, the occurrence of a mistake by one or
both parties, the need for valid offer and acceptance, the absence of frustrating acts etc. They discuss the conditions required for a valid offer, whether
certain events were reasonably foreseeable and so forth. Without too much
imagination, one can raise significant and deep questions about the operation
of these ideas which gradually unveil broader perspectives of thought. Should
contracts be seen as arm's length arrangements of an essentially commercial
nature, in which each party's interests remain entirely individual and merely
conjoined to the interests of another through the presence of the contract?
Or are contracts correctly viewed as a kind of limited partnership in which
the risks of non-performance are to be considered as somehow distributed
between the parties?[4] In the former case, a contractual promise is treated not
as an absolute guarantee of performance, but a promise to restore the prom-
isee to a position equivalent to one in which the contract had been performed
by the promisor: a position to which the promisor is otherwise indifferent. In
the latter, reference is made to the point or purpose of the contract, and the
contract is treated as an instrument for determining the apportionment of
losses between both parties where some frustrating act intervenes.

Having gone as far, one might press further the idea (or ideas) of justice that
underlie these alternative viewpoints. One may indeed raise questions about
the extent of the state's title to interfere in otherwise private arrangements,

---

[4] See *Hadley v Baxendale* (1854) 9 Ex 341. See also the discussion of J Finnis, *Natural Law and
Natural Rights*, 2nd edn (Oxford, Clarendon Press, 2011) 181–83.

perhaps leading to the development of sophisticated theories concerning the moral and political justification of the state itself, and the place of law within the life of the community. Hence, we are brought to general theories of the nature of law, of the kind considered in jurisprudence.

The point is that, whilst ordinary, everyday considerations of courts raise these deeper implications, it is hardly necessary for the court to devote time to reflect upon them. The judge's deliberations on the relative merits of the litigants' claims do not await the articulation of a general theory of law and state, even if they unavoidably presuppose one. One might say that the judgment of the court does not have to *ground* itself in philosophical claims, deducing specific conclusions from the most fundamental questions of political philosophy. There are no doubt occasions on which these deeper questions rise close to the surface of ordinary legal thought: where judges are confronted with the necessity of having to set out what it means to deal fairly, avoid unnecessary risk, act reasonably and so forth. The law of tort is one area in which questions of the extent of personal responsibility demand direct and principled consideration. But it remains that (as one might think) judges in discharging their function do not first have to resolve everything that lies between Plato, Aristotle, Kant, Locke and others before determining the narrower issues of the instant case.

THE PHILOSOPHER-JUDGE

In his most celebrated book, *Law's Empire*, Dworkin develops in detail an idea of law based not upon rule or right, but upon principle. It will be recalled that positivists regarded rights with a certain suspicion. Unwilling to accept that rights form the basis of legal order, early positivists such as Bentham decried the idea that one could determine the substance and boundaries of rights in the absence of coherent and clearly established rules. There are no 'natural' rights. 'Rights' can only be understood as implications arising from the application of posited rules. Dworkin wishes his readers to 'take rights seriously', but he too disavows any notion of 'natural rights'. Instead, he claims that the substance of legal rights is determined on the basis of principle.

Whilst sharing with the traditional common lawyers the idea that there is no firm distinction between doctrinal reasoning and more directly jurisprudential concerns, Dworkin wishes to move our deliberations in the opposite direction to that suggested a few paragraphs ago. I suggested that doctrinal concepts and ideas readily give rise to the most profound philosophical questions, but that these questions precisely *arise from* legal reasoning rather than forming its *ground*. In consequence, it is very often possible for lawyers and judges to prescind from an examination of those more general questions. There is not a definitive point beyond which legal deliberations become philosophical. One should instead think of philosophy merely as asking questions at progressively deeper and more comprehensive levels. At each stage of thought, further reflection is possible, so that there is no end to the enquiry. Courts reach their decisions usually without endlessly examining the basis of the reasons given in the judgment. The focus of the judgment is neither so wide nor so deep as it is possible to go. The deepest questions invited by the judgment (what is the basis of the state's authority to intervene?) are not explored. The focus is narrower. For Dworkin, on the other hand, philosophical ideas form the basis of legal thought. In his view, 'any judge's decision is itself a piece of legal philosophy'.[5] Even though the philosophical principles might lie hidden beneath the 'visible argument', with its citations and lists of facts, 'Jurisprudence is the general part of adjudication, silent prologue to any decision at law'.[6]

It might seem all one whether philosophical principles are said to arise from legal argument, or otherwise lie beneath it. But by adopting the latter image, Dworkin propels philosophy into the very heart of law. One does not move *from* the law, as it were, reaching ever higher and more abstract levels of thought. Doctrinal concepts and legal decisions are instead 'surface' or 'visible' features of deeper ideas into which it is possible to delve. In this way, the philosophical underpinnings of Dworkin's theory are very different from those of Hart. Hart avowedly adopts a descriptive approach, going so far as to describe his book as a contribution to 'descriptive sociology'. He wants to describe the practices that make up a legal order, coming to an understanding of their philosophical significance.[7] His jurisprudence is a contribution to practical deliberations only insofar as precise analysis offers clarity to those deliberations. (By realising that the law is a set of conventional rules rather than a set of 'natural' rights, we will not be led into false trains of reasoning.) Dworkin's concern is practical from the outset. The goal of legal philosophy is to provide a *justification* for legal decisions, indeed of law itself. There are no neutral descriptions of the object of enquiry, law. Law is nothing if not practical. It is intrinsically a domain of interpretation and of justification. Accordingly,

> it is essential to the structure of such a practice that interpreting the practice be treated as different from understanding what other participants mean by the statements they make in its operation. It follows that a social scientist must participate in a social practice if he hopes to understand it, as distinguished from understanding its members.[8]

---

[5] R Dworkin, *Law's Empire* (London, Fontana Press, 1986) 90.
[6] ibid.
[7] See in particular the discussion in HLA Hart, *The Concept of Law*, 3rd edn (Oxford, Clarendon Press, 2012) ch IX.
[8] Dworkin, *Law's Empire* (n 5) 55.

Hart had set out an idea of law in which judges apply the law according to established criteria of validity. In doing so, they need neither to entertain nor express any views about the nature of 'law' in general. For Dworkin however, enquiry into nature of legal institutions and the conditions under which they form a system, 'is part of the controversial and uncertain process of assigning meaning to what we find, not a given of the preinterpretive structure'.[9] To pronounce upon the law, the judge needs to hold some general theory that

> aim[s] to interpret the main point and structure of legal practice, not [merely] some particular part of department of it'. Such theories are 'constructive interpretations [which] ... try to show legal practice as a whole in its best light, to achieve equilibrium between legal practice as they find it and the best justification of that practice.[10]

To understand Dworkin's point, consider the following example. Suppose that within a community, people habitually remove their hat on solemn occasions, or upon entering churches. If asked, they claim to do this out of 'courtesy'.[11] The origins and meaning of the practice are lost in the mists of time: people just comply without stopping to consider or question the rules. Gradually however, attitudes to the practice change. People develop what Dworkin calls an 'interpretative' attitude to the rules.[12] To start with, they begin to assume that the rules have some point or purpose behind them, which can be formulated as a principle. But they also believe that the forms of behaviour demanded by this principle are not necessarily or conclusively those that have been traditionally accepted as belonging to the practice. The thought is that the behaviour called for must be related directly to the perceived point, and as such capable of amendment or variation. (Perhaps some traditional actions insufficiently serve that principle, or there may be others that seem to lack any explanation in terms of it.) In adopting this attitude, a community 'impose[s] meaning on the institution—to see it in its best light—and then [proceeds] to restructure it in the light of that meaning'.[13]

It is not difficult to imagine a scenario along the lines Dworkin suggests. People may come to believe that acts of 'courtesy' are performed out of respect. But respect for what, or whom? Is respect due on the basis of rank, or age or gender? Or is respect finally directed towards individual achievement? People may over time shift in their views about the proper grounds of respect. Or they may change their minds concerning the actions that express respect, or indeed whether respect is expressible at all. Might respect not after all be

---

[9] ibid 91.

[10] ibid 90.

[11] ibid 46–49.

[12] Dworkin actually uses the curious truncated form 'interpretive', but I will avoid this unless in direct quotation.

[13] ibid 47.

a matter of inner feelings rather than outward actions? If respect is to be manifested in outward acts, may this not be a matter of a *pattern* of behaviour towards the ones respected, rather than a single, conventional token (removal of one's hat)? If so, distinct 'rules' of courtesy will all but vanish from society. Courtesy 'will then occupy a different and diminished place in social life, ... the interpretive attitude will languish, and the practice will lapse back into the static and mechanical state in which it began'.[14]

The dynamics of interpretation present in this example are distinguishable into three stages. The first is a 'pre-interpretative' stage, which Dworkin equates to a kind of robotic observance or 'runic traditionalism'. The second (at which the practice is deemed to possess some point or purpose) is the 'interpretative' stage. But there is finally a 'post-interpretative' stage, in which the very interpretations being offered (at stage two), the different conceptions of the purpose or point, are themselves subject to criticism, evaluation and critical reinterpretation. It is this final stage in particular that Dworkin sees being manifested in the judicial consideration and application of laws and precedents.

A number of questions immediately arise. For instance, how (on Dworkin's view) should one respond to the positivist concern that law must be distinguished from open-ended moral deliberation, and embody clear, ascertainable rules? How shall law be separated from other forms of moral and political discourse?

As a domain of practical reason, law is the subject of what Dworkin calls 'constructive interpretation'. It is at once a body of practices that demand to be 'constructed' through human effort and deliberation (rather than naturally existing, and 'discovered' by the intellect alone); and in being practical, it requires interpretations that advance its purposes, improving them rather than eroding or worsening them. The values that one draws on in constructively interpreting a body of practices must be appropriate to those practices. In the case of law, this will not mean non-moral excellences (such as beauty), but moral-political values. In the absence of neutral descriptions, legal reasoning is in part a reflection on the moral-political theory that lies at the heart of the law, but also (in being 'post-interpretative') in part a substantive contribution to the further refinement and improvement of its excellence.

What prevents law collapsing into other forms of moral or political argumentation? At the 'pre-interpretative' level, we are bound to the traditional practices and conventions of legal practice. Included in this intellectual inheritance is the practice of deciding the law according to enacted legislation and

---

[14] ibid 49.

decided cases. Lawyers 'move within' these practices. Their deliberations are structured according to them. As Dworkin says:

> Law cannot flourish as an interpretive enterprise in any community unless there is enough initial agreement about what practices are legal practices so that lawyers argue about the best interpretation of roughly the same data. That is a practical requirement of any interpretative enterprise.[15]

If you and I are to have a meaningful argument about the correct interpretation of a painting, then it is necessary that we have the same painting in mind. If you are looking at the *Mona Lisa* and I am gazing at *Portrait of Balzac*, then we will end up talking past one another. Dworkin says that there must be *rough* agreement on the object of interpretation because, clearly, jurists may disagree about such things as the relative priority of statute and precedent as sources of law, or even (as in Bentham's case) whether precedent properly functions as a source of law at all. Nevertheless, there must in some sense be an agreed object of interpretation.[16]

One key determinant of legal reasoning—that by which law is distinguished from other forms of political and moral reasoning—is that substantive moral and political principles must be 'fitted to' the features of law that are generally recognised at the pre-interpretative level. In the same way that my interpretation of the *Mona Lisa* must be, as it were, an interpretation *of that painting*, and not another, so interpretations of the law must be interpretations *of the law* as it exists. I cannot put forward a theory of law that denies the enforceability of contracts, for example, if this would gainsay all that courts and legislatures have said on the subject in previous decisions and statutes. It does not matter whether the non-enforceability of contracts would enhance justice in the community, or be commendable on its own grounds; if it does not adequately fit with the existing body of laws and decisions, it cannot plausibly be offered as an interpretation of the law. At the same time (as was seen in the case of courtesy), it might be that no theory, and no set of principles, fits with every past decision of the courts, or every legislative provision in force. Indeed, lawyers are well aware of the existence of divergent lines of authority that cannot always be successfully reconciled. This is why Dworkin speaks of seeking 'equilibrium' between the constraints of 'fit', and the search for sound moral-political values. The judge must seek to articulate the most morally appealing

---

[15] ibid 91.

[16] It is nevertheless worth noting that this agreement extends, in Dworkin's view, only to agreement on instances, not the criteria that underpin those instances. We may agree that the established body of statutes and precedents are law, without endorsing the picture of 'criteria of validity' supplied by an agreed 'rule of recognition' for example. It is not open to positivists therefore to suggest that Dworkin's views do not conflict with their own in being addressed to a different, normative stage of enquiry.

interpretation that consists with the requirements of 'fit'. It is in this sense that Dworkin speaks of the law as a domain of principle.

Taken together, the requirements of 'fit' and 'soundness' constitute a distinct political value, which Dworkin calls 'integrity'. Again, this carries overtones of both the law's systematic or 'integrated' nature, but also the moral value placed on a person whom one judges to possess integrity. Aware that the requirements of 'fit' might sometimes conflict with our views about the demands of justice, Dworkin suggests that it would be wrong to equate law with justice in an unqualified sense. He therefore sometimes speaks of integrity as embodying 'justice in the real world': justice as it can be applied in a world that is imperfect, and subject to all kinds of limitations. At the same time, the constraint of 'fit'; (though it can indeed qualify justice) is also an intrinsic aspect of the administration of justice. 'How can it be fairer for judges to enforce their own views about the best future, unconstrained by any requirement of coherence with the past, than the more complex but no less controversial judgments that law as integrity requires?'[17]

This elaboration of the law in terms of principle falls above all into the hands of judges. Dworkin imagines an ideal, philosopher-judge (Hercules) as a model of what legal judgement should be. Imagine that you have superhuman powers of intellect, memory, patience, and virtues such as impartiality. These are not to be considered as bestowing godlike attributes, but recognisably human characteristics taken to indefinite lengths.[18] Without having privileged access to any higher plane of understanding, you can nevertheless read, take in, memorise and integrate the whole of Western thinking on philosophy, politics and morality. Your mind's eye has in simultaneous view all past court decisions, and all statutory provisions in force, in all their detail and permutations. Would you not then be ideally placed constructively to interpret the law? You would resolve, in a more profound and conclusive way, the outstanding questions of political and moral theory, and understand exactly to what degree different systems of moral principle 'fit' with the previously decided law. You would have weighed and considered every possible argument and counter-argument, and brought in every possible legitimate consideration. Could there be any greater hope for justice (or 'integrity')?

One should not be misled by Dworkin's suggestion that this ideal is a 'model' for ordinary judgement. Dworkin is of course aware that actual judges are

---

[17] Dworkin, *Law's Empire* (n 5) 264. The title of Dworkin's later book, *Justice in Robes* (Cambridge MA, Harvard University Press, 2006) suggests a similar qualification on justice, though he does in later work articulate his ideas more frequently in terms of 'justice' than earlier.

[18] Hercules 'has no vision into transcendental mysteries opaque to [ordinary people]. His judgments of fit and morality are made on the same material and have the same character as theirs'. ibid 265.

more fallible, finite in their intellectual capacities and virtues, than this. No person could possibly hold knowledge of the whole history of human thinking on politics and morality in their head. No person's knowledge of the law is so complete or so systematically detailed. The image of the ideal philosopher-judge is 'more reflective and self-conscious than any real judge need be or, given the press of work, can be'. But although actual judges decide cases in a far less methodical way, the ideal 'shows us the hidden structure of their judgments and so lays these open to study and criticism'.[19] For example: the case of *Riggs v Palmer* involved a murderer who claimed that he was entitled to inherit under the will of his victim.[20] Existing law on testamentary succession contained no provision debarring a person from inheriting in this situation. It might seem therefore as if the murderer (Palmer) had a clear right to the deceased's estate, despite the moral objections that might arise. If one thinks of the law as being primarily an 'affair of rules', then there seems to be no possibility of avoiding the application of the relevant statutory rules and awarding the bequest under the will. The majority opinion was nevertheless that the bequest should be withheld from the plaintiff. Dworkin's insistence that the law must be considered to form a domain of principle seems to make sense of this decision. It shows the courts considering and attempting to balance the weight of different principles: on the one hand, the principle that courts are bound to apply statutes as they find them, and on the other, the principle (drawn from consideration of other cases and doctrines) that a person should not legally be allowed to profit from their own wrongdoing. If weight is given to the latter principle, then one can understand that statutes cannot be construed so as to facilitate wrongdoing. Equally, the minority opinion calls upon principles in the elaboration of the judgment: in this case, the view that the withholding of the estate would constitute an *additional* punishment for the murder beyond the penalty received under the criminal law.

It is not difficult to imagine successive courts giving shifting consideration to these principles (and perhaps others), in the light of particular circumstances, creating exceptions and elucidating distinctions based upon the differences between cases. This process could continue indefinitely without it ever being possible to hammer the underlying principles down into a final, fixed form. They would need to be constructively interpreted in each case. Each new decision, in drawing inspiration and guidance from such principles, would truly represent a decision *in law*, rather than a piece of judicial legislation aimed at the filling of 'gaps' in the established legal rules.

One might nevertheless ask whether Dworkin's image of the ideal philosopher-judge really assists our understandings. The idea of an intellect, memory and

---

[19] ibid.
[20] *Riggs v Palmer* 115 NY 506 (1889).

understanding that can contemplate and systematise vast areas of our philosophical inheritance might seem attractive, but would the result of such deliberations not be just as likely to lead to intellectual and moral paralysis? The image might suggest that philosophy can be represented as a domain of arguments and counter-arguments. Would a person in command of all possible arguments, who genuinely and impartially allowed themselves to feel the pull of conflicting ideas, feel that they had resolved that domain? Philosophical questions are not in this sense amenable to final resolution. The most that one can do is steadily deepen and expand one's reflections upon those questions, a process that can often increase one's perplexity and qualify one's certainties. It is true that Dworkin speaks of judgments as inherently controversial, but it is far from clear that the continual addition of more considerations would diminish rather than enhance that sense of controversy. Would the ideal philosopher not grow steadily less confident about his opinions, in the face of all that could be said against them?

More than anything, if morality is a matter of the 'integrity' or coherence of one's inner voice or conscience, what possible basis is there for saying that legal or social practices 'embody' a moral philosophy? Are not legal practices then (as the positivists said) not simply inert phenomena open to evaluation according to different, radically detached, considerations? And if so, why should it be imagined that different individuals will (in conscience) ever converge in their judgements of the moral significance of such phenomena?

In early writings (and less visibly in more recent works) Dworkin had insisted that there is always a 'right' answer, or at least a 'best' answer, to any case to come before the court. This indeed is the logic of law understood as a domain of constructive interpretation directed towards the value of 'integrity'. One might argue in Dworkin's defence, therefore, that the ideal philosopher-judge does not need to resolve all that lies between different moral and political standpoints. The judicial task is to interpret the *law* in the light of the most appealing body of principles that 'fit' with extant statutes, cases and so forth. But one might say two things about the dimension of 'fit'. The first is that it is unclear that the ideal judge's 'superhuman' knowledge of law would enhance his ability to assess the satisfactoriness of 'fit'. Imagine that you could know and remember all details of all statutes and cases, in all their nuances, such that they were simultaneously present before the mind. Would this not severely hamper one's ability to determine which were the *relevant* or *important* ideas, concepts or doctrines in a given case? Memory and forgetting go absolutely together: the capacity to forget is indeed in this way a function of intelligence, allowing one to process and sieve the important or significant from the irrelevant. To the objection that the ideal judge would be able to prioritise or 'weigh' different aspects of different cases, the answer is that all such activities (even the construction of a simple list) must operate on the basis of some criteria of inclusion or exclusion. The second point is that therefore the idea of 'fit' cannot easily be understood simply as a set of 'constraints' on otherwise open-ended moral-political thinking. Meaning and significance are not bestowed upon doctrines, ideas and rulings in the light of opposing 'general' theories of morality or politics, but they instead already articulate and embody a certain regimentation of thought: they represent 'accumulated wisdom', in the language of the classical common lawyers.

Such regimentations of thought run throughout the common law, but they are not of course unchallengeable or even univocal. One question we can ask about the law of contract, for example, is whether it demands recognition as a systematic part of a 'law of obligations' (that branch which deals with voluntarily assumed obligations), and thus as concerned with moral ideas such as promise, reliance and duty; or whether it is better understood as an aspect of commercial law, and is therefore guided by economic considerations and the structure and needs of the market. One can readily imagine that particular judgments may turn on the reading that is adopted. But the adoption of one understanding over the other does not really seem to be a matter of formulating very general 'moral-political theories', and then seeing which best 'fits' the existing cases. Instead, judges and others (such as doctrinal writers) regard previous decisions of the court as the starting point for such an enquiry, and set out to trace its wider implications in the manner suggested at the beginning of this chapter: steadily increasing the scope and the level of abstraction of the enquiry, and (often) illuminating the tensions within the extant law.

Dworkin's insensitivity to this point is illustrated by his thesis of 'local priority'.[21] A 'special feature' of the ideal philosopher-judge's practice is that his

> judgments of fit expand out from the immediate case before him in a series of concentric circles. He asks which interpretations on his initial list fit past emotional injury cases, then which ones fit cases of accidental damage to the person more generally, then which fit damage to economic interests, and so on into areas further and further from the original … issue. This procedure gives a kind of local priority to what we might call 'departments' of law.

This passage is significant in its treatment of such categorisations as considerations of *fit*, rather than reflecting substantive moral ideas. But as we have just noted, division of the law into distinct 'departments' is not at all a pre-theoretical matter of local 'convenience'. What after all counts as emotional injury? Why should this be distinguished from other forms of injury? Why should damage to the person be considered a more immediate matter

---

[21] Dworkin, *Law's Empire* (n 5) 250. Perhaps 'insensitivity' is too strong a word: 'misreading' might be closer.

than damage to economic interests? Indeed, on what basis should one differentiate between the two? The response that these categorical divisions form part of a 'pre-interpretative' background, subject to 'post-interpretative' revision, entirely obscures the point: such divisions are not instances of 'runic traditionalism', but exist (or existed) for a purpose. Where such divisions are deeply ingrained in a society's thought, and the purposes largely forgotten, this tends to be because of their successful and uninterrupted operation giving no cause for deeper reflection. Only when new developments come to challenge the existing assumptions (the recognition that 'emotional harm' is real, for example), do lawyers and jurists become aware of the need to justify and articulate reasons for their arrangements. But again, this is not usually out of a desire to apply to the law the lessons of some grand moral-political theory.

There is something deeply unsatisfactory about the general orientation of Dworkin's remarks on adjudication. Hard to pin down, it comes across most clearly in the terminology, especially prevalent in earlier writings, of right, or best *answers*. Moral and political philosophy are above all domains of enquiry, not of answers. Practical reason, especially in law, is of course closely concerned with outcomes; but here the traditional language has always referred not to 'answers' but to *judgments* being handed down. Making judgements and returning answers are not the same thing. The mathematician clearly makes a judgement in saying that $2 \times 2 = 4$, and thereby returns an answer. But when I reason that harms against the person are more serious than harm to economic interests, I make a judgement without in any way providing an 'answer' that 'settles' a moral question. Too easily is it possible to forget Aristotle's dictum that one should not expect a greater level of certainty than is appropriate to the subject matter.

COULD THE LAW BE AN EXPRESSION OF SOMETHING OTHER THAN 'INTEGRITY'?

Having arrived at the idea that law is a domain of constructive interpretation, it becomes necessary to ask: what is the interpretative point of law? Such interpretations will always be a controversial matter, but in a revealing passage Dworkin clearly distances the process of constructing this point from any sense of philosophy being an irenic endeavour. The legal philosopher offers 'tentative paradigms to support his argument and embarrass competitors' in a way that will 'allow them to see their arguments as having a certain structure, as arguments over rival conceptions of that concept'.[22] One might reflect upon the innately adversarial, lawyerly approach to philosophical reflection that this

---

[22] ibid 92.

image suggests. But there are in fact deeper currents at work: in Dworkin's hands, political morality 'becomes a more protestant idea: fidelity to a scheme of principle [that] each citizen has a responsibility to identify, ultimately for himself, as his community's scheme'.[23]

Before proceeding to elaborate that 'scheme', philosophers of law would benefit (Dworkin suggests) by agreeing upon some abstract description of the law's purpose as a kind of 'plateau' on which the rival interpretations can vie and compete. Remembering that governments possess enormous power in the form of a monopoly on the use of coercive force, Dworkin puts forward the suggestion that:

> Our discussions about law by and large assume ... that the most abstract and fundamental point of legal practice is to guide and constrain the power of government in the following way. Law insists that force not be used or withheld, no matter how useful that would be to ends in view, no matter how beneficial or noble these ends, except as licensed or required by individual rights and responsibilities flowing from past political decisions about when collective force is justified. The law of a community on this account is the scheme of rights and responsibilities that meet that complex standard.[24]

Although offered as a basis for 'organising further argument' about the law's character, this abstract conception is not indeed neutral as between possible arguments: something that Dworkin, who repeatedly emphasises the contentious nature of all interpretations, can be supposed to accept.[25] The sharp-eyed reader will have immediately noticed (for example) the identification of 'law' with a 'scheme of rights'; but the question of whether rights form the basic phenomena of legal thought or are implications arising from something yet more fundamental, is one of the central questions one can ask about the nature of law. But one could also ask whether the 'most fundamental' point of legal practice is indeed the constraint of governmental power, or whether other phenomena such as the maintenance of order, or the creation of a body of stable and authoritative rules, may not occupy a more significant position? Indeed, it is necessary to ask whether the establishment of political order is a more fundamental achievement than the creation of a *just* political order; or whether political order is impossible if it does not conform in some measure to demands of justice.

These are not idle questions. A considerable portion of *Law's Empire* is given to the development of three rival interpretations of this abstract conception, termed by Dworkin 'conventionalism', 'pragmatism' and 'law as integrity'.

---

[23] ibid 190.

[24] ibid 93, paragraph break suppressed.

[25] In fact, Dworkin sees it as 'sufficiently abstract and uncontroversial', though nonetheless 'provisional': ibid.

'Conventionalism' can be regarded as a 'constructive' reworking of legal positivism, aiming not at the neutral description of the legal order, but at the interpretation of a domain of practical reason in the light of esteemed moral-political ideals of which it is considered to be the expression. Having accepted the provisional image of law as a constraint upon governmental power, it is necessary to enquire into the reasons that such a constraint should be deemed to be important. What purposes or values does it serve? (The interpretative stage.) But then what does it mean to say that the law 'licences' the use of power, and exactly when do they 'flow from' past decisions? (The post-interpretative stage.) Conventionalists, on Dworkin's definition, interpret the point of the law's constraint of power as being grounded in considerations of consistency and above all predictability. The law embodies published standards that give citizens 'fair warning' about the circumstances in which that power will be used against them, in the form of sanctions. Giving priority to the protection of expectations, conventionalists post-interpretatively construct the idea of 'consistency' quite narrowly, so that 'a right or responsibility flows from past decisions only if it is explicit within them or can be made explicit through methods or techniques conventionally accepted by the legal profession as a whole'.[26] Regarding law as a body of enacted rules, judges must limit themselves to interpreting and applying the explicit provisions of the rules. They may not attempt to derive general rights from the presence of allegedly systematic considerations in the law as a whole. Thus, if the rules do not offer a clear answer, judges are obliged to find 'some wholly forward-looking ground of decision'. In this way, conventionalism 'protects the authority of convention by insisting that conventional practices establish the end as well as the beginning of the past's power over the present'.[27]

Conventionalism, according to Dworkin, runs into certain problems. The notion of a 'convention' calls to mind fairly limited, settled rules upon which there is firm agreement. But when people begin to take an interpretative attitude towards their practices, they will complicate the situation considerably by calling into contention exactly what the conventions really require. (What actions, and on what occasions, does courtesy require?) In particular, is one's understanding of a conventional requirement in fact separate from the soundest interpretation of it? Faced with this question, Dworkin suggests that conventionalists will opt for one of two explanations. On the one hand, they might insist that the law of a community includes everything that lies within the implicit extension of its conventions ('soft' conventionalism). On the other, they may seek to maintain that conventions include only that

---

[26] ibid 95.
[27] ibid 118.

which it is virtually impossible for the community to disagree on, so that the law is restricted to the explicit wording of its statutes and precedents ('strict' conventionalism).

Strict conventionalism in this sense offers very little that is of importance in actual litigation. Seldom do the words of a statute admit of only one meaning, irrespective of the context of application. There is not usually one interpretation in the minds of all legislators who created it (so many statutes involving processes of compromise and refinement),[28] nor one common interpretation of its meaning in the minds of judges called upon to apply it. Much that we think of as being central to legal reasoning, in the context of judicial deliberation, would be propelled outside law, into the domain of 'discretion'. The idea of ratio decidendi—decisions at law—would have to give way to reasoning on the basis of moral and political opinion. The strict form of conventionalism therefore does not reflect the established patterns of ordinary legal practice. Paradoxically, a strict conventionalist judge

> would lose interest in legislation and precedent at just the point when it became clear that the explicit extension of these supposed conventions had run out. He would then acknowledge that there was no law, and he would have no further concern for consistency with the past; he would proceed to make new law.[29]

Perhaps there are some 'conventionalists' who would attempt to maintain this standpoint in the face of such criticisms. For them, the surface appearance of judicial argument acts as a means of obscuring what is really going on. Despite the court's detailed considerations in *Riggs v Palmer*, perhaps the judges should have swiftly found that the plaintiff was entitled to inherit, or else justified their contrary decision on the basis of considerations of a clearly extralegal, moral-political character. But in so doing, in propelling so much of legal thought and practice into the extralegal realm of politics, they would succeed only in establishing (paradoxically, as Dworkin says) the relative unimportance of conventions in the legal-political life of modern societies. 'Soft' conventionalism, by contrast, diminishes the idea of convention in another way. Nothing in it, Dworkin suggests, 'guarantees, or even promotes, the ideal of protected expectations, that past decisions will be relied on to justify collective force only so far as their authority and their terms are made uncontroversial by widely accepted conventions'.[30] It is in fact nothing less than an 'underdeveloped form of law as integrity' in which the field of legal vision is said to take in not only the explicit provisions of statutory rules and decisions, but the concepts,

---

[28] See O O'Neill's discussion of the 'Christmas tree effect' in 'Will Making Laws Better Make Better Laws?' (2012) 3 *Jurisprudence* 1.
[29] Dworkin, *Law's Empire* (n 5) 130.
[30] ibid 128.

ideals and ideas understood to be implicit in the system of rules considered as a whole.

If conventionalism does not 'fit' with legal practice as presently constituted, would it nevertheless provide a 'sound' or appealing ideal at which to aim? No. The ideas behind conventionalism are both positive and negative: positive in the sense that judges should apply the terms of clear, dispositive provisions which apply unambiguously to a case (in line with 'fair warning'); negative in that where no clear convention determines the outcome of a case, no right flows from previous decisions. Thus, if the protection of expectations truly lies at the centre of conventionalist concerns, the application of conventions should occur in a 'unilateral' way. That is to say, only in the case that a claimant can draw upon a clear rule to support their case should they win. In all other cases, they should lose. This process of thought is one that again clearly does not 'fit' with the way courts actually deliberate the relative merits of the litigants' positions. But more than this, it does not seem to embody a very just procedure. If the existing law does not clearly support either side, does it not severely abridge the enquiry to end deliberations at this point? Do we not expect judges fully to reason out the respective claims of the litigants in justice?

Perhaps one could therefore adopt an alternative strategy. One could respect the positive aspect of conventionalism by demanding that if *either* of the litigants can call upon a clear rule in their favour, the court must apply that rule (ie, they should win the case). But if neither party has a clear case in law, the court should not invariably interpret the negative aspect of conventionalism as demanding that the claimant loses. Although this might protect expectations in the sense that innovative forms of legal remedy do not spring forth unannounced from novel circumstances, the protection of expectations is not the *only* consideration to be considered. Equally important is the sense that the law must be responsive to the full variety of situations that confront it. The importance of predictability should not blunt the law's capacity to respond to the specific claims of those who appear before it, diminishing its ability to deal justly with litigants. Dworkin suggests that this is unsatisfactory. Why should the court be considered free to devote a full and exhaustive consideration to the justice of competing claims only in situations where the law is prima facie unclear? Indeed, in one sense, rules of law can only be deemed 'clear' when understood in context, ie, when all salient arguments have been heard and considered. To say that the claimant has a clear case is the same as saying that the defendant has no good case. Thus, a full and exhaustive attempt to do justice to the litigants cannot avoid considering the meaning and implications of the various applicable rules, in ways which (in responding directly to the opposing claims) include the potential for granting remedies in situations where none were previously awarded. It involves, in other words, an understanding of past decisions not only as establishing explicit rules, but also as a ground of individual *rights*.

On the one hand, therefore, this latter 'bilateral' approach to conventionalism once again collapses into a rudimentary form of the very conception of law that Dworkin wishes to defend: law as integrity. But on the other hand, if conventionalists of this kind wish doggedly to stick to the claim that explicit conventions are exhaustive of rights, then they must defend a position in which judges are conceived as balancing two opposing considerations in their application of law to specific cases. First, they must have due regard for the protection of expectations; but in certain situations, this consideration must give way to the need for innovation and flexibility in the law. This second consideration is then thought to license departures from the 'clear' rules where the needs of fairness or justice so demand. But if conventionalists do adopt this explanation, then their position has collapsed into a different conception of law: pragmatism.

Pragmatists on Dworkin's definition deny that past political decisions in and of themselves provide a justification for the use or withholding of the state's coercive power. (As alert readers may have realised, pragmatism therefore actually amounts to a denial of the 'abstract conception' of law rather than an interpretation of it as initially suggested.) For pragmatists, it is the justice or efficacy, or political value, of a given coercive decision that justifies that coercion. In contrast to bilateral conventionalism, consistency with previous rules and decisions is not in itself taken to constitute a requirement of justice. It need not in this sense be balanced against pragmatic considerations of efficacy, innovation or flexibility. But at the same time, consistency with the past has a pragmatic value of its own, so that it may appear as a residual consideration in juridical reasoning:

> [C]ivilization is impossible unless the decisions of some well-defined person or group are accepted by everyone as setting public standards that will be enforced if necessary through the police power. Only legislation can establish tax rates, structure markets, fix traffic codes and systems, stipulate permissible interest rates or determine which Georgian squares should be protected from modernization.[31]

Just as Hobbes reminded us that a world without law would leave everyone in a worse situation, pragmatism recognises the pragmatic value of consistency in decision-making.

It might be more difficult to convince a committed pragmatist that this form of pragmatism fails to 'fit' with existing patterns of judicial practice. Certainly, judges reason and behave as if litigants do possess legal rights which it is the purpose of adjudication to define and uphold. But it would be possible to put this 'surface' feature of legal argumentation down to a constant appreciation

---

[31] ibid 153.

of the pragmatic value of consistency ('consistency in strategy' as opposed to 'consistency in principle'). The overriding concern of pragmatism is to make the future less unjust in its treatment of individuals. For this reason, it cannot avoid amending or departing from previous decisions when strategic conditions permit. 'Bad' precedents can be confined to their facts, or at least to a narrowly circumscribed range of situations. The law contains so many divergent lines of authority. Judgments in 'hard' cases are invariably controversial. Should the sense of controversy not therefore attach to the most important consideration: which decision will result in the greatest efficiency or the fewest occasions of injustice in the future? Above all, 'How can consistency in principle be important for its own sake, particularly when it is uncertain and controversial what consistency really requires?'[32]

Amongst the responses it is possible to give to this question is the following: does the pragmatist truly understand what would be lost by treating rights, in effect, as purely pragmatic considerations? The law absolutely has to treat parties to a case as bearers of genuine rights and duties. By limiting the possibility of recovery to those situations in which another has infringed an 'entitlement', the law ensures that not all damage or loss caused to a person will result in the award of a remedy. Recognition of pervasive and infinitely variable forms of *damnum absque iniuria* is essential to the maintenance of that freedom from the will of others that is central to liberal (and indeed tolerable) societies.[33] Part of that freedom consists in the freedom from constant or frequent interference by others who find one's daily activities objectionable even if they do not cause legally recognised forms of injury: the loss of customers to one's business caused by the opening of a rival store next door being a clear example, but also including a person's practising of a religion that her neighbours deem to be against truth and objectionable on that ground. Imagine a situation in which a white male feels harmed, or wronged, or threatened by living next door to a new neighbour who is black. Or gay. Suppose that this triggers genuine medical anxiety or depression. Suppose that the claimant correctly complains that the presence of an Islamic neighbour has lowered the market value of their house. Such complaints are rightly excluded. But they can only be excluded by the presence of genuine rights, functioning as the measure (in judgement) of what is due to each of the litigants. Pragmatic considerations cannot function as the ground of legal duties without utterly destroying the boundary between actionable harms and those which, as a direct consequence of living in close and permanent relations with others, have to be endured, absorbed or manoeuvered around. To eliminate this distinction is to render everyone potentially liable (on pragmatic grounds) to others in all respects.

---

[32] ibid 163.
[33] See NE Simmonds, *Law as a Moral Idea* (Oxford, Oxford University Press, 2007) chs 3 and 6.

Lacking any true freedom from the will of others, individuals would no longer enjoy a 'private' life nor a stable basis for an ordered, secure existence.

Dworkin's criticisms could be expressed as the realisation that questions of justice cannot be isolated from a systematic context of reflection. The very practice of judgement demands the treatment of particular situations as belonging to a broader horizon within which they possess significance. Law can implement justice only by embodying the systematic *administration* of justice. At the same time, we know that the law is not a perfect expression of justice. The very systematic considerations that prevent each case being regarded wholly in isolation can produce particular outcomes that seem less than just.

In fact, Dworkin explains the situation differently. We know that not every legal decision seems wholly just in our eyes. The demand that we make of the law is, he says, therefore not that it instantiate a perfect justice, but the weaker demand that the law exhibit 'integrity': coherence and consistency of principle in a world in which we remain divided about the demands of justice. Indeed, integrity might come into conflict with the demands of justice. In Western societies, for example, some people are deeply committed to the principle that abortion is morally wrong, and that the law should not permit such a practice (unless perhaps in very restricted circumstances). Others just as vehemently insist upon the right of choice in such situations attaching to the pregnant woman. In such circumstances, why should not the state enact a 'checkerboard statute' that allows (say) every second application for an abortion to succeed, and turns the rest down. Dworkin points out that such a solution could be deemed to be fair in giving equal weight to each person's view. Indeed, he argues that such a solution fits in with the demands of justice, since those in favour of allowing abortions would surely prefer (as being less unjust) such a statute to one that banned all abortions; whilst those who oppose abortion would regard the outcome as more just than a situation in which *all* abortions were permitted. Dworkin suggests that our instincts nevertheless condemn the idea, because it conflicts with the virtue of integrity. In order to defend the solution, one would need to appeal to principles (such as those of individual liberty, autonomy and women's right to choose) in order to justify some of its outcomes that one would be obliged to oppose directly when defending its outcomes in other cases.

Perhaps we should not be so easily convinced of this. The reason why Dworkin is able to suggest that checkerboard solutions may be in line with considerations of justice is that such strategies 'will prevent instances of injustice that would otherwise occur, and we cannot say that justice requires not eliminating any injustice unless we can eliminate all'.[34] He is able to say this

---

[34] ibid 181.

because, in his view, 'Justice is a matter of outcomes.'[35] Is it? In the classical treatments of justice, that idea is not restricted to the denotation of a particular situation, nor confined to the description of an outcome (the *iustum*), but is (in Aquinas's terms) simultaneously an aspect of *prudentia*: practical wisdom. It thus pertains to the process of reasoning itself. Indeed, one can ask how one can possibly comprehend whether a situation is just or otherwise until it has been fully reasoned out in justice. Surely the 'checkerboard' solution is a severe abridgement of the enquiry that has to take place, an enquiry into *what is due to each person*. Does not the checkerboard solution simply ignore that question? Whatever one's position in relation to abortions, a situation in which a key demand of justice (the formal equality of treating like cases alike) is so flagrantly absent should not be defended *by anyone* as representing a more complete satisfaction of the demands of justice.

One might question whether the idea of consistency and coherence of principle represents a useful ideal for guiding juridical deliberation. On the one hand, to isolate these values from broader considerations of justice is to short-circuit the very difficult enquiry that has to be undertaken. If one believes in justice, one believes it to demand more than mere consistency of principle. But on the other hand, the attempt to state coherent principles can easily bring about a rather legalistic and inflexible attitude to morality in which principles begin to enjoy intellectual priority over a very sensitive and textured concern with the complexity of human situations. The traditional approaches to justice had considered justice first and foremost as a virtue (*iustitia*), the possession of a habit of mind, coexisting alongside other virtues such as temperance, *humanitas* and mercy. The requirements of justice in specific situations would therefore emerge in the deliberations of one whose interpretation of the situation is guided by those right habits of mind.[36] Such knowledge may be of a kind that does not reduce, without great distortion or impoverishment, to a set of principles.[37]

The processes of deliberation in the common law seem to exhibit some of the characteristics of ethical reflection as outlined by Aristotle. When the Court in *Hadley v Baxendale*[38] set down the basic principle for determining the scope of consequential damages arising from a breach of contract, it did not put to an end the process of speculating about the limits, the appropriate criteria, or even the very basis of the principle. Already in the later case of *Victoria*

---

[35] ibid 180.

[36] See, eg, Aristotle, *Nicomachean Ethics* VI.11.

[37] See Aquinas, *Summa Theologiae* I–II.100.11; I–II.94.4. Aquinas distinguishes the foundational aspects of justice and common morality from ends and values that are open to disagreement by distinguishing 'the most general precepts' open to *prudentia* (practical wisdom) with the considerations that these precepts point to as their ends. See further below, chs 9 and 10.

[38] *Hadley v Baxendale* [1854] EWCH J70.

Laundry (Windsor) Ltd v Newman Industries Ltd[39] issues surrounding the remoteness of damages were a topic of considerable controversy. Over a century after *Hadley*, Lord Goff in *Satef-Huttenes Albertus SpA v Paloma Tercera Shipping Co SA (The Pegase)*[40] revisited the entire rationale of the decision:

> [T]hough the principle stated in *Hadley v Baxendale* remains the *fons et origo* of the modern law, the principle itself has been analysed and developed, and its application broadened, in the 20th century ... The general result ... is that the principle in *Hadley v Baxendale* is now no longer stated in terms of two rules, but rather in terms of a single principle—though it is recognised that the application of the principle may depend on the degree of relevant knowledge held by the defendant at the time of the contract in the particular case. This approach accords very much to what actually happens in practice; the courts have not been over-ready to pigeon-hole the cases under one or other of the so-called rules in *Hadley v Baxendale*, but rather to decide each case on the basis of the relevant knowledge of the defendant.

One can see these constant revisitations as reflective of grounds of decision that are entirely resistant (unless with great loss) to finite statement in the form of principles. In yet other examples, it is (as all law students know) an intellectually challenging exercise to state precisely what the ratio decidendi is. This is not because judges are inept or unclear about stating the principles underlying their decisions, but because the contextual considerations that inform the grounds of the decision may not be capable of being extracted in a way that allows a clear general principle to be stated.

As already mentioned, Dworkin pays insufficient attention to the fact that part of the requirements of justice is the systematic administration of justice. We consequently find him arguing that the 'value' of 'justice' (which is 'a matter of the right outcome of a political system') must be intellectually separated from the value of 'fairness' ('a matter of the right structure for [a political] system') and that of 'procedural due process' ('the right procedures for enforcing rules and regulations the system has produced').[41] It is the potential for 'conflict' between these values that produces the concern for 'integrity' as a distinct political value. The result is a vision of law that not only distorts the image of justice, but divests the law itself of moral significance as the essential *form* in which justice is to be implemented in society. Thus, the operation of precedent and stare decisis, the 'practices of legislative history' and doctrinal judgements of 'local priority' are not themselves considerations that are relevant to justice.[42]

---

[39] *Victoria Laundry (Windsor) Ltd v Newman Industries Ltd* [1949] 2 KB 528.

[40] *Satef-Huttenes Albertus SpA v Paloma Tercera Shipping Co SA (The Pegase)* [1981] 1 Lloyd's Rep 175, 181.

[41] Dworkin, *Law's Empire* (n 5) 404–05.

[42] ibid 405: they are matters of 'procedural due process' which might compete with or impinge upon the requirements of justice. See also the interesting discussion of 'associative

This might lead us to ask: is the form of law itself not morally significant? Beyond questions of the fairness of the operation of social institutions, are there not questions we can raise about law as a distinctive kind of social institution? In chapter ten, we will encounter the views of the jurist Lon Fuller, who regards legality itself as morally significant, as distinct from the actual substance of legal rules.[43] But we have already touched upon one aspect of this significance. The law's imposition of coercive rules, its recognition of rights and obligations as operatively linked to the existence of such rules, guarantees a situation in which the individual legal subject is offered the protection of specific dimensions of privacy and freedom, and is treated as the bearer of certain capacities of rational choice and self-determination. It is arguable that to obliterate these freedoms, to deny the exercise of these capacities, requires more than the enactment of repressive laws: it requires a departure from the practices of legality itself.[44]

OBJECTIVITY, TRUTH AND SCEPTICISM

The above line of criticism differs significantly from the two main types of objection that Dworkin in fact anticipates: 'internal' and 'external' scepticism.[45] An internal sceptic (on Dworkin's definition) is one who asserts that the complexity of the law, the plurality of its various aims, the presence of divergent lines of precedent etc, precludes the possibility of discovering a consistent moral-political theory within the law of the kind Dworkin promotes. Dworkin's response is to accuse the internal sceptic of overestimating the significance of conflicts between differing values in particular situations. Our convictions are themselves complex, and it is entirely possible to feel the pull of competing considerations in reaching one's moral judgement. But nothing about these competing values should suggest that the law is finally morally incoherent or self-contradictory. To make such a declaration is simply to have terminated one's reflections at an arbitrary point, leaving unexplored the extent to which those values can be regimented within an overarching vision of the law's coherence (or 'integrity').

obligations' ibid: 195–206. This discussion, to my mind the most interesting in the book, is informed by the idea of integrity, and makes no mention of ideas that seem absolutely central to the duties to which Dworkin wishes to draw attention, and which specify their basis and extent: commutative and distributive *justice*. I will postpone discussion of these ideas to their logical place in chs 7 and 8.

[43] See ch 9 below.
[44] See in particular the discussion in ch 9 below.
[45] Dworkin, *Law's Empire* (n 5) 78–85.

External scepticism questions the very coherence of relying upon 'moral' values, suggesting that all such values are in the end subjective. The dimension of 'soundness' in interpretation is obliterated, forcing Dworkin's account of law back upon varying preferences which are alone responsible for our 'values'. Here, Dworkin points to the internal inconsistency of the sceptical position. Suppose I agree that murder is morally wrong. Is it open to me to assert that this is simply 'my opinion', and not an objective fact? There is no doubt that there are true and false opinions, and that we distinguish between truth and opinion for that very reason. But Dworkin nevertheless argues that I cannot *commit* myself to the statement 'It is wrong to murder' without also committing myself to the claim that 'It is true that it is wrong to murder'. My opinion might well turn out to be wrong; but I cannot assert claims as *mere* opinion. In saying that I have no room to deny the second proposition, Dworkin adheres to a position in which the two statements, 'It is wrong to murder' and 'It is true that it is wrong to murder' express the same claim (mean the same thing). One cannot honestly and sincerely assert a claim without honestly and sincerely asserting its truth. Dworkin believes that all 'meta-ethical' statements ('There are such things as moral truths', 'Murder *really is* wrong', 'It is a *fact* that murder is wrong' and so forth) thus boil down to moral commitments; they are a way of giving more emphatic emphasis to one's ordinary moral claims.[46]

The line of argument I pressed above embodies neither of these forms of scepticism. But it demonstrates the shortcomings of Dworkin's responses to the internal and external sceptics. I suggested that Dworkin misunderstands the nature of justice (as grounded in practical reason), and of the implementation of justice as connected to the very form of law: namely as a piece of work that is never finished, and as a value that is never fully realised in human efforts, and never entirely visualised without distortion. If it is true that our reasoning about the justice of practical means and ends does not reduce, except at the cost of great impoverishment, to a set of coherent principles, then it remains open to suggest that Dworkinian 'integrity' in law can only be bought at the price of artificiality. That is to say, the law can only be rendered coherent and consistent through the suppression of distinctive and competing concerns that lawyers have believed and continue to believe are important.[47]

---

[46] See R Dworkin, *Justice for Hedgehogs* (Cambridge MA, Harvard University Press, 2011), 25: 'I reject the idea of an external, meta-ethical inspection of moral truth. I insist that any sensible moral scepticism must be internal to morality'. See further *Justice for Hedgehogs* chs 2, 3 and 5; see also R Dworkin, 'Objectivity and Truth: You'd Better Believe It' (1996) 25 *Philosophy and Public Affairs* 87.

[47] We might ask, in this context, whether the 'coherence' of law (or of morality itself) is a matter of conformity to a body of principles, or instead of the collective intelligibility of discrete and divergent practices that belong to a shared form of life.

On the other hand, it seems perfectly intelligible to ask whether the human capacity to reason about practical ends may not itself be corrupted, whether on the basis of 'original sin' or of Kantian concerns about our failure to demonstrate true 'autonomy', such that justice can never be fully implemented at the level of human institutions. The questions that it is possible to ask about human beings' ability to perceive moral truth do not seem directly reducible or equivalent to 'ordinary' moral commitments. Dworkin's relentless suppression of this metaphysical perspective (despite the considerable complexity of his argument) is nothing other than the presentation of a specific conception of morality (morality understood as a set of law-like principles deriving from individual 'convictions') as the only possible understanding of morality. It is to present a vision of Protestant individualism as the inevitable basis of political-moral theory, by suppressing the metaphysical and theological assumptions which make it possible.

Similar considerations can be levelled against Dworkin's own vision of 'law as integrity'. The idea traditionally at the heart of liberal politics was that of the 'open' society. There are no 'ideal' social arrangements upon which everyone can agree. In the absence of consensus, law must permit the coexistence of numerous opposing ideologies, without allowing any one of them to become the sole principle of social organisation. The future is itself 'open'. Law can ensure the subsistence of social peace and order in such conditions only to the extent to which people remain willingly subject to considerations of justice and shared rules. One may regard Dworkin's theory as nothing other than the conversion of this liberal vision to the point where the open society is itself deemed to represent 'the ideal society', and its underpinning ideological commitments are elevated to the status of universal moral-political demands: praising the ambition of his 'country's most fundamental contribution to political morality', Dworkin proudly notes:

> We have been envied for our adventure and we are now increasingly copied all over the world, from Strasbourg to Capetown, from Budapest to Dehli. Let's not lose our nerve, when all around the world other people, following our example, are gaining theirs.[48]

The political vision at the heart of *Law's Empire* is an imperial vision indeed.

PHILOSOPHER-KINGS AND PHILOSOPHER-JUDGES

Where does this leave us? Plato's image of the philosopher-ruler in the *Republic* is premised upon an essentially pessimistic vision of politics. The philosopher who has escaped the Cave of conventional understandings perceives things

---

[48] Dworkin, *Justice in Robes* (n 17) 138–39.

aright, in their proper form, and is thus in a much better position to govern according to justice than those whose eyes are clouded and deceived by false images. Constantly people mistake justice for that which offers fulfilment to their dearest interests and desires. But Plato suggests that, so radical a revision of ordinary understandings is necessary to place society onto the right path, the philosopher will fail in his endeavour. Either the people will scorn and abuse him, treating him as a corrupting influence as they did Socrates, or the philosopher will himself become gradually corrupted by the very power he wields for the public good, sliding gradually back into unenlightened practices.

Dworkin's image of the philosopher-judge entertains no such doubts and anxieties. Where Plato worries whether the proper course for the philosopher is not to withdraw from public life altogether, seeking a kind of monastic purity, Dworkin crowns the servants of the law as 'Justice in robes'. Plato ultimately suggests that the philosopher must, in the end, seek to serve the City, lest his achievements amount to a beautiful but sterile life. But there is no sure way to protect oneself against the worst and most corrupting aspects social life, in the all too difficult task of bringing justice to the world, unless it be to walk constantly with humility and avoid intellectual pride. The image of Hercules seems scarcely to acknowledge the existence of the problem: as if the excellence and argumentative cleverness of the principles themselves (in embarrassing opposing viewpoints) is proof enough against moral failure. Beware their terrible certainties, 'O wretched generation of enlightened men, Betrayed in the mazes of your ingenuities'!

SUGGESTED READING

INTERPRETATIVE METHODOLOGY AND INTEGRITY

R Dworkin, *Law's Empire* (London, Fontana Press, 1986) chs 1–7.
—— *A Matter of Principle* (Oxford, Oxford University Press, 1985) chs 5 and 6.
—— *Justice in Robes* (Cambridge MA, Harvard University Press, 2006) chs 6–7.
—— *Justice for Hedgehogs* (Cambridge MA, Harvard University Press, 2011) chs 6–8 and 19.

Background Reading

HLA Hart, *The Concept of Law*, 3rd edn (Oxford, Clarendon Press, 2012) Postscript.
—— 'The New Challenge to Legal Positivism (1979)' (2016) 36 *Oxford Journal of Legal Studies* 459.
S Hershowitz, *Exploring Law's Empire* (Oxford, Oxford University Press, 2006).
G Postema, 'Integrity: Justice in Work Clothes' in J Burley (ed), *Dworkin and His Critics. With Replies by Dworkin* (London, Blackwell, 2004).
A Ripstein, *Ronald Dworkin* (Cambridge, Cambridge University Press, 2007).

Approach to Scepticism and Objectivity

R Dworkin, *A Matter of Principle* (Oxford, Oxford University Press, 1985) ch 7.
—— *Justice in Robes* (Cambridge MA, Harvard University Press, 2006) ch 4.
—— *Justice for Hedgehogs* (Cambridge MA, Harvard University Press, 2011) chs 2–5.
—— 'Objectivity and Truth: You'd Better Believe It' (1996) 25 *Philosophy and Public Affairs* 87.

Background Reading

R Hanson, 'Objective Decision Making in Lonergan and Dworkin' (2003) 44 *Boston College Law Review* 825.
NE Simmonds, *Law as a Moral Idea* (Oxford, Oxford University Press, 2007) ch 1 and pp 74–77.

8

Justice and the Liberal State: Rawls

FROM ONE VISION of justice to another: that of John Rawls. It is at first tempting to say that whereas Dworkin asserts the impossibility of realising justice in the imperfect conditions of the 'real world', preferring instead the value of 'integrity', Rawls (1921–2002) offers a concrete image of the ideally just, but nonetheless earthly, society. One should not, in a sense, read too much into these differences. Both outlooks, for example, are underpinned by a conception of practical reasoning informed by the method of 'reflective equilibrium'. Both are critical of, and are conceived in part as responses to, utilitarianism. But more than anything, the initial abstraction of Rawls's argument eventually (and remarkably) gives way to a vision of the ideal society that is in many respects the mirror of that which Dworkin thinks should be celebrated beyond all others: liberal democracy.

Rawls's great book, *A Theory of Justice*, is actually a response to two different intellectual traditions within liberalism: utilitarianism and intuitionism. Of intuitionism, I shall say more shortly. But why, one might ask, was it necessary to challenge the two great pillars of liberalism's moral philosophy, the traditional bases of its justification, in the first place? The fact was that utilitarianism was capable of differing interpretations, and was capable of being called into the service of very different political ideologies. In its original and 'classical' form, it served as the basis for liberalism. If all persons are equal, then the differing sources and opposing kinds of their 'happiness' must also be considered equal, and given equal priority. There is not one form of 'the good' that is common for all people in a society, but many kinds of thing experienced as good by many persons. Lacking anything by way of intrinsic value, these causes of happiness are to be measured by way of the levels of wellbeing produced. They are simply neutral 'units of utility'.[1] Liberal society should not discriminate between sources of utility, apart from their effect. It should not set limits upon the pursuit of utility in any of its forms except insofar as the resultant harms outweigh the positive utility produced: freedom, like utility, should be maximised. Or rather, freedom should be permitted to exist to the highest extent that is compatible with the maximisation of utility.

---

[1] See ch 6 above.

The focus on measurability almost inevitably produces a society that gives priority to rather venal tendencies and objectives. Property and consumption are easier to take account of than such phenomena as satisfaction or spiritual fulfilment. The close association between liberalism and the free market is not an accident: the liberalisation of the land and labour markets, the mobilisation of capital, break down fixed hierarchies that would otherwise disrupt the human being's pursuit of his or her wants. The emphasis is placed firmly upon the distribution of the needs and luxuries of material life. Market forces are a more effective maximiser of material satisfactions than any centralised scheme. The 'rights' which are given to such persons are primarily economic rights, and human equality is primarily an equality of entitlement in this respect.

But utilitarianism can also be given a collectivist interpretation. Socialists could point to the fact that true equality demands a more substantial fulfilment of each person's needs, for which mere property rights are insufficient. True equality demands equality of income, of opportunity, of resources: the communistic sharing of property.[2] But one cannot produce a communistic state without revolution, without sacrificing the interests and perhaps the needs of the minority. Communism cannot take root without the suppression of dissidents, and the immolation of those considered as being neither 'workers' nor 'comrades'. The communist tyrannies of the East represented a kind of Machiavellian utilitarianism in which the sacrifice of minorities was justified as being a necessary step towards the ultimate wellbeing of the majority.[3] Pain in the present would pave the way for a future bliss, or at least a future justice.

It became necessary for Western moral theory to seek a surer foundation for its moral doctrines. Liberal utilitarianism could not effectively respond to communism insofar as the latter could be seen as its logical fruition.[4] One could argue endlessly about which variant would be vindicated by history. Liberals therefore took the only path open to them: they denied the very premise of Machiavellian political theory, the idea that the ultimate tribunal of politics is none other than History itself. The means can only be justified by the ends if history itself possesses a certain meaning. Only if the communist state is the 'culmination' of human history can one morally justify the violence

---

[2] See E Perreau-Saussine, 'The Moral Critique of Stalinism' in P Blackledge and K Knight (eds), *Virtue and Politics: Alasdair MacIntyre's Revolutionary Aristotelianism* (Notre Dame IN, University of Notre Dame Press, 2011) 139. Also *cf* the discussion of Finnis's theory of justice, ch 9 below.

[3] Perreau-Saussine (n 2) 138.

[4] Perhaps this lies behind the thought, expressed by Rawls in 1990, that 'The primary reason for wanting to find such an alternative [to utilitarianism] is the weakness, so I think, of utilitarian doctrine *as a basis for the institutions of constitutional democracy*'. J Rawls, *A Theory of Justice*, rev ed (Oxford, Oxford University Press, 1999) xi–xii (hereafter *TJ*).

that attends its production: morality must itself be subordinated to history, and given a purely historical meaning. For communists, history cries out for urgent solutions whilst men of 'moral wisdom' pursue their pleasing thoughts in their ivory towers. The production of just conditions cannot be achieved without a fight. Those who stand in the way of progress must be dealt with. The revolution demands bloody deeds. It is necessary to suppress conscientious indignation, which achieves nothing and prevents every useful thing, and to tear out bleeding hearts. The plane of 'abstract morality' must give way to the concrete realities of politics. History itself would vindicate the communist state.

Those communists who followed the doctrines of Marxism liked to contrast the 'abstract purity' of morality with the relativity of all actions, the sense that every human effort is fraught with ambiguity and that none is unalloyedly 'good'. What use is such a morality, when it cannot be applied to the actions of this life, when it permits injustices to reign out of fear of making everything worse?[5] Rawls's response was to reassert a conception of morality that emphatically demands universality in the face of these imperfect relativities. The lesson to be drawn from humanity's imperfection is not that 'perfect' morality shall be replaced by history, that the status of all means is determined by their ends, but that history itself is totally unsuitable as a tribunal of judgment: human actions are judged by a morality that transcends history, are subject to a moral law of which the world has not seen a perfect example.

The basis of the political vision in *A Theory of Justice* is Kantian. One who follows the Categorical Imperative is incapable of viewing history as normative, and cannot derive principles of action from the concrete circumstances of any particular body politic. Nothing less than universality is demanded. Hence, Rawls begins his treatment of justice by asking us to imagine a situation in which a group of rational agents faces the task of determining the basic structure and institutions of their society. As a Christian brought up on images of the Fall, Rawls would have been keenly aware of the propensity of such agents to create structures which are tilted, in ways both conscious and unconscious, in favour of their particular interests. The best intentions of men are nothing if not infinitely corruptible. He might have drawn from

---

[5] Though this line of thinking is most closely associated with Leninist-Marxism, I feel justified in attributing it more widely as the ultimate logic of Marxism in practice. It is true that dictatorial communist regimes persecuted academics not for their failure to espouse or defend Marxist doctrines, but for their all too close support (Pashukanis is a good example). But one cannot ultimately separate convincingly an intellectual position (ie, Marxist *doctrine*) from the concrete political movements and actions that are carried on in its name. All political systems have their ideal forms; one learns more about the practical operation of their doctrines (including their resilience, immunity from corruption, commitment to justice etc) from the historical record of their achievements and travesties.

Kant the thought, painted so vividly and with such urgency in *Religion Within the Boundaries of Mere Reason*, but present also in the *Groundwork of the Metaphysics of Morals*, that human reason is endlessly subject to distortion arising from the immediacy of one's fleshly wants and interests, the attainment of which is so easily mistaken for a demand of justice (of what is due to one).[6] One must therefore imagine such agents as conducting their deliberations behind a 'veil of ignorance', deprived of all specific knowledge of themselves: all those personal characteristics (such as able-bodiedness or disability, health or sickness, intelligence or slow-wittedness, wealth or poverty, sexual orientation, gender, political or moral standpoints etc) that distinguish one individual from another. Deprived of such knowledge, agents would obviously lack any sense of the particular conception of the 'good life' that they would hold when properly embodied. Their deliberations, therefore, would be conducted under conditions (or within limitations) that would seem to guarantee fairness, that is to say, lack of conscious or unconscious bias towards certain favoured values or states of affairs. Such agents could not afford to be anything other than strictly neutral towards opposing conceptions of the good.

In this way, Rawls seeks to persuade his readers that the conditions of this 'original position'—conditions upon rational choice—are fair ones, so as to guarantee that the results of the deliberation will be just. If this sounds plausible, then it is all the more remarkable that having begun from such an abstract and ahistorical position, and having embarked upon over 500 pages of systematic argument, Rawls arrives at a theory of justice—that is, of the 'basic structure' and institutional organisation of society—that resembles very closely the current political arrangements of the United States: a commitment to representative democracy, liberal individualism and the rule of law centred upon an idea of human rights.[7] Liberalism is vindicated after all! The culmination of human history turns out not to consist in communist dictatorship but liberal and democratic governance.

RATIONAL REFLECTION AND QUESTIONS OF METHOD

The other great pillar of liberalist moral theory was intuitionism. In attending to the fact of liberal disagreement, one might suppose that there are simply a number of alternative and irreducibly conflicting principles of justice between which some collective choice is nonetheless necessary. Can one do better than

---

[6] I Kant, *Groundwork of the Metaphysics of Morals*, M Gregor and J Timmermann trans (Cambridge, Cambridge University Press, 2012); *Religion Within the Boundaries of Mere Reason*, A Wood and G Di Giovanni trans (Cambridge, Cambridge University Press, 1998).

[7] See R Geuss, *Outside Ethics* (Princeton NJ, Princeton University Press, 2005) chs 1–3.

attempt to weigh and balance the opposing principles against each other, hoping in this way to arrive at a considered judgement as to which, on balance, appears the most just or reasonable? Aside from this considered judgement, there exist no more fundamental or overarching criteria of rationality for preferring one idea of justice to another. This is 'intuitionism'.

Is it true to say that reason reaches no deeper than this, that it supplies no more fundamental grounds for decision than an ultimately ungrounded choice between different, seemingly reasonable proposals? Rawls is aware that people in a liberal society disagree, apparently fundamentally and intractably, about a range of complicated and often highly tangled issues. But his suggestion is that, faced with such dilemmas, one should proceed by abstracting from the concrete particulars of disagreement, seeking agreement on more general principles that will seem reasonable or defensible to all persons, no matter what their particular views might be. Proceeding in this way, various principles and proposals may seem plausible, though in mutual opposition. A choice is certainly needed: but Rawls wants to demonstrate that the choice is not at the same time 'ungrounded', but rational; not arbitrary, but reasoned.

I shall say more on the subject of the original position below, and of the particular constraints on reasoning that it entails. For the moment, one should note two things. First, if one accepts those restraints as imposing 'fair' conditions upon rational choice, then one must presumably accept that the deliberations and their outcome will likewise be fair, and not simply arbitrary. This leaves open the question, however, whether those placed in the original position will be capable of agreeing upon anything at all: might their discussions not result in deadlock or paralysis, as between a number of reasonable sounding alternatives between which a decisive rational choice seems impossible? As is made clear from the body of Rawls's text, discussed below, this is not a situation that Rawls considers likely, perhaps even impossible given the conditions established. But in case our confidence is less than Rawls's, it is important to remember the second thing: the original position is not the only device that Rawls employs to convince us of the validity of his position. Rawls equally insists that a theory of justice must be grounded in, and guided by, our moral intuitions 'considered in reflective equilibrium'.[8]

Having arrived at what we think to be a plausible conception of justice, it is not sufficient to find arguments in its favour deriving from the original position. There are, as Rawls says, 'several things to do': one of which involves working out the consequences of its principles for institutions and note their implications for social policy.[9] In doing so, our perception of the plausibility of the principles might shift, as they are applied directly to concrete institutional

---

[8] For an account of reflective equilibrium, see *TJ*, 42–45.
[9] ibid 132.

realities, causing certain revisions to the conception of justice itself. But at the same time, the principles of justice, in being abstract, guide our understanding and interpretation of the concrete realities from the perspective of justice, allowing us to engage in critical reflection upon them.

This hints at a solution to the problem of why individuals deliberating about the basic structure of their society should ever converge in their judgements: but it is a solution that raises as many questions as it answers. Rawls invites his readers to reflect upon the difference between 'considered judgements' and others that people tend to make in less favourable conditions. Where people feel under pressure, or threatened, or upset, or know that they stand to gain or lose a great deal, their judgements are in general less trustworthy, as being in a natural way focused on self-interest and prone to error. Considered judgements are those rendered under more congenial conditions, allowing for a greater sense of proportion, objectivity, perhaps even detachment. Under these conditions, one may be presented with interpretations of social institutions that conform substantially to one's initial judgements (one's sense of justice), with perhaps only certain minor variations and amendments. Whilst the process of reflective equilibrium under these conditions may result in a modest change in views, no great or radical change in outlook is likely to take place. One would, in effect, have before one a range (maybe only a small range) of interpretations of the institutions of liberal political order. On the other hand, one could be presented with all possible interpretations that might be said to relate to one's initial judgements, when considered in the light of the philosophical and moral arguments that could be advanced in support of them. Here, one's initial sense of justice may or may not undergo a radical shift: images of the basic structure might present themselves that are suggestive of quite significant departures from the features that typify one's present regime.

The methodology of *A Theory of Justice* endorses a procedure of the second, broader kind. The original position is a heuristic device that neatly encapsulates some of the conditions required for deliberation along these lines. Prescinding from all contentious images of 'the good life' as such, rational deliberators should set themselves the task of identifying principles that could be held by anyone who possessed such a conception; and the appropriate way to do this is to imagine such persons as being deprived of the knowledge of which conception they possess, whilst retaining the knowledge that they possess one. It nevertheless remains that the effect of this 'broadening out' is just as likely to engender disagreement as to bring people together. With the whole of moral philosophy to consider, would not agreement in fact prove more difficult to procure?

In later work, Rawls can be seen as offering a change of direction, or at least of emphasis. In his book *Political Liberalism*, he admits that the theory put forward in *A Theory of Justice* (that which is agreed upon by those in the original position) cannot be advanced as a 'comprehensive philosophical doctrine'. Not only would such a level of agreement be highly unlikely in a society characterised by wide variations in philosophical, political and religious beliefs, but it may indeed be incompatible with the very idea of liberal society. The 'open' society is characterised by an ongoing market in ideas: the point at which consensus is achieved and one set of ideas becomes the sole principle of political and social organisation, is one that represents the effective closure of society. More than that, Rawls came to believe that such a consensus could only establish itself, and would certainly only be maintained, through coercion or repression of dissident viewpoints. *Political Liberalism* therefore presents the doctrines of *A Theory of Justice* (together with certain changes of emphasis and detail) as a political theory for a specifically liberal society: a doctrine that can be supported by persons who possess deeply-held but competing outlooks, and who (precisely in being passionately committed to their outlook) wish to maintain the conditions that allow for the holding of opposing views. To this extent, the theory is presented as an idealised interpretation of liberal political order: closer in spirit to the narrower of the two characterisations of reflective equilibrium above.

This shift of emphasis from the rationality of his principles to their political acceptability comes at a price. For it makes it very difficult to accommodate the traditional critical role that conceptions of justice play in evaluating the soundness of practices and institutions, and the validity of the understandings that maintain them in place. Drawing itself from those very understandings, how can the theory of justice evaluate liberal political order as itself just, or unjust? This sense of uneasiness is perhaps most keenly felt in relation to Rawls's treatment of international relations in *The Law of Peoples*. In that book, Rawls suggests that liberal societies must play a leading role in developing a just 'law of peoples': one that is fair in establishing a place within a 'reasonable' world order for 'decent' or 'benevolent' states which are not liberal, yet which ought to be 'tolerated' by liberal states, but at the same time allowing liberal states to attack, and maintain a nuclear deterrent against, 'outlaw states' where necessary to defend human rights.[10] It is not difficult to appreciate the significant loss of theoretical scope and power resultant upon the lack of a robust and comprehensive defence of liberal political order.

These reflections provide some context in which to evaluate the arguments of *A Theory of Justice*, and to consider the scheme of justice that it puts forward. It is to these that we must now turn in detail.

---

[10] J Rawls, *The Law of Peoples* (Cambridge MA, Harvard University Press, 1999) 80–81.

THE PROBLEM OF JUSTICE

Human societies are characterised by a certain identity of interests (social cooperation results in a more fulfilling and commodious life than can be brought about if we each live by our own efforts), but also a certain conflict of interests: people are not indifferent as to how the benefits of cooperation are to be distributed, each in general preferring a larger share to enhance pursuit of their own ends. The problem of justice arises directly out of the need to choose between the various distributional proposals. These are principles of 'social justice' in that they result in the definition of social arrangements for the division of advantages.

For this reason, 'the primary subject of justice is the basic structure of society', due to the fact that men born into different positions have different expectations of life determined precisely by their political, economic and social circumstances.[11] The classical arguments about justice had centred upon the question of what is due to each person; but Rawls objects that the very pervasive and deep inequalities that arise from disparity in social situations cannot possibly be justified by reference to merit or desert. Rawls points out that Aristotle's definition of justice, as the avoidance of *pleonexia* (the gaining of an advantage by seizing that which properly belongs to another), is parasitic upon a prior identification of how property is to be distributed in the first place. It is impossible to determine whether I have unjustly taken another's property, or have failed to accord due respect, repay a debt, fulfil a promise and so on, unless we first have some notion of what properly belongs to, or is due to, the other. Such entitlements, Rawls argues, 'very often derived from social institutions and the legitimate expectations to which they give rise'.[12] Shall we know whether a person's entitlements are justly identified until we have satisfied ourselves of the justice of the social arrangements from which they derive?

Rawls suggests that Aristotle would not disagree with his approach. But the arguments of *A Theory of Justice* belong to a tradition of thinking that sees questions of *distribution* as logically prior to those questions referred to under the banner of 'corrective' justice (or 'commutative justice' in Aquinas's terms). The idea is that, once a fair distribution of resources, offices, responsibilities and so on has been determined, matters of 'correction' or compensation arise only because human beings have failed fully to comply with the demands of the distributional scheme. Such matters pertain only to the restoration of a fair distribution. In a society that strictly complies with the demands of justice, these questions would not arise. I shall take up the relationship between

---

[11]   *TJ*, 6–7.
[12]   ibid 10.

distributive and commutative justice in chapter nine, in the context of Finnis's political philosophy. Let it suffice for the moment to say that Rawls's theory is confined to the (imaginary) case of a 'strict compliance' society (ie, one in which everybody acts justly), and is criticised by Finnis precisely for the artificiality that flows from this.

In regarding justice as the *first* 'virtue' of social institutions, Rawls wants to isolate the discussion from the principles that might define other political virtues such as efficiency, liberality and so forth. A consideration of all the virtues of social institutions, and the potential ways in which they may compete or require balancing against one another, would go beyond the theory of justice and amount to a political ideal. But the theory of justice is yet a part of such an ideal insofar as it cannot be isolated from a conception of the way in which the aims and purposes of social cooperation are to be understood. Competing conceptions of justice 'are the outgrowth of different notions of society against the background of opposing views of the natural necessities and opportunities of life'.[13] That is to say, conceptions of justice are relative or responsive to political ideals. Accordingly, Rawls suggests that it is necessary analytically to separate the 'concept' of justice from the various 'conceptions' of justice (the concrete sets of principles) that instantiate the concept.

Rawls's own conception of justice is called 'justice as fairness'. This is not meant to suggest an equivalence between those two ideas, but calls attention to the conditions in which the initial selection of principles takes place. We are to imagine that the principles of justice for the basic structure of society are the object of the original agreement, taken by those operating behind the 'veil of ignorance' in the 'original position'. The conditions are fair because:

> Among the essential features of this situation is that no one knows his place in society, his class position or social status, nor does any one know his fortune in the distribution of natural assets and abilities, his intelligence, strength and the like. I shall even assume that the parties do not know their conceptions of the good or their special psychological propensities. The principles of justice are chosen from behind a veil of ignorance. This ensures that no one is advantaged or disadvantaged in the choice of principles by the outcome of natural chance or the contingency of social circumstances.[14]

Actual societies are not voluntary associations, but the original position responds to the demands of freedom and moral autonomy in meeting the principles that free and equal persons would impose upon themselves in circumstances that are fair. The Kantian inspiration of this should be obvious: it approximates to the demands of autonomy (genuinely self-standing,

---

[13] ibid 9.
[14] ibid 11.

self-legislation of the moral law) by appeal to a categorical imperative. It is, despite Rawls's actual dogmatic commitments, but in keeping with the Kantian heritage of the theory, specifically Protestant: the autonomous choosers of the original position are both rational and mutually disinterested, that is to say, lacking any interest in each other's interests. As such, their distinct and opposing conceptions of the good must even include the presumption that 'their spiritual aims may be opposed, in the way that the aims of those of different religions may be opposed'.[15]

In another way, however, Rawls departs quite radically from the Kantian tradition of thinking about justice. The condition of autonomy, it will be remembered, was for Kant a condition in which the individual acts for the reason of the moral law alone, abrogating from his principles of action all selfish or self-interested considerations. Consider, by contrast, this rather remarkable passage:

> Now obviously no one can obtain everything he wants; the mere existence of other persons prevents this. The absolutely best for any man is that everyone else should join with him in furthering his conception of the good whatever it turns out to be. Or failing this, that all others are required to act justly but that he is authorized to exempt himself as he pleases.[16]

It is, Rawls says, only because other persons would never agree to such an arrangement that such forms of egoism must be rejected. Further on, Rawls seems to suggest (in a section entitled 'The Circumstances of Justice') that questions of justice indeed only arise due to vestiges of such radical self-interest: if resources were infinite, or if I valued yours and my interests equally, it would not matter where the resources ended up. I would be equally content whether you have them or I do.

Is this correct? Suppose my tastes run to fast cars, money, women and fine wine and food. Suppose I enjoy treating others as personal slaves, and laugh in my wasteful plenty as the rest of the world starves. Suppose everyone else is content to fall in with my preferences, and ready to further them insofar as it lies within their power (perhaps I am very charismatic). Would that represent 'the absolutely best' for me? It is remarkable, in such passages, how far Rawls's vision of justice is removed from the classical tradition of Aristotle and Aquinas, for whom justice was above all else a virtue. The classical equation of the 'good life' with the life of virtue was forged precisely out of a sense that a life in which one's every desire is granted is one in which the individual has

---

[15] ibid 12. See also 131. Catholicism does not of course oppose the idea of religious freedom (freedom of conscience); but Rawls's Protestantism asserts itself in the idea that religious divisions are explained by association with genuinely distinct and opposing forms of the good.

[16] ibid 103.

become a 'natural slave' to their passions, rather than master over them.[17] The 'circumstances of justice' were not merely a response to a particular political problem, but part of the circumstances of human nature itself. Questions of 'the good' were not subordinated to questions of entitlement (Rawls's so-called prioritisation of the right over the good),[18] but formed the central question of ethics and political theory.

In some of his later works, Rawls repeatedly emphasised that his theory of justice is intended to prescind not only from contentious ideas of 'the good', but from the whole metaphysical framework in which reflection on the good takes place: images of the human being as an 'autonomous agent', radically free in his soul, or as *homo economicus*, or as a moral being whose freedom is circumscribed by the duty to lead the right sort of life. All such deep philosophical questions of the human being's status are suspended. What matters is not the fundamental nature of human beings as social or moral creatures (or as atomic 'individuals'), but their status as citizens. Justice pertains only to the human being's political, and not his metaphysical, situation. Nevertheless, Rawls is forced to admit that even the original position itself demands some idea of what is good for human beings. The notion of the 'fairness' of the conditions of deliberation presupposes precisely that nobody is advantaged or disadvantaged by the various procedural constraints. But these ideas, advantage and disadvantage, presume in turn an idea of the good: the very idea that men have 'interests' that they will ultimately 'pursue' requires a conception that there is something that is good for the human being, something that is worth pursuing. The activity of choosing principles of justice (ie, designing a 'basic structure' for the community) has no point unless it is good for men to do so, or will lead to their being better off. Indeed, the choice itself only becomes significant, even intelligible, if one can distinguish good choices (those which redound to human interests, even if the specifics of them are hidden) from bad ones (which will retard one's interests, ruin one's life, whatever its actual direction). Consequently, Rawls founds his vision of justice on what he calls a 'thin theory of the good'.

Rawls argues that certain 'goods' are 'primary' in the sense that '[r]ational individuals, whatever else they want, desire certain things as prerequisites for carrying out their plans of life'.[19] Remembering that individuals in the original position do not know what these 'plans of life' are, to what goods would they commit themselves? What will they regard as prerequisites of any worthwhile life? Rawls suggests that they will 'prefer a wider to a narrower liberty and

---

[17] The same is also definitive of Kant's notion of 'heteronomy', or lack of autonomy (self-standing).

[18] *TJ*, 347.

[19] ibid 348.

opportunity, and a greater rather than a smaller share of wealth and income'. In addition, a central place must be given to self-respect and self-worth: perhaps the precondition for pursuing anything at all, except extinction. That these are good 'seems clear enough'.[20] But their goodness is 'primary' (in supplying the motivation to pursue a 'plan of life' at all), as distinguished from 'final ends'.[21]

It is clearly possible to dispute the neutrality of these primary goods in giving unbalanced priority to individualist, even consumerist, styles of living over (for example) spiritual or communally orientated forms of life. A certain caution is nevertheless necessary. It must be remembered that the goods under consideration pertain to the individual's status as a citizen and not the enrichment of his soul as a moral being. The fact is that (as Rawls suggests) social virtue consists not of neutrality as such, but of *fairness*. It is important to distinguish these ideas. No society, even a permissive one, is neutral as between the life of the entrepreneur (for example) and that of the rapist. Indeed, the freedom characteristic of liberal societies cannot be taken so far as to permit forms of life that set out to destroy social freedom: a problem that the political philosopher Leszek Kolakowski termed 'the self-poisoning of the open society'.[22] Fairness instead pertains to the question of whether the primary goods give greater assistance to certain contentious, but nonetheless legitimate, forms of the good life, whilst offering less support to others, or even throwing obstacles in their way. The conditions of liberal society make the entrepreneurial, acquisitive lifestyle easier than the communal one, for the simple reason that the individual bent on acquisition does not need to recruit anyone else to the service of his projects; whereas the founder of a spiritual community must obviously rely upon the willingness of others to join in with the venture, devoting some significant proportion of their time, energies and resources. Does this signal the contentiousness of 'liberty' as a primary good? No: because the founder of the community cannot legitimately intend a compulsory, coercive community, but one founded on willing and voluntary participation. To that extent, the promotion of individual liberty gives assistance to both forms of life.

At the same time, however, it is not simply that wealth and opportunity are less central to a spiritual life of community and meditation. As Aristotle reminds us, no community is self-sufficient except the *polis* itself. No spiritual community based around the rejection of consumerism or consumption could entirely close itself off from the realities of a consumption society, but is obliged in numerous small and significant ways to share (via participation in)

---

[20] ibid.
[21] ibid 350.
[22] L Kolakowski, *Modernity on Endless Trial* (Chicago IL, University of Chicago Press, 1997) 162.

its values. Is this tendency of liberty to throw obstacles in the way of the spiritual life any different from the obstacles typically thrown in the way of all rational plans of life by the fact that liberties frequently and ordinarily collide? Perhaps this is not after all concerning, but more evidence of the fact that liberal societies, precisely in being liberal, cannot possibly give equal priority to all forms of life. But it remains that the status of liberty as a primary good includes for Rawls the notion that individuals will prefer a wider to a narrower experience of it. This is clearly far from the case. If I hold to a scale of values that places little emphasis on pursuit of worldly goods and successes, and much upon the notion of simplicity, duty and 'unspottedness'[23] then it might be that a narrower liberty is to be preferred, not only for myself, but for others too. Denied of personal knowledge, of any sense of my worldly outlook, can I be certain that I shall not regard liberty as an execrable idea, full of danger and promising to 'spread ruin in civil and sacred affairs'?[24]

One could not dismiss this, as some philosophers are inclined to do, as embodying an 'illegitimate' preference (preferring something for others aside from oneself), as the very conditions of the original position, in excluding self-knowledge, have the result that what is preferred by 'individuals' in that condition is indistinguishable from what is preferred by or for all individuals. One must accept either that the 'thin theory of the good' is tilted in favour of certain worldly priorities or scales of value, or else that the exclusion of richer (and of course contentious) visions of the good life do indeed, despite what Rawls says, qualify the rationality of the decision. Rawls asserts that 'in order to advance their aims, whatever these are, [individuals] normally require more rather than less of the other primary goods'.[25] But can even this much be asserted with confidence, without 'looking ahead to other questions' for which 'a more comprehensive account of the good is essential'?[26]

It is nevertheless from this characterisation of primary goods, on the basis of the thin theory, that individuals in the original position derive their understanding of justice. Reasoning from these premises, those in the original

---

[23] See M Oakeshott, 'Religion and the World' in T Fuller (ed), *Religion, Politics and the Moral Life* (New Haven CT, Yale University Press, 1993).

[24] See the encyclical *Mirari vos* of Pope Gregory XVI, 15 August 1832, s 14: 'Thence comes transformation of minds, corruption of youths, contempt of sacred things and holy laws—in other words, a pestilence more deadly to the state than any other. Experience shows, even from earliest times, that cities renowned for wealth, dominion, and glory perished as a result of this single evil, namely immoderate freedom of opinion, license of free speech, and desire for novelty.'

[25] *TJ*, 349.

[26] ibid. In later work, such as *Political Liberalism*, Rawls seems to acknowledge this concern to some degree, suggesting that the 'thin theory' pertains specifically to the individual's ability to develop powers of autonomous insight and decision; characteristics especially prized by *liberal* societies. See J Rawls, *Political Liberalism* (New York, Columbia University Press, 2005) 187–90, and my discussion above.

position will be driven to adopt two distinct and foundational principles of justice:

1. Each person is to have an equal right to the most extensive scheme of equal basic liberties that is compatible with a similar scheme of liberties for others.
2. Social and economic inequalities are legitimate only when both of the following conditions are met: (a) such inequalities can be reasonably expected to operate to everyone's advantage; (b) they are attached to positions and offices open to all.

Both of these principles pertain in different ways to the 'basic structure' of society. The first principle defines and secures the framework of basic liberties, whereas the second concerns questions of distribution: the regulation of social and economic inequalities. The principle captured by 2(a) is known as the 'difference principle'; that embodied in 2(b) equates to equality of opportunity.[27] In terms of logical priority, equality of opportunity takes priority over the difference principle, and both of these are subject to the basic scheme secured by the first principle. Thus, 'infringements of the basic equal liberties protected by the first principle cannot be justified or compensated for, by greater social and economic advantages'.[28] One must think of the basic liberties as open to limitation or qualification only when they come into mutual conflict: none, in being open to clashes, is therefore absolute.

In summary therefore: the basic structure of society secures and distributes certain primary goods, understood as being desirable by all individuals no matter what their other preferences, in the light of which injustice is any inequality in the distribution of such goods that is not to the benefit of all.

THE FIRST PRINCIPLE OF JUSTICE

At various stages in the text of *A Theory of Justice* and elsewhere, Rawls reformulated his two principles of justice. The first in particular gives rise to a general problem of interpretation: in saying that each person is to enjoy an 'equal right to the most extensive scheme of basic liberties' compatible with 'a similar scheme of liberties for others', is the central concern with liberty here, or with equality? The presence of the second principle (the difference principle) might incline us to believe in equality as the more important notion, embodying as it does a specific departure from otherwise formally equal relations. But it is

---

[27] Readers should note that Rawls restates and qualifies these principles at points throughout the work; to avoid complications I have drawn the statement of the principles above from *TJ*, 53.
[28] ibid 54.

necessary to remind ourselves that the difference principle comes into play only once the first principle has been *fully* satisfied, suggesting that liberty is indeed the uppermost concern. Rawls's later reformulation of the principle in *Political Liberalism* also seems to reinforce this reading: there, he speaks instead of a 'fully adequate scheme of basic liberties' as the requirement, not merely the most extensive.

In its original formulation, the first principle suggests that a basic liberty 'can be limited only for the sake of liberty itself'[29] and not for any other consideration of welfare or adjustment in the name of social equality. Reformulated, it suggests that such adjustments must await not merely the fulfilment of an ordinally equal scheme of liberties, taken to its maximum extent (ie, the calibration of 'the one system of liberties in the best way')[30] but the manifestation of a scheme of liberties that completely fulfils the purposes for which such liberties exist: to enable pursuit of a freely-chosen conception of the good. This demand is more extensive than the demands of earlier thinkers concerned with liberty (such as Kant and Rousseau), who generally specified only the attainment of equality of liberty and not some specific threshold of freedom taken as indispensable; but also less exacting, in applying only to a certain class of liberties ('basic liberties') conceived to underpin the very possibility of pursuing a good life.

The classic objection to those earlier approaches, which insisted on equal liberty, was that one cannot effectively *measure* liberty: a certain amount of freedom of speech cannot be quantitatively compared with a certain amount of freedom of organisation. If one society has members that are entirely free in the first respect (lacking any legal restrictions on what can be said) but highly unfree in the second, whilst the citizens of another state have very little freedom of speech but almost unrestricted rights of assembly and organisation, which society enjoys more freedom? Any comparison is in reality qualitative; a question of which set of freedoms (given the need for choice) is more valuable, or preferable.

Aware of the difficulties facing the attempt to measure liberties against one another (an impossible task unless measuring their relative importance), Rawls asks instead for a set of *basic* liberties to be equally manifested. Though it remains that one cannot measure, say, freedom of speech against freedom of movement regarding relative extent, one might hope to compare the relative ability of two individuals to formulate and freely adopt conceptions of the good. The purpose of the basic liberties is precisely to secure this end: those in the original position in being deprived of the knowledge of which 'conception

---

[29] ibid 179.
[30] ibid.

of the good' they possess, require above all those liberties that will allow them freely to choose and pursue a conception of the good that conflicts with those of others. In particular, the possibility that one may change one's mind about the good life means that it is essential that a person's 'original allegiance and continued devotion to [their chosen] ends are to be formed and affirmed under conditions that are free'.[31]

It is difficult, however, to understand how a person's ability to adopt and pursue a given range of ends, deemed by them to be good or worthwhile, can possibly be separated from questions surrounding the availability and distribution of social and economic resources, postponed by Rawls to considerations falling under the second principle. (We must remind ourselves again that resort to the second principle is only sanctioned once the first has been fully achieved.) Poverty is obviously a significant factor in shaping the opportunities that are open to each person, cutting off certain opportunities and thus restricting a person's options. Rawls's response to this problem is to separate questions of liberty (legal protection from interference by the state or by other citizens) from questions of the value, or worth of liberty. The scheme of basic freedoms established by the first principle holds equally for every person: the state does not prevent me, for example, from entering into commercial relationships with a view to profit. But such opportunities are not equally *valuable* to every person, since lack of material resources, capital or knowledge may qualify or altogether prevent their exercise. Whilst this situation may be unsatisfactory, it is a question for the difference principle rather than one of a community's failure to instantiate the first principle.[32]

How convincing is this response? At one level, it might be true to say that two individuals are 'equally free' to donate £1 million to a charity, even if one of them lacks the resources: true in the sense that the state does not interfere to deprive either person from so acting, should they be in a position to do so. But it is easy to overlook the fact that such political freedoms (freedoms from interference) mean nothing unless backed up by and manifested through the law. When looked at on the concrete plane of legal rights and duties, are two individuals, abstractly equal in this way, genuinely equally protected from interference? A specific example will illustrate the point. A person who owns a particular plot of land has numerous liberties that can be exercised in relation to it, liberties that are meaningful only because they are protected by law by an array of *rights* that can be asserted against others: infringement of which would amount to trespass, civil or criminal damage, fraud, nuisance and so on.

---

[31] ibid 131.

[32] In pondering this question, we might wonder whether the purpose of the difference principle is indeed primarily distributive rather than corrective; or whether the distinction between these two kinds of justice is fully sustainable: see further ch 9 below.

The majority of these rights are designed to exclude others from the use of the land (so that one's liberties may be exercised without interference by others). The range of liberties possessed by the landowner are obviously exercisable with respect to that particular piece of land; so it would seem to follow that one who does not own any land possesses fewer liberties, being excluded from all privately owned land.

Could one go further? The basic liberties create conditions which allow individuals freely to adopt and pursue contentious conceptions of the good life. But is one's ability to conceive of particular ends not partly a function of one's education, of the development of one's intelligence and one's other capacities? Does the lack of developmental capacities not reach down into the very possibility of exercising free choices? Such questions have led some modern writers, such as Martha Fineman, to accuse political liberalism of engendering a 'structural tilt': concentrating privilege and structuring disadvantage in a way that compounds the social divide between 'haves' and 'have-nots'. The language of the 'autonomous subject', or the free and equal agent who is formally equal to others, permits an all too plausible conception of formal equality to hide or disguise substantive inequalities which, in real terms, erode individual autonomy for many disadvantaged people.[33]

It might be supposed that Fineman's concern is misplaced: these matters are addressed by the difference principle, so does it really matter that the first principle suspends or excludes them? But a closer examination reveals the extent of Rawls's problem. Fineman's concern is precisely to question whether the kind of 'formal' approach to equality pursued by a theory like that of Rawls results in conditions that allow each person to manifest and express the autonomy that lies at the heart of the first principle of justice. Can the first principle indeed establish a 'fully adequate scheme of basic liberties' whilst suspending distributional questions? Moreover, her question stands as a challenge to Rawls's entire methodological approach in giving the first principle 'lexical priority' over the second. Rawls (it will be remembered) states that the basic liberties can be adjusted or restricted 'only for the sake of liberty itself' and not for the purposes of improving the position of the most disadvantaged, or so as to ensure greater material equality of resources. The question is what would happen if it turned out that considerations of disadvantage and material inequality directly impinge upon 'liberty itself', and not simply its 'value'.

These thoughts highlight one of the latent ambiguities of liberal theory. Individual freedom is prized above all else; but is the 'autonomy' that is treasured conceived as a condition inherent to the human condition, and qualified

---

[33] See, eg, M Fineman, 'The Vulnerable Subject: Anchoring Equality in the Human Condition' (2008) 20 *Yale Journal of Law & Feminism* 1.

through the existence of coercive laws that are nevertheless deemed to be necessary to the survival of community? Or is it instead an aspiration, manifested only by degrees and *established* by the conditions created by the law? Rawls's discussion of the first principle of justice indicates that his theory is orientated more towards the first assumption: questions of justice arise at all only because 'the absolute best for man', that 'everyone else should join with him in furthering his conception of the good whatever it turns out to be', is unlikely to materialise.[34] Deprived of knowledge of their conceptions of the good, knowing that they will differ and conflict, rational persons in the original position will realise that the safest course is to select a principle that sets the greatest store by personal liberty, and minimises interference, qualifying 'natural' autonomy as little as possible. Fineman's argument invites us to question this assumption: the condition of *autonomia* (literally, of giving to oneself one's own law) implies the capacity of a rational individual to make an informed decision that is free from coercion. If we think of this capacity as itself essentially social, and hence as the product of social goods, is not the distribution of such goods, and the material resources needed to pay for them, an essential precondition for genuinely autonomous citizens?

THE SECOND PRINCIPLE

It will be recalled that Rawls's second principle of justice has two parts: the first part justifying social and economic inequalities where the result is to the benefit of the least advantaged; the second pertaining to equality of opportunity. Though the latter takes priority over the former, it is the difference principle that dominates Rawls's discussion, and which has attracted more critical comment.

To understand the relationship between these requirements, one must first understand that they operate essentially as limitations upon an entirely free and unrestricted market. Rawls assumes, quite reasonably, that the idea of a completely unrestricted market would be intolerable to most people. Rawls's theory is a liberal, but nonetheless moral, critique of the market in that it wishes to inject a certain morality into transactional behaviour: a motive in any case historically at the root of contract law doctrine and other areas of private law. These branches of law were never absorbed wholly by concerns of economic efficiency, but were orientated simultaneously by other concerns, such as fairness, proportionality, justice and so on. The undesirability of a completely unrestricted market lies in the thought that the distribution of assets in the very long term should not, in most people's eyes, be left to the

---

[34] *TJ*, 103, and discussion above.

play of forces that are arbitrary from a moral point of view. In the modern world, the market is not simply a domain for entrepreneurs and venture capitalists. Increasingly, all persons are forced to engage with the market in fulfilment of their basic needs. It follows that a market in which the distribution of resources is patterned after historical or entirely accidental factors such as inherited wealth or one's class background, place of birth etc, would operate to structure the lives of those subject to it in ways that seem morally indefensible (or at least non-optimal).

The traditional principle of equality of opportunity was advocated by liberals (and others) as a way of counteracting these tendencies of the open market. The market should principally reward those who exercise their talents and efforts, responding to merit and industriousness rather than accidents of birth or circumstance. This applies as much to the distribution of offices and positions of power and influence as anything else. Rawls supports this principle, noting that any exclusion of certain individuals or groups from the powers or privileges of offices is not to be tolerated even if the result were an improvement in everyone's situation overall. Such restrictions would not only arbitrarily close off the benefits and rewards that come from holding certain offices, but would be unfair in preventing certain people 'from experiencing the realization of self which comes from a skilful and devoted exercise of social duties'. In this way, they would have been 'deprived of one of the main forms of human good'.[35]

At the same time, Rawls parted company from many of his contemporaries in regarding this requirement as insufficient on its own to produce just outcomes. For with what reason do we think of natural talents and abilities as any less arbitrary than historical accidents of birth and position? If the latter are irrelevant from the perspective of justice, giving us no special entitlement to a greater slice of benefits and rewards, are not the former also? Abilities in being 'natural' are not, in that respect, 'deserved'.

A certain care must nevertheless be taken in speaking of natural talents and abilities. Many of the capacities people exercise are at least as much 'constructed' products of work and effort as they are 'natural'. To say that a person is a gifted musician, say, ought not to suggest that one accomplished in the playing of some instrument does not need to practise hard, develop and nurture skills through great effort and sacrifice etc. Improvement, indeed any development or acquisition of skill, demands resources of time and hard work, as well (often) as material resources. It follows that if social resources such as education, healthcare and the like are distributed unevenly, so that certain groups who would benefit from them are arbitrarily excluded, to the

---

[35] *TJ*, 73.

cost of their development, then those deprived would by ordinary standards have been victims of injustice. This is one reason for agreeing with Rawls that equality of opportunity must be supplemented by the difference principle.

It remains, however, that talents and abilities are far from being purely proportional to effort and hard work. There is no doubt that by a very deep commitment of time and energy, devotion to long hours of practice and boring repetitive exercises, I would become a more competent pianist than if entirely untrained. Through sufficient practice, I might even develop my piano-playing skills to a very high level, which may allow me to obtain a reasonable living as a concert pianist. Nevertheless, my skills are never likely to be as great or as accomplished as the person of natural flair and genius, assuming such a person also practises assiduously and does not waste their talents. 'Natural' variations in talent will remain. Rawls deems these natural variations to be a question for justice, not because such variations are themselves unjust (one cannot help having one's talents any more than one 'deserves' them), but because we are faced with the question of what (if anything) a society should do about their existence:

> The natural distribution is neither just nor unjust; nor is it unjust that persons are born into society at some particular position. These are simply natural facts. What is just and unjust is the way that institutions deal with these facts.[36]

Aristocratic and caste societies are on this understanding unjust precisely because they take certain contingencies (birth, skin colour, rank) as the basis for its distributions. In so doing, '[t]he basic structure of these societies incorporates the arbitrariness found in nature'.[37] But it is not necessary for men to resign themselves to such structures. If accidents of birth and ability are not deserved, then neither is a society that reflects and rewards such variations 'owed' to those blessed with them. We must, Rawls argues, rid ourselves of the habit of thinking of the social system as 'an unchangeable order beyond human control' and begin to understand it as 'a pattern of human action': something human beings themselves bring about. The basic structure absolutely need not reflect and reinforce such variations.

Understood in this context, the difference principle effectively represents an agreement to regard natural talents 'as in some respect a common asset' rather than a matter of private good or bad fortune.[38] Obviously those blessed with talent will only be motivated to exercise their skills if they feel duly rewarded; but the difference principle ensures that such rewards are not automatic but conditional and qualified: skilful persons 'may gain from their good fortune only on terms that improve the situation of those who have lost out'.[39]

---

[36] ibid 87.
[37] ibid 88.
[38] ibid 87.
[39] ibid.

It should not be imagined that Rawls intends by this to propose a very aggressive form of redistribution of assets across society. The difference principle is stated in such a way as to ensure that inequalities are perfectly permissible, so long as the situation of the least advantaged is alleviated. There is no question, therefore, of personal talents and efforts being understood as wholly yoked to or subsumed within collective efforts to improve the common good. The gap in earnings between senior bankers and those who clean their offices may be huge indeed; but it can, in Rawls's eyes, be justified if large salaries and magnificent bonuses are required to attract the best people to the top jobs, thereby maintaining a flourishing and dependable banking system to the benefit of all. Similarly, high salaries for company directors may stimulate productivity and efficiency; whereas attempts to equalise directorial salaries and those of shop-floor workers may erode these gains, leading to an economic decline that results in a lower actual income for all. These are familiar arguments, not always borne out by experience: the difference principle can in one sense be regarded as a corrective to highly generalised arguments of this kind, but this itself invites the question of the level of generality at which the difference principle is itself supposed to apply. Rawls measures benefits for the purposes of the second principle by reference to an 'index of primary goods', but this does not establish a neutral context for its operation: for example, should the question of bankers' bonuses be addressed separately from questions of high managerial salaries, or ought these questions be considered as linked in virtue of an overarching economic strategy designed to stimulate productivity?[40]

One question to ask is why those in the original position should be thought to favour a principle of this kind. It is in one sense obvious that rational persons deprived of specific personal knowledge have good reasons to favour equality of opportunity; but is it equally obvious that they would also favour the difference principle, the principle that reward for one's talents and efforts (whatever these turn out to be) is limited and conditional? We need to remember that Rawls does not characterise natural variations in ability as intrinsically unjust, but wants to make clear that the social response to this situation lies very much open to choice. But would rational persons behind the veil of ignorance necessarily believe that individual talents are (to some extent) common assets?

Rawls has a specific argument for this, known as the 'maximin' argument. The circumstances of the original position are extremely stringent in what they exclude from the knowledge of the parties. These parties are forced to make rational decisions and conduct their reasoned deliberations whilst deprived of

---

[40] ibid 84: Rawls concedes 'a certain arbitrariness in actually identifying the least favoured group', noting that 'Any procedure is bound to be somewhat ad hoc. Yet we are entitled at some point to plead practical considerations'. See also 136.

the knowledge of themselves, their conceptions of the good, position in society, the affluence of that society and so forth. This makes it all but impossible to enter into calculations of probability or estimations of outcome, as there is simply no data on the basis of which to found such calculations.

Conditions of this kind accordingly tend to promote very conservative thinking: if I do not know how particular decisions will affect me, it is advisable to rank various alternatives by their worst possible outcomes, and to select that which produces the least-worst outcome, ie, the alternative in which the worst outcome is superior to the worst outcomes that result from the other alternatives. To illustrate this, suppose I am faced with three alternatives: I can become a teacher, a businessman, or a thief. Being a teacher will likely guarantee a minimum annual income of £18,000 and a relatively modest maximum of £50,000, but with pretty good job security. As a businessman, I could expect to earn up to £200,000 in a year, but in a bad year I may only make £15,000, or even a net loss; and there may be the permanent spectre of redundancy or unemployment. If I become a thief, my annual income may exceed the other alternatives considerably, but in the worst case I end up in prison, and with nothing. Applying maximin, I would elect to be a teacher, since it delivers the best-worst outcome.

Rawls notes that the maximin rule is not ordinarily a suitable one to employ in conditions of uncertainty, holding only in highly specific circumstances. These are nevertheless circumstances that the original position exhibits to a very high degree. The exclusion of knowledge of likelihoods is one such feature, essential (in Rawls's eyes) because of the need for the choice of principles to be acceptable to others: in particular, the descendants of the choosers, whose rights and responsibilities will be deeply shaped by them. Secondly, Rawls thinks that the workable theory of social justice provided by his two principles is compatible with other reasonable demands (such as efficiency), and therefore constitutes a satisfactory minimum that leaves little reason for risking everything for the promise of greater economic or social advantages. (The grass is always greener.) Finally, Rawls thinks that it will be apparent to those in the original position that the other alternatives contain the possibility of worst outcomes that are scarcely tolerable: the principle of utility, for example, potentially justifying serious infractions of liberty in exchange for greater social benefits.[41]

The fact is that all available alternatives have a best and a worst outcome for each person. In selecting any solution to the question of justice and distribution, I may find myself in a more advantaged and insulated position, or a less advantaged and exposed one. If I genuinely do not know which of these

---

[41] ibid 134–35.

situations will be mine upon the lifting of the veil, should I not choose the one that seems the most favourable to those in the latter situation? Perhaps Rawls is correct to say that the tolerability of such a situation would be considerably eroded under a principle of utility: knowing that my misfortunes were a necessary price to pay for the benefits of the better off. Could one genuinely believe that one's own stoicism would be sufficient to bear that outcome, if it turned out to be one's own? Indeed, mindful of the need for a conception of justice to seem reasonable to those in positions of disadvantage, would it be possible for the least advantaged in a utilitarian society to think of their disadvantages, need to sustain in place the advantages of others, as required by justice?

This reasoning is certainly not without considerable power. But one might wonder at the same time if it is not dubious, somehow, to rely on a principle of reasoning (maximin) acknowledged to be a poor guide to thinking in most situations involving uncertainty. In comparing the principles of 'justice as fairness' with the principle of utility, Rawls remarks that the full meaning and application of the utilitarian's doctrines 'may be highly conjectural'.[42] Since the latter involve the possibility of specific trade-offs between individual liberties and general social goods, 'it seems that the parties [in the original position] would prefer to secure their liberties straightaway, rather than have them depend upon what may be uncertain and speculative actuarial calculations'.[43] Perhaps so. But does not Rawls ignore the fact that concrete knowledge of social and economic conditions might lend considerable precision or confidence to those calculations? Such knowledge may at least have the effect of removing from the sphere of immediate, or even long-term, possibility some or all of the very worst outcomes, otherwise to be feared in the abstract. If the promise of gains held out by utilitarian arrangements were very great, might it not be rational to accept a comparatively small risk that liberties may be qualified; or accept certain, but small, qualifications to personal freedom in exchange for a more commodious lifestyle? Rawls's approach in *A Theory of Justice* is of value in raising such troubling questions, but it does not altogether resolve them.

We thus arrive back, via a long route, at the questions raised at the beginning of this chapter. *A Theory of Justice* was intended in part as a rational defence of the concept of justice against utilitarian and intuitionistic political theories. Rawls's ambitions for the arguments of his most famous book were grand indeed: to suggest a rational basis for judgements of justice, culminating in the defence of justice-as-fairness. Initially conceived as a method for securing reasonable agreement on the 'basic structure' of society, the approach became more modest in its expectations, merely offering 'a way of continuing public discussion when shared understandings of lesser generality

---

[42] ibid 138.
[43] ibid 138–39.

have broken down'.[44] Deeply attached to, and expressive of, liberal values, the net effect of Rawls's work is to leave the ethical status of liberal society ultimately unclear.

THE BASIC STRUCTURE IN CONTEXT

There can be no doubt that the single most significant aspect of Rawls's theory of justice is its focus upon the 'basic structure' of the community. As noted earlier, this focus (effectively upon distributive justice) leads Rawls to believe that other significant questions of justice that might be asked (pertaining to the justice of private transactions for example) are to be deferred until the basic structure has been settled. In one sense, this is correct: the enforceability of contractual rights, or of rights to restitution, remuneration for labour or compensation for harm etc, are all dependent upon a framework of legal institutions and doctrines against which they are given specific form. Rawls invites his readers to remember that the basic structure from which our specific entitlements and obligations derive, is malleable after all kinds of considerations and ideas, and is neither natural nor innately 'given'. Nothing about the status of our entitlements as just or unjust is clear, therefore, until the justice or injustice of the basic institutional structure itself is resolved.

Fuller, whom we shall come to in chapter ten below, could be said to share something of this concern with social forms, but he connects these forms (as means) more firmly with the ends they are presumed to pursue. For the moment, I would like to place Rawls's views in contrast with those of the classical and early-modern natural lawyers, and with those of the modern natural law thinker we shall examine in chapter nine: John Finnis.

The older natural lawyers would certainly not have suggested that the 'basic structure' of the community is quite as open to negotiation as Rawls would have his readers believe. Rawls wants to say that there is nothing innate about a social structure which rewards merit, or which regards the fruits of a person's labour as their entitlement. To take my example above, if I train relentlessly and with great dedication and become a great pianist, it is not the case (for Rawls) that I am inevitably owed the fruits of this labour. But equally, they are subject to the operation of the difference principle *if* we adopt that principle as a means of organising the basic structure. If we do not, that is equally a choice we make. However, the classical natural lawyers would have said that certain rights belong to a person *suum ius*: they are innately 'one's own'.[45] Thus, the question of 'what properly belongs to a person' is not the subject of an original agreement (hypothetical or otherwise) but derives from

---

[44] Rawls, *Political Liberalism* (n 26) 46.
[45] See, eg, Grotius, *De Iure Belli ac Pacis*, I.1.5; I.II.1.iv; Proleg. s 8; and discussion in ch 5 above.

'essential traits implanted in man'.[46] However a regime might ultimately order itself, amongst the laws necessary for the 'maintenance of the social order' will figure 'the abstaining from that which is another's; the restoration to another of anything of his which we may have, together with any gain which we may have received from it; the obligation to fulfil promises; the making good of a loss incurred through our fault; and the inflicting of penalties upon men according to their deserts'.[47] Note that although Rawls would treat these as considerations of commutative justice, posterior to determination of the basic structure, Grotius understands them to contain also elements of distributive justice, and in being essential to the social order, pertaining directly to the 'basic structure' or institutional organisation of the community.

In the broadest terms, natural lawyers (such as Grotius) would not have regarded as a valid possibility (that is to say, as being in accord with natural law) a regime which enforced unrestrained sharing of material wealth. This rules out certain forms of utilitarian thinking, as well as forms of communism, which might otherwise 'adopt' principles of justice which regard one's labour as a social rather than individual asset.[48] Deliberators in an original position are not free to choose or not to choose this 'principle' of justice. But equally, one's labour and one's material property are not entirely private, but *must* be distributed to (ie, can be lawfully taken by) another where that other is in the direst need.[49]

To be fair, Rawls does not characterise those in the original position as being presented with an open choice in which everything is negotiable (although this would be the 'ideal' situation).[50] They are required to rank and choose between certain families of conceptions of justice, as a reasonable procedure for decision given the need for provisional agreement on a range of alternatives (a procedure which Rawls admits is 'unsatisfactory'). Still, even this more limited list presents as choices or proposals, conceptions of justice that are invalid according to doctrines of natural law, as well (perhaps) as distributive proposals that in being *demanded* by natural law are not objects of choice.

I alluded above to the location of certain considerations of justice in 'essential traits implanted in man'. This is not an idle phrase, for the early natural lawyers devoted considerable attention to the examination and analysis of these traits (such as sociability). In chapter nine, we encounter the work of a modern natural law writer, John Finnis. Finnis elucidates these 'essential traits' by reference to what he describes as basic forms of human flourishing. The account of justice which flows from this analysis is one of great subtlety and

---

[46] ibid Proleg. ss 10 and 12 respectively.

[47] ibid Proleg s 8.

[48] ibid II.22.xvi: there is no right on the part of the poor for the rich to donate their wealth in charity.

[49] ibid II.2.vi.

[50] *TJ*, 105 (where he speaks of choice between 'all possible conceptions of justice').

power: one that is certainly not confined to the community's 'basic structure', but which would with equal certainty regard elements of that basic structure as non-negotiable (if they are to serve justice), whether by agents in an 'original position' or others.

SUGGESTED READING

THE THEORY OF JUSTICE

J Rawls, *A Theory of Justice*, rev edn (Cambridge MA, Harvard University Press, 1999).
—— *Justice as Fairness: A Restatement* (Cambridge MA, Harvard University Press, 2001).

Background Reading

M Fineman, 'The Vulnerable Subject: Anchoring Equality in the Human Condition' (2008) 20 *Yale Journal of Law & Feminism* 1.
S Freeman (ed), *The Cambridge Companion to Rawls* (Cambridge, Cambridge University Press, 2002) chs 3, 5 and 9.
C Kukathas and P Pettit, *A Theory of Justice and its Critics* (Cambridge, Polity Press, 1990).
T Pogge, *Realizing Rawls* (New York, Cornell University Press, 1989).
M Sandel, *Justice: What's the Right Thing to Do?* (London, Penguin, 2009) chs 2 and 6.
A Sen, *The Idea of Justice* (Cambridge MA, Harvard University Press, 2009) ch 2.
L Wenar, 'Rawls' in *The Oxford Handbook of Political Philosophy* (Oxford, Oxford University Press, 2012).

POLITICAL LIBERALISM AND INTERNATIONAL RELATIONS

J Rawls, *Political Liberalism* (New York, Columbia University Press, 2005).
—— *The Law of Peoples* (Cambridge MA, Harvard University Press, 1999).

Background Reading

S Freeman (ed), *The Cambridge Companion to Rawls* (Cambridge, Cambridge University Press, 2002) chs 1, 8, 12 AND 13.
R Geuss, *Outside Ethics* (Princeton NJ, Princeton University Press, 2005) ch 2.
J Mandle and D Reidy (eds), *A Companion to Rawls* (Oxford, Blackwell, 2013).
A Perreau-Saussine, 'Immanuel Kant on International Law' in J Tasioulas and S Besson (eds), *The Philosophy of International Law* (Oxford, Oxford University Press, 2010) 53.

9

Justice and the Common Good: Finnis

> There are human goods that can be secured only through the institutions of human law, and requirements of practical reasonableness that only those institutions can satisfy. It is the object of this book to identify those goods, and those requirements of practical reasonableness, and thus to show how and on what conditions such institutions are justified and the ways in which they can be (and often are) defective.[1]

S O BEGINS *NATURAL Law and Natural Rights*, one of the most significant and intellectually rich books on jurisprudence of modern times. This opening announcement gives some sense of the structure of the book. Its concerns lie first of all in political and indeed moral philosophy, identifying and elucidating the nature of human goods attainable only in common (the common good), and requirements of practical reason directed towards the pursuit of those goods. Only having established these arguments does the focus turn specifically to *institutions*, to the matter of how these goods are to be secured through law, and whether (in securing them or not) such institutions can be justified.

Indeed, *Natural Law and Natural Rights* can be divided into both a political and a legal philosophy. It is broadly speaking the former that attracts the attention of most jurisprudential writers. The book itself has roughly the following form: two initial chapters discuss first the proper methodology for jurisprudential enquiries, and its implications, and then the tradition of natural law thinking from which the book's own arguments draw inspiration. Chapters III to VIII set out the book's political philosophy. Chapters IX to XII centre upon topics in legal theory; and a final chapter, XIII, sets both the political and the legal theory in a broader, eschatological context. In this chapter I will confine myself to the book's political philosophy, which is better known amongst legal theorists, deferring a discussion of Finnis's legal philosophy until chapter eleven.

INTRODUCING THE POLITICAL PHILOSOPHY

The political philosophy of *Natural Law and Natural Rights* reasserts the traditional Aristotelian/Thomist understanding of human individuals and

---

[1] J Finnis, *Natural Law and Natural Rights*, 2nd edn (Oxford, Clarendon Press, 2011) 3 (hereafter *NLNR*).

human society over the Protestant images of politics that proliferated after the Reformation. It will be recalled that, whereas Aristotle had begun the *Politics* with the assertion that man is a political animal, both intellectually and bodily fitted for living the life in common, and pursuing a form of life (the 'good life') that can only be realised in common, post-Reformation philosophies characterised human societies as domains of disagreement, in which the focus is upon each individual's final responsibility for formulating and pursuing their own conception of the good life, in competition with others. In the absence of shared conceptions of the good, law cannot be understood as securing a 'common good', but as offering a method for securing tolerable levels of peace and social stability, and at the same time refraining from giving priority to any specific (and contestable) conception of the good. In this way, legal order can be said to constitute an agreed basis for the coexistence and simultaneous pursuit of many different ideas of human flourishing.

In this vein, Hart in chapter IX of *The Concept of Law* suggested a vision of human society in which human beings can agree upon the desirability of survival (at least of preferred groups), even if they agree on nothing else. The very desire for survival, however, is itself regarded by Hart as contingent, perhaps differing from other contingent desires only in the depth to which it has penetrated in our thought and language. In chapter six above, I suggested that this is an inadequate explanation of the significance of survival amongst human aims. If the elimination of that aim would indeed, as Hart suggested, do extreme violence to 'whole structures of thought and language', ruining our notions of harm and hurt, exterminating all intelligible priorities and assumptions, then does not that very fact justify us in referring to survival as a *necessary* aim for human beings? Indeed, might not other aims, beyond 'mere' survival at any cost, and therefore linked to ideas of the 'good life', enjoy a similar status? Might we not see the purpose of law, as Finnis says, as an endeavour to secure such ends, and try to identify them precisely? Would they not amount to a rich, satisfying vision of a collective good, a form of the 'good life' that is irreducibly, unarguably, common?

One of the principal obstacles to accepting a rich notion of the common good, for many people, is the fear of moral imperialism. In asserting that certain goals or ends are 'good' (and that by implication others are 'bad' or perhaps even 'evil') we appear to assume that the basic features and perspectives of our own culture are superior or privileged in relation to others. How can we be so sure that our 'values' are the right ones, and that the different (to us troubling or abhorrent) values of other times or places are wrong? What gives us the right to assert this?[2]

---

[2] See my discussion in ch 1 above.

As the political philosopher Leszek Kolakowski once pointed out, such anxieties tend to arise from a desire to respect other cultures, to regard their values, claims and priorities as equally valid with our own, or with others that might be imagined. But he went on to observe that an attitude of moral relativism in fact subverts that very respect. If all cultures or value systems are equally valid, then none are valid: there is nothing permanent, essentially true or valuable in any of them. All are entirely disposable, all equally worthless and devoid of any priority whatever. To assert this is not to accord respect to different cultures, but to annihilate the value of all culture.[3]

That is a very negative thought. Instead, let us remember that the fundamental direction of post-Reformation politics was towards a sense of the rich variety of conceptions of the 'good life', and how these may differ from one another or come into conflict.[4] Where this is the case, we may find that the divergent conceptions are underpinned by a divergence in moral outlooks, or in the very moral principles that define those outlooks. This fact of divergence does not in itself *remove* the possibility of enquiring into the soundness of those principles. (Indeed, it is the prerequisite for that enquiry.) And when we undertake that enquiry, what we are really asking is whether the moral principles that underpin a set of cultural practices serve the needs of human flourishing, in the sense of enabling human beings to progress towards some aspect of a good life. In that context, the notion of a 'good life' is not endlessly flexible, despite its obvious diversity. The manner and means by which human beings 'flourish', by which they lead lives that are genuinely worthwhile, are not without limitation. Thus, if a state enacts rules or provisions which remove reproductive or sexual capacity from young women, exclude certain castes or sections of society from basic benefits of society such as freedom or education, or the capacity for self-direction, then it can be said to be acting against a basic dimension of human flourishing, or withholding this from some of its members. Precisely in virtue of the fact that (as Hobbes noted) the various differences between human beings are not of ultimate significance, and are contained firmly within a broader sameness and equality, it is not open to particular societies to justify their trespasses against basic human needs by appealing to the fact of cultural difference. Cultures, as bodies of human practices, are not somehow beyond or above moral judgement.

[3] See L Kolakowski, *Modernity on Endless Trial* (Chicago IL, University of Chicago Press, 1997) ch 2.

[4] The effect of the inculcation of Christianity into Europe was first to suggest that man's final 'good' was not of this world, but represented salvation in the next. Only the Church could guide souls towards this eternal reward. The theologians of the Reformation were instrumental in upending this picture: the Church has no special insights into the good. Each individual has his own encounter with the Bible. As a result, individuals had to take thought concerning the proper way to live in *this* life, paving the way for images of the good life that genuinely vied and competed, and were not simply alternative proposals for realising a 'common' good in the next.

In *Natural Law and Natural Rights*, Finnis (1940–) seeks to persuade us that there are indeed objective grounds on which to evaluate ideas of the good life. The first part of the book undertakes the task of identifying these forms of the good. In all, Finnis claims that there are no more or fewer than seven 'basic goods', constituents of a flourishing life: knowledge, life, play, aesthetic experience, sociability, practical reasonableness and religion. These, correctly understood, amount to a vision of the common good, when the latter is understood as an 'ensemble of conditions' in which all members of a community are enabled fully and meaningfully to participate in and pursue such goods. This, he thinks, both satisfies the demands of the common humanity that Hobbes and other philosophers attempted to identify, whilst leaving sufficient scope for diversity in the way that each individual might choose between, and give differing priority and expression to, the basic goods.

It is to be noted, therefore, that the direction of Finnis's argument does not run from a consideration of what is supposed to be 'natural' to an understanding of what is thereby 'reasonable and right', but instead from 'what is reasonable and right' to what is 'therefore natural'.[5] The central role of 'human flourishing' in the account indicates its orientation in human inclinations: human beings are inclined towards certain goods (which are fundamental to a flourishing life), grasped by the intellect, once experienced, as good in themselves even aside from further instrumental or emotional satisfactions they might bring. Actions which pursue such goods are *therefore* intelligible (and acts merely destructive of them *therefore* unreasonable); and whilst no person can possibly pursue every instantiation of every basic good, such goods provide intelligible ends for human action: the necessity of choosing between them in practice, and of rationally managing a situation in which *each person* is similarly involved in pursuing instantiations of those same goods, gives rise to a series of practically reasonable and ultimately *moral* principles for the direction of human conduct. (Note, therefore, that Finnis's basic goods correspond to—though without deriving from—a conception of human function(ing), in itself pre-moral; whereas the form of enquiry initiated by Aristotle, and later Aquinas, seeks to explain the ultimate validity of human action by reference to *purpose*, final ends [*telos*] or proper goals.)[6]

---

[5] See J Finnis, *Aquinas: Moral Political and Legal Theory* (Oxford, Oxford University Press, 1998) 153n.

[6] See my discussion at the end of this chapter, and in ch 11 below, for the suggestion that Finnis therefore mischaracterises Aquinas's first principle of practical reason (*Summa Theologiae* I–II.94.2) that 'good is to be done and evil avoided', ie, that a sense of what is practically reasonable must be taken to include the governance of human action by the virtues, not as mere 'modes' of realising basic goods but as essential to our *nature* as rational beings. Finnis therefore overstates the position in making 'nature' a mere conclusion of the enquiry.

Basing the account in human tendencies (ie, in a sense of what is *good for* people) undoubtedly gives Finnis's theory a huge intuitive appeal. He can avoid, on this basis, invoking at the outset any difficult metaphysical or theological assumptions in his account of practical reasoning. Are you disposed towards Finnis's outlook on the basic goods? Let us examine the account in greater detail.

THE BASIC GOODS

The seven basic goods referred to above are, according to Finnis, both objective and self-evident. We might begin, as Finnis does, with the good of knowledge. In what sense is knowledge 'good' for human beings? Obviously, there are many useful reasons for attaining a piece of knowledge. Suppose somebody asks you why you are reading *Natural Law and Natural Rights*. You might reply that you are reading it in order to clarify your understanding of a set of jurisprudential problems, perhaps in order to pass an examination in jurisprudence. Or you might say that you are mining the book for useful ideas and phrases with which to impress people at dinner parties, when you drop them into conversation. Perhaps you are reading it in order to look sophisticated and interesting. There is nothing starkly irrational in any of these reasons. Now suppose that you have started reading the book for one of the above reasons, or perhaps a mixture of them, but that part way through the book, you begin to develop an interest in the book's ideas, its claims and arguments. You begin to read the book simply in order to know what those ideas and arguments are, to know whether they are persuasive, sound, coherent and so on. Would reading the book for that reason be any less rational, less intelligible, than reading for the sake of any of the other reasons mentioned above?

Finnis does not deny at all that people seek knowledge for specific instrumental purposes. It is necessary, for all sorts of reasons, to gain information, avoid error or confusion and so forth. But this desire for information, and for the avoidance of error, is not *exhausted* by the instrumental ends or the practical utility of the information. It is, Finnis suggests, valuable in an unbounded sense. This applies to sophisticated forms of knowledge, such as wanting to read the novels of EM Forster (without any other end in view), or knowing what distant stars are composed of, how Titian came to paint *Venus of Urbino* etc, but also to more mundane pieces of information, such as the truth or otherwise of some rumour or piece of gossip. We are, it could be said, simply better off by knowing the truth of things than if we lack knowledge, labour under error or confusion and so forth.

In so saying, it is necessary to remember that the idea of 'good' or being 'better off' in this context does not equate immediately to the idea of 'happiness' or 'contentment'. Clearly, the knowledge that one's partner is conducting a secret affair, or that a trusted friend is lying to you, are unpleasant, even hurtful, and one may in such situations find oneself thinking that one would have been happier by remaining in ignorance. Here however, the sentiment is surely better expressed as wishing that one's partner were not being unfaithful behind one's back, or that one's friend had not proved to be dishonest or unreliable. Would it really be true to say that one would be *better off* by living in ignorance of such things? Similarly, suppose that a person has held strong beliefs in astrology all their life. They consider that their fate is written in the stars, governed by the planets and revealed through newspaper columns by experts capable of divining the celestial movements. All their actions, deliberations and decisions are made on the basis of the advice in these columns. It is easy to see how the revelation of the utter falsity of astrology would be devastating to such a person. But again, are they really better off living under confusion and superstition? Even supposing the person suggested that they had been better off before the revelation: would this not actually just amount to a childish wish to abrogate responsibility for one's actions, avoid facing up to choices etc? Would that person not be made genuinely better off by overcoming childish attachments? Is the adherence to superstition, error and the like not a pitiable condition?

It might be objected that one who experiences the 'good' of knowledge in discovering the truth of some matter, or reading for pleasure, aside from all practical ends is in fact experiencing the satisfaction of curiosity. Is not the pursuit of such satisfaction an instrumental reason for gaining the knowledge? Here we seem once again to come close to Hart's conception of desire, as something primary in order of explanation: that things are desirable *insofar as* one desires them. A tradition of philosophical reflection does indeed hold this to be the case. But consider the following: suppose I wipe my hand along the surface of a window, collecting grime and dust in the palm of my hand. Suppose I then say to you that I treasure this dust, love it, value it beyond price. You ask me whether any dust (from a different window, or a television screen perhaps) would do just as well, and I reply that it would not: it is *this* dust that I desire. You might go on to ask me *why* I find the dust desirable. Is it because of the interesting patterns it makes on my skin; or does it feel nice to hold the dust; or do I intend to do something with the dust (and so on)? To each question, I reply that, no, my desire is only for the dust itself. Is this intelligible?

Contrast this with the situation of one who sits absorbedly in front of the Titian painting, contemplating the brushwork, the composition, the allegorical significance and meaning of the painting and so forth. If that individual claims to find the painting desirable, moving, endlessly interesting, delightful etc, that seems instantly more intelligible, indeed more sane, than the previous example. Why? The answer seems to be that, whilst the painting *has the property of being desirable*, the dust does not. There is nothing valuable about the dust: nothing about it, no property it possesses, contains any value. The painting, by contrast, has all sorts of properties that it is possible to value: beauty, profundity, meaning, metaphorical and historical significance and so forth. Therefore, if we value an object it is because the object *has value*, is capable of being valued. Our desires do not, as it were, place values *onto* or *into* otherwise neutral and inert objects, but instead discover the value *of* or *within* the object. Knowledge is not good *because we desire it*, but rather we desire it *because it is good*. The curiosity that we feel, and which demands satisfaction, is nothing other than an experience of the 'pull' of the good of knowledge.

All of this is to say that knowledge has *intrinsic* value: its value is not exhausted by association with the numerous practical ends or specific occasions for which it might be useful. It is therefore rational (ie, not irrational) to pursue it without reference to any of these other ends, and to pursue it without restriction. Knowledge is in this way an 'objective' good: it is good irrespective of whether, or to what degree, we subjectively feel its pull in relation to specific instances or circumstances. Its goodness is 'self-evident' in being graspable, in experience, in itself: the good of knowledge is intelligibly present without reference to any further thing, or in relation to any further end. For this reason, Finnis speaks of such goods as 'basic goods': their goodness is not relative to any further reason.

If it seems difficult to accept this, try reflecting on your own reasons for action, or on the reasons for action you impute to others in rendering their motives and deeds intelligible or explicable. Can any reasonable, sane course of action be genuinely and sincerely said to deny, or set out to destroy, the good of knowledge? Or do all actions invariably presuppose it as a value? Insofar as we are better off with knowledge than if we are ignorant, in error, muddled etc, it is possible to speak of knowledge as an aspect of human wellbeing.

One question that Finnis leaves unexplored is whether the significance of knowledge *ends* with its goodness. Consider, for example, the death of Socrates, which was an instance of self-sacrifice in the name of truth. If it is good to have knowledge, and if this ultimately translates into a moral demand— indeed a *right*—to pursue knowledge, might there not also be circumstances in which one also has a *duty* to know, to pursue knowledge? It is the latter aspect of the human relationship to knowledge that the death of Socrates expresses, but it is one that is not much explored in *Natural Law and Natural Rights*. As the title of the book suggests, its focus lies in examining the reasons for which, and conditions under which, institutions of law and instruments of 'right' are required for establishing and maintaining human access to the basic goods. Does an excessive focus on rights distort the moral basis of the book's natural law vision? Indeed, does the book's own title suggest an accommodation between *law* and *right* that disguises the tension between a moral vision based exclusively on human flourishing, and one based on moral duty? To what extent would such a shift in focus (to a morality of duty) transform the book's doctrines and outlook?

Let me pass over these questions, important though they are, in favour of glancing at the other basic goods. Finnis regards each of these as equally fundamental and underivable from any further consideration. It therefore follows that none of the goods derives from any of the others. Instead, each represents a dimension of value that is distinct from and irreducible to any other.

Life. By life, Finnis means not only 'survival' in the thin, Hartian sense, but more broadly freedom from the pain of organic malfunctioning. The same sorts of argument apply here as to the case of knowledge. Can one intelligibly deny that life is an aspect of the good? There may be some occasions, or some causes, for which one might choose to act in a way that threatens or erodes this aspect of the good: the hero's death in battle to save the lives of others, for example. But it remains that one would be irrational to court such pain or illness for its own sake, for no further reason. As Hart said, the value of life, as an aspect of human good, seems to be confirmed by the deep structure of our languages and ways of thinking; but it is also presupposed by our practices, particularly medical practice, and acts of procreation.

Play. This refers to the value that can be derived from undertaking an activity for its own sake, aside from any serious point or purpose. This is not about knowledge, but about the *performance* itself. Again, there may be very many reasons to play the flute: for money, for the entertainment of others, to block out unpleasant noises etc. But it is not irrational to play for no further reason than enjoyment of the performance itself. It is not, in this context, the joy itself that defines the good (for joy may be produced in other ways), but the specific joy *of performance*: I may derive pleasure from hearing the music of Bach, but I gain something more, some distinct fulfilment, from producing the music myself rather than listening to a CD.

Aesthetic experience. 'Many forms of play', Finnis says, are the occasion of aesthetic experiences, an experience of wellbeing that is distinct from the value of play itself. It is both a matter of the contemplation of the beautiful form external to one, and the 'inner' experience that attends the appreciation of its value. Obviously, the form must genuinely possess beauty for it to be possible to appreciate it or receive impressions of its satisfying form. That is to say, it involves both an intellection of the quality of a particular form, as well as the capacity to be moved by it. I have touched on this question before in relation to knowledge, where one may distinguish what is read when reading a novel (knowledge) from appreciation of the cleverness, or beauty, or satisfaction, of the structure of the sentences.

Sociability. The 'good' of sociability is of course remarked upon by Aristotle, Aquinas, Grotius and many of the major philosophers of the Western intellectual tradition. But Finnis wants to draw particular attention to the self-evidence of the good of sociability, aside from the instrumental significance of cooperation for the achievement of one's goals. Though sociability is present by varying degrees, from 'minimum peace and harmony amongst persons' through to close and full friendship, it is in the latter idea that we encounter the good of sociability in its most complete expression. Here, one acts not simply for one's own ends, but at least in part out of a concern for the wellbeing of the other person. This ability to be moved by the wellbeing of another (and for another to be moved by concern for your wellbeing) is good in and of itself: so that a society devoid of this value would be impoverished even aside from the numerous luxuries that cooperation makes possible. The good of sociability plays a very significant role in relation to the book's political philosophy, and so like Finnis I will defer a longer discussion of sociability to a later point.

Practical reasonableness. This refers to the ability to bring order and coherence, or intelligent purpose, to one's actions and deliberations. Its primary satisfactions are delivered in the form (a) of freedom from the will of others (the ability to think, choose and act for oneself: to be self-directing); and (b) of the harmony and order of one's inner life, which does not need therefore to be induced by drugs, indoctrination, the suppression of one's mental faculties and so forth. Again, this is obviously highly significant for the argument of Finnis's book generally, as I shall make clear shortly.

Religion. In one sense, this dimension of the good need not be taken to refer to any specific doctrinal or credal position (such as Roman Catholicism), but given Finnis's own Catholic beliefs and the presumptive need to avoid false religion, one could say that Finnis would ultimately want religious reflections to guide us towards a vision of the truth that he sees as being captured (perhaps not uniquely) by Catholic doctrine. In this context, however, 'religion' refers merely to an openness to the contemplation of ultimate questions about life. A thoughtful person looking at the other six goods might be struck by the fact that our engagement with them is transient and seemingly insignificant. We are born, grow old and die within such a vanishingly short time, when considered against the background of the history of the world (or even merely of human history). What then does it matter whether or not we have managed to 'flourish' in our time here? Unless we are exceptionally good, or exceptionally evil, history will cease to remember us. What purpose is served by engagement with 'forms of the good', when our time is so fleeting? Concern with these questions, Finnis argues, can transform (essentially, deepen) our engagement with the other goods, especially if we are led to believe in an order to the cosmos that is independent of us, and which makes all that passes within significant. Then, our fleeting engagements might be seen as working to, or within, some broader purpose even if we, imprisoned in the temporal world, cannot perceive its workings or its ends.

THE STATUS OF PRACTICAL REASONABLENESS

Are you convinced by these explanations? (If not, ask yourself what you would take as satisfactory grounds for their explanation; or try to scrutinise the assumptions required for their rejection.) Finnis asserts that these seven basic forms of the good are *exhaustive* of dimensions of human wellbeing. Any other imaginable dimensions of human flourishing will turn out to be, on reflection, aspects of these seven goods, or else ways of engaging with them in combination. Is this correct? What about 'meaningful labour', or 'dignity', for example?

At all events, the basic goods are dimensions of human wellbeing that can only be secured *in common*, so that taken together, Finnis say that they represent a 'common good' in the classical sense. Individuals (who are practically reasonable) are able to participate in these dimensions of the good in an endless variety of ways, giving priority through their choices now to some goods, and now to others; and finding endless new and old ways of realising the good through this engagement. Thus, a person may elect to pursue the life of a scholar, giving priority to the good of knowledge perhaps above all others on many occasions (and always in relation to a particular *field* of enquiry); whereas another may pursue sporting excellence, giving most priority to the value of 'play', and necessarily also to that of 'life' (interpreted in Finnis's broad sense). Finnis is thus able to resuscitate the classical idea of human society as organised around a good that is irreducibly common, though endlessly flexible and diversified, rather than a world in which essentially private, individual 'forms of the good' compete with one another.

Obviously, however, there are certain limits to each person's ability to choose and pursue certain aspects of the basic goods on certain occasions. I may hold myself to the highest standards of scholarship, exhibit the greatest dedication to my researches, but it would clearly be irrational (unreasonable) for me to continue to prioritise my reading if the library in which I am sitting is burning down around me. It is one thing to give general priority to knowledge over other aspects of the good, but quite another to give it exclusive priority. In extreme cases such as this one, my priorities seemingly *must* shift 'to the good of life as such'. But we might also regard as unreasonable the person whose devotion to academic perfection results in the neglect of health, for example. Or suppose, finding joy in books but not in other people's company, I neglect altogether the good of sociability. Have I, in this case, unreasonably cut myself off from a valuable dimension of human flourishing, or reasonably given priority to one form over another? Is life really about balance, and moderation in all things? What, indeed, if I witness a person drowning? Should I risk my own life in recognition of the value of theirs? What factors enable us to make decisions between alternative courses of action?

It is recognition of the need to make such decisions (and thousands of others like and unlike them) that leads Finnis to claim that the good of 'practical reasonableness' has a kind of special status amongst the other goods, in that it structures our pursuit of, and engagement with, them. The alert reader will have worked out that, until the preceding paragraph, discussion of the basic goods did not allude to any specific sense of 'moral goodness', but merely talked about what it is good for human beings to have, or to do, in the sense of what redounds to their wellbeing. The good of practical reasonableness translates these 'non-moral' goods into moral ones, by drawing attention to the consequences and contextual factors in the light of which practical decisions must be made. Of the long, involved and very rich discussion provided by Finnis, I draw attention only briefly to a few considerations:

i.   Each basic good has value, and none should be engaged with in a way that eliminates or devalues any of the other goods. There will be certain situations in which, for example, my priorities must shift towards considerations of bodily health, as above. Equally, one cannot reasonably engage in forms of play (for example) that are essentially destructive. The reason that it is wrong to 'murder for fun' (to take an extreme instance) is that the good that comes from 'performance' is here being directed *against* the good of life. If one is so insane or twisted as to find the performance of such acts enjoyable, it is only because one has failed to understand the basic good of life (and sociability etc).

ii. Goods must not be pursued in a way that harms other people. Indeed, practical reasonableness furnishes no grounds for arbitrarily valuing one's own wellbeing more highly than that of others, in the sense of viewing one's own priorities as demanding that others abrogate their own welfare in deference. Nothing whatever can be drawn from the fact that person A is person A, and not person B. However, in the context of this premise of basic equality (so to speak), it is nevertheless entirely reasonable to have regard first and foremost for one's own wellbeing, and allow others to look after theirs. It is reasonable to do this, not because one's wellbeing is more valuable than that of others, but because it is *one's own*. Nevertheless, this dimension of practical reasonableness 'remains a pungent critique of selfishness, special pleading, double-standards, hypocrisy, indifference to the good of others whom one could easily help ... and all the other manifold forms of egoistic and group bias'.[7]

iii. Pursuit of the basic goods takes place in a world of limited resources, so that account must be taken of distributive questions. How, in such a world, is it possible to decide what is reasonably due to me, or when

---

[7] *NLNR*, 107.

certain things, opportunities, resources and so forth are owed to others? This is at the heart of enquiries into justice.

iv.   In attempting to understand the extent and limitation of one's reasonable opportunities, one must have regard to the fact that these goods are a common good, often demanding that at least part of the satisfaction that is derived from the goods must not be regarded as exclusively one's own. Take again the good of knowledge: as a scholar, my pursuit of knowledge is of obvious benefit to me (in satisfying curiosity and the thirst for understanding); but my pursuit of knowledge involves written and verbal reflections on the knowledge attained. This occurs not only when I write books, or give lectures, but when I talk to family or friends, voice knowledgable opinions on topics of common concern etc, and generally share ideas with others. My pursuit of knowledge is therefore in part directed to the *common good* of society, not just my own personal wellbeing (though, as we shall see, the bonds of sociability link these together).

These last considerations, on justice and the common good, go to the heart of Finnis's political philosophy in *Natural Law and Natural Rights*. Finnis's discussion of justice in *Natural Law and Natural Rights* is very intricate, but it helps to remember that it is premised upon the relationship between three ideas: order, community and justice.

ORDER, COMMUNITY AND JUSTICE

Let us begin with the concept of order. That human communities exhibit or depend upon order is in one sense obvious, since community is precisely the antithesis of anarchy. But how is 'order' to be understood? Borrowing from Aquinas, Finnis says that there are four kinds of order that it is necessary to comprehend:

i.   First, there is an order to the world that is not the product of human efforts or a mere by-product of human energies, but which human beings can nevertheless come to know and to understand (so-called 'natural order'). The world is not a random collision of unrepeatable, ever-contingent events, but exhibits regularity: objects possess a certain chemical structure, which can be broken down or analysed into more basic elements, or otherwise combined into compounds. The subject of chemistry is the study of the laws governing such structures and reactions, and their properties, just as the subject of physics systematises knowledge of the properties of energy, motion etc. Newton's and Faraday's Laws are precisely examples of human understanding of an order that exists entirely independently of human beings, but which brings regularity and intelligibility to the world we inhabit.

ii. The second kind of order is the very order of human thought and reason itself ('rational order'). The human mind is obviously capable of coherent, ordered thought. We do not experience thinking as simply an endless sequence of random images which flash before the mind without any connection to each other. The capacity for reason is exactly the ability to marshal one's thoughts into some kind of order, to link one thought to another and to form propositions (or questions), or chains of argument. It is scarcely possible to deny the existence of this capacity, for any such attempted denial would constitute nothing other than the exercise of the capacity being denied. Equally obviously, we could not appreciate order of the first kind were we unable to organise thoughts into coherent chains of reasoning.

iii. Human beings are also capable of bringing further order into existence, of reducing aspects of the world to order ('sub-creative order'). The wheel is not a form that exists in nature, but had to be invented and *produced* by human effort. Cakes can be made by combining various ingredients and introducing a chemical reaction (through mixing and heating, for example). Again, the capacity to bring about such instances of order relies both upon natural order (one cannot subvert the laws of chemistry nor the properties of physical forces), and upon rational order (coherent ideas about the ways in which such properties can be utilised or manipulated). All of this depends upon the ability to organise our actions into non-random chains: the churning of butter, the combining of flour and cream, the lighting of a flame etc. exhibit order in being directed *as steps* towards a specific end.

iv. Finally, much that human beings create is not achievable by one person acting alone (however orderly their actions). Think about a university classroom. Consider the number and variety of different materials that go into its construction. Many of these, including the bricks themselves, must be manufactured. Each brick must be of the same size, be capable of sustaining the same load and so on. The mass-production of bricks requires the cooperation of a production line. Indeed, the skills of brick-making need to be taught and learned. The building itself is obviously not a haphazard jumble of materials, but an organised and ordered construction, following detailed plans created by architects and civil engineers amongst whose skills are intricate understandings of physical forces and mathematical calculations. Again, those skills must come from somewhere, must be taught and passed on. The transfer of materials to the building site requires lorries and other forms of transport: again, these are not naturally occurring units but manufactured machines, requiring the same skills, modes of production and construction etc. And to operate, there must be road and rail networks, bridges, viaducts, cuttings and the organisation of labour and planning that went into their creation. It should be apparent, therefore, that even the erection of a building, which might seem quite mundane, involves a collective effort so complex that it is impossible to trace the totality of efforts that contributed to its realisation. This fourth kind of order, therefore, is the order of choice and decision: the ability (or perhaps one should say availability) to organise and direct not only individual efforts but also to combine them into large-scale patterns which produce new forms of order that otherwise could never come into existence.

One might ponder at length the ways in which these different forms of order interrelate; but it is important to understand that none of the four kinds of order *reduces to* any of the others. Each forms a genuinely separate kind of order. How do these ideas of order relate to that of community?

It might be recalled that Hobbes regarded community as a kind of artifice: the 'natural condition' of mankind was one of 'freedom' from any kind of structure, and the foundation of society a kind of compact that introduces order and stability to human affairs. Order is not natural, but demands to be produced. It might therefore be imagined that there is nothing 'natural' about human community: in the absence of any inherent structure or order, one must be invented. For Finnis this is not the case. If we bear in mind the first kind of order, we may be led to recall that human beings are composed of biological material that itself has a certain kind of structure. The creation of life demands the transmission of this biological material, and the life that is created derives from and shares certain characteristics with those whose union produced it. Human society, even in a very primitive sense, is therefore not simply a 'random' collection of otherwise unrelated, 'equidistant' individuals. It is a collection of family units defined by shared blood. This unity at the genetic level is inescapable, but it may be observed to have certain effects. Normally, the parents who gave life to a child will have the closest connection, will feel the strongest need to ensure its survival or wellbeing. Obviously, human beings are capable of subverting or interrupting this natural order, by acting against it or without thought for it. But it remains that human community is not without a natural mode of ordering, an in-built structure that cannot be eliminated simply by being denied.[8]

If community depends upon order in the first sense, it also requires unity in the second. Aside from the special genetic unity of the family, the human race itself is defined by certain physical and physiological continuities: in possessing the same organic structure, we experience the world in broadly the

---

[8] In Aquinas's terms, such departures from order are precisely *subversions of* order, and hence parasitic upon that order. See also Finnis's distinction between the primary or 'focal' meaning of concepts versus those usages that are *secundum quid*.

same way. Possessing eardrums of a similar kind, and having a particular type of vocal chord, we hear and are capable of generating a certain kind of sound. No doubt again there are various interruptions of this unity (deafness, for example) but it is nevertheless the case that human beings can vocalise sounds to produce noises that, for example, lions or even apes cannot. But it is only the unity that we can bring to *understanding* that allows us to interpret the sounds thus produced as *words*, organised into propositions, claims, arguments, explanations, questions and so forth. Here, the unity or order is certainly only ever partially realised. Perhaps, in a lecture, you might understand everything the lecturer has said. But the chances are that not every student in the room will have understood every explanation, grasped every implication that the lecturer intends to draw to the audience's attention. Misunderstandings are clearly possible. Even amongst those who have understood, there will be differences of interpretation, significance, emphasis and suchlike: lecture notes are not a verbatim transcript of the lecture, and it would be decidedly odd (indeed, practically impossible) for each student's notes to report exactly the same thing, in the same words. Despite such variations in understanding, however, the presence of unity, of coherence in understanding amongst those present, is undeniable. It is not as if half the audience thinks the lecture is about Finnis's discussion of community, whereas the other half think the topic is the eating habits of the diplodocus.

Finnis points out that the family has again a special unity in this regard: its members will be quicker to grasp exactly the subtleties of the speaker's intention, knowing more intimately the other's concerns, viewpoints, interests etc and having a certain common fund of experience as a shared background. In-jokes and the ability to anticipate the other's point are examples of this. This shared background obviously becomes more diluted outside the family, but it is never completely absent, as the discussion of Hart's jurisprudence earlier perhaps served to show. The same special unity of the family is exhibited in relation to the third order: these subtle modes of communication between family members spill over into a broader 'cultural' unity, shared skills, ways of dealing with situations, as well as the presence of common assets and possessions. But in a similar way, the lecture audience understands the language of the speaker (as being English, or French, for example), can understand gestures and facial expressions as well as the words and so on.

Finally, community obviously depends upon the possibility of coordinating action and directing that coordinated effort towards ends of various kinds. The lecturer and audience come together with certain common assumptions in play: they expect to hear arguments and explanations, regard the occasion as one part of a larger effort, and realise that this requires certain commitments. On the part of the lecturer, it demands the accumulation of thought and knowledge, and the steady effort and willingness (for whatever reason) to communicate this to others; on the part of the audience, it is to commit certain amounts of time and energy to acquiring and processing the knowledge, again for numerous possible reasons.

Community cannot exist without the presence of some measure of unity in respect of all four kinds of order. But insofar as reflection is directed towards understanding the place of *justice* in society (that is to say, the distinction between just versus unjust forms of social order), it is the fourth kind of order that is of most immediate significance. How in other words, having understood how community is related to order, can one distinguish bad ordering from good order (*eudaimonia* in Aristotle's terminology)?

We were brought to the concern with community in view of the fact that the basic goods discussed earlier are fully capable of being pursued and secured only in common. Though all are important, the good of sociability obviously has a particular claim on our attention. It is necessary to consider, then, the various ways and degrees to which sociability can be manifested.

Finnis invites us to imagine a situation in which two students, A and B, are having a seminar with their tutor. Suppose that A and B are in direct competition with each other: A wants to do better than B in the examination they must both sit (perhaps to beat B to the award of a prize, or a position of employment); whereas B wishes to outdo A for the same reasons. In this situation, A is at best indifferent to B's aims, and at worst hostile to them (and vice versa). Nevertheless, A and B have every reason to cooperate with one another for the purposes of advancing their own aims. If each talks constantly over the other, competes aggressively for the tutor's attention, or otherwise disrupts proceedings, neither will derive very much benefit from the seminar. On the other hand, if A allows B to converse with the tutor (ask or answer questions, clarify points etc), A will gain the same knowledge that B thereby gains. Thus, each student 'has an interest in the maintenance of the ensemble of conditions … for the pursuit of his or her own objective'[9] such that the combined interests in the maintenance of that state of affairs might be called a 'common good' that exists between them.

Obviously, this form of sociability is quite rudimentary and not very deep. A deeper expression might therefore be present in the context of two parties who enter into a contract in order to pursue an end that is jointly desired, and jointly beneficial. (Perhaps by agreeing to cooperate, study together, test one another and correct each other's mistakes, A and B will both do better in the examination.) The example of a contractual relationship differs from the seminar situation described above, in that the parties are coming together to cooperate because their interests temporarily align: they are not in competition in relation to some end, but jointly endeavour to bring it about. This is

---

[9] *NLNR*, 139.

still a far cry from saying that Party A has any real or lasting concern for the wellbeing of Party B, but unlike the first example, the situation demands that Party A exhibit *some* interest in Party B's welfare, insofar as the joint realisation of the goal demands it.

Capable of expression at various levels of depth, sociability can be considered on a sliding scale: Party A and Party B are clearly linked more closely if involved in a regular course of dealing, than if signatories to a one-off contract. Here, there might come into existence what Aristotle called 'business friendships': relationships of reciprocity that exist for mutual advantage, but which involve a degree of genuine affection. However deep such relationships go, or might become, Finnis nevertheless says that the highest expression of sociability is that of true friendship, which involves a different kind of reciprocity.

For A to be the friend of B, it must be the case that A genuinely desires the welfare of B. It might be asserted by very cynical people that in all such cases, what A really desires is his own wellbeing, and that the concern for B is simply a function of the fact that A enjoys B's company and wishes to continue to do so. There might indeed be such instances of friendship, but they are not really the ideal Finnis has in mind (they approximate more to the business friendship of two individuals who use each other for fulfilment of private ends, which might generate affection along the way). At any rate, it does not seem to be impossible or absurd to suggest that A might come to be genuinely moved (motivated etc) by a concern for B, in ways that do not immediately focus upon or come back to considerations of A's own benefit. At the same time, there is no need to think of friendship as being *devoid* of self-interested motives. A is not a deserving object of B's affection if he is only interested in B as a means to fulfilment of A's own ends; but neither is A a deserving object of affection if he devotes all his time, energy, reserves of affection and so on, to B, at the expense of his own wellbeing: he becomes an object not of affection but of pity. The point is that within a true friendship, A's interests and wellbeing become so bound up with B's interests and wellbeing, that the motivation for action (on the part of both A and B) terminates neither with A's interests nor with B's, but is directed towards the 'common good' that exists between them.

In short: if A genuinely cares for B, then B's wellbeing becomes a dimension of A's wellbeing (in that A will be moved to sorrow, or pity, or distress, or anxiety, if B suffers), just as A's wellbeing becomes a dimension of B's. But if this is the case, then A has good reasons to secure his *own* wellbeing *as a dimension of B's* and not simply for entirely private, selfish reasons. But similarly, B's wellbeing is an intelligible source of motivation for A since it advances A's wellbeing (or 'flourishing' in Finnis's terms). There is no end to this oscillation of focus. It becomes intelligible to speak of a common good between them, for the sake of which it is coherent to act, plan, deliberate, cooperate and so forth: it is, in Finnis's own words, 'the common good of mutual self-constitution, self-fulfilment, self-realization'.[10]

The world has known many examples of relationships that fail to embody fully this image of friendship; but it would be overly cynical to suggest that the ideal is completely absent from experience. No doubt again it is to the family that we should look for its clearest expressions: the parent's pain, anxiety, concern and love for a child addicted to drugs, or terminally ill, or depressed, is not simply a mirror for the parent's selfish desire for happiness. The concern for the child to flourish, to overcome obstacles, is not down to the parent's wish to treat the child as a source of happiness, satisfaction, fulfilment etc. The concern is *for the child's sake*, and the anxiety (and so on) that is felt is due to the child's welfare being an aspect of the parent's. Those things that adversely impact upon the one will ipso facto adversely impact upon the other. That there are clear examples of selfish or bad parenting, ungrateful children, families at war with themselves, families torn apart by long and bitter divisions etc, does not detract from this point. They are precisely departures from the expression of sociability in its highest form (its 'focal meaning').

Aristotle's lesson, in Book I of the *Politics*, was that the family, like the individual, is not a complete community. It is not self-sufficing. This is true even at a biological level. The ongoing life of the family, the production of future generations, can only be secured through genetic diversity, and cannot be sustained if there is interbreeding only between family members. But it is also manifested in more mundane ways: there are vast resources of knowledge, of practical skills, of culture and of 'things', that can only come to the members of a family from outside. The family's own fund of such resources is too limited in general to secure the complete flourishing of its members, its ability to deal with illness, with scarcity, its capacity to absorb the consequences of harmful events, generate income and so on. (Aristotle's example is more dramatic: whereas a community can repel an invasion by an enemy nation, a family cannot.) Families which band together to forge permanent communal or trading links, who share knowledge, come together for the purposes of defence etc, are better equipped in this regard. But even neighbourhood, as Aristotle points out, is hardly sufficient as an economic unit, can scarcely provide or sustain the material conditions necessary for the health and cultural needs of its members. Only the *polis* itself, the political state, is self-sufficing in this sense.[11]

---

[10]   ibid 141. Recall Aristotle's dictum that man is a social animal, not self-sufficient but requiring others for his flourishing.

[11]   Following Eric Voeglin, Finnis regards Aristotle's assessment as premature: it ignores alike the spiritual needs of men that fall to be fulfilled by the community of the universal Church, and the material needs of economic health and political stability that find expression in the international community of states: *NLNR*, 160.

With this in mind, an idea of justice immediately arises. Throughout the history of Western thought, a consistent definition of justice has been the notion of 'giving to each person their proper due'. We might therefore say that *if* there are certain things, required for human life and self-constitution, that *cannot* be secured or produced by individuals or family units (or other small forms of association), which therefore *must* come to those individuals from outside, *then* it is a requirement of justice that those things be given to them. Certain things are due in justice to each member of the community.

The theory of justice is the theory that asks what is owed to each person, and from whom those things are owed. Perhaps some may quarrel with the assertion in the previous paragraph: perhaps it will be said that each person's wellbeing is their own affair, and it is no responsibility of mine, or of the state, to ensure the welfare or even survival of members of society who lack the ability to take care of themselves.

There are various levels at which we might break down this objection. At the most general level, if we accept the argument (as seemingly we must) that many or all of the 'goods' we depend upon can only be secured in community, and cannot be pursued in complete isolation from the society of others, then to have any sort of entitlement to those communally secured goods entails a duty on behalf of all those who enjoy or partake of them to foster that common good for the sake of their community. This is, admittedly, unlikely to move the stony-hearted advocate of the law-of-the-jungle view of human society. So perhaps we need to draw upon more specific examples. We might recall that those who regard themselves as 'self-sufficient' are really not so. Anyone who has wealth must have acquired it from somewhere. The 'self-made man' is not really self-made, but worked his way into an affluent position on the back of dealing with others. One might say that he contracted his way to a wealthy situation. But if this is the case, it is because certain duties, services, goods and so on were due to him under the terms of the contracts: he was owed certain things by other people. This is a dimension of justice know as *commutative justice*: those duties, services and so on that are due to a person in virtue of being owed by other specific individuals.

Commutative justice is of enormous importance, speaking directly to the notion that human beings are social animals reliant on others for their existence and flourishing. Its effects are felt not only in the world of business transactions and contract, but in a different way in broader social contexts. There are bonds of trust and affection that are in some sense 'due' to members of the same family. The marriage relationship itself is a kind of contract: a set of promises that create obligations of care, attention and very often material sharing. When the self-made man objects to the idea that the community owes duties of justice to its members, it is probably because of an instinct that rails against any generalised notion of 'material sharing' in society. As Finnis points out, these instincts are far from being entirely wrong. Perhaps the most famous image of communistic sharing is that of Plato's ideal society in *The Republic*. Plato envisages a society in which there is the widest possible sharing: not only of property and land, but of children and sexual partners, decision-making and all the things that contribute to the material life of the community. Nothing would be privately owned, but everything would be held in common for the whole community. The instinct that drives this suggestion is no doubt an enthusiasm for the most expansive expression of the 'sharing' that seems to lie at the basis of friendship, the thing that epitomises the highest form of sociability. But Plato's image is terrible! Why?

The fact is that although the image of the ideal republic might seem to embody the deepest expression of sociability, in reality it erodes sociability almost completely. The opening passages of Aristotle's *Politics* are a reminder of the fact that friendship is more than anything the steady willingness to commit oneself to the good of one's friend. But to 'commit' oneself in this sense is precisely to commit certain energies and resources to one's friend, and this implies that one *has* something to commit, that one has things *of one's own* to share. Plato's image is a catastrophic watering down of friendship, because it renders everybody mutually and equally responsible to everyone else. This cannot be just: suppose for example that I devoted no more of my time, my energy, reserves of affection and concern, my resources etc, to my wife than I devote to strangers I happen upon in the street. It would I hope be agreed that to do so would be to treat her with great injustice. Similarly, if I gave no more thought or priority to the reasonable demands or needs of my colleagues, or to students of my university, than I give to students or academics in other institutions, with whom I have no previous or lasting connection, then it seems quite clear that I would be failing to live up to my professional duties, ie, failing to render to students and colleagues what is due to them in virtue of being students or colleagues *of mine*.

Much of the time, the majority of one's efforts and one's resources are of such a character that they can only be given to a few, and only fully given to those with whom one has a special and permanent connection. That being the case, one is forced to recognise that the complete absorption of every individual's efforts to secure the wellbeing of others into some grand social scheme will do little except suppress the very possibility of self-constitution through the making and selecting of commitments. A society in which there are no wives or husbands or close friendships and partnerships of any kind, in which one labours always and only for the benefit of 'society' and not any individuals within it, in which excluded from one's life is the possibility of any deep personal connection, is truly a horrific image: a radical emaciation of human flourishing. Drawing on the social teaching of the Catholic Church, Finnis calls attention to the principle of 'subsidiarity' and its importance in thinking

about justice. This is the principle that wherever possible, larger forms of association (such as the state) should not assume functions that are more efficiently
performed by smaller associations, such as the family (which after all have
a much more intimate knowledge and understanding of the needs of their
members).[12] In short:

> It is therefore a fundamental aspect of general justice that common enterprises
> should be regarded, and practically conducted, not as ends in themselves but as
> means of assistance, as ways of helping individuals to 'help themselves' or more
> precisely, to constitute themselves. And in all those fields of activity, including eco-
> nomic activity, where individuals, or families, or other relatively small groups, can
> help themselves by their own private efforts and initiatives without thereby injur-
> ing (either by act or omission) the common good, they are entitled in justice to be
> allowed to do so.[13]

At the same time, however, it is simply not possible to derive all that one needs
from specific individuals. Though the marriage contract contains promises to
care for one's spouse in sickness, and not just in health, it is obviously beyond
the resources of most individuals to treat or cure serious illnesses. One's partner is taken 'for richer, for poorer', but it is not usually within the power of
the other to generate employment opportunities, or (in the broadest sense) a
safe and stable society in which to live. The same is true of business relationships. The power does not lie with either of the contracting parties to compel
the performance of contractual duties, or to extract equivalent compensation:
the practice of contracting itself relies upon a centralised system ensuring the
determination and enforcement of individual rights. It requires the backdrop
of a stable and effective legal order. These matters can be determined only
at the level of the state itself. They require nothing less than a political community, with an organised system of governance. Hence Aristotle's dictum
about the *polis* being the only truly self-sufficing community. Insofar as this
is the case—insofar as certain conditions *must* be established and maintained
by the state itself—it is absolutely a demand of justice that the members of a
community are given assistance in the form of resources and efforts necessary
for securing their wellbeing, which it is beyond their capacity to produce or
secure for themselves.

Subsidiarity in this context refers to the assistance or help that the community owes to the smaller units within it that are not self-sufficing in Aristotle's
sense: individuals, families and other forms of fraternal association that might
exist to secure the wellbeing of their members. This is, in effect, the reverse
side of the principle that such small forms of association should in justice be
allowed to self-constitute. Again, it is clear that there is no possibility of the

[12] *NLNR* 146–47.
[13] ibid 169.

state performing such functions if it lacks resources of its own to distribute. Hence, the principle of subsidiarity calls into play another dimension of justice: *distributive justice*.

As the name suggests, distributive justice takes as its focus the question of how goods in society should be distributed, and on what conditions. 'Goods' in this context refer not only to material resources, but also opportunities, profits and other sorts of advantages, and also things like offices and responsibilities, roles etc, and burdens. The example of Plato's ideal society in the *Republic* demonstrates that very many of these goods will fail to serve or be mobilised for the common good, unless they lie in private hands. Efficient use, careful management and sensible husbandry of resources derive principally from considerations of private advantage, the love of one's own and so on, and are less easy to replicate or promote in relation to goods held in common: a point of which Aristotle was very well aware.[14] Given this persistent characteristic of human community, and despite the obvious abuses to which it is subject, Finnis regards a regime of private property as a requirement of justice.[15] But because the common good always requires forms of collaboration and coordination of resources and efforts, property is so to speak never *absolutely* private: each person owes a duty in justice to foster the common good of their community.

The question of distributive justice is again the question of what is due (or owed) to each person. One obvious proposal, the simplicity of which perhaps explains its enduring appeal in certain sectors of politics, is that goods, offices and such like should be divided equally amongst the members of a community. Such levelling ambitions ought to be rejected, for numerous reasons. For one thing, equality itself is an endlessly adaptable idea. To take up again my example from chapter six, suppose I am faced with the task of dividing up a birthday cake between party guests. 'Equality' might suggest that each person should receive a piece of the same size. But if some guests are small children whereas others are large adults, might 'equality' not entail a larger piece for some and a smaller piece for others in accordance with their size? What if some guests bought expensive gifts, whereas others made only a token effort? Or should one take account of the thoughtfulness, rather than the expense, of the gift? Should equality be construed at all in terms of reward? One could go on indefinitely in this vein (closeness of relationship,

---

[14] Aristotle, *Politics*, II.2. See Finnis, *NLNR*, 170–71.

[15] ibid 170: 'a theory of justice is to establish what is due to individuals in the circumstances in which they are, not in the circumstances of some other, "ideal" world'. Thus, 'my theory is not restricted (like Rawls's) to the ideal conditions of a society in which everyone complies fully with the principles and institutions of justice': ibid 164.

relative wealth of the guests etc), so that the idea of 'equality' itself leads us nowhere (or everywhere).

For Finnis, however, the objective of justice is not equality, but the common good: the flourishing of all persons within a community. From this point of view, there is nothing wrong per se with inequalities of wealth, but the presence of such inequalities is suggestive of the rich having failed to live up to their duties in justice by failing to mobilise the part of their wealth that is better used by others, through acts of redistribution. This view is neatly encapsulated in the following passage:

> If redistribution means no more than that more beer is going to be consumed morosely before television sets by the relatively many, and less fine wine consumed by the relatively few at salon concerts by select musicians, then it can scarcely be said to be a demand of justice. But if redistribution means that, at the expense of the wine etc, more people can be preserved from (non-self-inflicted) illness, educated to the point where genuine self-direction becomes possible for them, defended against the enemies of justice, etc, then such redistribution is a requirement of justice.[16]

The fact is that all means and manners of flourishing, of engaging with the basic goods, demand the expenditure of resources: not only time, but very often money or other material assets. Suppose I am fortunate enough to be able to pursue opportunities, reasonably or otherwise exhaustively, to engage with the basic goods (ie, to pursue my own flourishing), before my wealth is exhausted. Other portions of my wealth may go towards the satisfaction of obligations in commutative justice: the wellbeing of dependants, or payment for services under contract and so forth. In addition, I may mobilise other assets so as to insure myself against risks, including the ability to bear losses which result from communal enterprises, or to provide a cushion against future loss of income or capacity. If after all this I still have wealth left over, serving no useful end, then is it not just that this portion of my wealth should be mobilised by or on behalf of others who could thereby seize opportunities to flourish in ways otherwise denied to them?

Finnis acknowledges that there are 'no very precise yardsticks' for addressing these issues. As his own example suggests, it may not always be in line with justice for a person to use their wealth to secure for themselves even reasonable opportunities for flourishing, if they live in a society where many are unable to fulfil even basic needs. How far should a society go in effecting redistribution? Should a society cease to offer subsidies to the arts, or maintain public libraries or sports facilities (enjoyed by the relatively few) so as to pay for more doctors or teachers (which will benefit the relatively many)? In deciding what portion of individual or corporate wealth is 'better used by others', to what extent should a society interfere with, regulate or otherwise limit obligations in

---

[16] ibid 174.

commutative justice? Should there be, for instance, a maximum wage as well as a minimum wage?

Amongst the other possible dimensions of the problem (such as desert, contribution, need, ability to insure oneself and so on), Finnis mentions capacity: 'Flutes to flute-players'.[17] Not everybody will benefit fully or equally from higher education, for example. It therefore seems reasonable to distribute opportunities only to those capable of deriving benefit from them. But in thinking about capacity, how far should our thought reach back into questions of 'structural tilt', or perhaps better the 'structural disadvantage' that is imposed upon people who for all sorts of socio-economic reasons fail to manifest or develop capacities?[18] To what extent is the ability to insure oneself, ability to contribute and so on, a matter of systematic or structural patterns of disadvantage and privilege? How radical a redistribution is necessary? Indeed, how radical a redistribution is even possible? The redistributive ambitions of even the most left-thinking governments in liberal and democratic societies eventually come down to the willingness of a vast middle class to vote increased taxation upon itself. (There is also the question of considerable erosion to individual privacy consequent upon the state having to 'drill down' into an examination of people's capacities and vulnerabilities: would we give up our privacy, in exchange for greater state intervention and assistance?)

One must also reflect upon the economic complexity of modern capitalist societies. We may feel outrage against corporations that are in some cases richer than the governments of their communities. How can such a situation be permitted to exist in adverse economic conditions in which the state cannot secure even the basic needs of some people? Putting aside crude demands for 'equality', we might question whether, once a corporation has been duly rewarded for its efforts and innovations, and once account has been taken of the needs of inward investment, insurance against risk, and after its obligations in commutative justice have been honoured, if that corporation still has reserves of, say, $76 billion, ought it not to be seen as a failure to do justice if such wealth is not somehow mobilised or redistributed for the common good, through taxation or other means? But the fact is that the immediate economic effect of such huge profit reserves is to increase the value of the shares for individual shareholders. This wealth is then open for circulation, capable of being borrowed against, or even used for the common good. The idea of 'stored wealth' is therefore problematic: were the $76 billion to be distributed to the shareholders, this would put an extra $76 billion in circulation, but would simultaneously decrease the value of the shares by the same amount, taking

---

[17]   ibid 175.
[18]   See, eg, M Fineman, 'Evolving Images of Gender and Equality: A Feminist Journey' (2009) 43 *New England Law Review* 437.

$76 billion out of circulation. Liquid shares would have converted into liquid cash with no net alteration to the 'wealth' in circulation.[19] Of course, one could validly object that such shares are owned disproportionately by those who are already very wealthy, and used more for private benefit than anything else. But this simply returns us to the problems of taxation and of structural privilege and disadvantage alluded to earlier.

JUSTICE AND RIGHTS

Perhaps this is what Finnis means by saying that his theory considers the problem of justice in an imperfectly just world. Perhaps this also lies behind Finnis's assertion that 'the modern language of rights' is both a 'supple and potentially precise instrument for sorting out and expressing the demands of justice' but also 'a hindrance to clear thought' in working out what justice requires.[20] It is, on the one hand, extremely difficult to determine what is due to each person without precise notions of what can be claimed 'as of right' or demanded 'as per duty'. One can regard the law as establishing and in some cases clarifying the boundaries of people's entitlements, through the operation of numerous doctrines, principles and concepts. Rules regarding foreseeability, legal capacity, principles of duties of care and so forth all clarify the scope of duties and the rights that correspond to them. Rights, when clearly made out, have a kind of conclusory force that does not always operate in relation to broader concepts of morality. If A breaches a contract with B, B has certain enforceable rights (and thus remedies) against A, which obtain irrespective of wider considerations as to whether, say, B is of good character, more able to absorb the loss than A, and therefore a 'deserving' recipient in a more general sense. But precisely because of this conclusory force, rights can often obscure enquiries into justice, because they represent a closing-off of further moral enquiry. Another part of the enquiry into justice, in other words, is: *should* people have rights of a certain kind? Do certain kinds of right (such as rights relating to the testamentary transfer of property) operate to sustain or reinforce structural privilege and disadvantage?

The fact is that human wellbeing is a many-sided affair; and the actions, modes of collaboration, coordination and mutual forbearance involved in the pursuit of the common good can lead to inescapable, unpalatable and finally incommensurable choices. *Natural Law and Natural Rights* does not resolve these questions, if indeed they are resolvable: it is not, as Finnis admits, a

---

[19] I am grateful to Dominic de Cogan for discussion of the themes of this paragraph.
[20] *NLNR*, 210.

book on justice.[21] But it nevertheless contains an important theory *about* justice. Departing significantly from most other treatments of the subject, Finnis resists the idea that commutative and distributive justice represent separate 'kinds' of justice. He instead supposes that they are discrete parts of a single enquiry—the enquiry into what is due to each person—and the distinction more a matter of analytical convenience than anything else. In this sense also, both commutative and distributive considerations alike are directed ultimately to the question of how the common good is to be fostered and maintained.

One can see Finnis's point in various areas of legal life. Consider tort law, for example. If A accidentally but negligently knocks B down a flight of stairs, so that B becomes paralysed, the law will typically (through the operation of a duty of care) render A liable to B in damages, for example, for pain and suffering, loss of future earnings, shock and so forth. This involves an aspect of commutative justice in the fact that there are things that are due to B directly from A: the law makes A, and not the community as a whole, directly responsible in virtue of having caused the accident. But at the same time, if B needs constant medical attention, social care and so on, these are things that it is beyond A's resources to provide (especially if A has a low-income job). Thus, through the operation of social security, housing benefit, a national health service, and other resources (such as the provision of disabled access to buildings, buses etc), the state provides facilities that are due to B (in fulfilling essential needs) that derive from the community itself, through taxation, insurance schemes and other measures. In doing so, it might be said that the state recognises that there are always risks in social life, and that it is unfair to visit the consequences of such risks entirely upon the hapless individuals who run afoul of them. This is an act of distributive justice: a distribution of such risks and attendant responsibilities. Indeed, private insurance schemes that pay out in the event of accidents (especially in the context of motor insurance) also simultaneously exhibit the ideas of commutative and distributive justice: consider the position of an individual who causes a motor accident whilst driving uninsured.

These questions arise at all levels of legal and political debate. If we see contract or tort as instruments for correcting wrongs arising from a breach of obligations, then we will see them as serving the needs of commutative justice. The natural interpretation of the law is then one that regards property rights as essential, or of primary importance for the polity, and infractions of these as inviting forms of redress. Questions of distributive justice will accordingly be confined largely to implications arising out of the exercise of the rights of ownership: transfers, gifts, succession and so forth. Alternatively, law can be regarded as the principal means by which the state's, and by extension the community's, distributive goals are realised or implemented. The legal rules

---

[21] ibid 175.

and doctrines concern the patterns after which goods, offices, risks, responsibilities, real property and so on are to be distributed throughout society. If that
is the case, branches of the law such as contract and tort are seen as primarily
distributive in aim, with commutative justice being confined to the secondary
role of restoring balance when some action, accident, or event disrupts a pre-
existing distribution.

Finnis reminds us that the act of adjudication itself reflects both forms of
justice simultaneously. It is rich in significance for distributive justice in that
the raising of an action before the court creates a common subject matter
between the parties upon which the judge is required to adjudicate. Given
that the judgment will allocate gains and losses between the parties, any bias
or negligence on the part of the judge will violate the requirements of distributive justice that operate in that context. But at the same time, the judge's
conscientious carrying-out of his duties is an aspect of commutative justice
insofar as his official capacities and responsibilities bring him into a relationship with the litigants, who can justly demand due consideration of their rights.
Perhaps, therefore, to assert that some branch of law (such as contract) has as
its ultimate aim the fulfilment of commutative justice, or is principally concerned with matters of distributive justice, is to close off the enquiry at too
early a stage, before all matters relating to the question of what is 'due' to the
litigants have been thoroughly and exhaustively reasoned out in justice.

Be that as it may, Finnis argues that rights, which are so good at reminding
us that a decision involving more than one person requires a clear understanding of exactly what is demanded of each person concerned, and of how each
person can affect these demands, also hinder the reasoning process because
their conclusory force can all too easily cut off the investigation prematurely.
The assertion that one 'has a right' can mislead the mind into concluding
that the demands of justice in a given situation have been fully considered or
met, when we know that aspects of human wellbeing are in fact complex and
competing. This is a very significant problem, which Finnis faces head-on:
are there *absolute* rights? That is to say, are certain types of action absolutely
forbidden in all situations, and therefore certain rights inviolable, or does the
admitted complexity and many-sidedness of the human good entail that acts
become good or bad, permitted or otherwise, only when considered against
given contexts of action? Finnis's answer (like that of Grotius and other earlier
natural law thinkers) is that some rights are inviolable, thus justifying the terminology of 'natural' or 'human rights'.

What can be said in support of this? If we ponder the true complexities
of the private and collaborative projects, commitments, actions and forms
of mutual restraint that are necessary for realising the human good in community, it may become clear to us that there are nevertheless factors relating to public peace and good, stable order that *must* be met if any significant

level of human flourishing is to be secured. The Church's declaration *Dignitatis Humanae* of 7 December 1965 brings these considerations together under the notion of 'public order':[22] a notion which requires an environment which is physically healthy and structured by stable expectations and reliances in which weaker members of society can move about without fear from the whims of the strong or the powerful. These aspects of public order, which would include dimensions of commutative justice,[23] pertain to the prohibition of acts such as inciting hatred towards or amongst sections of the community, rioting and acts of terror, or of public nuisance: all of which threaten the rights of every person in the community with a future of violence and other potential violations of right. Clearly the maintenance of a social space which holds such violations in check requires an understanding that each individual's rights belong to a *system* of rights which may need to be delimited or specified according to mutual limitations and accommodations. In asking how rights are to be specified—that is, how much interference with a person's enjoyment of their right by others in the exercise of the same right is to be permitted—Finnis says that

> [t]here is ... no alternative but to hold in one's mind's eye some pattern, or range of patterns, of human character, conduct, and interaction in community, and then choose such specification of rights as tends to favour that pattern, or range of patterns.[24]

We must bear in mind, in other words that, for example, toleration is preferable to hatred and bias, that privacy and reputation are essential constituents of the good, and that culture and art are superior in succouring wellbeing than ignorance, impoverishment and trash.

This might strike some readers as paternalistic. But Finnis reminds us of the ruin that would come from the idea that there are 'no fixed points in that pattern of life which one must hold in one's mind's eye in resolving problems of rights'.[25] Utilitarians would avow that there are in this sense no absolute rights: no rights that cannot be limited or overridden for the sake of the community in its last need. Indeed, Finnis warns that none are the governments in this world whose practice genuinely manifests belief in absolute human rights, for example, through torture and erosion of freedoms, and the killing of non-combatants in times of extremity. But we must not forget, Finnis says, that the seventh of the requirements of practical reasonableness prohibits actions which directly harm one of the basic goods, whether for oneself or for others.

---

[22] Dignitatis Humanae, s 7.
[23] *NLNR*, 230n.
[24] ibid 219.
[25] ibid 224.

Correlative to the exceptionless duties implied by this requirement are absolute human rights, prime amongst which would include the right not to have one's life terminated as a means to any other end.

Here we run into a serious problem, however. Finnis's earlier discussion of this requirement makes clear that he does not intend 'direct harm' only to mean actions which have no other object than the destruction or erosion of a basic good. All actions that are in any way intelligent are undertaken for the purposes of securing one or more of the other basic goods, and this requirement must be understood as operating with that assumption in play.[26] The actions Finnis has in mind are therefore actions which, for example, seek to save lives *by extinguishing a life* (murdering a person one knows with certainty is about to embark on a killing spree, or is about to press the button which launches a nuclear attack), euthanasia and the like. Such actions, however well intentioned, are prohibited by the requirements of practical reasonableness as direct assaults on a basic value. But at the same time, it must be acknowledged that *all* actions are capable of impoverishing or inhibiting basic goods in complex and unpredictable ways: my decision to become a scholar rather than a doctor may mean that some lives that might have been saved are not so; and my devotion to research into a particular field comes at the cost of furthering knowledge in others. Finnis therefore claims that actions which *indirectly* sacrifice or damage basic goods, scarcely avoidable in any event, are morally and rationally quite different from actions which perpetrate direct and immediate damage.

But here is the problem: aside from the difference in severity, what justifies the judgement that the sacrifice of knowledge entailed by my devotion to a particular research field, or the sacrifice of medical cures by my training as a historian (say) rather than a doctor, is any less a *direct* consequence of choice than in the case where I shoot the person about to kill others? The difference cannot lie in the positive nature of the action of shooting, because the example is easily adaptable to one in which my *omission* directly kills the person. (A famous problem in philosophy asks whether you should or should not pull a lever to divert a train, when doing so will kill a person on track A whilst saving five people on track B.) Or, to adapt Finnis's own example, if a state launches an attack on a military target in the knowledge that civilians will die in the blast, but the result of which is to save millions by bringing about an early surrender that will save millions of innocent people, is the killing of the civilians a 'direct' or an 'indirect' assault on a basic good (their lives)? Nor can the difference lie in the foreseeability of consequences arising from one's actions, for the level of impoverishment to the good of knowledge (and of life etc)

---

[26] ibid 119.

in not undertaking cancer research, may be just as unquantifiable, at least in advance, as the number of innocent lives that will be lost in striking the military target.

Finnis elsewhere puts the problem in other, more familiar terms, by equating the seventh requirement with the thought that the ends do not justify the means. This does help to clarify some instances of the problem: the targeting of the facility is a 'means' to the 'end' of preventing greater bloodshed, whereas the undertaking of research into history is not, by ordinary lights, a 'means' either to or away from the 'end' of curing individuals of cancer. But this way of looking at the distinction should not make us too comfortable. For one might say that the destruction of a military target is a legitimate means in warfare, at least if one is prepared to accept (as we must) that certain wars are undertaken for a just cause. We can then ask whether that 'act' is or is not separable from the killing, to whatever extent foreseen, of innocent persons by the fallout, on the grounds that it is, similarly, not an intended 'means' to the 'end' of killing civilians. The reference to intention here is dubious at best: if an action is undertaken that will, with reasonable certainty, result in collateral death, then would one not say that the action had intentionally sacrificed those lives, whether or not the deaths were specifically *desired*? Can one really draw a sharp distinction between intention and foreseeability in this way?

I do not propose to go any further into these questions here, but hope to have indicated some of their complexities. Both Finnis's standpoint, *and* the standpoint that he rejects, are deeply troubling in their implications and in the difficulties they raise. But they undoubtedly offer further support for the suggestion that utilitarian calculations which try to quantify the rationality of an action by reference to the overall net good that it brings about, are wholly inadequate as a response to the problem of justice.

Perhaps we are left with a very troubling predicament that seems to have been foreseen by Augustine. It must not be forgotten that the context of this problem is the rational choice between particular patterns of rights, given the complexities and competing considerations involved in the realisation of the common good. Finnis's deliberations might point us towards the conclusion that, after all, no system of rights will perfectly achieve justice in this world, but all shall, in various ways, perpetuate forms of injustice even as they strive to eliminate it. It is for this reason that the citizen should not place too much faith or pride in earthly arrangements, which will fail to embody a perfect justice despite our best efforts. Finnis's arguments are a salutary reminder that failures of justice are the result not only of unwisdom in our actions, but also shortcomings in our efforts of practical reason. Those efforts must never be closed off prematurely or ever taken as the last word as to how individuals and communities must act. But neither must we therefore allow ourselves to slide into arbitrariness or consequentialist thinking; rather we must be prepared to think through as many of the complexities that may be thrown into our path as possible, seeking always to understand how even the most seemingly 'private' decisions we make may resonate beyond our own situation, causing injustice and deepening the plight of others. One need only try to imagine the exhausting efforts that would be required, in the modern economic market-place, to act as a truly ethical consumer, to perceive the extent of the problem.

THE OVERALL DIRECTION OF FINNIS'S ACCOUNT

This chapter has resolutely focused upon the political philosophy of *Natural Law and Natural Rights*. But I want here to pick up (albeit briefly) on a question relating to the very basis of Finnis's philosophy, which I shall take up again more fully in chapter eleven below in considering his specifically legal philosophy.

Finnis regards his philosophy as proceeding from an interpretation of Aquinas's remarks on natural law and upon what Aquinas calls the 'first principle' of practical reason: that good is to be done and pursued, and evil avoided.[27] In his later book *Aquinas*, Finnis insists that in the course of this passage, Aquinas's reference to the 'ultimate end' of human life (*ultimus finis*) should be interpreted in the plural, as referring to *ends*, or (in other words) 'goods' that are basic in not being derivable from any further ends.[28] Hence, the basic goods provide the substance for Aquinas's first principle, which becomes therefore a *moral* obligation only when it 'is followed through ... with a reasonableness which is unrestricted and undeflected by any sub-rational factor such as distracting emotion'.[29] But that which bridges the gap, in Finnis's words, from mere prudence (on the near bank) to moral obligation (on the farther shore) is in fact the workings of practical reasonableness, which themselves, in excluding arbitrary preferences, acts of mere destruction etc, come down to a commitment to the fullest and most genuinely unrestricted openness to all of the basic goods.[30]

Although Finnis is correct to note that Aquinas's use of *finis* sometimes translates in the plural, his interpretation of this passage is deeply questionable. For earlier in the *Summa*, at I–II.1.4–7, Aquinas has already stated that there is only one possible final end of human life, that of happiness: *beatitudo*. Finnis equates this reference to 'happiness' with precisely the full and unrestricted participation in the basic goods that is the object of his discussion.[31] But Aquinas very

---

[27] Aquinas, *Summa Theologiae* I–II.94.2.
[28] Finnis, *Aquinas: Moral Political and Legal Theory* (n 5) 79.
[29] ibid 87.
[30] ibid 111ff.
[31] ibid 104.

clearly distinguishes between *beatitudo*, by which he denotes the individual's personal relationship with God (brought to fullness in the beatific vision of the afterlife), and the merely temporal *felicitas* or *beatitudo imperfecta* that is possible on earth.[32] Whereas Finnis regards happiness as intelligible only on the basis of these goods, and defined in relation to them, Aquinas *contrasts* these forms of happiness (genuine though they are) with the end that is ultimate for human beings, and which can scarcely be understood apart from the life of virtue. As I mentioned earlier in passing, Finnis's understanding of the basic goods, although it is not derived from any prior considerations, is premised upon the intellect's grasp of the goods as self-evident once they have been experienced: that is to say, our understanding of their goodness is not innate, but flows from a rational appreciation of their role in human flourishing. As such, the basic goods can scarcely avoid implicating some underlying understanding of human *functioning*. But this does not of itself turn Finnis's philosophy into a continuation of the Thomist/Aristotelian natural law theory, precisely because of the latter's placement rather of *purpose* or *proper end* at the heart of the enquiry.

The loss of this teleological framework changes everything: Aristotle does not *derive* virtue from human happiness, nor does he depict the virtues as 'ways ... or modes' for realising basic goods.[33] Humans find satisfactions in all manner of things: for example, in pleasures of the appetite towards good food, or in sexual release, or in the aesthetic enjoyment of objects. The practice of virtue demands of the individual that they withdraw from at least certain instances of these goods (and possibly from certain sorts of satisfaction altogether). In so doing, the virtuous individual will come to a rational understanding that, for example, moderation, fidelity and charity (giving up of objects that one could oneself have enjoyed) are themselves good, and a source of satisfaction that is deeper and more profound than the goods or satisfactions from which the individual withdraws in the name of virtue. Yet the pursuit of these deeper satisfactions is undoubtedly also *harder*, and more demanding than a life centred upon other goods. Thus, the virtuous life is the happy life because the one who diligently practises the virtues comes to love things aright (including virtue itself as its 'own reward'): his loves, as Augustine would say, are directed to the proper objects; proper because they point to the ultimate fulfilment of human *nature*, directed to its proper *end*. This is the intention of Aquinas's statement that it 'pertains to right reason' that 'one must make use of those things that lead to an end in accordance with the measure that is appropriate to that end', which finds its ultimate expression in 'the wellbeing of the soul'.[34]

---

[32] See *Summa Theologiae* I–II.3.8 and I–II.1.7, and elsewhere.
[33] See *NLNR*, 90–91: though they are 'not means'.
[34] *Summa Theologiae* II–II.152.2.

Does it finally matter whether Finnis's account is fully faithful to the Aristotelian and Thomist traditions? In chapter eleven below, I will take up this question (though only in part), by exploring some of the consequences of Finnis's position with respect to the distinction between natural *law* and natural *right*. There, I will suggest that Finnis's equation of these two ideas (which is made possible by exactly those moves away from the intellectual preoccupations of Aristotle and Aquinas, discussed here) leads to a number of misconceptions, which qualify the success of his legal philosophy. Before doing so, however, I would like to turn to another legal philosopher whose work owes a good deal to the Aristotelian tradition: Lon L Fuller.

SUGGESTED READING

Human flourishing and the human good

J Finnis, *Natural Law and Natural Rights*, 2nd edn (Oxford, Clarendon Press, 2011) chs III–V.

Background Reading

Aquinas, *Summa Theologiae* I–II 90–97.
S Coyle, 'Natural Law and Goodness in Thomistic Ethics' (2017) 30 *Canadian J of Law and Jurisprudence* 77.
J Crowe, 'Natural Law Beyond Finnis' (2011) 2 *Jurisprudence* 293.
J Finnis, *Aquinas: Moral, Political, and Legal Theory* (Oxford, Clarendon Press, 1998) chs 3 and 4.
E Fortin, 'The Political Thought of St Thomas Aquinas' in E Fortin, *Classical Christianity and the Political Order: Reflections on the Theologico-Political Problem*, Collected Essays, vol 2 (Lanham MD, Rowman & Littlefield, 1996).
J Porter, 'Nature and the End of Human Life: A Consideration of John Finnis's *Aquinas*' (2000) 80 *Journal of Religion* 476.
—— 'The Common Good in Thomas Aquinas' in PD Miller and D McCann (eds), *In Search of the Common Good* (New York, T & T Clark, 2005).

Justice, community and the common good

J Finnis, *Natural Law and Natural Rights*, 2nd edn (Oxford, Clarendon Press, 2011) chs VI–VIII.

Background Reading

Aquinas, *Summa Theologiae* II–II 57–122.
J Finnis, *Aquinas: Moral, Political, and Legal Theory* (Oxford, Clarendon Press, 1998) chs 6–8.

R George, *Natural Law Theory: Contemporary Essays* (Oxford, Clarendon Press, 1992).

C Orrego, 'Natural Law Under Other Names: *de nominibus non est disputandum*' (2007) 52 *American Journal of Jurisprudence* 77.

Pope John Paul II , Encyclical *Centessimus Annus* of 1 May 1991.

Pope Leo XIII , Encyclical *Rerum Novarum* of 15 May 1891.

Pope Pius XI , Encyclical *Quadragesimo Anno* of 15 May 1931.

10

Justice and Legality: Fuller

A T THE OUTSET of *Natural Law and Natural Rights*, Finnis announced that '[t]here are human goods that can be secured only through the institutions of human law, and requirements of practical reasonableness that only those institutions can satisfy'; stating that the object of his book was 'to identify those goods and those requirements of practical reasonableness, and thus to show how and on what conditions such institutions are justified and the ways in which they can be (and often are) defective'.[1] Legal philosophers often think of Finnis as being distinctive amongst modern writers in wishing to place this question at the very centre of jurisprudential enquiry. It is not a focal concern that is very often connected, in philosophical reflections, with the legal philosophy of the other prominent opponent of legal positivism, Lon Fuller. Nevertheless, Fuller (1902–78) was unwavering in his insistence that there is something distinctive and important about legal *forms*. To him, this meant that there are aspects of the human condition, of incalculable importance to us, that can be (as Finnis said) 'secured only through the institutions of human law'. Also like Finnis, Fuller connected this distinctiveness of form with the issue of practical deliberations, of the manifestation and respect of human agency.

Fuller's writings in legal philosophy are informed above all by 'eunomics': the theory of 'good order'. His abiding concern lay in identifying the characteristics of good order, and in how this is manifested and distinguished from bad order. Fuller wanted to demonstrate that there are aspects of law ('desiderata') that are intrinsically and specifically promotive of good order. Wherever there is law, these desiderata will be found to be manifested to some degree, indeed to the extent that good order is unimaginable without law. Bad order is characterised by the relative absence or disruption of these desiderata, so that bad order does not indeed represent the absence of law, but a situation in which law has been corrupted to serve the ends of repression or injustice. Whereas positivists typically believe that law is an instrument that is equally serviceable for both sorts of ends (good and bad), Fuller believed that his arguments demonstrate that law more fully serves the good.

---

[1] J Finnis, *Natural Law and Natural Rights*, 2nd edn (Oxford, Clarendon Press, 2011) 3.

Fuller's characterisation of 'bad order' in terms of repression emphasises the second of the concerns mentioned above: human agency. Fuller shares a belief in the importance of what Finnis called fully 'authentic' practical reason as an intrinsically necessary foundation for the good life. But his over-arching absorption with agency leads to certain significant differences of form and focus. He exhibits much less interest in the other 'basic goods' examined by Finnis; and whereas Finnis's account begins with a very abstract explora-tion of these goods, before turning to the question of legal institutions, Fuller explores agency from an institutional perspective: patiently examining the meaning and import of the variety of legal forms, and the distinctive ways in which these forms (of contract law, of property, of adjudication itself) pro-mote the exercise of human agency. Fuller is above all a lawyer who wants to understand what marks these out, and what makes them significant, as forms of governance.

LEGALITY AND JUSTICE

The reader of Finnis's *Natural Law and Natural Rights* quickly understands the substantial role played by justice in its intellectual scheme. Pursuit of the basic goods, which only institutions of law can successfully secure, demands the maintenance of an 'ensemble of conditions', a common good, which jus-tice takes as its object. It is therefore unsurprising to find a long and intricate account of justice at the heart of the political philosophy of *Natural Law and Natural Rights*. The place of justice in Fuller's writings is somewhat more dif-ficult to pin down. In speaking about the nature of law as a mode of govern-ance, Fuller's starting point is the neglect shown towards 'the morality that makes law possible': a subject often dismissed, according to Fuller, 'with a few remarks about "legal justice", this conception of justice being equated with a purely formal requirement that like cases be given like treatment'.[2] Legal philosophers all too often fail to recognise that this problem 'is only one aspect of a much larger problem, that of clarifying the directions of human effort essential to the maintenance of any system of law, even one whose ultimate objectives may be regarded as mistaken or evil'.[3]

Does Fuller regard this larger problem as itself a problem of justice? Is he suggesting, in this passage, that legal philosophers have studied justice in much too narrow terms? Or does he intend to say that the problem of justice is simply one aspect of a larger problem which demands to be understood in other ways, and according to other values? Recent interpretations of Fuller's

---

[2] L Fuller, *The Morality of Law*, rev edn (New Haven CT, Yale University Press, 1969) 4.
[3] ibid.

legal philosophy have largely assumed the latter view, regarding him as being concerned with the identification and analysis of a separate value, that of 'legality'.[4] It must be admitted that Fuller's discussion both in *The Morality of Law* and elsewhere is not articulated in terms of justice, and in none of his published writings does one encounter a fully developed theory of justice. His reference in the above passage to systems of law that pursue mistaken or evil objectives further strengthens the sense that Fuller's interest is not immediately connected to the identification of justice in law, but instead to the value of legal order even in circumstances where justice is absent or imperfectly manifested.

In another way, Fuller's intention is intelligible only when considered as having justice as its final object. For the aspiration that is embodied by the principles of legality cannot relate to the imposition of legal order only. His book begins with a contrast between two propositions on the idea of sin. The first, recalled by Fuller from some forgotten source, is: 'Die Sunde ist ein Verksinken in das Nichts' (roughly, 'the sinner falls ever further into nothingness'). The second, from the theologian Karl Barth, states: 'Die Sunde ist ein Versinken in das Bodenlose'. Fuller observes that:

> '*das Bodenlose*' implies a loss of limits or boundaries and therefore suggests a transgression of duty. What I have sought is an expression of the concept of sin as viewed by a morality of aspiration—sin as a failure in the effort to achieve a realization of the human quality itself.[5]

This distinction, between a 'morality of duty' and a 'morality of aspiration' is the subject of the first chapter of *The Morality of Law*, and the foundation for its subsequent discussion. Suppose I frequently gamble for very high stakes. One may look at this activity in two different ways. On the one hand, although gambling can sometimes provide harmless and innocent amusement, it certainly possesses more virulent and harmful forms. If we focus on these harmful or potentially harmful effects, we might come to regard gambling (at least for high stakes) as immoral, and thus accuse one who gambles obsessively for having fallen away from widely accepted minimum standards of moral duty. On the other hand, one might regard gambling as the deliberate cultivation of *risk*: a phenomenon that is present throughout life in many forms, and which often must be faced in order to achieve great and significant works; but which in the context of gambling is celebrated for its own sake and removed from any positive or edifying venture. In this second case, the source of the moral complaint is not the transgression of a duty, but the sense that gambling is not an activity that is befitting of human capacities.

---

[4] See, eg, NE Simmonds, *Law as a Moral Idea* (Oxford, Oxford University Press, 2007) esp chs 5 and 6.

[5] Fuller, *The Morality of Law* (n 2) 3.

One might consider the rule of law in a similar way. In one sense, the law establishes the minimum standards necessary for people to act as good citizens. The goods of social peace and stable order absolutely require freedom of action to be limited, but they do not require virtue. It does not matter whether I pay my taxes, perform contracts, respect property and avoid committing crimes all with great disapprobation and resentment, so long as I do in fact meet these obligations. The creation and application of law can therefore be considered from the perspective of the judgements that must be made concerning the relative boundaries of personal freedom and legal duty. (Do the potential harms of gambling justify a law prohibiting all gambling, or one limiting stakes, or otherwise offering restrictions or disincentives? Or ought one to be free to ruin one's character as one chooses, the law stepping in only where this leads one to transgress property rights, breach contractual obligations, offer violence to the innocent, or perpetrate other harms?) For the most part, workable standards of legal judgement require a morality of duty, but 'there is no way by which the law can compel a man to live up to the excellences of which he is capable'.[6]

Very often, when contemplating the relationship between law and morality, it is these kinds of judgement that are in issue: judgements which pertain to the law's 'substantive morality', the justice (or injustice) of its demands. But as Fuller points out, a morality of aspiration is nonetheless 'pervasive in its implications' for the law, for:

> In one aspect our whole legal system represents a complex of rules designed to rescue man from the blind play of chance and to put him safely on the road to purposeful and creative activity … [T]here is no way open to us by which we can compel a man to live the life of reason. We can only seek to exclude from his life the grosser and more obvious manifestations of chance and irrationality. We can create the conditions essential for a rational human existence. These are the necessary, but not sufficient conditions for the achievement of that end.[7]

How therefore should one understand the 'whole legal system', and in what do these 'essential conditions' consist? In the famous second chapter of *The Morality of Law*, Fuller enumerates eight principles or 'desiderata' that, in his view, characterise a legal system. These are to be understood as desiderata which particular systems of law manifest to some greater or lesser degree, but in the total absence or failure of any one of which we would no longer

---

[6] ibid 9. The ideal society of Plato's *Republic* represents a partial march towards a direct legal manifestation of aspirational morality: one's personal freedom and choices are subordinated to one's duty as a citizen, so that one's talents as an inspirational and excellent teacher would lead to one's performance of that role even if one's desire was to pursue the life of an artist, if the needs of the community so dictated.

[7] ibid.

consider a set of social arrangements to embody governance *through law* (as opposed to, say, governance by arbitrary fiat or some other absence of recognisable legal processes). Thus, taken together, the eight desiderata represent a rational reconstruction of our intuitive understanding of, or concept of, law:

1. For a legal system to exist, there must be rules.
2. Such rules must be published or otherwise made known to the citizens to whom it applies.
3. The rules must be sufficiently clear/free of ambiguity so as to be intelligible.
4. The rules must not be retroactive in effect.
5. The obligations established by the law must not be contradictory.
6. The law must not establish duties that it is beyond the power of citizens to perform.
7. The law must be relatively stable (not subject to revision with bewildering regularity).
8. The law as administered and applied must not diverge from the law as written or published.

Each of these desiderata, taken in turn, is straightforward enough, and all are sufficiently obvious not to require much further explanation. Fuller presents them as eight ways in which a law-giver could fail to create a functioning legal system. (Notice, however, that contraventions of some of the desiderata simply fail, by ordinary understandings, to create legal obligations—such as in the case of 3 or 5—whereas others seem to belong to our understanding of law because their transgression embodies such a flagrant departure from justice—as in 4.)

Here, Fuller treats the idea of 'law' as an ideal to which actual manifestations of legal order approximate only to some degree. (Consider for example the common law's partial fulfilment of desiderata 2 and 4: often decisions at law clarify and 'establish' the relevant obligations *as they are being applied*.) In a similar way, mathematicians possess a precise criterial definition of a geometric figure such as a circle. Real-world manifestations of circles only approximate to the purity of the ideal: the circle that I sketch freehand on a piece of paper is likely to be very imperfect (though recognisably a circle); that drawn with compasses or precision instruments more perfect, but still flawed. All manufactured circular forms, when viewed under high magnification, will be seen to possess flaws or irregularities of line, even if very minute. This does not prevent us from recognising them for what they are meant to be; but none of them exactly, fully and perfectly realises the ideal geometric form.[8]

---

[8] See NE Simmonds, 'Jurisprudence as a Moral and Historical Inquiry' (2015) 18 *Canadian Journal of Law & Jurisprudence* 249.

Fuller's eight desiderata can therefore be read as a reminder that justice is not only a matter of the substantive provisions which make up the 'complex of rules' to which the citizen is subject. It relates no less to the forms and procedures through which the rules are created and administered. Justice, in other words, requires an institution to deliver it, and the eight desiderata speak to the health, or appropriateness, of the particular institutional forms that a society erects in this regard.

I would like to return to the question of how these desiderata connect to the idea of justice in due course. Fuller himself speaks of them collectively as embodying an 'internal morality' of law, in contrast to the 'external' or substantive morality of specific legal provisions. Legal positivists have not been slow to object to this idea: both Hart (with whom Fuller had an extensive debate) and later positivists have insisted that the eight desiderata amount only to considerations of 'efficiency' in law-making, but not of morality. One might concede that many of the desiderata do promote the value of efficiency. If I am a law-giver and want my rules to be obeyed, then it is necessary for the rules to be published (for example). Keeping them secret will not promote efficiency in getting people to behave in the way that I want. Similarly, if I produce a set of standards that are hopelessly ambiguous, failing to express exactly the form of behaviour that I intend to enforce or prohibit, or if I constantly change my mind about what I want people to do, then I will not succeed in promoting my aims efficiently.

The question, however, is not whether the desiderata promote efficient government (they may well do), but whether they serve that end *alone* without promoting any other value. The core of Hart's suggestion was that the allegedly moral dimension to the desiderata was entirely incidental: that they give assistance in reality to all purposive activity, to be distinguished from morality as such.[9] All imaginable types of purposive activity invite practical considerations of the kind suggested by Fuller: one could easily speak of desiderata of poisoning (including the avoidance of poisons that induce vomiting, or perhaps the use of poisons which would lead to the rapid identification of the poisoner), but this is scarcely intelligible as an 'inner morality' of poisoning! Similarly, the kinds of procedural virtue embedded in the eight desiderata could be observed in a society 'devoted to the highest refinements of sin'.[10]

Hart's analogy is not as straightforward as it appears, and it is not immediately clear what it establishes. Yet it does help to uncover something of great importance. Fuller's response is to refuse the underpinning assumption that evil aims have as much coherence as good ones, or to put it another way, that

---

[9] HLA Hart, *Essays in Jurisprudence and Philosophy* (Oxford, Clarendon Press, 1983) Essay 16.

[10] See L Fuller, 'Positivism and Fidelity to Law: A Reply to Professor Hart' (1958) 71 *Harvard Law Review* 630, 636.

'coherence and goodness have more affinity than coherence and evil'. Fuller accepts that this assertion leads to extremely difficult issues in the epistemology of ethics. But initially, we might think that Fuller is simply mistaken about this. Is not Hart surely correct to observe that the practical considerations that give coherence to purposive activities are not invariably promotive of moral ends? A coherent technique of poisoning is nothing other than a refinement and more effective promotion of an evil end. However, the remainder of Fuller's argument makes clear that he has in mind, not *every* context of practical activity, but a specific subset of practical activities with which Hart's example is disanalogous in significant respects: namely, practices of *reasoning* and practices of *justification*. Hart's example is more analogous to activities such as piano playing (where a coherent technique of hand placement, timing etc, will refine one's playing) than to the question of justification for one's activities. The use of the word 'technique' in relation to the desiderata that inform the latter practices (of reasoning and justification) can be misleading: it corresponds not to the Greek *techne* ('art' or craftsmanship) but rather to *phronesis* (wisdom or intelligence in practical thought), the virtue of intelligent thinking about ends and not simply of the means of reaching them. The eight desiderata advance our understanding of the end being sought, because they embody ideas about the best way in which to achieve or manifest that end. Only by reflecting on what could cause that end to fail, do we gain a richer understanding of the nature of the end being pursued. Hence, they involve some measure of understanding of, and reflection upon, what one wants to achieve; whereas the poisoner does not wish to obtain, through his criteria of efficiency, a firmer understanding of *what poisoning is*. Coherence in the context of justification is thus not simply a consideration of the ease of bringing about some end, but a dimension of the coherence of the end itself. Fuller is therefore not being naive in saying that he believes

> that when men are compelled to explain and justify their decisions, the effect will be to pull those decisions toward goodness, by whatever standards of ultimate goodness there are. Accepting these beliefs, I find a considerable incongruity in any conception that envisages a possible future in which the common law would 'work itself pure from case to case' toward a more perfect realization of iniquity.[11]

(In a sense, to believe in morality at all is to commit oneself to this suggestion. For belief in morality is the belief in the existence of definitive reasons for acting in certain ways: reasons that can be coolly and patiently, but above all relentlessly and finally, advanced against supposed justifications for immoral action; reasons so finally irresistible in belonging to any reasonable or tolerable form of life, that one who clung to immoral justifications would become

---

[11] ibid.

embroiled eventually in incoherence or contradiction. This is not to say that evil is not cunning, and there will always be opportunities for deliberations to be ingeniously twisted. The task of straightening out the lies can be a long labour indeed.)

It is, therefore, far from clear that the desiderata enumerated by Fuller straightforwardly reduce to considerations of efficiency, equally good for both wicked aims and virtuous ones. Indeed, it is arguable whether some of the desiderata would even represent the most efficient way for a tyrant to impose his will. Suppose I wanted to stamp out all acts of dissidence. Defining 'dissidence' is extremely difficult, because it is of course possible to imagine endless possibilities for dissident action: there is no closed set of actions that manifest dissidence. In this case, would it not be much more efficient for the tyrant to punish all perceived acts of dissidence, presently outlawed or not, thus breaching principle 4? Would it not serve tyrannical ends better to enforce as crimes against the state actions that do not appear in any established legal documents (in contravention of principle 8)? As Nigel Simmonds has argued in considerable detail, our normal understanding of the eighth principle involves the idea that the coercive machinery of the state (its use of force as a punitive measure against citizens) will be employed only where the official rules have been transgressed. Whilst a repressive regime would have every reason to publish and enforce its rules, it would have no compelling reason for restricting the use of force to instances in which the rules have been broken; the reason being that there are many other contexts in which coercion can be effectively employed: overcoming lawful resistance to the regime's aims, demoralising or scattering opposition, removing all impediments to the regime's ideals, creating a climate of fear which makes organisation of resistance vastly more difficult and so on.[12]

It is not very difficult to see how these considerations relate to Fuller's suggestion that the law's function is to 'rescue man from the blind play of chance' and secure a 'rational existence'. The presence of a system of rules that conforms to the eight desiderata gives people notice of their obligations, and in doing so establishes very significant domains of permission (or liberty) in which individuals remain free to order their lives as they would wish. Reflection upon the eight desiderata amounts to reflection upon the *purpose* of law, and thus the purpose of governing through law. Against the positivist belief that law, as an instrument of governance, does not possess one single purpose (such as securing the good life) but all kinds of purposes dependent upon the will of the law-giver, Fuller asserts the *coherence* of purpose embodied in the eight desiderata. In this respect, Fuller's theory is very powerful, because the eight

---

[12] See Simmonds, *Law as a Moral Idea* (n 4) ch 2; also Fuller's remarks on the Nazi tyranny, discussed below.

desiderata themselves do not arise from some detached theoretical perspective, but articulate the tacit assumptions that underpin our legal practices, and become visible when we reflect upon that practice. It is for this reason that reflecting more directly on the desiderata further illuminates the suppositions of these practices.

Fuller uncovers this sense of the purpose of law precisely by considering the disasters that are consequent upon the failure of the desiderata. We can begin by imagining a form of governance that proceeds, not by established rules, but by resolving disputes and handing down decisions ungoverned by rules. Perceiving the extreme difficulties with this approach, the law-giver devises a legal code but fails to publicise it. Upon publishing it, the rules are worded in a way that renders them retrospective rather than prospective in effect. The rules are subsequently re-drafted to make them apply prospectively, but they are ambiguous and ultimately unintelligible in what they require. A further re-drafting renders the rules clear and intelligible, but reveals that the entire system of obligations is riddled with contradiction and inconsistency (the performance of every duty being prohibited by another). A revised code is produced that is internally consistent, but inconsistent with human powers of compliance, demanding the impossible. A code is then produced which is in principle possible to comply with, but constantly changing in a way that people cannot practically remain up to date with its present demands. Finally, a system of rules is produced that steers clear of all these earlier failures, but which is impossible to interpret in such a way as to reconcile it with the judgments of the courts which purport to apply it.

We can see from this that the eight desiderata are not independent criteria that happen to come together in explanation, but are systematically linked in pursuing a single purpose: removing from human life the 'grosser and more obvious manifestations of chance and irrationality'. This purposive mode of explanation is one that we tacitly employ in the description of all sorts of artefacts in everyday life. Consider how difficult it is to describe something like a chair or a table in purely physical terms: some chairs, and some tables, have four legs, but some have three, or even one attached to a base. Tables and chairs come in a very wide variety of shapes and sizes, and materials and forms of construction. There are armchairs and occasional tables, bar stools and dining tables, computer desks and office chairs, chairs with backs and chairs without, and many others besides. A single physical description is not available to cover all such instances; and even if it were, such an explanation fails to convey what a chair, or a table, actually *is*. For this, a description of the *point* of a table or chair ('a chair is something for sitting on') is really inescapable.

Once in possession of such an understanding, two things become possible. In the first place, we are able to a greater extent to say whether a particular example is a *good* table or chair: the extent to which it fulfils its purpose (by being stable, comfortable, durable, suitable for intended use etc). But secondly, it becomes possible to see that artefacts are often capable of being turned to unintended uses. When objects are misused in this way, they are seldom capable of fulfilling the secondary purpose as fully or successfully as in respect of their original and intended purpose. Aside from acting as a platform for sitting on, a chair can be used in place of a ladder for reaching books off high shelves, or as a weapon (for example). But although it is indeed possible to use a chair in this way, it does not offer the height and stability of the ladder, nor the effectiveness and speed of a sword, say. A table used for perching upon is similarly less comfortable (less satisfactory for sitting upon) than a chair. (One could go on.) Fuller's argument is that law, similarly, can be perverted or bent away from its intended purpose (rescuing man from irrationality and promoting the ends of self-expression and self-development), but will achieve the purposes of repression or tyranny less effectively than other means.

The world, as Fuller knew, always was (and remains) all too full of examples of regimes in pursuit of unjust or repressive ends. Certain societies pursue the good of some privileged or powerful group at the expense of minorities who are persecuted or dispossessed. Others significantly erode or extinguish freedom, repressing the entire population. Law is indeed, as Hart observed, compatible with great iniquity. But here we are considering not the law's 'internal morality' but its external (or substantive) morality. It is true that nothing in the law's internal morality prevents the creation of rules that exploit or deprive minorities of rights afforded to other groups. Without in any way diminishing the horror of situations of this kind, Fuller suggests that adherence to the rule of law in such situations nevertheless prevents certain kinds of injustice by limiting the evil being pursued. Most obviously, the exploited group cannot be oppressed in ways not deliberately specified by the established rules: people can continue to plan their existence even within the much narrower limits allowed by the law, taking advantage of whatever opportunities still exist for self-development, and avoiding imprisonment or punishment through compliance with the law. Less obviously (but no less importantly), the operation of the rule of law in demanding clear rules, and the public offering of reasons for decision in the application of the law, restricts opportunities for corruption on the part of public officials which is often a consequence of grossly unjust or persecutive regimes. On a broader scale, Fuller clearly thought that the requirements of legality render the pursuit of injustice more difficult in laying open manifest inequalities or repressive laws to international criticism and other more concrete forms of international pressure, so that tyrannous governments may be forced to moderate their aims to maintain at least a pretence of legality.

Do historical examples bear out this suggestion? Perhaps it is the case that people tend to regard Apartheid-era South Africa, for all the terrible reality of its injustices, as having fallen short of the evil of Nazi Germany, or Stalin's Russia, where adherence to the rule of law was itself compromised to a considerable extent. Perhaps the 'restraint of reasons' (as we might call it) does indeed do something to restrain the ferocity of the most ruthless tyrants. But if so, this is less a matter of the direct difficulty of formulating repressive or racist laws in clear terms, and more a matter of the moral pressure that is applied (either domestically or internationally) to regimes in open pursuit of unjust ends. The totalitarian regimes of Eastern Europe finally fell, not because their laws were unclear or inconsistent, but because the economic and social realities being pursued were themselves inconsistent, causing the system to crumble under the weight of its own contradictions. It would be a mistake to think that the ideal of legality can do very much to improve the substantive values of an unjust government; its importance lies exactly in cabining the pursuit of such ends by imposing an order that preserves vital pockets of liberty.

Fuller's analysis forces us to revise certain intuitions we might otherwise have entertained about the legal systems both of totalitarian regimes and of liberal ones. Prior to reflecting upon the value of the eight desiderata, we might have supposed that the consistent application of oppressive rules would be worse than their constant adaptation or interpretative perversion by judges seeking to mitigate their effects in the cases that come before them for decision. Fuller reminds us very forcibly that the limited good achieved by such mitigations has to be put into the balance against the damage that is done where people's expectations are robbed of stability and certainty, leaving each person in doubt as to the nature of the rules that will be applied to them. Thus, in seeking to ameliorate the oppression of tyrannical laws, liberal-minded judges who depart from the rule of law would in fact abolish liberty for the subjects of law.

This last point is sometimes contested on the ground that the judges in the situation described are not seeking to erode such liberties as the law actually permits to the oppressed group or population. They are merely endeavouring wherever possible to avoid the oppressive consequences of the very laws that restrict liberty. Surely this results in an overall increase in the number of liberties each person possesses. It may be true in certain situations that the judges would indeed succeed in increasing liberties in this way, or at least decelerate their erosion. But the fact is that 'liberty' is not really amenable to ordinal measurement as the objection suggests. The judicial practices described, *precisely* in departing from the consistent application of the rule of law, actually place the fate of citizens at the mercy of individual judges, making them entirely subject to their will. Howsoever good the intentions, we would have abolished the rule of law in favour of the rule of men. Fuller's argument is taken up and developed by Nigel Simmonds, who points out that the difference between the slave and the free person is not reckoned according to the number of options or occasions of oversight and interference to which the slave is subject (the slave might indeed have a liberal master who permits considerable licence); it is instead the fact that this licence is entirely dependent upon the will of the master. Slavery is the very embodiment of the absence of liberty because the one person is fully subject to the will of another.[13]

If we turn attention towards liberal regimes, the same concern is evident. The law establishes various rights and freedoms for liberal subjects, either directly (through human rights instruments, employment legislation and such like) or indirectly (by opting not to prohibit certain actions or render the actor liable to civil remedies). These rights correspond directly to legal duties: to possess a right to some advantage is to be owed that advantage by another, through the performance of a duty (eg, of delivery or service); to have a right against interference with some project is for another person or persons to possess a duty not to interfere with one.[14] It is of course obvious that the legal rules which establish these rights and duties may sometimes be regarded as unjust, sometimes significantly so. Yet for judges to depart from these rules, even in pursuit of a more perfect justice, is to eliminate or restrict duties by simultaneously limiting or annihilating rights; or conversely, to expand rights only by simultaneously expanding duties. Even if the needs of a just society were to involve the curtailment of rights or the expansion of duties (eg, by demanding payment of higher taxes), it is a greater injustice to vary each person's obligations without adequate prospective notice. Similarly, the ends of greater liberty are not served by ad hoc revisions to the relative legal positions of citizens, for this is actually the elimination of liberty. Irrespective of the ideological orientation of a political regime, there are no shortcuts to justice.

JUSTICE AND THE INSTITUTIONAL REALITY OF LAW

To engage with Fuller's ideas on the inner morality of law is to consider a relationship between law and justice quite unlike anything to be found either in modern positivism or its other prominent critics. A reader of the eighth chapter of Hart's *Concept of Law* cannot fail to observe the essential superficiality of the law's association with justice in Hart's account of it. Hart connects

---

[13] ibid 99ff.

[14] Rights must in this sense be distinguished from 'mere' liberties (or 'privileges' in the language of Hohfeld), which may indeed conflict: my right to be free from physical assault is thus of a different nature from my freedom to carry on a business, since the latter carries no implication of a duty on the part of others not to interfere, eg, by setting up and running a rival business across the street offering lower prices.

the idea of formal justice ('treat like cases alike and different cases differently') with the very activity of rule-following, and in so doing he divests it of any deeper moral significance. *Any* activity in which rules are followed generates considerations of equality and analogy in their application, but there is not for that reason any specific point of reflective connection between the practice of adjudication and the production of justice in the community. Our attention is directed away from the specific institutional conditions that the law creates and maintains, and towards the source of law: politics! The 'justice' done to the litigants' interests is in part a function of the formal aspect of rule-following, but overall a question of the substantive policies or political 'values' that the legal rules serve, for the law is ever the instrument of a politics. Consequently, we are presented with an apparently inescapable image in which the legal justice administered by the courts (justice 'according to law') must often be distinguished from justice as it appears in our own conception of it.

Fuller endeavours to remind his readers that the formal dimension of justice is not as neutral or insubstantial as this image implies. Its significance lies in 'the view of man' implicit in the very form of law and practices of adjudication:

> [L]egal morality can be said to be neutral over a wide range of ethical issues. It cannot be neutral in its view of man himself. To embark on the enterprise of subjecting human conduct to the governance of rules involves of necessity a commitment to the view that man is, or can become, a responsible agent, capable of understanding and following rules, and answerable for his defaults.[15]

That is to say, the administration of law involves something other than the simple *subjection* of human beings to control, a mere 'acting upon' men as one may act upon mere objects. The very premise of law as a distinctive form of social order (as opposed, eg, to military rule) is its treatment of citizens as capable of responding to direction through the exercise of reason and agency. Indeed, Fuller says that the idea that persons are 'judged' by law becomes all but unintelligible where this respect for agency is absent, where they are reduced to objects for manipulation.[16]

To understand this point fully, it is necessary to reflect upon the immediacy with which the institutional realities of law, for Fuller, are connected

---

[15] Fuller, *The Morality of Law* (n 2) 162.

[16] See Fuller Papers, box 2/16 (letter to Dorothy Emmet dated 7 October 1966): 'Unless I am seriously mistaken [Hart] displays a truly formidable blindness to the simple notion that holding down a job carries with it moral responsibilities that, in some measure, are peculiar to that job'. In fact, the same insight can be derived from what Hart has to say about the need for communication of general standards in his passage on 'the open texture of law': see my discussion in ch 6 above. Fuller is correct however that Hart does not seem to perceive the full significance of this insight.

with autonomy. One might almost say that it is through such institutional realities that human beings manifest agency in a way that becomes visible or tangible to them. In some notes for a lecture on 'Traditions of Justice Among Western Peoples', Fuller asked whether in achieving justice, it is institutions or public attitudes that are more important. His answer is that whilst both are essential, it is institutions which require most emphasis: no moral attitude (such as respect for human dignity) can realise itself directly, but needs mechanisms for its expression and manifestation.[17] The sustaining attitudes that are necessary are not simply attitudes towards 'freedom' or 'dignity' (or justice), but towards *institutions*. Quoting Michael Oakeshott, Fuller states that therefore the writ of *habeas corpus* is not to be thought of as an expression of the spirit of freedom, or a way of protecting freedom, but instead one must recognise that it *is* freedom, in the context of a particular problem.

In a similar way, the 'morality which makes law possible' is also the morality that makes not only justice, but also human agency and dignity possible. Fuller's discussion of the eight desiderata is full of anxieties about the many ways in which their pursuit can be impaired or rendered deeply problematic by circumstance and human failing. Though he clearly thought of the eighth desideratum as the one most difficult to put into effect (being open to prejudice, misinterpretation of precedents and indeed the capacity for law to 'become a snare for those who cannot know the reasons of it as fully as do the judges'),[18] all the desiderata in seeking to realise justice and rational agency can potentially also undermine those very values: the effort to meet the complex demands created by those values is subject to all sorts of unforeseen calamities, requiring the sacrifice of the same dimensions of legality through which they are ordinarily realised. Fuller's extensive discussion of retrospective laws indicates the complexities he foresaw in the issue. Even retrospective laws may be an important 'curative measure' in legal systems facing a bitter crisis.[19] For example, suppose that Parliament having legislated to permit homosexual marriages later discovers that a little-publicised formality requirement (such as the affixing of an official stamp) has often been overlooked in practice, perhaps exacerbated by the fact that the government department responsible for distributing the stamps suffers a technical breakdown so that no stamps are in fact printed. Parliament therefore enacts another statute conferring validity on marriages that were legally void by the terms of the first statute. Fuller urges us not to be too hasty, in regard to examples of this kind, to derive the

---

[17] Fuller, Notes for a talk on 'Traditions of Justice Among Western Peoples' to be delivered at the University of Vermont, 13 July 1959, Fuller Papers, box 11/8.

[18] Fuller, *The Morality of Law* (n 2) 83. He cites the principle in *Heydon's Case*: that to understand a law one must first understand the 'disease of the commonwealth' it was appointed to cure.

[19] ibid 53. I adapt the following example from Fuller.

general lesson that retroactive laws are justifiable where their intent is to cure formal irregularities: he goes on to cite the Roehm Purge of 1934, in which Hitler took a trip to Munich to oversee the shooting of nearly 100 Nazi party members viewed by him as standing in the way of progress. Hurrying back to Berlin, Hitler passed a statute converting the murders into lawful executions, claiming that during the affair 'the Supreme Court of the German people consisted of myself'.[20]

Calling attention to the importance of institutional realities, Fuller is thus not forgetful of the terrible uses to which they can be put. 'More than any other in history', Fuller wrote, 'the Nazi dictatorship came to power through the calculated exploitation of legal forms'.[21] The Nazi tyranny was not merely the eruption on the terrain of European politics of an 'atavistic savagery' but precisely a determined corruption of historic social realities: 'they would never have achieved their control over the German people had there not been waiting to be bent to their sinister ends attitudes toward law and government that had been centuries in the building'.[22] Consequently, whenever Hitler's aims conflicted with the demands of legality, he circumvented legal processes and acted directly through the party, in the streets.

Again and again, Fuller pulls his readers back down to earth: away from very abstract discussion of the eight desiderata, and towards the concrete realities of institutions. One can learn very little from the desiderata except by devoting considerable attention to the nuanced and highly problematical ways in which they are worked out at the level of actual institutions. Neither morality nor its more specific procedural form, legality, is to be understood as enshrined only in 'principles' but must come to be explored as an active sensibility. In a letter to William M Evan dated 29 March 1965, Fuller wrote that *The Morality of Law* 'is an attempt to conceive law, not in terms of the formal structure of authority within which it occurs, but as an *activity*'.[23] He went on:

> Instead of speaking of 'the internal morality of law' I could have spoken of a 'humane attitude'; 'a recognition that law impinges on people's lives and that the law-giver and law-administrator has an obligation to act with due recognition of this fact', etc.

Explored in this way, the eight desiderata (the notion of legality) give a sense of just how complex and difficult is the task of erecting conditions for a just society. Fuller was innately suspicious of theories which in pursuing the clarity

---

[20] ibid 54–55.
[21] L Fuller, 'American Legal Philosophy at Mid-Century' (1954) 6 *Journal of Legal Education* 457, 465.
[22] ibid 466.
[23] Fuller Papers, box 2/16 (emphasis in original).

of systematic understandings impose upon us an 'impoverished reality'. In an especially beautiful passage in a letter to Alburey Castell in 1958, Fuller wrote:

> I have sometimes said in class that as we read the Book of Life or of Experience we come upon many passages that are relatively clear, as well as some that are almost unbearab[ly] obscure. I said that there are in vogue two general ways of dealing with these obscure passages. One is that of the mystic, who bows down before them, and concludes that all that seems clear (including unpleasant things such as death) must not really be so. The other is that of the self-consciously 'scientific' modern who simply tears the obscure passage from the book and pretends it was never there.[24]

Neither is justified. Instead, according to Fuller,

> we ought to respect the obscure passages, work to clarify them, and face courageously the possibility that a solution of them might also modify what now seems clear.

These passages and others make clear the inadequacy and extraordinary bluntness of jurisprudential discussions which attempt to trace (or deny) clear connections between the idea of legality and that of agency. Fuller emphatically defended the presence of such connections, but repeatedly offered up examples to demonstrate how problematic they are in practice, how easily they can be perverted or destroyed, and how often circumstances can frustrate good intentions, producing cross-cutting considerations even amongst the eight desiderata. One must as it were separate the gordian complexities and reversals of the immediate present from the longer-term trend of legal institutions, always remembering that the long-term trend is nonetheless shaped by the present efforts. Reflecting on Hart's accusation that the eight desiderata are compatible with 'great iniquity', Fuller's response is to agree that of course they are, in very many possible senses. The most obvious example would be one in which the iniquity in question was not subject to legal regulation at all, but simply permitted to exist. Hart's statement becomes objectionable at the point at which it asserts, as a perfectly general thesis, that respect for the desiderata in no way impairs the law's capacity for *producing* and *supporting* iniquity.[25]

Fuller's thought is at this point almost Augustinian in outlook, comparing the iniquities of even our purest and most excellent institutions in the here and now, the goodness of which is irrevocably mixed with worldly snares until the end of time, with the hope that these institutions offer to the world. Christianity itself is, as Fuller reminds us, historically associated with slavery (and a thousand other vices), but nevertheless 'it demands to be realized that

---

[24] Fuller Papers, box 2/7 (letter dated 4 April 1958).
[25] See Fuller Papers, box 11/17 (letter to Walter F Burns jr dated 14 October 1964).

the morality implicit in Christian belief tended—in some measure at least— toward an eventual elimination of slavery'.[26]

EUNOMICS: THE THEORY OF GOOD ORDER

These observations leave us with a very difficult problem. Institutions of law and legal government can give support to civility and the realisation of human potentialities, but they can also be perverted towards tyranny and suppression. Law is implicated both in the greatness of Athens and the terror of Berlin, just as it presided over Rome's glory as well as its descent into decadence and folly. What then distinguishes good order from bad order, and what methods or ideas will help us to evaluate our situation?

A very great deal of hesitation is felt about approaching such questions arising out of a fear of imputing some specific 'end' or 'nature' to man as such: an imputation considered as unscientific in virtue of the realities of choice to which men, and thus social forms, are subject, and because of the unwillingness (as Hart said) to believe in higher laws of nature to which the actions and ends of men are subject. Society is 'just what men choose to make it', whether this choice turns out to be the conscious expression of collective 'interests' or the intangible product of class—and other biases.

Against the picture of limitless social forms implied by these thoughts, Fuller opposes the assumptions that structure other domains of human activity, such as corporate management and economics.[27] Take the example of a factory, the accepted purpose of which is to produce goods. In any factory there will be production processes, either mechanised or otherwise, essential to the manufacture of the goods in question. Where machines are involved, all kinds of human interventions remain necessary: cleaning, oiling, maintaining, feeding in the materials, removal of debris, handling and removal of the finished product, quality control and the like. Such operations can be divided amongst the workforce in numerous ways. Perhaps a single worker is given responsibility for all the above tasks with respect to each separate machine. More likely, a number of workers will be given responsibility for discrete tasks (such as maintenance) in the factory generally, or more likely still with respect to some particular subset (such as administration of computer-controlled systems). Perhaps some workers have responsibility for several tasks or operations, others more or less. The factory's output efficiency is a direct function of the manner in which these tasks are allocated; hence the

---

[26] ibid.
[27] Fuller, 'American Legal Philosophy at Mid-Century' (n 21) 457, from which the examples below are drawn.

importance of management lies in the selection of the particular solution, out of the various that are available, which produces the most optimal results. This question of 'optimal solutions' is undoubtedly constrained by the nature of the organisational possibilities available, as well as being shaped by the end in view, in terms of which there are 'good' and 'bad' methods of organising production. Similarly, it is broadly understood that in economics generally, the forms through which economic objectives are achievable are not unlimited, and that (for example) the maximal satisfaction of diverse preferences out of scarce resources demands some variety of market mechanism.[28] The forms of economic life and activity through which a society might successfully pursue the goal of choice-maximisation differ from those which are appropriate to a concern based upon equality of welfare as the primary outcome.

This concern with social forms, specifically as a means to the realisation of ends or purposes, is termed by Fuller 'eunomics': a term it seems of his own invention, but clearly deriving from the Aristotelian conception of *eunomia* (good order). Fuller to some extent distances himself from Aristotle by professing to be less interested in ultimate ends, placing the focus upon the means by which the ends are explored and pursued. At the same time, his euonomics bear a certain resemblance to aspects of *phronesis* (the wisdom of practical deliberation) in that a focused exploration of the means available to a society to pursue its aims will simultaneously clarify the ends being pursued. Indeed, it may reveal that certain ends, regarded in the abstract as desirable, are in reality unviable for the lack of a social form, devised for their pursuit, which does not involve disproportionate costs of one kind or another. Can one decide whether euthanasia should be legalised, Fuller asks, without first considering the social manageability of the task of selecting the right people to put to death? Alternatively, if one's goal is that of equality of income or of resources, it is necessary to investigate the questions of how manpower is to be allocated once the inducement of wage differentials has been removed, how efficiency is to be maintained and waste, indolence and other economic vices avoided, how prices are to be structured so as to avoid hidden subsidies (since man-hours are not all equally productive), and how a market can cope in the face of equal purchasing power. Unless one has resolved all these issues, can one claim even to have understood the end of 'equality'? If they are irresolvable, or if their resolution brings about significant unfreedoms in social and economic terms, would this not demonstrate the end of equality to contain an inherent contradiction: one that can perhaps be brought to light in different guises, and with differing effects?

---

[28] See M Polanyi, *The Logic of Liberty* (Indianapolis IN, Liberty Fund, 1998) for the claim, which Fuller quotes, that even socialist and communist economists are logically forced to accept a market, whatever the controls or restrictions they ultimately place upon it.

Fuller's project of eunomics recalls attention to a problem that is all too often forgotten in academic philosophy. It is that the possibilities that are open to academic discourse are frequently closed to the realities of politics, which is situated in time, in a way that philosophical concerns are not. As Raymond Geuss has observed, within idealised philosophical discourses, such as Habermas's theory of 'communicative action' or even Rawls's original position, possibilities are mooted and discussed in a principally endless way, from the most detailed and concrete concerns to the highest levels of abstraction. Nothing is left off the table, and arguments which have been heard and determined can be revisited and reopened at future stages as need arises.[29] Real politics is not like this: events are often structured in such a way as to demand immediate responses, and the effect of this is to remove certain possible lines of thought from the table permanently. Others will be interrupted before being fully heard; inequalities of power amongst those deliberating will have all sorts of distorting or even corrupting effects on the arguments and positions being urged. Misunderstandings will arise and be acted upon, with the mistake being uncovered too late, if at all.

The philosopher's perspective can incline us to take an 'ethics first' view of politics. One resolves all ethical dilemmas first, thereby gaining an 'ideal' theory of how one ought to act, and only then seek its implementation in the world of concrete fact and circumstance. Meeting with resistance and all manner of corrupting influences, the moral philosopher then laments the world which will not bend itself to the norms of the model. Fuller's and Geuss's views belong to a perspective which endeavours to highlight the need to recognise those very distorting influences, those very conditions which interrupt and shape practical discourse, as dimensions of the problem which needs to be resolved: they are not extraneous problems lying in the path of a solution to an overall problem that is perceived clearly on its own terms. This once again recalls Augustine's words to Nectarius: nothing can be easier than devising ideas of justice which remain aloof from the world of human practice. The part of the good person is not to comfort himself of herself with such dreams, but to set about the bitter and unending task of realising true justice in the imperfect terrain of this life.[30]

Fuller was above all a lawyer. His interest in the problem of social forms does not remain in the abstract, but leads him to analyse the nature and functioning of specific modes of legal ordering, such as contract and adjudication. His analysis on the subject of what makes a particular social form especially suited to the resolution of a particular problem is extremely rich and many-stranded, but a common thread is his concern with the mode by which

---

[29] R Geuss, *Philosophy and Real Politics* (Princeton NJ, Princeton University Press, 2008) 23ff.
[30] See ch 1 above.

participation is made possible through the employment of such forms. Despite all that distinguishes legislation, election, mediation, adjudication, custom, management and contract as forms of ordering, that which underpins them and sunders them from the order of a concentration camp, is the possibility of self-constituting participation. Forms of *good* order represent social arrangements that are 'just, fair, workable, effective, and respectful of human dignity'.[31] In Finnis's terms, considerations of dignity and self-constitution supply the focal meaning of sound forms of legal ordering: their absence (as Fuller says) is what leads us to 'stigmatize certain forms of social ordering as *perverted* and *parasitic*'.[32] The form of legislation, for example, is disclosed not in the idea of enacted orders demanding compliance, but in the establishment of base lines against which to order one's life with one's fellows, each person remaining free (within those base lines) to pursue his own goals.[33] The law (as noted above) does not simply *act upon* the citizen, laying down specific requirements for compliance, but establishes a mode of participation, 'a pattern of living', as Fuller said elsewhere, 'that is satisfying and worthy of men's capacities'.[34]

These 'baselines' are however just one element in the fabric of social relationships which men forge in their daily lives: irreducibly necessary but insufficient for all the social commerce that passes between citizens in a flourishing society. Amongst the numerous devices which sustain such relationships, contract is of especial significance. Fuller devoted many papers to the law of contract, which retained a particular interest for him. For him, the contractual form was vital in bringing into being certain 'sustaining attitudes' which both define and maintain in existence the specific type of contractual relationship by which so much in society is accomplished. To participate in this form of relationship is to put on such attitudes, which in allowing one to comprehend the demands of others and the extent to which they can be qualified, resisted or negotiated away, are key to the possibility of private ordering.[35] In this way,

---

[31] L Fuller, 'Means and Ends' in K Winston (ed), *The Principles of Social Order: Selected Essays of Lon L Fuller* (Portland OR, Hart Publishing, 2001).

[32] ibid 62 (emphasis added).

[33] L Fuller, 'Human Interaction and the Law' (1969) 14 *American Journal of Jurisprudence* 1, 24, 34.

[34] Fuller, 'Means and Ends' (n 31) 68. Compare this treatment of legislation with that of Hart in his discussion of 'open texture' (see ch 6 above). Fuller and Hart shared a private correspondence in addition to their public exchanges, though it is difficult to draw from it the extent to which Fuller's thoughts helped to shape Hart's treatment of 'general standards of communication'. It is likely that Hart was already coming at this problem independently and from a different angle.

[35] See, eg, L Fuller, 'The Role of Contract in the Ordering Processes of Society Generally' in K Winston (ed), *The Principles of Social Order: Selected Essays of Lon L Fuller* (Portland OR, Hart Publishing, 2001), and 'Consideration and Form' (1941) 41 *Columbia Law Review* 799, where Fuller speaks of the 'channelling function' of the contract form.

contract 'brings home to man graphically the fact of social cooperation, and forces him to take a conscious part in that process'.[36]

This concern with participation carries over into the other social forms examined by Fuller. It is telling, for example, that Fuller distinguishes contract from adjudication not in terms of the latter's underpinning guarantees of the enforceability of the former, but in terms of the distinct 'mode of participation which it accords' to those who submit to the law for decision.[37] The 'integrity' of adjudication as a form is maintained only where this mode of participation is maintained; namely, the opportunity to submit proofs and reasoned arguments in favour of one's position before the courts, and to have them seriously heard and considered as part of the decision. 'Whatever destroys the meaning of that participation' Fuller said, 'destroys the integrity of adjudication itself'.[38] Bribery, prejudice, carelessness, systematic corruption: these are only some of the ways in which adjudication can be caused to fall away from its 'optimum expression'. Again, this form of social ordering is the realisation of personal autonomy, of individual freedom and self-constitution, in only one of its dimensions, and in relation to only certain classes of problem to which it is subject. The very distinction between adjudication and contract discloses one important limitation on adjudication, which remains unsuitable as a form for expressing certain kinds of private ordering. On the other hand, adjudication is typically unsuited to the resolution of what Fuller, drawing on Polanyi, terms 'polycentric problems', such as the complex repercussions that may arise from attempts to adjust prices or wages:

> We may visualize this kind of situation by thinking of a spider web. A pull on one strand will distribute tensions after a complicated pattern throughout the web as a whole. Doubling the original pull will, in all likelihood, not simply double each of the resulting tensions but will rather create a different complicated pattern of tensions. This would certainly occur, for example, if the doubled pull caused one or more of the weaker strands to snap. This is a 'polycentric' situation because it is 'many centered'—each crossing of strands is a distinct centre for distributing tensions.[39]

In such situations, where each set of consequences would result in different sets of parties being 'affected' by the decision, other social forms seem more suited to producing an overall outcome: legislation, election, or the market for example.

---

[36] Unpublished manuscript of Fuller, quoted by K Rundle, *Forms Liberate* (Oxford, Hart Publishing, 2012) 40.

[37] L Fuller, 'The Forms and Limits of Adjudication' (1978) 92 *Harvard Law Review* 353, 364.

[38] ibid.

[39] ibid 395.

At the same time, Fuller wishes his readers to be alive to the 'covert polycentric elements almost always present in even the most simple-appearing cases'. Suppose A is the parent of a child who suffers injury due to a road traffic accident, and avers negligence on the part of B, a local authority, for failing to take reasonable steps to protect children from traffic dangers outside a local authority school. Amongst the failures alleged are inadequate signage, lack of a speed camera or speed bumps or other traffic-calming devices, or the refusal on grounds of local or environmental interest to construct a bypass to re-route heavy traffic outside the town. A decision which attempts to locate the rights and duties of the litigants represents an inept solution to a polycentric problem, because some of its elements cannot be fully argued before the court in relation to the suit brought by the injured party against the defendant: for example, the true extent of the environmental or economic costs to the town due to the building of a bypass or of slowing or redirecting traffic flow; the statistical likelihood of construction worker injuries in the building of a bypass; the potential impact on local authority budgets and spending commitments arising from the precedent created by the ruling if negligence is found; the effect these consequences will have on provision of other amenities or services, taxation and so forth. The fact is that, as Fuller observes, there are polycentric elements in virtually all problems submitted to adjudication, if only because it is impossible for courts to predict what effects a precedent will have on future decision-making in contexts as yet unforeseen. Here he says, 'If judicial precedents are liberally interpreted and are subject to reformulation and clarification as problems not originally foreseen arise, the judicial process as a whole is enabled to absorb these covert polycentric elements'. The question is therefore one of knowing when the polycentric elements have become so pronounced that the proper limits of adjudication have been reached.[40]

Eunomics therefore relates not only to the well functioning of distinct modes of social ordering, but also to the appropriate selection of the correct or optimal method for resolving or managing social problems. The latter question, no less a question of 'means', is just as firmly a question of justice as the substantive 'values' realised through the operation of such social forms.

THE DIRECTION OF FULLER'S THOUGHT

Throughout Fuller's published and unpublished writings, one encounters evidence of deep frustration on the part of Fuller that his critics persistently failed to understand both the substance and direction of his thought. Much of this impatience arises from the tendency of the critics to see in his work a version

[40] ibid 398.

of 'natural law' thinking, the associations of which Fuller was far from comfortable with, and regarded as resulting in significant misinterpretations of his claims. There is much truth in this, but it is also fairly clear that Fuller's own understanding of natural law was imperfect, and thus his own judgements as to how his work related to the natural law tradition are not completely sound.

I briefly take up here the question of the extent to which Fuller was, or intended to be, a natural lawyer for two reasons: first, students often desire an answer to it; and secondly, for the (albeit limited) further light it sheds on his thinking.

So, was Fuller pursuing a natural law position? Certainly, he repeatedly distanced himself from what he called the 'imperative theory' of law, the idea that law is finally a body of rules sustained in place by power, as distinguished from the claim that law is grounded in (what Aquinas calls) the *iustum* (the just thing itself). In a significant essay on the intellectual orientation of American legal thought, for example, Fuller noted that Austin's jurisprudence was motivated precisely by the wish to deny that law is that which is right and just, but is merely an instrument of social order.[41] But even if obedience to law is ultimately guaranteed by physical compulsion (arrest and detention for example), the organisation of government as a whole is not, and cannot, be founded upon structures of physical constraint but upon corporate action. As Austin himself seems to realise, individuals acquire the capacity for corporate action only by adopting rules that prescribe modes and forms of their common action: rules that are accepted and adopted in practice, and indeed obeyed habitually in practice, because they are deemed to be right or necessary, or both.[42] Hence, Austin is led back to the very notion he wished originally to avoid: the consideration of that which is right or just.

Despite this interest in the *iustum*, Fuller did not, in most moods, wish to be associated with the tradition of natural law, which he regarded as mistaken in its focus. To a large extent, this was due to a misguided image on his part as to what that 'tradition' (or rather cluster of traditions) actually stands for. Fuller's principal concern was that one's conception of the *iustum* should not be taken to refer to some domain of higher law or *droit naturel*. For example, amongst a number of working notes in his private papers is a list of definitions of 'natural law' to which Fuller emphatically dissents: 'a code of divine origin'; 'a code deemed perfect for all times and all places'; the 'assumption that for any particular country, as of any time, there is one best system of law'. 'I repudiate natural law', Fuller writes. 'I don't think there is a single code best

---

[41] See Fuller, 'American Legal Philosophy at Mid-Century' (n 21) 460–61. It should be noted that Fuller does not use the language of *iustum*, but it is the correct term for capturing his meaning in making this contrast.

[42] ibid, referencing Austin, *Lectures on Jurisprudence* [1869] Lecture six.

for all times and places'.[43] Speaking in *The Morality of Law* of his notion of an inner morality of law, in place of the idea of a higher law Fuller wanted an idea of 'lower law' if indeed 'any metaphor of elevation is appropriate'.[44] Elsewhere, he wrote that 'The great mistake of the natural law school was ... not to keep the problem of ends in a sufficiently intimate contact with the problem of means'.[45]

The sources from which Fuller derived these images of natural law seem to have principally figured various nineteenth-century treatises, as well as a few twentieth-century revivals drawn from the field of international law.[46] Fuller certainly avoids some of the more gross errors perpetrated by these writers, to which Finnis later adverted in chapter II of *Natural Law and Natural Rights*. But his image of higher law is nonetheless deficient in numerous respects. Aquinas for example notes that only the most general precepts (which are to be considered more in the character of the point or end of the precepts) are capable of universal recognition, since they apply not as such to contingent predicaments, choices and circumstances, but to the very basic aspects of human existence which must be pursued in any context, whatever specific dilemmas or obstacles their pursuit might practically or concretely entail.[47] But because practical reason is 'busied with contingent matters', 'the more we descend to matters of detail, the more frequently we encounter defects', so that 'practical rectitude is not the same for all, as to matters of detail'.[48] For example, it is true that one must act according to reason, and reason generally demands that goods entrusted to another are restored to their owner. But this principle can become unreasonable, for example, if the owner will use them to fight against one's country. Thus, 'this principle will fail ever the more, as we descend further into detail'.

Unlike strictly juridical religions such as Islam, which directly specify a code by which the citizen is to conduct himself *as a citizen*, and hence create a particular kind of regime, Christianity laid down general ethical principles that do not immediately indicate or attach to a particular political form. Precisely because it does not specify the form of a specific regime, the natural law can

---

[43] Single sheet headed 'Natural law', Fuller Papers, box 15/8.

[44] Fuller, *The Morality of Law* (n 2) 96.

[45] Fuller, 'American Legal Philosophy at Mid-Century' (n 21) 479. Another manuscript of eight lines headed 'Natural law' in box 12/1 says 'Much that is written today in the name of natural law I find superficial, ignoring as it does such vital problem[s] [as] the institutional implementation of social ends and the interaction of means and ends in the actual ordering of society'.

[46] In a letter to Daniel A Dignan dated 20 April 1972, declining to act as doctoral examiner, Fuller writes that he is not 'really familiar with the basic theoretical elements of St Thomas's thought' (though some of the discussion in the letter suggests this to be an exaggeration).

[47] Aquinas, *Summa Theologiae* I–II.100.11; I–II.94.4.

[48] ibid.

therefore be said to be concerned not only with the ends to which human life is ultimately connected, but also (and directly) with the problem of evaluating and selecting appropriate means for their realisation. The 'problem of means', as Fuller puts it, is therefore connected in natural law theorising intimately with the problem of ends.

There is nothing as such in the project of eunomics that contradicts natural law. Fuller indeed points out that the considerations that objectively restrict the number of (for example) managerial models of organisation that are suitable for promoting productive efficiency might be termed 'natural laws' of production. Taking the same terminological approach, one could equally refer to the legal forms which secure freedom and self-constitution as 'natural laws' of freedom. Fuller would probably hesitate here only because the association of 'natural *law*' with *law* itself, as a social form or instrument, suggestively inclines us towards a picture of 'higher law' that he, on the whole, wished to resist. Fuller is indeed ultimately unclear about the status of freedom as an end. Clearly he believed it to be a rational end, one morally significant and worthy of pursuit in being specifically suited to (and befitting of) the character of man, and not something that men 'happen to choose' for themselves as Hart ultimately suggests. Freedom arises and is assured through forms of social order that men erect for themselves,[49] but its superiority to repression or lack of order is, for Fuller, unarguable. Freedom is natural to order, just as order is natural to man. But he does not give expression to such thoughts by suggesting that freedom is 'given' as an end, to man. Rather than suggesting that reason supplies or is capable of discovering this end, as an independent starting point for reflection, he is more likely to say that reason *is* an aspect of the free operation of the mind, so that our comprehension of this end is shaped through the very experience of reflecting upon its implications, and the conditions that make this possible.

SUGGESTED READING

LEGALITY AND THE EIGHT PRECEPTS

L Fuller, *The Morality of Law*, rev edn (New Haven CT, Yale University Press, 1969) chs 1 and 2 and 'Reply to Critics'.
—— 'Positivism and Fidelity to Law—A Reply to Professor Hart' (1958) 71 *Harvard Law Review* 630.
HLA Hart, 'Positivism and the Separation of Law and Morals' (1958) 71 *Harvard Law Review* 593.

---

[49] See, eg, L Fuller, 'Freedom—A Suggested Analysis' (1955) 68 *Harvard Law Review* 1305, 1322.

Background Reading

J Finnis, *Natural Law and Natural Rights*, 2nd edn (Oxford, Clarendon Press, 2011) 270–81.

L Fuller, 'Reply to Professors Cohen and Dworkin' (1965) 10 *Villanova Law Review* 655.

R Henle, 'Principles of Legality, Qualities of Law in Lon Fuller, St Thomas Aquinas, and St Isidore of Seville' (1994) 39 *American Journal of Jurisprudence* 47.

NE Simmonds, *Law as a Moral Idea* (Oxford, Oxford University Press, 2007) chs 5 and 6.

R Summers, *Lon L Fuller* (Stanford CA, Stanford University Press, 1984).

THE THEORY OF GOOD ORDER

L Fuller, *The Principles of Social Order*, K Winston ed, rev edn (Portland OR, Hart Publishing, 2002).

—— 'American Legal Philosophy at Mid-Century' (1954) 6 *Journal of Legal Education* 457.

Background Reading

K Rundle, *Forms Liberate* (Oxford, Hart Publishing, 2012).

O Williamson, *The Mechanisms of Governance* (Oxford, Oxford University Press, 1996) chs 1–3 and 8.

W Witteveen and W van der Burg (eds), *Rediscovering Fuller* (Amsterdam, Amsterdam University Press, 1999).

11

Justice and Legal Order: Further Reflections

I N THIS FINAL substantive chapter, I want to try to tie together some strands of thought that have been running throughout this book. They might be said to concern the extent to which justice is specifically a *legal* virtue. The focus, as will become clear, falls upon the (sadly too often neglected) *legal* philosophy of Finnis's *Natural Law and Natural Rights*. But its starting point is the concern which came to the fore in the closing pages of chapter ten: the character of justice as the *iustum*, the 'just thing itself'.

NATURAL RIGHT AND NATURAL LAW

The themes I am about to discuss necessitate some historical explanation. Throughout the history of Roman law jurisprudence, even up to and beyond the era of scholastic philosophy, the distinction between *ius* and *lex* (right and law) was never fully clear or ever resolved. Hobbes's announcement, in *Leviathan*, that 'they [who] speak of this subject use to confound *ius* and *lex*, right and law', is an occasion for him to offer a new and radical conception of the relationship between these ideas:

> [Y]et they ought to be distinguished, because right consisteth in the liberty to do, or to forbear, whereas law determineth and bindeth to one of them: so that law and right differ as much as obligation and liberty, which in one and the same manner are inconsistent.[1]

But both before and after Hobbes, the dominant juristic conception has been that rights are intimately associated with law. What is the nature of this association?

In probably the first systematic treatment of the subject, Gratian's *Tractatus de legibus*, written sometime early in the twelfth century, the *ius* which is appointed for the governance of human beings is said to be contained in the *lex* (*naturalis*) and the Gospels. The result is that *ius* is a synonym not only

---

[1] Hobbes, *Leviathan*, ch 14.

for 'right' but also for 'law',[2] which leads Finnis to state that *lex naturalis* is the same thing as *ius naturale*.[3] However, although these terms are equivalent in extension, they differ in their connotations. *Lex* is derived from the Latin *ligare* ('to bind') and in its origins connotes a written form of bond; *lex naturalis* was therefore the law that was (to use a scholastic metaphor) 'written on the heart' of human beings in virtue of their rational nature.[4] *Ius* was somewhat more complex, Aquinas amongst others noticing that it already possessed a number of distinct but related meanings. Its primary meaning, Aquinas says, is 'the just thing itself', but meanings are not static, and its use was distorted to encompass 'the art by which it is known or determined what is just' (ie law), as well as the place in which such matters are decided (the courts) and finally the award itself, handed down by the judge 'even if [the ruling] is unjust'.[5] All these meanings were present in Roman legal practice, which thus failed to resolve an important tension between 'what is right' in an objective sense ('the thing which right requires'), in the first of Aquinas's meanings, and 'right' in a subjective sense of what is owed to one by right (*suum ius*), in something like the final one of Aquinas's meanings. Thus, references to *ius* in Roman case law make it clear that the term embraces both the modern sense of 'right' (as the thing to which one is entitled) *and* the modern sense of 'duty' (as the thing which is owed by the defendant to the claimant): the *ius* of way refers not only to the right of the dominant tenant to walk a path across the servient tenement, but also the duty of the servient tenant not to interfere with the exercise of the right. It is therefore clear that the Latin term *ius* is not straightforwardly translatable as 'right' in the modern sense (one would not speak of a 'right' to have one's land walked on)!

Before going on to examine the importance of these shifts in meaning, I want to draw attention to the fact that the equivalence of *lex naturalis* with *Ius naturale* is thus only an *extensional* equivalence. To speak of *Ius naturale* is to indicate one's concern with the situations of justice which the natural law is concerned to identify, or perhaps (to use a more modern idiom) with the principles of justice or the body of rights which the law embodies. *Lex naturalis* specifies a concern with the *leges* which determine those *iura* and make them present to the intellect as *binding* standards. The metaphor of laws 'written on the heart' is probably ultimately unhelpful, but the difference suggests that the very clear

---

[2] See my discussion below. Where the context demands it, I will use the capitalised form '*Ius*' when referring specifically to 'law', but my initial discussion will perforce depart from this convention.

[3] J Finnis, *Aquinas: Moral, Political, and Legal Theory* (Oxford, Clarendon Press, 1998) 135.

[4] The first occurrence is in Romans 2:15, but it resurfaces at several points in the natural law tradition.

[5] Aquinas, *Summa Theologiae* II–II.57.1.

teachings of reason as to what is required in justice must be understood as binding requirements before any considerations of their promotion of the good for human beings enters the picture, at least in so far as their obligating force is concerned. (Perhaps just punishment for criminality is an example of this.) The full importance of this will be made plain below, but suffice for the moment to note that Finnis's equation of the two terms disguises part of the story. For it is quite clear that, although the system of legal rules and the body of legal rights within a jurisdiction must come to the same thing, understood as a whole, the focus on one or other of these aspects of the law indicates different ranges of operative 'norms'. As a simple example: my right to be free from bodily assaults can be to some extent individuated from other rights that I possess. But tracing the rather complex system of legal rules and principles which define the scope of this right (even if they do so exhaustively) is by no means an easy task. For (as Finnis himself later points out)[6] the law does not take the simple form of a rule prohibiting assault (or murder), but must also indicate the nature of the offence not only as a crime, but also as a tort, as the ground of expulsion from political or other office, or forfeiture of property, or a relevant consideration by which insurers or others can lawfully void an otherwise sound contract etc. (This is before we even consider applicable rules of evidence, and the legal principles which operate to ensure a fair trial etc.) This disparity is indeed the principal reason why the question, whether the law is *ultimately* a system of rules which determine rights, or a systematic body of rights which are delineated through rules, is of such importance.

However: to return to the question of *ius*, the scholastic and early-modern philosophers who came after Aquinas increasingly adapted the notion of 'right' to refer to the subjective sense of right by which it becomes correct to speak of 'a person's rights', ie, a person as a *holder* of, or owner of, rights. Suarez in *De legibus* writes of the 'proper signification of *ius*' as pertaining to 'a kind of moral power which each person has over his own property, and generally over that which is due to him'.[7] To some extent drawing upon Suarez and other sources, Grotius refers to 'another meaning of *ius*' which is distinguished from Aquinas's primary meaning ('the just thing itself') by 'reference to the person … [as] a moral quality of the person enabling him to have or to do something justly'. This, which he treats as the term's 'proper meaning', is the one which grounds his own discussion. It represents a *competens* (ability) to claim something to oneself, but is distinguishable into a *facultas* (roughly

---

[6]   eg J Finnis, *Natural Law and Natural Rights*, 2nd edn (Oxford, Clarendon Press, 2011) 282–83; 287–88. (I shall again adopt the practice of referring to the book as *NLNR* throughout this chapter.)

[7]   Suarez, *De Legibus* I.ii.5. 'Moral power' is used here to translate from the Latin *facultas*.

a legal power or entitlement over one's own) and an *aptitudo* (roughly, one's suitability as a receiver of benefits distributed from elsewhere, to which one has no strict entitlement).[8] Between Aquinas and Grotius, therefore, is an important shift in usages, in terms of the way conclusions of reasoning about justice are expressed. Justice refers not only or exclusively (or even primarily) to a *situation* which must obtain, but to a pattern of individual *entitlements* which demand satisfaction. Finnis argues that, notwithstanding this intellectual 'watershed', 'there is no cause to take sides as between the older and the newer usages, as ways of expressing the implications of justice'.[9]

This is the basis of Finnis's argument that there is no intellectual breach between the 'natural law' tradition and the tradition of 'natural rights'; so that everything that has been claimed about justice in the discussion of the basic goods can be suitably expressed in the language of rights; the reference to *law* in natural law being 'unhappy' and merely 'analogical'.[10] However, I am not so sure that this analysis is complete. The shifts in terminological usage surrounding *ius* were, as Aquinas's own text makes clear, well established in medieval scholarship, and it is indeed unclear whether the innovations introduced by Suarez, Grotius and others amount to a significant watershed.[11] For we can think of 'the just thing itself' in both a general sense (ie, what justice demands, altogether and generally all things considered) and a more specific sense (what justice demands as between the litigants presently before the court, in relation to the issue between them). Without disrupting the extremely complex (and perhaps practically unfathomable) connections in distributive (or even commutative) justice that might tie the situation of these litigants to others known and unknown, living and yet to be born, it may seem possible to abstract the demands of justice that are particular to these litigants, so that their part in (and of) 'the right thing' might be referred to as 'their right', in the sense of their ownership of those things (chattels, duties, immunities, powers etc) that are demanded by that right situation.

---

[8] Grotius, *De Iure Belli ac Pacis* I.1.3. My explanation differs slightly from the one offered by Finnis: cf *NLNR*, 207–08.

[9] *NLNR*, 210. See also Finnis, *Aquinas: Moral, Political, and Legal Theory* (n 3) 133 for a more emphatic version of the argument: by now, he is attributing to Aquinas an essentially modern view: 'When Aquinas says that *ius* is the object of justice, he means: what justice is about, and what doing justice secures, is the *right* of some other person or persons—what is due to them, what they are entitled to, what is rightfully theirs'.

[10] *NLNR*, 374, 280. See also the discussion below.

[11] Thus eg William of Ockham (1287–1347) speaks of 'right' as a *licita potestas* (lawful power); but it needs to be explained why the early moderns (such as Hobbes and Machiavelli) deemed themselves to be making a decisive break with the past: a past that included examples such as that of Primasius of Hadrumetum (d 560) who writes of *naturalia locorum iura* ('the natural rights of places'): *Commentarius in Apocalypsin* II.5.

However, as I mentioned in chapter two, Aquinas's notion of the *iustum* is not immediately equivalent with the goods that are at stake here, and which enable this transition. The heart of the matter for Aquinas was the ability to distinguish between good and ill modes of living: both are in a sense products of 'human nature', so that not everything that human beings do is by definition good. But just about everything human beings do is concerned with pursuit of 'good' things in some sense of that term. Natural *laws* for human conduct cannot in consequence be straightforwardly 'read off' from human nature or human 'goods' in this wide sense. When Aquinas states that the first principle of natural law is that good be done and evil avoided, he is not therefore envisaging any *specific* form of life as the fulfilment of this nature: 'so that whatever practical reason naturally apprehends as man's good (or evil) belongs to the precepts of the natural law as something to be done (or avoided)'.[12] The common good, then, is always the expression of a distinctively human form of life, but this does not point to one specific communal form as the one to which all others aspire.[13] There will be certain commonalities, irreducibly necessary to any good way of living in community (such as security, recognition of kinship ties, the meeting of basic needs, circumstances which make it possible to make a living etc), but it remains that the common good is vastly impoverished if confined at this level. In other words, the common good of a community when fully expressed is its culture. But a culture is not a work that is completed or frozen, but is always being built. Consequently, the common good is itself never finished or fixed, so that the *iustum*, the 'right thing' for that community is never fixed even if it must exceed certain base lines. If that is so, however, it is impossible to isolate elements of that total situation so as to enable talk of 'rights' in the conclusive sense intended by Finnis.

For alongside this we must place the innovations introduced (partly as a reflection of natural rights thought) by the common lawyers of the medieval period. As noted in chapter one, the legal processes of the common law were for the longest time organised rather unsatisfactorily around formal heads of pleading, but otherwise exhibited no underlying systematic properties. It was indeed some considerable time before jurists sought to arrange and commentate upon these procedural heads in anything more ambitious than alphabetical order. The most significant development within common law scholarship in the post-medieval period was therefore the shift from its conception as (essentially) a body of procedures and remedies to one understood as a systematic body of *rights*. For this shift in thinking to occur, more was required than a recognition of discrete conclusions of justice: there was needed also the

---

[12] Aquinas, *Summa Theologiae* I–II.94.2.
[13] J Porter, *Ministers of the Law: A Natural Law Theory of Legal Authority* (Grand Rapids MI, Eerdmans Publishing, 2010) 156.

development of a conception of rights as legal *instruments*, actual counters in legal argument in the form of conclusive claims that could be asserted against, and defended from, the actions of defendants: already-held instruments that litigants bring to the court for enforcement or remedy, and which do not await the fathoming of a general situation of justice.

The lawyer's sense of right is indeed conclusive. For consider that the *Ius positivum* is itself never complete or finished. New legislative provisions come into force all the time, and old ones are repealed or fall out of use. At the same time, the courts' use of stare decisis unfolds the common law according to an endless process of development, refinement and restatement. Yet the rights that are created, decided and thus stated at any given point *are* decisive for all time. The settlement at law between the litigants, once all possible avenues of appeal are explored, is dispositive and final. The courts' decisions are not open to later revision as the *Ius positivum* itself undergoes changes and transformations. Similarly, criminal convictions are not subject to being overturned due to changes in the law (eg, if convicted of tax evasion practices which are later decriminalised), but only if mistakes as to relevant procedures in force at the time come to light later, or if later evidence reveals a mistake of fact. One's rights (and duties) are crystallisations of this law at a specific point in time, but they possess an absolute conclusivity.

As long as the law continued to be understood as a set of remedies, one could speak of litigants seeking the enactment of the *iustum* as it pertained to them, as the conclusion of practical deliberations about the demands of justice. But where the law is itself understood to be composed of rights, in some sense 'owned by' or owed to the litigants, one must speak of those rights not as conclusions but as predetermined starting points for deliberation: elements of the *iustum* already, as it were, separated off and determined as against further considerations (though no doubt falling to be delimited by legal reason). As Dworkin reminds us, to take rights seriously is precisely to understand rights as possessing exclusionary force against other demands of justice, morality or utility.

Of course, because such rights are crystallisations of a law that is acknowledged to be in constant development, and never fully just, there is always intelligible room for mercy in the exercise of one's rights, which must not be mistaken for a final justice.[14] But the crucial point that is overlooked in Finnis's discussion of natural right is that the *iustum* itself, in Aquinas's treatment of it, is not a fixed or static situation. Finnis's own treatment of the common good differs in this respect from Aquinas, for it is constituted by a set of principles

---

[14] See the discussion in S Coyle, *Dimensions of Politics and English Jurisprudence* (Cambridge, Cambridge University Press, 2013) ch 13.

of practical reasonableness, coupled with 'modes' of pursuing basic goods. Now, one can scarcely avoid the analysis and enumeration of human goods, rightly said to be incommensurable with one another; for without identifying them, how would it be possible for a community to secure them? But only in being so fixed is it possible to effect the transformation of the common good (the 'ensemble of conditions' identified by practical reason as securing each individual's opportunity to pursue the basic goods) straightforwardly into 'the situation that right demands' (*iustum*) and thus into 'rights'. By contrast, Aquinas has in mind an idea of the common good as more an activity of finding rationally practical ways to configure and sustain, amid diverse and often very turbulent socio-historical conditions, that which is required for human life to flourish as it ought to: it is in this context that one must learn to distinguish good and evil modes of living. If 'forms of flourishing' act as a kind of gravitational pull upon persons and communities, what brings order to these forces, and sets them in the correct condition? Aquinas's answer, like that of Aristotle, puts virtue and the requirements of a morally good life at the centre: these are indispensable for an understanding of justice, of the *iustum* that must pertain in any community concerned with human flourishing, and without which 'forms of the good' are inadequate to explain what can be demanded as of *right*.[15]

For precisely these reasons, 'right' understood (as in Grotius) as a *facultas*, or moral power to claim that which is owed to one in justice, is distinguishable from the ownership or possession of the very instruments ('rights') themselves, precisely in awaiting the procedural innovation of the common lawyers. But this very procedural innovation, which gives rise to genuinely *conclusive* rights, makes impossible any direct equation of 'natural rights' and the *Ius naturale* ('natural law') as postulated by Finnis. (Grotius's reference to such moral powers as 'perfect rights' is thus sadly and all too easily misleading.)

Admittedly, as noted in chapter nine above, Finnis regards the conclusivity of rights as both their great strength and their great weakness.[16] The equivalence of natural law and natural (or human) rights depends entirely upon there being absolute, exceptionless rights. But as we have seen, when it comes to determining these rights, Finnis himself claims that there is 'no alternative but to hold in one's mind's eye some pattern, or range of patterns of human

---

[15] Note that Aristotle is able to establish all this moral framework without invoking God precisely because of his insight that the final good of human beings is the *virtuous* life.

[16] He actually speaks of 'rights language' here, presumably to distinguish between what we know and assert about rights (which is not conclusive of their true nature) and the rights themselves. But if our thought and talk of rights exhibits this ambivalence, then the rights of which we are talking suffer from the same problem: for they cannot be imagined or delimited except in our speaking of them, and they are moreover 'fixed' against other countervailing aspects of justice even as much as are our propositions.

character, conduct, and interaction in community, and to choose such specification of rights as tends to favour that pattern, or range of patterns'.[17] At
the end of all, the instances of absolute (exceptionless) rights mentioned by
Finnis extend only to the following: the right not to have one's life extinguished
'directly' as a means to some other end; the right not to be lied to in communications reasonably believed to be factual; the right not to be condemned on
knowingly false charges; the right not to be deprived of procreative capacity,
and 'the right to be taken into respectful consideration in any assessment of
what the common good requires'.[18]

Do these rights seem too thin? If so, it must be remembered that the
Christian teachings at the heart of the Gospels do not point towards any specific form of political regime (eg, liberal democracy) as the essential context
of their fulfilment. It is for precisely this reason that the earlier writers such
as Aquinas and Grotius stressed that a great many different forms of association were possible, and in accord with the law of nature insofar as justice is
respected.[19] I argued earlier (in chapter nine) that the true lessons of Finnis's
argument should point us towards a teaching of Augustine, that the demands
of true justice are very often too admixed with earthly priorities to be asserted
conclusively with any great assurance. The task of elaborating the demands
of justice, of fully reasoning out what is due to each person in justice, is an
awe-inspiring task in which one must participate even without hope of ever
reaching the end wherein all labours cease. Thus, in our practical deliberations and decisions about matters that have to be decided in the here and
now, ie, which cannot await the fulfilment of that task, one must accept all
conclusions as provisional. But it was in part exactly in order to alert us to this
gap, between our sincerest and gravest efforts to deliver justice and what is
actually thus demanded, that the classical writers and scholastics asserted the
existence of a natural *law*: a *lex* which gives validity to *right* reason, and distinguishes and condemns all false reasoning. Thus, Finnis is not quite so close as
he appears to believe to Fortescue, when he says that 'Where Fortescue speaks
of the law of nature, I have preferred to speak of the principles of practical
reasonableness'.[20]

---

[17] *NLNR*, 219.

[18] ibid 225. It should be acknowledged that Finnis does describe this list as comprising the
'most obvious' rights. See also Finnis, *Aquinas: Moral, Political, and Legal Theory* (n 3) 163ff.

[19] Are even these 'thin' rights truly absolute? The fortunes of a culture (its skill-base, intellectual inheritance, material and genetic resources) can rise and fall. Suppose the gene pool of a
species were eroded through disease or some other cause to the point where it is no longer viable
if confined to monogamous reproduction. Would each person then still have an 'absolute' right
to fidelity? Or suppose threats to a community's security demand acts of espionage: would one
still assert an 'absolute' right of all persons to truth in communications purporting to be factual?

[20] *NLNR*, 251.

THE ORIGIN OF THE LAW'S AUTHORITY

Wishing to understand further the extent to which the idiom of 'law' is 'unhappy' and merely 'analogical', we must turn to Finnis's discussion of authority in chapter IX of *Natural Law and Natural Rights*. Finnis's account of the origins of legal authority is both subtle and important. His discussion begins by distinguishing between the authority of custom (in international relations) and the authority of domestic rulers, but the underlying considerations are broadly the same.

Asking what justifies the existence of authority (ie, makes it necessary), he observes that authoritative determination is the only alternative to unanimity when it comes to complex decisions about the common good, the problem of 'reconciling aspects of justice with each other' in a context where every dimension of that good 'is potentially affected by every aspect of every [individual] life-plan'.[21] The principle of subsidiarity, itself a dimension of justice, recognises that particular individuals and groups have their own interests as their prior concern, so that one can hardly avoid the need for some person or body to act as the custodian of the overall common good of the community. Obviously, the more complex the overall good (ie, the overall demands of justice), the less realistic it will be to suppose that unanimity shall suffice to resolve conflicts of interest. The crystallisation of customary rules of international law provides a useful theoretical starting point, for they pertain to that domain in which there is neither unanimity nor an overall authority established over states for the governance of their actions.

Here I shall simplify the argument, but without destroying what is essential to it for present purposes: the basis of custom is not the derivation of an 'ought'-statement from a factual premise, but a series of practical judgements that are associated with certain empirical conditions. The practical judgement that immediately grounds the custom is the judgement that it is desirable for there to be, in a present context, a determinate, stable and shared pattern of conduct articulable as an authoritative rule, and that some particular pattern P is or would be appropriate in the circumstances. The empirical circumstances (no less judgements) are that P is in fact a widespread form of behaviour amongst states, and most seem to concur or at least acquiesce in this (ie, there is state practice), and that most states endorse the above practical judgement (ie, there is *opinio iuris*). Finnis notes that all this presupposes a foundational judgement, itself practical in nature, that

> the emergence and recognition of customary rules (by treating a certain degree of concurrence or acquiescence in a practice and a corresponding *opinio iuris* as sufficient to create such a norm and to entitle that norm to recognition even by states

---

[21] ibid 232–33.

not party to the practice or the *opinio iuris*, is a desirable or appropriate method of solving interaction or co-ordination problems in the international community.[22]

The desirability of accepting *this* judgement is thus itself conditional upon a sufficient number of other states also accepting it. Finnis rightly observes that there is no regress here. The ground of custom, of its very possibility, remains (in effect) the promotion of the common good between the various actors: 'this opportunity [for furthering/safeguarding the common good] is the root of all legal authority, whether it be the authority of rulers or ... of rules'.[23]

Let us for a moment stay with the authority of customary rules. The foundational judgement referred to above is quite clear in requiring (as a practical matter) widespread consensus or at least acquiescence amongst those actors subject to its rule, but not unanimity. As Finnis later says, if the establishment of authority is demanded (made necessary) by the absence of unanimity as a means of decision, then unanimity is unlikely to exist sufficiently to provide a foundation for that very authority. There will be states, then, that could conceivably and intelligibly object to this judgement because it fails to respect that state's own internal power to govern its own people. This language of 'interference in internal matters of the state' by the international community is not inevitably the language of tyrants. The first duty of a domestic government is to secure the common good of the people. One could readily imagine developing or economically struggling nations which would suffer considerable disadvantage through the operation of internationally agreed tariffs, trading rules (or customs), rules governing production etc. It is not at all clear in such contexts—that is to say, contexts in which the overall wellbeing of a particular nation would be diminished or perhaps fatally compromised by the subscription to international customary rules—that the foundational rule above would be correctly regarded (*by the affected state*) as a 'desirable' and 'appropriate' method for establishing order. This is indeed especially the case if it can be demonstrated that such rules inherently favour the interests of larger, more developed or resource-rich states. Inevitably, a state in an economically fragile position would (as actual examples attest) regard the presence of the rule as an act of political (perhaps leading to, and certainly in the final analysis underwritten by, military) interference in the domestic affairs of the nation, grounded not in 'authority' but in hegemonic *power*.[24]

---

[22] ibid 243.

[23] ibid 244.

[24] An intellectual basis for this can be found in Aristotle's assertion in Book 1 of the *Politics* that the *polis* is the form of community to which human beings are finally (and thus naturally) ordered. Compare Finnis's assertion, discussed in ch 8 above, that Aristotle should have considered the international community, rather than national communities (or peoples) as the only genuine self-sufficing community.

Finnis, as shall be seen, does not entirely stray from this conclusion: it is 'the sheer fact of effectiveness that is presumptively (not indefeasibly) decisive'.[25] But the point is then that such states (and states generally) require some other foundation for their authority to determine the internal circumstances of their peoples. From whence therefore does the authority of domestic rulers arise? In the classical natural law theories, it is the image of the Prince as holding the reins of power by divine *law* that settles the question of authority. But Finnis has this to say: when confronted with the claim to title, power or right to rule, lawyers understandably, but incorrectly, enquire after the root of the alleged title, searching for the instrument or act of conveyance by which the title was transmitted, and wondering whether those who donated the power or author-ised the transference themselves had authority to do so. It is from this lawyerly but inappropriate mode of thinking that

> arise the theories of governmental legitimacy and political obligation which tac-itly assume that the present authority of particular rulers must rest on some prior authority (of custom; or of the community over itself, granted away to the ruler by transmission or alienation; or of individuals over themselves, granted away by promise or implied contract or 'consent').[26]

Finnis rightly points out that such notions run immediately into problems, since the 'consent' or 'authority of the community over itself' presuppose the very unanimity or authority the absence of which in fact necessitates the establishment of authority. Authority emerges without prior authorization; it requires only the fact that the dictates of X will be, in the main, complied with or acquiesced in, to the exclusion of any rival source. As Finnis admits:

> The effort to bring everyone to at least an acquiescence in this judgment is usually very taxing and exhausting for all concerned, and makes very clear ... that those general needs of the common good which justify authority, certainly also justify and urgently demand that questions about the location of authority be answered, wher-ever possible, by authority.[27]

Finnis cites with qualified approval a passage from Fortescue, who observed in *De Laudibus* (c 1470) that 'amongst nearly all peoples, realms have come into being by usurpation, just as the Romans usurped the government of the whole world'.[28] This did not affect the truth, for Fortescue, that the governing power (however base or corrupted its origins) has its origin in the 'law of nature', and continues at all times to be under the governance of that law. One might therefore say that, for Fortescue, 'politics' (in the widest signification of

---

[25] *NLNR*, 247.
[26] ibid.
[27] ibid 249.
[28] Fortescue, *De Laudibus* ch XII.

that term, ie, as including forms of governance like *regimen regale* which were in Aristotle's thought to be contrasted from *political* rule)[29] is an eternal form, even though it takes terrible forms as well as good. Similarly, Augustine taught that human societies will always and inescapably stand in need of a politics, which is in that sense a requirement of nature, even though political systems will in practice lead to all kinds of injustice.

Is authority thus explained by virtue of an 'opportunity to further the common good', by the overwhelming necessity for political arrangements if the good is really to be secured in any form? Is authority built upon the fact that one shall arise who seeks power over others, whether out of benevolent concern to secure their interests, or in pursuit of some ideological vision, or to satisfy his own cravings of power? Here again, Finnis could be understood as following a teaching of Augustine, who observes in Book XIX of *City of God* that there are no natural kings of men. Earthly government is not intrinsically justified (and is never fully justified), but can claim a kind of justification in the absolute necessity of political-institutional arrangements for the distribution of material needs. But again, whereas Finnis places authority finally within a context of practical reasonableness (ie that practical reasonableness shows authority to be necessary for securing the common good in the absence of unanimity), the older natural lawyers would have advanced an explanation in terms of *natural law*. I do not refer here to the tradition of 'divine right': a tradition very much informed by the lawyerly fictions of which Finnis speaks. For Augustine's teaching points to an explanation (not fully articulated by him) which places the image of natural law at the centre, and which differs from that offered by Finnis.

Consider that wherever human beings live in close and permanent relations with one another, power will always be present (and in this sense without origin, without depending upon prior 'authorisation'). For each person's actions and choices (pertaining, eg, to the consumption of perishable resources) will have an effect on the available options of everybody else. In this very broad sense, each person's (free) will is shaped and conditioned, in numerous ways, according to the (free) will of others. Without some centralised authority, or some means of developing stable rules to govern interaction, the operations of this power are rather chaotic and extremely difficult to trace fully. This is why, for example, Fuller speaks of law as 'rescuing man from the blind play' of such forces, by creating specific domains of liberty or freedom from interference. Augustine's teaching in Book XIX of *City of God* reveals that no person, or group of persons, has any intrinsic title to govern—to assume the mantle of government and to set about the task of regulating these operations of power, which can only be achieved if much of that power is reserved unto the one who wishes to rule. The one who thus decides to take up the reins of power

---

[29] See the discussion in Coyle (n 14) ch 7.

therefore (if his authority be genuine and not *mere* usurpation), through this very act of assuming power, also takes unto himself a duty to foster and secure the common good of the people.

It may strike lawyers as odd to suggest that a person can have a duty to do something that they are not entitled to do. But there is nothing mysterious about this. If we say that it is the moral duty of each human being to avoid evil, and to render unto others what is due in justice to them, then it is clear that each person has this duty insofar as he or she has opportunity or occasion to discharge it. The one who takes up the reins of government within a community thereby also takes to himself a vastly expanded duty, for he takes it upon himself to specify, that is to determine, the form that justice will take within the community. The possessor of power does not first need to be considered 'the chosen of God' in order to possess this duty. But neither is it the sheer existence of the opportunity to further the good which explains authority. It is the imperative rather, that this be done: it is this alone which can give any justification to the assumption of power where no natural title exists. For one who accumulates power thereby also magnifies his responsibilities in justice; so that he who would wield the power without acceptance of this responsibility is indeed nothing except a base usurper. Authority must ultimately be understood against the presence of a moral *law*.

In making this argument, that the duty of the ruler is an extension of the duty of all persons to act for the common good, I am again highlighting the neglect in Finnis's account of the idea of a moral law. Finnis does indeed speak of a duty to foster and to act for the common good of one's community. But what is the basis of this duty? For Finnis, it is (in the end) a combination of sociability (itself one of the goods to be pursued) and the requirements of practical reasonableness (eg, in making no arbitrary preferences amongst persons, or in avoiding direct harm to any basic good). These ideas help to explain what motivates a person to foster the good; but they do not fully explain what *obligates* them. As Finnis himself makes clear, it is entirely practically reasonable for a person to select from amongst the basic goods in a way that gives minimal priority to sociability (though never entirely escaping involvement in it). So, we must ask ourselves why, in the case of one who does not feel very strongly the pull of fellow-feeling, the demands of practical reasonableness are to be preferred to a narrower and self-interested prudence. Indeed, it has been suggested that the principles of practical reasonableness are themselves more sophisticated precepts of prudence: the realisation that certain things are good for me, but I shall not have them unless you have them too.[30]

---

[30] See E Fortin, 'The New Rights Theory and the Natural Law' in J Benestad (ed), *Classical Christianity and the Political Order* (Lanham MD, Rowman & Littlefield, 1996) 270. Fortin's criticism is overstated at a number of points (including this one), but the seeds of his concerns ought to be more disturbing to new natural lawyers than they have been in practice.

I will not explore here the criticism that Finnis's account leaves too little to the virtues, ie, gives insufficient priority to the inner life of the citizen. My point is rather the Augustinian one that one's duty to the common good is not simply an intellectual one: it is a duty that is grounded in a set of commandments that operate within a covenant of love.[31]

Partners within a marriage (for Finnis the highest expression of sociability) certainly owe things to one another: duties of care, of the sharing of certain resources such as time, duties of fidelity and so on. To this extent, justice operates within a marriage as much as anywhere in human relationships. There is no objection therefore to the proposition that each spouse has *iura* that are owed, in commutative justice, by the other. And yet if these *iura* become the focus of the deliberations of each spouse in deciding how to act towards the other, so that spousal arguments constantly refer to *what one is owed* by the other in relation to such-and-such a matter, then the marriage is really not a healthy one. But if (on the other hand) one spouse adores the other to such a degree as to give the other *everything* that she possibly desires, without any regard for his own interests, then this is equally a distortion of the meaning of marriage. Justice requires a mode of calculation of what is due to each, but the point is that these *iura* are neither simply 'grounded' in love, nor merely 'completed' by love, but must be utterly suffused with love at every level and in every respect. And this love is itself not ecstatic but reasoning, and intellectual as well as emotional. But we will not understand this love until it is perceived clearly as a *duty*, a right situation that goes beyond the shared goods or satisfactions which are its finite expressions, and which demand to be extended to neighbours and even enemies before it is fulfilled. Thus, here as elsewhere, *iura* can scarcely be understood except by virtue of a *Ius* (*naturale*) which is itself a *lex* (covenant) and not *merely* practically reasonable.[32] Practical reason is rather the mode by which human beings can participate in the *Ius* that is only partially revealed through its commandments (*leges*).

---

[31] ibid 272.

[32] It is important to understand that the love of neighbour spoken of here therefore does not equate to a diffuse fellow-feeling, but must come down to specific acts, demanding amongst other things *caritas* (rendering to others resources that one could oneself have profitably used or enjoyed); *misericordia* (forbearance from exacting the full measure of legal justice from one who has committed a harm); *fortitudo* (determination to confront intimidation, injustices, and fear); *patientia* (avoidance of wrath and violence) and so on. These virtues must be practised even in a world which constantly offers resistance to the love that is demanded, which seemingly at every turn corrupts, perverts and works against that love. The virtues of *prudentia* (the ability to judge between actions) and *iustitia* (giving to each his due) belong to, and cannot be understood in separation from, the workings of this love, and the demands that it makes upon each individual.

Those wishing to consider the manner in which the human good and earthly power are related to the *Ius naturale* may profitably ponder these lines of Donne:

That thou mayst rightly obey power, her bounds know;
Those past, her nature, and her name is changed; to be
Then humble to her is idolatry.
As streams are, power is; those blessed flowers that dwell
At the rough stream's calm head, thrive and prove well,
But having left their roots, and themselves given
To the stream's tyrannous rage, alas are driven
Through mills, and rocks, and woods, and at last, almost
Consumed in going, in the sea are lost:
So perish souls, which more choose men's unjust
Power from God claimed, than God himself to trust.[33]

LEGAL ORDER AND POSITIVE LAW

It will be recalled that Finnis at the outset of *Natural Law and Natural Rights* wanted to pursue not simply an understanding of the concept of 'law' as it appears across a range of ordinary usages, but to comprehend the *focal* meaning of law within that pattern of usages. That is to say: our employment of the term 'law' and of legal ideas and methods will encompass not only a primary signification but also many kinds of *secundum quid*. Whereas Hart's method sought to arrive at a concept of law which remained agnostic between (some of) these meanings, Finnis's seeks to identify the focal meaning in distinction from the rest.[34]

In chapter X of *Natural Law and Natural Rights*, Finnis discusses the main features of legal order when understood in this primary reference (namely, as a form of order which seeks to secure the common good). The presence of sanctions obviously differentiates law from other schemes of social ordering and types of rule (such as etiquette), but as Finnis observes, this is of itself insufficient to identify that focal meaning, recalcitrance and the restraint of criminality being only one of the matters which the law must

---

[33] John Donne, *Satires* III.100–110. Roughly: To obey power rightly, it is necessary to understand the bounds of its legitimacy. If those are exceeded, power changes its nature to tyranny, and it is wrong to cleave to it. Those who remain true to the source of power, in God's law, will thrive; but the farther from this source one travels, the more turbulent one's life will be, and one's soul will be lost.

[34] Neither, therefore, is Finnis's conception of law merely 'interpretative' of our 'convictions' in a way which lends them integrity: *cf* R Dworkin, *Law's Empire* (London, Fontana Press, 1986).

deal with in its pursuit of that objective. The five 'main features' of legal order are thus:

1. That it brings definition, specificity, clarity and therefore predictability into human affairs through a system of rules which define and constitute the institutions of law, at the same time as the institutions define and administer the rules.
2. Rules that have been validly created in this way remain in force until determined according either to their own terms, or through being subject to some valid act of repeal.
3. Rules also give scope for individuals to modify, in certain circumstances, their own legal position and that of others (eg, by executing property transfers, contracts, purchases, marriage, incorporation etc).
4. Precision in the rules is advanced by the treatment of past acts (including those of enactment and adjudication as well as private acts of individuals or of public powers) as giving sufficient and exclusionary reason for acting as the rules then in force provided.
5. The assumption that there are 'no gaps', ie, that every situation has been in this way 'provided for', if only by the existence of adjudicative procedures allowing for the operation of judicial discretion.

Finnis observes that these five considerations have significance and intelligibility even in a world where every person acts only for the good; but in the real world they operate also to meet the problems of fraud and abuse of power, where they are also conjoined to the law of torts and of offences, criminal procedure and punishment. At the same time, some account is needed of the way in which these considerations are *systematically* linked to the pursuit of justice and the common good (that is to say, against which standards they require to be interpreted and understood as *together* pursuing those goals). Such an account is supplied, Finnis says, by an understanding of the rule of law along the lines espoused by Fuller. Having devoted a chapter to Fuller's desiderata, I will not rehearse that account again here. Finnis himself provides very little discussion, but does indicate the bearing that he thinks the desiderata have upon our focal understanding of law: for example, the requirement of consistency between legal rules

> requires not merely an alert logic in statutory drafting, but also a judiciary authorized and willing to go beyond the formulae of intersecting or conflicting rules, to establish particular and if need be novel reconciliations, and to abide by those reconciliations where relevantly similar cases arise at different times before different tribunals'.[35]

---

[35] *NLNR*, 271.

He also hints tantalisingly at 'further desiderata' which historical experience have shown to be necessary, such as the independence of the judiciary, the openness of court proceedings, the power of judicial review, and access to justice.

Finnis's account is (as one might expect) remarkably similar to Fuller's at this point. Thus, he says that the main virtue of the rule of law is precisely that it allows individuals to constitute themselves as 'selves', by being both allowed and assisted to create a subsisting identity (*cf* life-plan) across a lifetime. This highlights further the fact that the virtue of the five formal features of law above is not exhausted by their ability to prevent harms (such as the injustice of despotic rulers) but extends to the positive good of respectful consideration to those subject to the law: a 'morality of aspiration' in Fuller's terminology. Thus, in Finnis's eyes, 'the five formal features of law ... are the more instantiated the more the eight desiderata ... are fulfilled'.[36] The rule of law embodied by those eight desiderata is hence amongst the demands of justice.[37]

At the same time, it would be foolish to think that the rule of law (in this sense) can insulate societies completely against the possibility of unjust rule. Unless a society is very careful, the very idea of the rule of law itself can be detached from a sober grasp of its importance for practical reasonableness, and made the subject of ideological enthusiasm. In this (distorted) form, the law can then become the instrument of ideology, so that 'conspirators against the common good will regularly seek to gain and hold power through an adherence to constitutional and legal forms which is not the less "scrupulous" for being tactically motivated, insincere and temporary'.[38]

Taken all together, these requirements place in our hands a conception of law that lies within the boundaries of common usage, but which excavates from this usage a *focal* meaning. This focal meaning, Finnis states, is only fully instantiated when all its component terms are themselves fully instantiated: terms such as 'making', 'determinate', 'effective', 'sanction', 'rule-guided', 'reasonable', 'community' and others. These component concepts also have focal and secondary meanings.[39] Here we have to recall Finnis's warning in chapter I of *Natural Law and Natural Rights* that 'focal' meanings are focal only as against one's purposes in undertaking an enquiry. Against this present focal meaning of law, references to chemical, biological, physical or other scientific 'laws' are only metaphorically laws. But this is not to oppugn the purposes

---

[36] ibid 273.

[37] See further my discussion of the relationship of legality to justice in ch 10, above.

[38] *NLNR*, 274. Finnis remarks that Fuller does not seem to have been sufficiently aware of this. As my discussion in ch 10 should demonstrate, this does disservice to Fuller's acute concern for this very problem.

[39] ibid 277.

of scientists, from whose perspective the idea of 'law' in the lawyer's central case is only metaphorical. It is against this background that Finnis says that 'Natural law—the set of principles of practical reasonableness in ordering human life and human community—is only analogically law, in relation to my present focal use of the term'.[40] For the natural law writers of the past, 'could, without loss of meaning, have spoken instead of "natural right", "intrinsic morality", "natural reason or right reason in action", etc. But no synonyms are available for "law" in our focal sense'.[41] I have in fact argued above that at least this last proposition is open to question. Each of these terms, 'natural', 'right', 'intrinsic', '*right* reason', requires more than a reference to practical reasoning in human affairs (ie, about the conditions for the human good), but demands to be grounded in a natural *law* which commands (and does not merely recommend, or point out opportunities for) the pursuit of certain ends. Prescinding from further discussion of this, however, it needs to be observed that the 'focal' meaning of law that Finnis gives thus far leaves it mysterious how or in what way the 'positive' law is supposed to be a derivation from 'natural law' principles (in whatever form, rights or *leges*, these are finally to be understood). How, in other words, is Finnis's understanding to be differentiated from Fuller's?

If we turn to what Aquinas has to say on the subject, we find him offering a distinction between rules that are derived from natural law 'in the manner of conclusions deduced from general principles', and others that are derived 'in the manner of implementations [*determinationes*] of general directives'.[42] The second form, which we can call 'specification', can be thought of as analogous to an architect's determination of (ie, making determinate, giving determinate form to) something such as a house, or a window: the general idea of which leaves open a huge potential for specification after all manner of different choices as to size, shape, aesthetic and other choices, but which certainly 'derive from' the general idea (a door fit for human beings must be confined within certain dimensions of width and height). In a similar way, we might think of the law prohibiting murder as deriving fairly directly from practically reasonable considerations about the good of life and the requirement that one's actions must not directly damage a basic good. But as noted above, professionally trained lawyers and draftsmen do not stop with the consideration that 'killing is forbidden'. This is (to repeat) because an act of murder is considered not in isolation but against the background of social order in general, where its effects extend to all sorts of considerations: commission of torts,

---

[40] ibid 280.
[41] ibid 280–81.
[42] Aquinas, *Summa Theologiae* I–II.95.2.

suspension of licences or liberties, confiscation of property, dismissal from office or employment, or future suitability for consideration for such offices, insurability, rescission of contracts, provisions of wills etc. As Finnis observes, 'Very many of these legal implications and definitions will carry legislators or judges beyond the point where they could regard themselves as simply *applying* the intrinsic rule of reason, or even as deducing conclusions from it'.[43] The process is much more akin to that of specification: that by which the laws are not positive only, but derive a *part* of their force from the natural law (or as Grotius puts it, in which the positive laws supply what was wanting in the natural law, by adding richness to its detail, so long as nothing is enacted which goes *against* the basic precepts).

Finnis and Grotius both offer a 'purer' example of specification: property law. Justice demands that material goods are distributed in ways that are efficient and appropriate to human wellbeing. This will normally require some recognition of private property, but this leaves open many different possible patterns of rules governing such matters as ownership, transfer, taxation, restitution, pollution, waste etc. Hence, 'precisely what rules should be laid down in order to constitute such a regime is not settled ("determined") by this general requirement of justice'.[44] In specifying such rules, what is it then that guides legislators or judges in creating and applying the appropriate standards? What guides discretion? Finnis argues that the answer lies in basic legal norms (juridical principles) which operate at two distinct levels.[45]

At one level, legislators and judges are guided by the desiderata of the rule of law, in conjunction with the basic goods and demands of practical reasonableness. In crafting and applying legal rules, it is therefore possible to identify basic legal norms of a law-abiding citizen: do not commit offences, pay one's debts, perform one's duties, abstain from torts, respect other's property etc. These are amongst the conditions that are necessary in order to secure the common good through the law. But there are also many second-order principles and maxims, specific to lawyers, which help to guide the creation and specification of the required conditions: principles such as *qui prior est in tempore, potior est in iure, in aequali iure*, for example. Finnis regards many of these principles as second-order crystallisations of first-order principles, so that

> legislators who ignore a relevant first order principle in their legislation are likely
> to find that their enactments are controlled, in their application by citizens, courts

---

[43] *NLNR*, 284.

[44] ibid 286.

[45] This idea of 'juridical principles' is quite distinct from Dworkin's idea of legal principle: a source of legal ideas which, as Finnis rightly says, it is impossible to understand the derivation: ibid 280 (*cf* 288), and which in virtue of interpreting 'convictions' threaten to turn law into an instrument of ideology, rather than practical reasonableness.

and officials, by that principle in its second order form, so that in the upshot the law on the particular subject will tend to turn out to be a *determinatio* of that principle (amongst others).[46]

So for example, the second-order precept that rules should be stable across time (Fuller's desideratum), or that authoritative force must be given to past rules and customs (the fourth of the five formal characteristics mentioned above), can be understood as securing the first-order principle that those human goods which are 'fragile and cumulative achievements of past effort, investment, discipline, etc' are not to be treated lightly in the pursuit of future goals or goods.[47]

The cumulative effect of these considerations is to demonstrate that, although the act of 'positing' law (whether judicially or legislatively) is one that can and ought to be governed by moral considerations, which are in themselves in no wise arbitrary, natural law theory does not seek to offer any general answer to the question whether particular rules of positive law are 'settled by' appeal to morality or exclusively by 'positive' conventions, or whether the 'correctness' of positive laws is determinable only by reference to moral norms.[48] The true intent of the tradition is not to ask whether morality 'affects' law, but 'instead seeks to determine what the requirements of practical reasonableness really are, so as to afford a rational basis for the activities of legislators, judges and citizens'.

Does this contradict Finnis's earlier assertion that it is possible to select various focal meanings according to one's theoretical intentions, and that his book's practical focus can be contrasted with an (equally viable) *theoretical* examination of law? We might at first be inclined to think so. But it ought to be remembered that Finnis has already demonstrated, by this point in the book, that such theoretical efforts can only be provisionally separated from practical concerns and understandings. Thus, an account of law motivated by (for example) historical or purely speculative reasons would, whatever it revealed about the nature of law, fall short of uncovering everything that might be said about the law as a social institution in the world of human practice.

SUMMING UP

Finnis's remark that 'natural law' is 'only analogically law' ought not to be misunderstood. Against any selected focal meaning, all other meanings are analogical; but as we have seen, this does not render references to, for example,

---

[46] ibid 287.
[47] ibid.
[48] ibid 290.

'the laws of physics' as non-focal against scientific purposes (in the light of which the lawyer's use of 'law' is itself 'only analogical'). I have argued that the difficulty with Finnis's claim, if one exists, is in the treatment of natural law as conceptually ('intensionally') as well as extensionally equivalent with natural right. I have suggested that the category of *lex* acts as the indispensable ground for regarding practical reasonableness, indeed the pursuit of the good itself, as normative.

There is no doubt that Finnis offers a significant and subtle 'focal' account of law. Its unjust neglect by modern legal and jurisprudential writers is a matter for regret. Perhaps its greatest service lies in offering a patient and powerful illustration that the attempt to secure justice in society can scarcely be understood apart from law, ie, apart from efforts to secure the systematic *administration* of justice. I remain unsure, however, of the veracity of Finnis's claim that 'no synonyms are available' for law in this focal sense. As I argued earlier in this book, it is a significant question whether the law is ultimately to be understood as a systematic body of positive rules which (precisely under-stood systematically) give expression to a body of rights; or whether one should regard the law primarily as a body of rights, understood as having been given partial and fragmented expression through the system of legislative rules and judicial decisions, doctrines etc. Is *Ius* the ground of (interpretation of) *lex*, or is *lex* the attempt to lay down a set of *iura*? What Finnis actually offers is a complex understanding of law in which it is emphasised that *both* processes of derivation occur: both deductions from the basic goods and pre-cepts of practical reasonableness, *and* the specification (*determinatio*) of laws which determine the shape of civil rights. It would thus appear that Finnis's 'focal' characterisation of law could be described both as *lex positiva* and *Ius positivum*, whilst being fully neither of these things.

Is this the end of the question? I wonder. For we must not forget that these processes of derivation and specification are grounded in the postulates and requirements, and the objects of, 'practical reasonableness'. The reader is therefore obliged to consider the ultimate character of these objects and requirements. For Finnis, as we have seen, these can be elaborated as an intri-cate tracery of *rights*. But for the understanding of these same *iura* it is neces-sary to invoke a *Ius*, which is normative not simply because of the goodness of its ends but because it is conceived precisely as a 'law': practical reason's elaboration of a *lex* that is presented as a set of commandments and moral teachings situated within a covenant of love.[49]

---

[49] See also R Hittinger, *A Critique of the New Natural Law Theory* (South Bend IN, University of Notre Dame Press, 1989) 195–96, who points out that in the absence of proper telic completions to human beings and to the goods for which they seek, 'there is no compelling reason to opt for Aristotle rather than Nietzsche'.

SUGGESTED READING

J Finnis, *Natural Law and Natural Rights*, 2nd edn (Oxford, Clarendon Press, 2011) chs IX–XII.
—— *Aquinas: Moral, Political, and Legal Theory* (Oxford, Clarendon Press, 1998) chs 5, 7–8.

Background Reading

A Brett, *Liberty, Right and Nature* (Cambridge, Cambridge University Press, 2003) chs 3 and 4.
S Coyle, *Dimensions of Politics and English Jurisprudence* (Cambridge, Cambridge University Press, 2013) chs 12–13 and 15.
E Fortin, 'The New Rights Theory and the Natural Law' in J Benestad (ed), *Classical Christianity and the Political Order* (Lanham MD, Rowman & Littlefield, 1996).
—— 'On the Presumed Medieval Origin of Individual Rights' in *Classical Christianity and the Political Order*.
R Hittinger, *A Critique of the New Natural Law Theory* (South Bend IN, University of Notre Dame Press, 1989).
J Porter, *Ministers of the Law: A Natural Law Theory of Legal Authority* (Grand Rapids MI, Eerdmans Publishing, 2010).
T Rowland, *Culture and the Thomist Tradition After Vatican II* (London, Routledge, 2003) ch 7.
R Tuck, *Natural Rights Theories: Their Origin and Development*, 2nd edn (Cambridge, Cambridge University Press, 1981).

There is also a symposium debate between Finnis and others, on the subject of subjective right (*ius*) in Aquinas in (1997) 20 *Harvard Journal of Law & Public Policy* 627.

12

Conclusions?

C AN ANYTHING BE concluded from all of this? If by this question
is meant, *finally* concluded, then the answer is 'no'. Philosophical
questions (in being without limit) are too all-encompassing and bring
in too many considerations to admit of conclusive answers. Nevertheless, a
reader who, like Aristotle's *spoudaios*, carefully reflects upon arguments and
allows them to work on his mind, might entertain the following observations.[1]

I asked, at the beginning of this book, what it means to live under the
governance of law in the modern world. Pertaining to the central concern of
modern jurisprudence, the relationship between law and morality, it might be
said that amongst the various opposing outlooks examined in this book, there
are broadly two possibilities. The first states that law is merely an instrument,
ultimately constituted by enacted rules backed in the final instance by the
threat of force and sanction. If we are lucky, then the rules that are enacted
will be just and morally agreeable in their demands. But there are very many
examples both of individual laws and entire legal systems that are unjust,
repressive, or immoral. In the face of this, we are forced to concede that legal
rules may exhibit either potentiality, and law might in that sense be the tool
either of good or of bad government. As such, there is no intrinsic connection
between the substance or content of laws, and demands of morality.

The second possibility reminds us of the intuitive connections that are
made, in ordinary thought, between law and justice. It is useless to deny the
presence of unjust laws and cruel regimes. Is this sufficient to sever all ties
between the idea of legal order and that of justice, leaving their relationship
entirely to the contingencies of political will? Are not unjust laws precisely
bad laws, perversions of the values that we look for in the law, and regard as
emblems of a healthy and well-functioning legal order? Would one, for example, apply the same logic in casting doubt on the goodness of adhering to
moral precepts, if it turned out that an inflexible and self-righteously puritan
regard for moral precepts perpetrated harms and perverted the sentiments

---

[1] See, eg, Francis Bacon, who observes that in relation to 'first principles and very notions ...
confutations may not be employed'. One can but press the truth 'quietly into minds that are fit and
capable of receiving it': *Novum Organum* [1620] I.35.

behind moral action? Or, similarly, ought one to deny that apples, as such, have health-giving properties because occasional apples are internally rotten? The law's connection to justice runs deeper than the content of its provisions.

These deeper connections can be revealed through a consideration of the law's establishment of social order. Hobbes brings to light some of the terrors of a world devoid of justiciable limits to freedom. The loss of such limits would represent the complete right of each person to everything: a situation which, as he reminds us, is the same thing as nobody's right to anything. The paradox of freedom is that restraining laws are necessary in order to bestow meaningful liberty on individuals. Without enforceable restraints upon action, no person would be free from the constant spectre of violence and dispossession. To amass to oneself any of the trappings of a comfortable existence would indeed invite and hasten such acts. Strictly speaking, one would have no possessions, since property is itself (as Hobbes again reminds us) a creature of laws. This latter admission reveals something that Hobbes himself did much to obscure: that rights are precisely a function of law, so that the loss of law is concomitantly a loss of rights. In this connection, Simmonds has spoken of the law's introduction of a domain of universality and necessity into human affairs.[2] The human being is indeed liberated by law, both from the 'blind play of chance' (as Fuller put it) and from the tyranny of other wills, so that he is given space in which to order things to his own will.

The very existence of law is therefore germane to the possibility of justice. Justice absolutely demands the introduction of an order based upon rationality, rather than the randomness of might-makes-right. But the law's liberation of the human being—and indeed freedom itself—signify nothing without the presence or possibility of ends to pursue. It is merely atavistic without some linkage to the development of human potentialities. Despite the wide differential that is presumed by many to exist between opposing moral 'points of view', there are some dimensions of justice (we must use that word) which are inescapably necessary if any particular ends are to be secured, and which in being irreducibly brought about in common again depend upon law. The internal peace and stability of the state are examples of such 'goods' as lie at the heart of justice, on anybody's vision of it. What do these goods involve? Surely, they involve a recognition of the need to organise social life in accord with what Aquinas called 'the most general precepts' open to *prudentia* (practical wisdom), and what these precepts point to as their ends. Minimally these precepts must include a collective decision to pursue a life founded upon elementary virtues of citizenship or sociability: a life that cannot proceed without the remuneration of work undertaken; payment of debts; performance of

---

[2] NE Simmonds, *Law as a Moral Idea* (Oxford, Oxford University Press, 2007) 55.

obligations; punishment of crimes and avoidance of civil disturbances etc—
ie, a life that is organised around the renunciation of those policies of 'war'
(in Hobbes's sense) that serve in the absence of all order, and a reminder to the
akratic person who wants to secure advantages at all costs that no viable social
scheme exists that would allow for this whilst securing anything good in the
long run.[3] At the same time, the *ends* of the precepts are helpfully elucidated
(exhaustively?) by the 'basic goods' spoken of by Finnis.

The considerations of legality elucidated by Fuller demonstrate that these
goods or ends can only be secured and delivered through the operation of legal
forms. It is important therefore to understand that law is intimately connected
with justice in both of these senses: justice concerns, and depends upon, not
only institutional forms and structures (the point at which Rawls leaves it),
but also the ends that are brought into view through the unfolding of those
structures within the stable but nonetheless highly negotiable conditions of
civil society. At the same time, those ends alone do not complete the work of
justice, which depends upon law in a literal and not simply 'analogical' sense.[4]
It is these thoughts which allow us to look upon the work of the courts as a
genuine and meaningful effort to do justice to the interests and rights of the
litigants, recalling Simpson's observation that in the common law system, no
clear line divides the thought that a particular solution is in accordance with
the law, and the thought that it embodies a rational, or fair, or just solution.[5]
Far from being at a loss to understand when a judgment serves the needs
of justice, the reasonable person reflecting on both the means and ends of
human life is in a good position to evaluate the law as good or bad. Morality
and justice despite being debatable do possess discernible lineaments. This is
not to suggest that the law achieves perfect justice, but those manifestations
of legal order which succeed in obliterating justice from society are obvious
as such to intelligent persons, and can be contrasted with the successes, sometimes modest, sometimes great, of just societies. Following Saint Augustine,
one could say that humanity is doomed to seek justice only as it exists in mixture with worldly priorities until the end of days. Humanity in consequence
occupies a kind of middle position, never knowing justice in its pure form; but
only the very wicked pursue earthly satisfactions in ways altogether alienated
from the good works of mercy, charity and compassion through which the true
justice of the 'heavenly city' gains a foothold on human experience in the here

---

[3] I am referring here to elements of what Finnis refers to as the limited and specific *public good*;
but see also T Schaffner, 'Pre-Modern Legal Philosophy for the Twenty-First Century? The Case
of Hugo Grotius (1583–1645)' (2016) 7 *Jurisprudence* 478.

[4] *cf* J Finnis, *Natural Law and Natural Rights*, 2nd edn (Oxford, Clarendon Press, 2011) ch II.

[5] AWB Simpson, 'The Common Law and Legal Theory' in AWB Simpson (ed), *Oxford Essays
in Jurisprudence*, 2nd Series (Oxford, Clarendon Press, 1973) 79: see also my remarks in ch 1 above.

and now. One who insists on contemplating 'law' in separation from these associations forecloses too early upon the attempt to understand the nature of law, and consequently fails to uncover all that may be discovered in it.

To be under governance of law, then, is to live in the presence of certain values (many of which are revealed fully only when understood as virtues): values which are not the exclusive property either of the ends nor of the means of their pursuit—and which can certainly be recruited (and distorted) by enemies of justice, and therefore have to be constantly built and rebuilt anew.

Liberals who believe in the negotiability of all moral values will not look kindly on these remarks. But it ought to be remembered that the instincts that originally underpinned liberal tolerance did not deny the existence of moral truth, but asserted the importance of each person's freedom to discover the truth on their own terms. But this very freedom can only be asserted, and its reality maintained, if the ethical basis of that form of life (justice and social peace) is recognised as an essential common morality. Liberalism will annihilate itself if it becomes forgetful of these values, or fails to renew them ever within the minds and hearts of its citizens:

> The men you are in these times deride
> What has been done of good, you find explanations
> To satisfy the rational and enlightened mind.
> Second, you neglect and belittle the desert.
> The desert is not remote in southern tropics
> The desert is not only around the corner,
> The desert is squeezed in the tube-train next to you,
> The desert is in the heart of your brother.
> The good man is the builder, if he build what is good.

So, what can be done? These conclusory remarks are not really a conclusion of thought, but indicate a mode of beginning. One's thought must have starting points, foundations upon which to build. But in philosophy, as in law, authorities are not all equal to one another. How ought one to orientate one's thinking? It is undoubtedly possible to advance understanding through the contemplation of any of the theoretical standpoints examined in this book. But the question is how far each of them in attempting to give expression to the truth thereby also propounds errors from which the mind must free itself in order to see clearly. Thus (as my conclusory remarks indicate) if you would understand law and justice, and determine their significance, you must finally turn away from Hart. Fuller is scarcely mentioned in *The Concept of Law*, but re-reading that book it is possible to see Hart's concerns, especially in the later chapters, as attempting to account for the important characteristics of law that are pointed out by Fuller, without invoking any of the significant moral commitments that Hart wanted so dearly to avoid.[6] As my arguments in chapters six and ten attempt to demonstrate, these efforts (though ingenious) are not successful. The perspective that results is impoverished and incomplete, or worse (if it is mistaken for the whole), a distortion. Similarly, Dworkin misunderstands the true nature of justice (and of juridical reasoning), sending our thinking in the wrong direction. Nor do I think that a correct understanding of the problem, nor a right conception of the labour that must be undertaken to address it, are to be found in Rawls's works. The great significance of these works for modern times, is that their errors teach us much more than does the wisdom of many lesser philosophers.

But I would say that the works of Fuller and of Finnis offer the soundest starting points for reflection upon the meaning of law and justice in modern times. To consider their arguments critically, in the light of the intellectual traditions of which they are part, is to give to one's thinking the most favourable orientation. Yet they remain foundations, and not the whole of the truth which is sought and must be made manifest in the difficult social conditions of our times. So: BUILD.

> And though I fail of my required ends,
> The attempt is glorious and itself commends.[7]

---

[6] Perhaps Hart's reason for retreating from objective moral truths is explained by his desire to remain a liberal. But as my remarks above are meant to indicate, liberals as much as any men have to make some rational moral commitments, if they are to make any kind of life for themselves, however 'free' it aspires to be.

[7] 'Elegy on Variety' (of uncertain authorship but attributed to John Donne).

Index

Aquinas, Thomas
  common good   40, 41, 95, 243
  definition of law   40, 42
  directionality of nature   28–9
  highest good   32–3
  ius/iustum concepts   49–50, 238, 241
  justice   49–50, 144
  natural law
    being, idea of   43–4
    eudaemonist tradition   42
    hierarchy of precepts   44–5
    human knowledge of   50–1
    kinds of law   42
    moral culpability   51
    practical reasoning   43, 44
    pre-political/non-ideological   44
    promulgation   43
    rationalisation of immoral acts   51
    secondary precepts   50–1
    speculative reasoning   43–4
    virtuous goods/ends   45–6
  natural/positive law relationship
    contract law   47–8
    criminal laws   47
    determinations from premises   46–7, 49
    fraud/bad faith   49
    property legislation   49
  positive law
    common good   40, 41, 95
    natural/divine precepts   40–1
    reasons for   40–1
    unjust law and conscience   41–2
  specifications   254–5
Aristotle
  Christian attitudes   27–8, 34–6, 54, 63, 68
  ethical reflection   144
  eudaemonist tradition   42
  the good life   23
  happiness/well-being   13
  and human condition   34
  and interpretation of law   29
  and modern political thought   67–70
  moral culpability   51
  natural philosophy   27–8
  philosophy of nature   34–6
  pleonexia   158
  political thought
    aspirational aspect   31
    civilised society   31
    highest good   31–2

minimum duty   31, 33–4
  nature of the good   30–1
  role of families   30
  social and political institutions   30
  state as creation of nature   30
Augustine, Saint
  love of neighbour/self   63–4
  political/institutional arrangements,
    necessity   248–9
  transitory/eternal objects   26, 261–2
  two cities (communities)   25–6, 54
Austin, John
  binding force of the law   99
  legal obligation   99–100
  legal positivism   93
  merits/demerits of laws   93
  perceived errors   39
  social fact   98
  sovereign rule, legitimacy   98

Bentham, Jeremy
  censorial/expository jurisprudence   97–8
  definition of law   11, 15
  exclusion of natural law   78, 96
  law as assemblage of signs   98
  morality, law and morality   74
  natural rights, suspicions of   127
  social fact   98–9
  sovereign rule, legitimacy   98
Blackstone, William
  legal rules   13–14, 15

Calvin, John, opposition to Aristotle   34, 35
case-law   1
Christian theology
  Aristotelian influence   27–8, 34–6, 54, 63, 68
  Saint Augustine's influence   54
  dualistic nature of man   87
  eschatology   86–7
  the Fall, images of   153
  God's free will   94–5
  good life, post-reformation notions   178, 179
  goodness and iniquity   226–7
  love of neighbour/self   63–4
  natural law, Catholic/Protestant   72
  original sin   53
  Saint Paul's influence   54
  positive law
    medieval period   94–5
    post-Reformation   95–6

public peace and good (*Dignitatis Humanae*)   203–4
redemption/salvation, need for   53–4
sin, idea of   213
social (Catholic) teaching   196–7
common good
  legal order   251–2
  positive law   94
  utilitarianism   96–7
  see also under Aquinas, Thomas; Finnis, John
common law   1
  artificiality of legal reason   125–6
  deliberation process   144–5
  nature of law   1, 3, 14, 104
  as systematic law   241–2
communism
  human history   152–3
  Marxism   153
community concept *see under* Finnis, John
consequentialism *see under* utilitarianism
contract law
  contractarian theories   69
  contractual relationships   230–1
  legal reason   126
  moral principles   120
  natural/positive law   47–8
conventionalism *see under* Dworkin, Ronald

Donne, John   251
Dworkin, Ronald
  adjudication   136
  checkerboard solutions   143–4
  conscience, integrity/inner voice   134
  consistency and coherence   144
  constructive interpretation   130, 134, 136–7
  conventionalism   138–41
    bilateral approach   140–1
    interpretative/post-interpretative stages   138–9
    soft conventionalism   138–9
    strict conventionalism   139–40
  courtesy   129–30
  ethical reflection   144–5
  external scepticism   147
  fitness requirements/dimension   131–2, 134–5, 140
  form of law, moral significance   146
  freedom from the will of others   142–3
  fundamental points of legal practice   137
  general theory   129
  Hercules image   132, 149
  integrity   132, 134, 139–40, 141, 148
  internal scepticism   146
  interpretative stages   130, 136
  justice
    implementation of justice   147–8
    sytematic administration of justice   143, 145

law/morality distinction   83
legal reasoning   127–8
legal rights   127
local priority   135–6
moral-political soundness   131–2, 140
morality   36, 83, 134, 148, 263
open society   148
philosopher judge ideal   125, 132–3, 135, 148–9
post-interpretative stage   130
practical interpretation   128, 130, 147–8
pragmatism   141–3
pre-interpretative stage   130–1
Protestant conception of morality   36
rational will   84
regimentations of thought   135
Riggs v Palmer, example   133, 139
scheme of rights   137
soft conventionalism   138–9
soundness, moral-political   131–2, 140
strict conventionalism   139–40

equality *see under* Hart, HLA
equity   1, 14
eunomics *see* Fuller, Lon, theory of good order (eunomics)

Fineman, Martha   167–8
Finnis, John
  absolute/exceptionless rights   244
  aesthetic experience, as basic good   184
  basic goods
    in common   186
    exhaustiveness   186
    limits to choice   186–7
    seven elements   180, 181–5
  common good
    as objective of justice   199–200
    precise identification   178
  community concept   190–5
    communistic sharing   196–7
    coordination/direction   191–2
    family   191, 194
    order   190
    sociability   184–5, 192–4
    unity   190–1, 192
    Aquinas' teleological framework   207–8, 209
    Aristotelian tradition   208, 209
    natural law/natural right, equation   209
    virtuous life   208
  effectiveness of legal authority   247
  first/second-order principles   255–6
  forms of human flourishing   32
  good life, post-reformation notions   178, 179
  human flourishing   180–1
  justice
    capacity for benefit   200

capitalism's complexity 200–1
common good as objective 199–200
commutative justice 195–6
distributive justice 198–9
and law 16
notion 195
and self-sufficiency 195
subsidiarity 196, 197–8
justice and rights 201–7
adjudication 203
commutative/distributive justice,
significance 202
conclusory force/conclusivity 201, 203,
243–4
direct harm to basic goods 204–5
indirect harm to basic goods 205–6
natural/human rights 203–4
public peace and good 203–4
utilitarian view 204
knowledge, as basic good 181–4
desirability factor 182–3
intrinsic value 183
moral duty 183–4
life, as basic good 184
moral duty 249–50
moral imperialism 178
natural law
as analogical law 256–7
governing power 247–8
hierarchy of precepts 45
and natural rights 240
order 188–90
natural order 188
organised/directed order 189–90
rational order 189
sub-creative order 189
play, as basic good 184
political philosophy 177–81
practical reasonableness
as basic good 185, 204–5
direct harm prohibition 204
legal authority 248
legal order 253–7
status 187–8
religion, as basic good 185
sociability, as basic good 184–5, 192–4, 250
specifications 254–5, 257
Fortescue, John 247–8
Fukuyama, Francis, human perfectibility 87
Fuller, Lon
natural law thinking 233–4
problem of means 235
status of freedom 235
good/bad order 211–12
historical experience 10
human agency 211, 212, 224, 226
justice and institutional reality of law
administration of law 223

agency 226
compatibility with iniquity 226–7
concrete realities 225–6
form of law 223, 261
habeas corpus 224
immediacy and autonomy 223–4
inner/internal morality 222, 225
retrospective/retroactive laws 224–5
tyrannous regimes 225
law working itself pure 28
legal desiderata 211, 214–19, 221, 252–3
coherence of evil/good aims 216–17
contravention as failure 215, 219
efficiency in law-making 216, 218
health/appropriateness of legal
forms 216
idea of law 215–16
internal morality/external morality
difference 216
legal positivist objections 216–17
purposive activity 216, 219
repressive regimes 218
legality and justice 212–22, 262–3
external (substantive) morality 220–1
idea of justice 212–13
justice as final object 213–14
liberal regimes 222
minimum standards for rule of law 214
morality of duty/morality of
aspiration 213–14
separate value, legality as 213
minimum duty 31, 33–4
morality
external (substantive) morality 220–1
inner/internal morality 222, 225
internal morality/external morality
difference 216
morality of duty/morality of
aspiration 213–14
natural law thinking 233–4
theory of good order (eunomics)
corporate management/economics,
optimal solutions 227–8
good order (*eunomia*) 228–9
good/bad order distinction 227
political realities 229
polycentric problems 231–2
social forms 227–8, 229–31

Geuss, Raymond 229
governance of law 1–2
Gratian, *ius/lex* distinction 237
Grotius, Hugo
Aquinas's influence 73
contract law 47–8
human being as social being 57
ius 239–40
natural law 75–9

Aristotelian influence   76
common life of community   78
limited rights   76–7
and positivist arguments   78–9
property as foundation of state/
    society   76, 115
sociable impulses   76
state power, restrictions   77–8
positive law   73–4
as Protestant   73
and rights   243
specifications   254–5

Hart, HLA
acceptance of a rule   101
adjudication, rule of   103–4
Austin's influence   99–100
    see also Austin, John
and Bentham   99
command notion   100, 103
common law   104
concept of law   9–10
descriptive sociology   128
hierarchy of sources   102
justice and equality   118–23
    complexity of issues   118
    cooperation/voluntary acceptance   121
    functionalist approach   122–3
    guides to conduct/standards of criticism,
        law as   120–1
    judgment, notions of   119–20
    master group/subject group
        inequality   119
    statutes/contracts and moral
        principles   120
law and morality   93, 110–12
    legal validity   101, 111–12, 129
    limitations on behaviour   110
    moral obligation to obey   111
    virtues as superogatory/ancillary   111
law's association with justice   222–3
legal desiderata (Fuller), objections
    to   216–17
legal positivism   93, 101, 111–12
legal validity   101, 111–12, 129
military commands   100, 101
moral scepticism   21–2, 262–3
natural law   112–18
    alternative images   112
    contingent/permanent features   114–16
    desirable purposes   113–14
    language/thought structures, changes
        in   116–17
    metaphysical view   112–13
    natural forbearances   115
    positive law relationship   47
    property/ownership conventions   115
    survival as end   114–18, 178

teleological assumptions   113–14
nature of law
    agreement in judgment   109
    autonomy   105
    common law   104
    communication of general
        standard   106–7
    criteria for judgment   109–10
    general standards of conduct   104–5
    interpretation   105, 107
    judgment process   107–9
    legal reasoning   107
    precedent/legislation   105–6, 109
obligation, meanings   100
official, concept of   102
ordinary language philosophy   99
popular acceptance of law   69
popular obedience   102
positive law
    deliberately created rules   104
    legal positivism   93, 101
    natural law relationship   47
    support   29
property/contract laws   103
right, concept of   99
rule of recognition   101–3
rules of adjudication   103–4
sources of law   102
sovereign commands   100–1
unjust law   41
    see also positive law
history
concept of law   9–10
cultural history   9
historical experience   10–11
significance of historical development   7
Hobbes, Thomas
Christian heritage   53–4
human condition   54–9, 70
    appetites/desires   55
    basic equality   76
    equalities in abilities/hopes   55
    insecurity of freedom   55–6
    moral values and social relationships   59
    preemptive attack as defence   56, 57–8
    primitivism   56, 62
    reason and passions   58
    rights of nature   57, 58–9, 76
    solitary nature   55
law and society
    absolutist reputation   61
    analysis of power   62
    artificiality   59–60
    authority through agreement   60
    background   59
    justiciable limits to freedom   260, 261
    sovereign ruler   60–1
    totalitarian regime   61

natural law theorist 72
political context
English Civil War 62–5
political authority 65–6
Protestant influence 63–7
religious toleration 66–7
social fragmentation 62–3
positive/natural law position 72, 73
state of nature 56, 58–9, 62–3
Hume, David, exclusion of natural law 78, 96

interpretation of law 29
constructive interpretation *see under*
Dworkin, Ronald
nature of law 105, 107
intuitionism 151, 154–5
Islam, code of conduct 234
ius
ius/lex distinction 237–8
litigants' demand for justice 240
natural law and natural rights 240
right/duty, in modern sense 238
specification 257
ius naturale
human good and earthly power 250–1
lex naturalis extensional equivalence
238–9
ius positivism, conclusivity 242
iustum
absolute/exceptionless rights 244
commonalities 241
concept 237, 241
demands of rights 242–3
and natural laws 241

James I, legal reason 125
judge-made law 1
judges, philosopher-judges 125
jurisprudence
black letter rules 3
debate 13, 17–18
judicial arguments and decisions 3
legal positivism 11–12, 14–15
morality 4, 259
natural law 11
as philosophy of law 3
situating of 16–18
justice
duties of state towards citizens 2
first principle of justice *see under*
Rawls, John
justice and equality *see under* Hart, HLA
justice and institutional reality of law *see under*
Fuller, Lon
justice and rights *see under* Finnis, John
legality and justice *see under* Fuller, Lon
problem of justice *see under* Rawls, John
relationship to law 1, 259–62

second principle of justice *see under*
Rawls, John
see also under Aquinas, Thomas; Dworkin,
Ronald; Finnis, John

Kant, Immanuel
autonomy 81–2, 84
categorical imperative 82, 83–4, 153
dualistic nature of man 81, 87
experience 81
interpretation of 83
free will 81–2
happiness and good character 88
human anthropology 79–80
human progress 85–7
human reason, laws of 80
morality
and the good 87–90
and human reason 79
nature of the good 85
nature of law 24
non-overlapping rights 82, 85
universal moral law 84
Kolakowski, Leszek 162, 179

law *see* nature of law
legal authority
customary rules, international 245–6
effectiveness 247
hegemonic power 246–7
moral duty 249–50
political-institutional arrangements 248–9
resource sharing 250
subsidiarity 245
unanimity 246–7
usurpation 247, 249
legal order
common good 251–2
desiderata 252–3
first/second-order principles 255–6
focal meaning 252–4, 257
main features 252
natural law 253–7
positive law 256
practical reasonableness 253–7
rule of law 252–3
legal positivism
nature of law 11–12, 14–15
see also under Austin, John; Hart, HLA;
positive law
legal reason
artificiality 125–6
contract law 126
legal reasoning 107, 127–8, 217–18
legal validity 51, 101, 111–12, 129
legal writing/scholarship 74–5
lex naturalis, intellectually binding 238–9
liberal societies, and law 1

liberalism
  common morality   262
  communism   152–3
  intuitionism   151, 154–5
  liberal political order   157
  utilitarianism   151–2
Locke, John, nature of law   14
Luther, Martin, opposition to Aristotle   34,
  35–6

Machiavelli, Niccolo   152
modern political thought
  diversity in society   67
  divided inheritance
    and collective government   69–70
    forms of the good   67–8
  human condition
    role of law   56
    as social beings   57
  law and society *see under* Hobbes, Thomas
  liberal values/open society   62
  limits to freedom   61
  Saint Paul's influence   54
  permissive society   63
  religious toleration   66–7
  social contractarian theories   69
Molina, Luis de   47
morality
  divergent opinions   4–5
  law and morality *see under* Bentham, Jeremy;
    Hart, HLA
  liberal societies   4
  live-and-let-live   5–6
  as mere opinion   5
  moral relativism   6–7
  moral scepticism   21–3
  see also under Bentham, Jeremy; Dworkin,
    Ronald; Fuller, Lon; Kant, Immanuel;
    Rawls, John

natural law
  Aquinas *see under* Aquinas, Thomas
  Catholic/Protestant distinction   72
  Finnis *see under* Finnis, John
  governing power   247
  Grotius *see under* Grotius, Hugo
  Hart *see under* Hart, HLA
  for human conduct   241
  human flourishing   96
  see also ius naturale; lex naturalis; positive law
nature of law
  common law   1, 3, 14, 104
  governance of law   1–2
  interlocking rights   14
  justice/law relationship   16, 260–1
  legal education   2–3
  legal positivism   11–12, 14–15
  natural law   11–12, 14–15

relationship to justice   1, 12
  social/historical context   12–13
  system of rules   13–14
Nozick, Robert, values' importance   22

Oakeshott, Michael   224
order *see under* Finnis, John

personal freedom   22, 104, 173, 214
Plato
  cave-dwellers analogy   25, 26, 37, 148
  dualism, type of   26–7
  ethics as moral truth   24
  the good life   23
  ideal society   196–7
  Ideas theory   25
  and interpretation of law   29
  moral culpability   51
  philosopher kings   125, 148–9
  reason as guide for behaviour   25
  pleonexia, avoidance of *see under* Aristotle
positive law
  Aquinas' view *see under* Aquinas, Thomas
  common good   94
  debate with natural law   39
  good order(*eunomia*)   94
  liberty as primary good   162–3
  past errors of thought   39–40
  philosopher-judges   125
  sovereign rule, legitimacy   98
  see also Hart, HLA; legal positivism; natural
    law
practical reasonableness *see under* Finnis, John
pragmatism   137–8, 141–3
precedent   105–6, 109
property
  contract laws   103
  legislation   49
  ownership   115
  state/society foundation   76, 115
Pufendorf, Samuel
  external governance   80
  moral ideas   36

Rawls, John
  basic structure of society   158, 164, 173,
    174–6
    commutative justice   175
    essential traits   175–6
  choice   155
  concrete institutional realities   155–6
  difference principle   168, 170–1, 174
  disagreement   155
  first principle of justice
    autonomy   167–8
    basic liberties   165–7
    liberty/value of liberty, separation   166–7
    measuring liberty   165

reformulations 164–5
social/economic resources, availability/
    distribution 166
foundational principles of justice 164
intuitionism 151
justice and law 16
Kantian vision 153–4
liberal political order 157
morality, universality of 153
moral scepticism 22
morality, Protestant conception of 36
problem of justice
    the absolutely best for man 160–1, 168
    autonomy 159–60
    corrective/commutative justice 158–9
    distributional proposals, choice
        between 158–9
    fairness, justice as 159, 161–2
    social entitlements 158
rational reflection 154–6
rational will 84
reflective equilibrium 155–6
second principle of justice 168–74
    aristocratic/caste societies 170
    difference principle 168, 170–1, 174
    equality of opportunity 169
    free/unrestricted market, limitations
        on 168–9
    maximin rule 171–3
    natural talents/abilities 169–70, 171
    redistribution of assets 171
    utilitarian arrangements 173
theory of justice 154, 155–6
two foundational principles of justice 164
utilitarianism 151–2
Raz, Joseph, concept of law 10
Reformation *see under* Christian theology
rights
    absolute/exceptionless rights 244
    human rights 203–4
    justice and rights *see under* Finnis, John
    natural rights 127, 203, 240

non-overlapping rights 82, 85
    state obligations 2
Rousseau, Jean-Jacques, nature of law 14
rule of recognition 101–3
Rundle, Kristen 121

Simmonds, Nigel 222
Simpson, AWB
    experience of history 10
    idea of justice 3
society, law and society *see under* Hobbes,
    Thomas
sovereign rule, legitimacy 98
statute law 1
Suarez, Francisco 40
    significance of *ius* 239
subsidiarity
    justice 196, 197–8
    legal authority 245

textbooks' role 15–16
theory of good order (eunomics) *see under*
    Fuller, Lon
tort law 47, 74, 93, 127, 202–3, 239, 252,
    254–5

utilitarianism
    collectivist interpretation 152–3
    common good 96–7
    consequentialist assumptions 97
    limitations on behaviour 110
    measurability focus 152
    units of utility 151–2

western jurisprudential tradition
    Aquinas 28–9
    Aristotle 23, 27–8, 29–30
    Augustine 25–6
    basic division 23–30
    moral scepticism 21–3
    Plato 24–5
    political theory 21